EVERETT PUBLIC LIBRARY
Everett, WA 98201

MAR   1991

D0435971

THE NORTHWEST COAST
A Natural History

THE NORTHWEST COAST
A Natural History

by
Stewart T. Schultz

Drawings by
John Megahan and Kathy Kellerman

TIMBER PRESS
Portland, Oregon

Acknowledgments

Jay Watson and Paul Barlow provided easy access respectively to U.S. Fish and Wildlife and U.S. Forest Service publications, manuscripts, and technical reports.

Bert Brehm, Ronnie Estelle, Susan Fry, and Paul Rudy proofread portions of the manuscript.

Karen Karelius generously donated her well-used Sears electric.

Among the many who provided transportation, accommodations, and various kinds of guidance in the field were Tom Atzen, Cal Baker, Cathy Baker, Bert Brehm, Pat Doak, Peter Eilers, Ronnie Estelle, Susan Fry, Jeff Goddard, John Greene, Mary Hektner, Alan Hoelzel, Joe Horton, Dick Huff, Dave Hull, Dave Imper, Stevie Leet, Bonnie Lindley, Irene Lucius, Nancy McGarigal, John Megahan, Malcolm Montgomery, Lee Perkerson, Sherri Prager, Reg Pullen, Paul Rudy, Rob Sandelin, Rick Scott, Mark Smith, Bruce Sutherland, Susan Thorpe, Floyd and Frances Vandervelden, Steven Veirs, Marge and Larry Warnberg, Al Wiedemann, and Carole Wiegardt.

© 1990 by Timber Press, Inc.
All rights reserved

ISBN 0-88192-142-4
Printed in Singapore

TIMBER PRESS, INC.
9999 SW Wilshire
Portland, Oregon 97225

Library of Congress Cataloging-in-Publication Data

Schultz, Stewart T.
    The Northwest coast : a natural history / by Stewart T. Schultz ;
drawings by John Megahan and Kathy Kellerman.
      p.   cm.
    Includes bibliographical references.
    ISBN 0-88192-142-4
    1. Natural history--Northwest Coast of North America.   I. Title.
QH104.5.N6S38 1990
508.795--dc20
                                                        89-39460
                                                             CIP

3 3056 00216 8469

CONTENTS

Color plates follow page 96.

INTRODUCTION

Life is wet. The ocean, the original wetness and once the cradle of life, still quenches the thirst of all living things, on land even to the mountaintops. Like other abrupt boundaries, the violent zone where ocean collides with land is a meeting place of two realms, and of all the diverse and colorful inhabitants of both, including we humans who sample its offerings and seek to understand its daily joys and tragedies. This is a book about such a place, one dignified with the last vestiges of seashore wilderness in the lower United States: the Northwest Coast. This is the region of jutting sea cliffs, fog-drenched forests, and sweeping dunes from Cape Flattery, Washington to Cape Mendocino, California, and from the Coast Range summits to the edge of the continental shelf. Though still blessedly pristine in many places, this territory is nevertheless faltering under the increasing burden of logging, development, and pollution, and it is with the hope that understanding and respect are as inseparable as the ebb and the flow that these pages have been written.

I realize the term "northwest" might amuse some Canadians and Alaskans, but it is used to avoid confusion in an audience predominantly of the lower U.S. The Canada-U.S. border is geologically as well as politically expedient, since it marks roughly the southern limit of the highly glacier-eroded outer shoreline.

The questions I have tried to answer include: How has the coastal environment molded the bodies and behavior of its inhabitants over the millennia? How have these creatures, in turn, changed their environment? What forces control their abundance, distribution, growth, and reproduction? How is our coastal community unique, and what makes it so? What impacts have people had on all this?

Many of the events and relationships recounted are unobservable to the casual naturalist, documented only by the slow, painstaking work of many experimental ecologists, natural historians, and paleontologists, and laid out in excruciating detail in scientific journals and government reports. This book is one interpretation of these sources, cleared of the equations, numbers, and technical language, and presented in a way that I hope makes the beautiful logic of nature, with all its daily struggles and crises, comprehensible to most everyone, regardless of their technical background. I have assumed an audience with the same interest and knowledge of biology as that of, say, the magazines *Audubon* and *Natural History,* although more knowledgeable readers might also find here much of interest outside their fields.

The book is organized by habitat, since overlap is small as a rule, and since different habitats have molded different adaptations. The chapters deal separately with the nearshore ocean, the intertidal zone, estuaries, sand dunes, and coastal forests. Rather than approaching each from the same perspective, the treatment varies with my own interests and the history of each discipline. I emphasize evolution and behavioral ecology of birds and mammals in the nearshore, community organization in the intertidal, primary productivity in estuaries, succession and diversity in sand dunes, and biomass and decay in forests. In addition, in Chapter 7 I present a sampling of the most obvious conservation problems on the coast, and suggest a few solutions.

Obviously, my subject is far too large for any more than a summary account of the most important issues, and although I've limited my treatment to those addressed recently by professional ecologists, I could have included countless more as well. With luck, my own interests and curiosity will jibe with those of my readers. Throughout I have tried to stay on the correct side of the fine line between clarity and brevity on the one hand, and oversimplification on the other.

These pages are not intended as a field guide, but rather as a preparation for field experience. Chapter 1 is necessary for a full understanding of the rest, which reads most smoothly as presented. I have written very little on the identification of species, and hope that the reader is already familiar with the more common ones, or can become so with the help of a few of the many superb guidebooks available, and a little time in the field.

1

EARTH, WIND, AND SEA

a hard rain all the last night we again get wet the rain continue[s] at intervales all day. Wind verry high from SW and blew a storm all day . . . .and our situation is truly a disagreeable one.
William Clark, Monday, Nov. 11, 1805

Some 17 million years ago, a sudden twisting of the earth's crust near the present Wallowa Mountains invited one of the greatest geological upheavals ever to befall the Pacific Northwest. The twisting motion tore open several deep gashes in the continent, and like blood from a wound, molten lava gushed out through the vents and down the ancestral valley of the Columbia River. The lava poured down the river until it reached the ocean and burrowed into the soft sea floor sediments. When the lava had cooled and hardened, the river valley was no longer a valley, but instead a long, snake like stripe of basalt rock painted across northwest Oregon, following the ancient Columbia channel south from The Dalles and across the young Coast Range to its outlet near present-day Newport. The basalt pushed the Columbia River slightly to the north, where it eventually cut a new valley. A new lava flow, however, soon filled the new valley with basalt. Successive flows pushed the river ever northward in this way, until 7 million years later, it had occupied its present course (Beeson, *et al.*, 1979).

These colossal lava floods left several arms of basalt buried beneath the muds and sands of the continental shelf. The constant pounding of the breakers soon washed away the soft sediments, and slow uplift raised these basalt columns from the mud as though from the dead, until they towered alone above the sea as magnificent coastal headlands. All the major capes and sea stacks from Cape Disappointment to Yaquina Head and Seal Rock came into being in this way, and each finger clearly marks the location and outline of an ancestral Columbia River valley, fixed in an instant of time (Plate 1).

As Tillamook Head and Neahkahnie Mountain emerged from the mud some 15 million years ago, they soon were clothed by portions of the vast metasequoia forests that flourished in the hot and

9

humid climate of the Northwest at this time. In all likelihood, these capes were populated by the three-toed horses, saber-toothed tigers, giant pigs, tiny camels, and other mammals of this period whose fossils have been found in the John Day area (Baldwin, 1981).

Now, Neahkahnie Mountain lies hunched over like the hulk of a beached sea lion, vertebrae exposed as rock outcrops along the sharp ridgetop, the head bathed in the breakers at Short Sands, and the limp hindquarters sprawled along the meandering Nehalem River Valley (Plate 2). A great variety of life clings resolutely to the stable basalt surfaces, mingling in a mosaic of associations that responds directly to the texture and pattern of the rock itself. In the zone cleansed by the tides, rock crabs and sea slaters find refuge in the crevices; the brilliant green alga *Enteromorpha* lines the fresh-water seeps; purple urchins honeycomb the tidepools to escape the waves; barnacles and mussels defy the battering surf on the outer cliffs; oystercatchers steal the soft limpet flesh and ruddy turnstones probe the barnacle beds; and harbor seals haul out and rest on the rocks and protected coves. Above the tides, wrentits flit furtively in the salal under the massive old growth Sitka spruce along the lower creeks, and broad grasslands and shrubfields blanket the middle slopes. A dense, wet hemlock forest clothes the shaded north face, while an open, dry spruce and salal community dominates the storm-exposed south. The rock outcrops at the summit support a colorful wildflower community; paintbrush, wild garlic, lomatium, daisies, and others extend their roots into the wet crevices.

Neahkahnie's natural history is just one of many examples of the tight dependency of our coastal life on the spatial and temporal patterns of earth, air, and sea. If not for the Columbia Basalt flows, the rocky tidepools and boulder fields might not exist here, nor would the sea stars, urchins or puffins; nor the rock gardens or headland prairies. The radically different topography, soils, and exposure to wind, sun, and waves would mold forests and beaches of radically different character, creeks of different shapes and sizes, and overall a much more uniform and monotonous landscape and biota.

Ecology as a science cannot be divorced from geology, oceanography, and meteorology any more easily than a starfish is pulled from its rock. Over vast stretches of time, our coastal inhabitants have winced and staggered under forces largely beyond their control, and those few who managed to survive did so by gluing their lives to the environment, or at least to small pieces of the environment that were more stable or predictable than the rest. The barnacles and other creatures of the tidepools are wonderful symbols of evolution, literally stuck to the solid substratum that gives them life, their success tightly intertwined with the stability of the rock and the utter predictability of the tides.

But permanence is just an illusion, perpetrated by our short lifespan and shallow perspective. Over the long run the earth is anything but tranquil: mountains rise and crumble; rivers shift; continents drift, collide, and overrun each other; the climate cools and warms; glaciers advance and retreat; the sea falls and rises; volcanoes erupt; and searing lava smothers the lowlands. While a single salmon may be oblivious to this long history of lumbering cataclysms in its native land, it carries the memory written in its genes. These are the genes that gave its ancestors the power to react, adjust, and compromise in the name of survival; to strap the species snugly in this lurching geologic roller coaster while the great majority of its neighbors were tossed, one by one, to the abyss of extinction.

So the shoreline we see today is just one frame in an ongoing motion picture that began, with the earth, 4 billion years ago. The creatures we see are the few tough survivors of eons of infighting and of battering by earth, wind, and sea; we can only guess which will endure as the film flickers on into the millenia. But we do know that the shore is a place where, unlike anyplace else on earth, these forces lay exposed in all their naked fury: breakers bite into the bluffs and chew great chunks of earth in the surf; rivers sweep sands onto the tideflats and beaches; furious winter storms flood the lowlands with rain and tidewater, and launch violent winds that scream across the dunes and up the valleys, threatening to conscript even the most detached observer into an active participant in the conflict.

If we peer closely into this latest picture frame, we can learn how these forces have shaped the shore and controlled the lives of the cedar, barnacle, and salmon; in so doing we may, as with the Columbia Basalt flows and the ancestral valley, see the process of adaptation frozen in an instant of time, as we explore the newest twist in the long thread of evolution that weaves tightly through the rough fabric of mountains, sea, and rain.

GEOLOGY

Slow, elephantine movements of the earth's crust over millions of years have determined the shape and texture of the land, and these in turn have set the boundary conditions for life. Such movements have given our coast its high relief, and with it, increased rainfall, productivity, and a variety of forest communities, most impressively the coast redwoods and Olympic rain forest. Earth movements also have released the lava flows that gave us coastal headlands and numerous mountains with their associated rock gardens, such as Saddle, Sugarloaf, and Onion Peak (Beeson, et al., 1979). Geologic and atmospheric processes have united to create the special soils our plants have adapted to; the famous Klamath serpentines underlie a bizarre and unique wildflower community.

What are these movements, and how is it that they shape the land and its inhabitants? The surface of the earth, including the floor of the oceans, is composed of several enormous rock slabs that fit together like a jigsaw puzzle. These slabs or "plates" range from 40 to 60 miles thick, and float passively on top of a layer of hot, near-liquid rock, like ice cubes in a glass of water (Figure 1). Where the plates break above the sea surface lie the continents, and where the denser rock sinks downwards the ocean basins have formed. Although several plates are composed entirely of sea floor, no purely continental plates are known to exist; every continent merges at some point with sea floor.

At the center of the earth, continual radioactive decay of the rocks releases tremendous amounts of heat, which radiates passively upward until it reaches the fluid layer that supports the plates. As these fluid rocks warm, they lose density, rise to the surface, collide with the rigid surface plates, then veer sideways, flowing parallel to the surface just underneath the plates, all the time oozing like thick molasses at about an inch per year (Figure 2). As these warm, fluid rocks move along, they drag the plates along with them

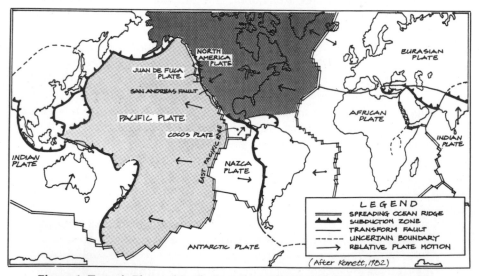

Figure 1. Tectonic Plates of Earth. Earth has seven major plates; those affecting Oregon and Washington are shaded. Plates diverge along ocean-spreading ridges, converge along subduction zones, and slide past each other along transform faults known as fracture zones. Plate boundaries do not necessarily coincide with continent or ocean outlines. Arrows indicate the relative motion of the plates. The North American Plate is moving westward away from the Mid-Atlantic Ridge. The Juan de Fuca Plate and the Cocos Plate are remnants of the ancient Farallon Plate now consumed beneath the North American Plate. (From Parmenter and Bailey, 1985.)

like a conveyor belt. Eventually the rocks cool off as they radiate heat through the plates to the atmosphere, then gain density, sink, and flow back underneath to complete the cycle. Several of these circular currents, or "convection cells," have been established in the mantle, apparently semi-permanently, and the rock plates above them drift along in various directions depending on the direction of the surface portion of the current (Anikouchine and Sternberg, 1981).

The slow creep of these enormous plates gives them an immense kinetic energy powerful enough to raise mountains, launch earthquakes and tidal waves, and rupture the earth with volcanic explosions. Most of the activity occurs along the plate margins, which often coincide with the shore. As two adjacent plates inch along, they may do one of four things: they may break apart from each other; they may slide alongside each other; they may collide head on; or one may sink underneath the other. Which actually happens determines the broad features and overriding character of the coast. Where two plates break apart a "trailing edge" coast emerges; where they slide by parallel to each other a "sliding edge" coast forms; where one wedges beneath another a "leading edge" coast appears; where two continents collide there is no coast (the heavier sea floor will always sink beneath a continent) (Anikouchine and Sternberg, 1981).

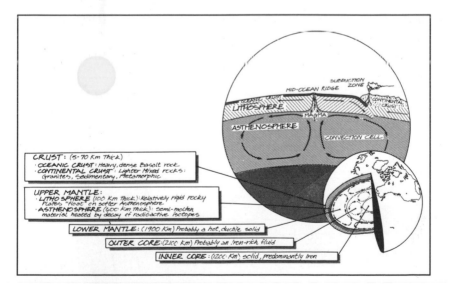

Figure 2. Earth's Internal Structure. The earth's internal structure is composed of several concentric layers. Scientists study how seismic (earthquake) waves change as they pass through these layers to determine their characteristics and thickness. Composition of the layers is still a subject of study and debate. (From Parmenter and Bailey, 1985.)

Each of the three coast types has its own peculiarities, and is both geologically and ecologically distinct; all three are present in the United States. The entire west coast of the Americas forms the west margin of the American Plate, which consists of North and South America and the western half of the Atlantic Ocean basin. The coast of Washington, Oregon, and northern California abuts a small piece of Pacific Ocean sea floor, the Juan de Fuca Plate, which for millions of years has been slowly moving eastward and wedging itself underneath these states, giving us our present leading edge coast.

The distinctive features of ours and all other leading edge coasts arise in a simple manner. Over time, the Columbia, Fraser, and other rivers and their tributaries have scoured the muds, sands, and gravels from the mountain slopes and dumped them on the Juan de Fuca Plate, where they have accumulated to a depth of over two miles, their sheer weight forcing the deeper layers to solidify into sedimentary rock (Baldwin, 1981). As in all other ocean basins, the platform upon which the sediments lie is solid basalt, whose greater density forces the Juan de Fuca Plate underneath the lighter continental rock of the Northwest Coast. As the Juan de Fuca Plate moves slowly eastward, however, the continental margin scrapes off most of the sedimentary rock, and the motion of the plate plasters this loose rock against the underside of the continent. As this wedge of plastered rock thickens over time, it gradually forces the edge of the continent upwards, creating a range of coastal mountains that now includes the Olympics, Willapa Hills, Oregon Coast Range, and Klamath Mountains (Figure 3; Plate 3). The Juan de Fuca Plate, meanwhile, continues to descend beneath the continent at an angle of about 45 degrees, dragging down some of the sedimentary rock as

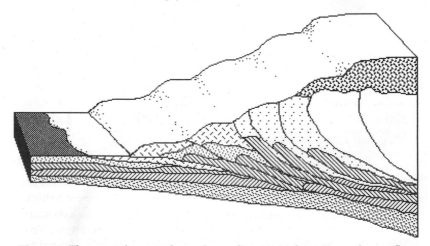

Figure 3. The coastal ranges formed as sedimentary deposits on the sea floor folded against the continental plate during sea floor subduction.

well. When the sedimentary rock reaches a depth of about 30–60 miles, it melts under extreme heat and pressure, loses density, and rises through the soft areas in the denser continental rocks; at the surface it erupts as basalt lava from a line of spectacular volcanoes, the Cascades, that stand about 100 miles inland and parallel to the coast (Dott and Batten, 1981). Similar lava flows erupted in eastern Oregon and elsewhere, giving us, as we have seen, the Columbia River Basalt and several coastal headlands (Beeson, *et al.*, 1979).

So a leading edge coast is marked by uplift, volcanism, and youth. Typical features include a range of coastal mountains a few miles from shore, rugged and spectacular sea cliffs and headlands, a steep gradient from coast range summits to the ocean, a narrow or nonexistent coastal plain, small bays and estuaries, a minimum of sand dunes, and a shallow layer of continental shelf sediments.

A trailing edge coast, on the other hand, is just the opposite in nearly every respect. About 200 million years ago, North America separated from Africa and South America, creating the North Atlantic Ocean and a trailing edge coast along the eastern margin of North America. When the continents broke apart, a deep rift opened between them, and molten lava welled up through the crack to the surface, where it solidified into hard basalt sea floor. As the continents continued to drift apart, more lava oozed up through the opening and the sea floor slowly widened while the rift remained stationary in the middle of the ocean, always serving as a conduit for lava and birthplace for new sea floor (Anikouchine and Sternberg, 1981). The newly formed Atlantic Ocean defined a new shoreline along the margins of the separating continents, but in contrast to the leading edge coast, here the continent and sea floor are firmly attached and move together as a unit; there is no grand confrontation between two neighboring plates that grinds, crumples, and uplifts the coastal landscape, no spectacular floods of lava that awaken the sleeping land with hot spikes of newborn rock.

Instead, the most important geologic process at work on a trailing edge coast is erosion; the slow, dull, weathering away and smoothing out of the hills and valleys. Over 200 million years, wind and rain have scoured and planed the east coast of North America, washing the mountains, pebble by pebble, down the rivers and into the Atlantic, where clays and sands have piled up to form broad beaches, sandspits, and barrier islands from New York to Texas. In stark contrast to the Northwest Coast, the wedge of sediments dumped on the Atlantic shelf stretches 180 miles out to sea at a thickness up to six miles. The broad coastal plain extends inland 200 miles to the Appalachians, and has allowed the formation of huge, lush estuaries such as Chesapeake and Delaware bays. Other prime examples of trailing edge coasts are the Gulf Coast, the east coast of

South America, and the entire coasts of Australia and Africa (Davies, 1980).

Ecologically, then, leading and trailing edge coasts are worlds apart. The ancient and serene trailing edge fosters broad intertidal flats teeming with productive salt marshes and eelgrass beds as well as burrowing invertebrates and their predators. Beach sands blow inland to form dunes that march easily across the flat lowlands that merge with the shore. In contrast, the steep seaslope of the Northwest Coast and other leading edges banish large estuaries and dunes. Instead, the lava flows have created spectacular mountain peaks, rocky tidepools, and seastacks that have welcomed the invasion, respectively, of unique plant and forest communities; dense, colorful beds of attached invertebrates; and breeding colonies of seabirds and sea lions. The uniform climate of the flat trailing edge coastal plain ensures a monotonously uniform forest, while the sharp gradients in temperature and precipitation from the sea to the leading edge Coast Range summits invites a great variety of intergrading forest types.

To complete the picture, consider the sliding edge coasts of central and southern California. Here the American Plate meets the Pacific Plate, which is creeping northward at about three inches a year. As the two plate margins grind against each other, they tear off chunks of the land that twist and buckle with the movement, so that the zone of plate contact is not a single sharp rift, but instead many odd-angled faults of various sizes, one of which is the famous San Andreas Fault. As the Pacific Plate moves along, some of these chunks catch against each other and momentarily stop, their rocks slowly stretching and bending with the unremitting plate movement. Eventually they reach their stress limit, suddenly break, and lurch forward. During the catastrophic San Francisco Earthquake, the Point Reyes Peninsula was thrust over 16 feet northwestward. A sliding edge coast is probably the most heterogeneous of the three types, with bizarre juxtapositions of rocks and soil types, many jagged and irregular landforms at odd angles, and frequent earthquakes. San Francisco Bay, Tomales Bay, the Baja California peninsula, and the Gulf of California were all created as the Pacific Plate slid along the margin of the American Plate, and drastic changes will undoubtedly result as the plate movement continues into the future (Davies, 1980).
1961) (Figure 8).

CLIMATE

Our unusual Northwest climate exerts a second dimension of ecological control superimposed on, and in part directed by, the shape of the land.

The most powerful climatic force on the Northwest Coast is probably the winter storms, more frequent in the Gulf of Alaska and Pacific Northwest than anywhere else on earth. The 12 feet of rain that these blow in each year have created lush, productive forests, not only on the coastal mountains (notably the Olympic rain forests) but also on the west slope of the Cascades. The gale force winds, laden with burning salt, control the shorefront vegetation, create sand dunes, and blow down old growth trees that then become nurse logs and wildlife nest sites. Storm winds also raise up waves and breakers, some of which each year exceed 20 feet in height. These in turn erode headlands and dunes, liberating sand for the winds to create parabola dunes; transport eroded sediments along the beaches; build bayfront sandbars, creating productive bar-built estuaries such as Willapa Bay, Grays Harbor, Netarts Bay, and Sandlake; and stir up lost nutrients from the continental shelf to the sea surface, where they increase the productivity of the plankton (Plate 4). Apart from the storms, the mild maritime climate also contributes to the luxuriance of the forests, and the warm winters unite with the dry summers to create a dominance of evergreen conifers unparalleled in any other temperate forest.

What is it about the Northwest that brings the starkly contrasting winter storms and summer drought? The earth is a great coughing, sputtering heat machine, whose seasonal shifts in wind and rain arise from global patterns of air circulation, powered by the sun, and their interaction with local topography. As usual, the story begins with the sun, which heats the earth's surface unevenly. On the average, the equator receives more heat than it radiates back out to space, and the poles radiate more heat out to space than they receive from the sun. But if this is true, then why don't the polar temperatures continue to drop until the glaciers spread down to Mexico, and why don't the tropical seas heat to boiling? The reason is that heat moves constantly from the equator to the poles via the air and water; roughly speaking, the mechanism for this movement is weather (Figure 4).

As the sun beats down on the tropics, it bakes the earth and warms the seas, which evaporate some of their moisture into the atmosphere. The warm earth warms the humid surface air, and this heat begins the first leg of its long trek to the poles as the hot air rises in great columns of thunderheads throughout the tropics. As the rising air expands, it cools, loses its water-holding capacity, and lets

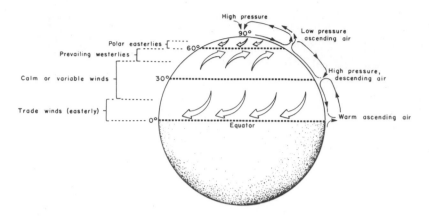

Figure 4. Atmospheric Circulation Patterns. Uneven heating and rotational (Coriolis) effect cause the generalized atmospheric circulation patterns shown in this diagram for the northern hemisphere. The Pacific Northwest Region is located in the zone of prevailing westerlies (40°–50°N).

loose with explosive thunderstorms and monsoons throughout the equatorial region. At about 6 miles altitude, the air stops rising and veers toward the poles. As it moves along, it radiates heat steadily out to space. By the time it reaches about 30° latitude, it has cooled enough to descend. As the air sinks, the increasing column of over-lying air compresses it, causing it to warm and dry. In two great rings that encircle the Northern and Southern hemispheres at 30° lati-tude, these columns of descending air pile up at the surface as high-pressure cells. The warm, clear air of these "subtropical highs" is responsible for the world's great deserts: the Saharan, Syrian, Gobi, Australian. As a rule, the air does not subside at random all along the 30th parallel, but rather in response to the topography. The rela-tively cool regions, generally the continents in winter and the oceans in summer, promote subsidence and hence high-pressure centers. The dominant high of the West Coast of the U.S., the "North Pacific High," occupies most of the eastern Pacific in the summer north of latitude 20 and west of longitude 160; its center lies some 1000 miles off San Francisco (Barry and Chorley, 1976; Hare, 1966) (Figure 5).

The air naturally diverges in all directions from the highs; some returns to the equator to complete the grand cycle, while some con-tinues poleward. As the latter moves along at the surface, it collects moisture evaporated from the warm subtropical seas. The furor com-mences between latitudes 40–50°, when this warm, moist air finally reaches the cold envelope of surface-hugging polar air (Barry and Chorley, 1976; Schneider and Londer, 1984).

The warmer, lighter air mass glides upward over the polar front, and as it gains altitude, it cools and loses its moisture, first as

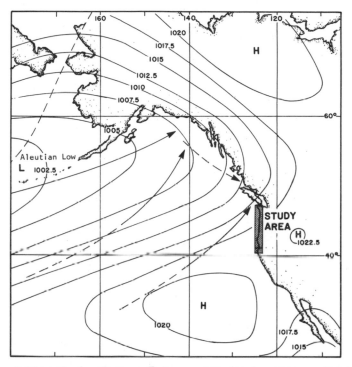

Figure 5. Mean Surface Pressure Pattern and Surface Low Pressure Tracks for January. Pressure isobars are in millibars (1000 mb = 750 mm-Hg = 29.54 in-Hg). The low pressure tracks (arrows) show general winter storm paths in the region. (From U.S. Department of the Navy, 1958.)

clouds, and then as rain. Moreover, as this air rises at the base of the polar front, it creates a low-pressure center at the surface, and the surrounding air rushes in from all directions to fill the low. But the entire system is rotating with the earth, counterclockwise in the Northern Hemisphere. When this converging air pulls inward into a smaller area, its rate of rotation increases in the same way that an ice skater accelerates a spin by pulling in his or her arms and legs to conserve angular momentum. The result is a large-scale air circulation around these polar-front lows, counterclockwise in the Northern Hemisphere. Meteorologists refer to this rotation as "cyclonic," and to the low-pressure cell as a "cyclone." Exactly the reverse process occurs as the air diverges from the subtropical highs, or "anticyclones," creating a clockwise flow around these systems. The cyclones, however, usually have much greater wind speeds because the continued inward movement accelerates the spin. As with the subtropical highs, the polar lows form in response to the topography, but in the reverse: generally over land in summer and ocean in winter. The low-pressure cells that dominate the Pacific Northwest,

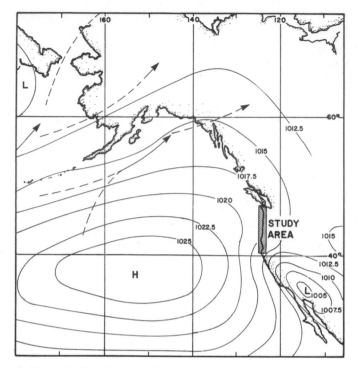

Figure 6. Mean Surface Pressure Pattern and Surface Low Pressure Tracks for July. Pressure isobars are in millibars (1000 mb = 750 mm-Hg = 29.54 in-Hg). The low pressure tracks (arrows) show general summer storm paths in the region. (From the U.S. Department of the Navy.)

collectively the "Aleutian Low," occupy most of the Gulf of Alaska and Bering Sea in the winter (Barry and Chorley, 1976; Hare, 1966) (Figure 6).

So the climate of the Pacific Coast is controlled by two systems: the North Pacific High to the south, and the Aleutian Low to the north. Since in the Northern Hemisphere the wind is from the west both along the northern margin of a high and the southern margin of a low, a prevailing westerly wind flow refreshes most of the West Coast the year around. And since the westerlies flow for hundreds of miles over the Pacific, by the time they reach the coast they have roughly the same temperature as the ocean. The high heat capacity of water prevents any wide fluctuations in ocean temperature, so both ocean and westerlies are cool in summer and warm in winter. Thus buffered by the ocean winds, the coast from the Alaskan Panhandle south to San Francisco enjoys a classic marine climate. Temperatures are comfortably mild, and on the average range from 38–54°F in January and from 50–67°F in August; the monthly mean increases only about 4° per month from January to July. Over most of the

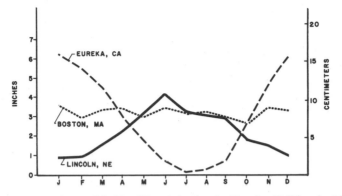

Figure 7. Normal Monthly Total Precipitation for Eureka, California; Lincoln, Nebraska; and Boston, Massachusetts. These patterns characterize the maritime Northwest, the Midwest, and the New England States. All stations are at approximately the same latitude. Eureka receives less precipitation than most of the Northwest coast, but the pattern of wet winters and dry summers characterizes the entire region. (Adapted from U.S. Department of Commerce, 1968.)

lowlands, the maximum temperatures ever recorded are in the 90s, and the minimum in the 10s; over 200 days per year are frost free. Ironically, these same westerlies bring harsh continental temperatures to the same latitudes on the eastern U.S. coast, since by the time they get there they have traveled some 3000 miles over the baked or frozen heartland. While at Brookings the average monthly temperatures range from over 40 in January to about 60 in July, those at the same latitude on the Connecticut coast range from 30 to 75, and less than 160 days per year are frost-free (Proctor, *et al.*, 1980; Trewartha, 1961) (Figure 8).

Occasionally, however, this pattern is disrupted, and the westerlies are temporarily replaced by easterlies that displace the marine air and bring in wider extremes of continental air. The causes of this depend on the season. In the winter, a high-pressure cell of arctic air sometimes spreads south into the Pacific Northwest, and the east winds along its southern margin bring frigid but mostly clear and dry weather. In the summer, the North Pacific High occasionally moves north and east over the continent, bringing the Northwest within reach of the east winds of its southern flank. This time, however, they carry hot, dry air from Idaho and Montana. An interesting consequence is the so-called "Brookings effect," in which the temperatures near the Oregon/California border are unusually high. After traveling over the Siskiyous, the east winds descend the western slopes, and in the process undergo all the standard changes of subsiding air (as for example in the subtropical highs): compression, warming, and drying. This pattern is centered on the Brookings

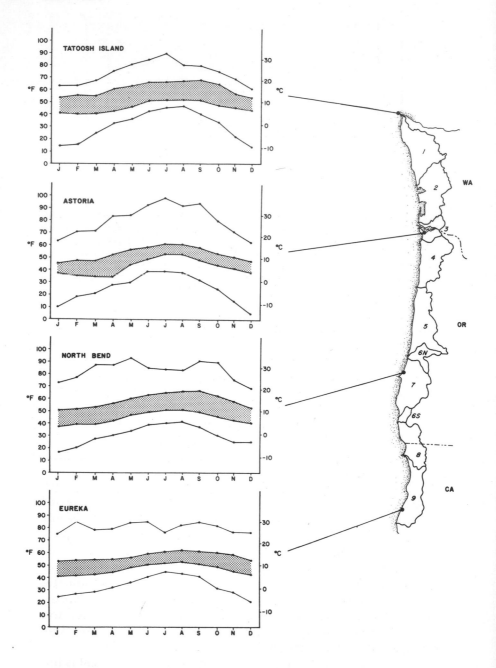

Figure 8. Temperature Data for Coastal Stations in the Study Area. Darkened band shows average temperature range. Top and bottom lines show extreme high and low temperatures that have been measured. (Adapted from: Phillips and Donaldson, 1972; U.S. Department of Commerce, 1968, and 1977C; and Oceanographic Institute of Washington, 1977.)

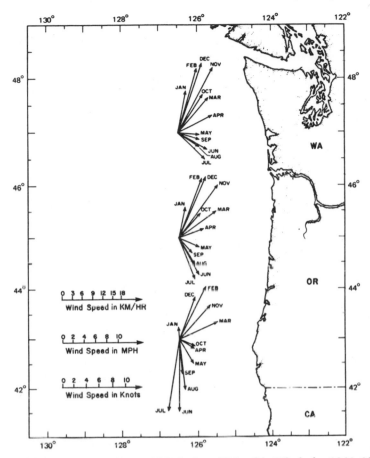

Figure 9. Average Direction and Velocity of Monthly Winds for 1961–1963. (From Duxbury *et al.*, 1966.)

area primarily because a summer low in the San Joaquin Valley of California attracts the east winds. In January, 1984, when the North Pacific High lay over the Northwest for nearly a month, precipitation was negligible and temperatures were near the summer averages; Brookings topped the list with an unbelievable 80° heat wave. When this happens in summer, temperatures can soar into the 90s and humidities plummet to near 20% along much of the Northwest Coast. Precisely these conditions were responsible for the catastrophic Tillamook Burns of the 1930s and 1940s. On average, though, moderation is the rule.

The other predominant climatic force in the Northwest is the famous cyclonic storms of winter. Where the moist subtropical air meets the cold polar front, the air ascends, pressure falls, winds and sea swells rise, and rain falls heavily, from latitudes 40–50° in both Northern and Southern hemispheres. The surface westerlies inten-

sify to a steady 100 mile-per-hour "jet stream" at about six miles altitude that tends to drag the cyclones eastward at about 20–50 miles
per hour. In the North Pacific, most cyclones form over southern
China and Japan, and in the winter move northeast to the coasts of
Alaska and British Columbia; usually the southern flanks, and occasionally the cyclone centers, pass over Washington, Oregon, and
Northern California (Barry and Chorley, 1976; Hare, 1966).

The result is not only the heaviest precipitation on the continent north of Guatemala, but also powerful winds exceeded only by
the hurricanes and tornadoes of the Southeast and interior. Between
capes Flattery and Mendocino, annual rainfall averages about 80
inches at sea level. As the cyclone moves inland, the Coast Range
raises and cools it at a rate of roughly 3.6°F per 1000 feet of elevation.
This squeezes out even more rain, about an inch for every rise of 50
feet. Every year 200 inches fall on the Coast Range slopes east
of Lincoln City, Oregon, and 250 inches near Mt. Olympus,
Washington; the latter amount is the highest in the continental U.S.
Along the coast, the lowest rainfall in the region is the 40 inches at
Eureka (Figure 10). By the time a North Pacific cyclone reaches the
coast, it has partially played itself out, and the rain it brings is almost
always a prolonged drizzle that merges imperceptibly into the next
system. Downpours are scarce; a fall of an inch in an hour occurs
only once every 50 years. On the average, the days per year of precipitation range from 55% at Cape Flattery to 32% at Eureka; in
winter, only 4–7 days per month are clear or partly cloudy (Proctor,
et al., 1980).

The warm westerlies restrict snowfall to the higher elevations;
in the Olympics snow forms usually above about 2000 feet and persists as year-around glaciers only above 4500 feet. Snow falls in the
lowlands only when the westerlies are disrupted between December and February, and rarely accumulates more than a few inches or
persists more than three days. Maximum amounts recorded are 36
inches at Tatoosh, 90 at Aberdeen, 31 at Astoria, and 3 at Eureka;
Olympic glaciers accumulate up to 40 feet (Proctor, et al., 1980).

Although the drizzle is unspectacular, the energy released by
the howling winds of the temperate cyclones each year exceeds 100
times the combined output of all mankind's electric generators, and
is the primary means of heat exchange from the equator to the poles:
in the Northern Hemisphere, the southward flow on the western
margin of a cyclone brings cold polar air in contact with the warm
subtropical air, and the northward flow on the eastern flank sweeps
the warm mass over the cold (Hare, 1966; Barry and Chorley, 1976).
When the storm winds hit the coast, they routinely exceed 40 miles
per hour, and as they continue inland commonly accelerate in the
mountain valleys to the 50s and 60s. Theoretical calculations predict

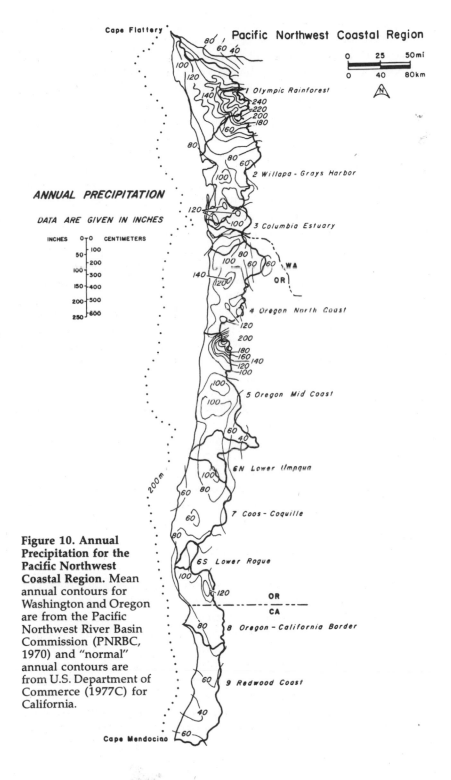

Figure 10. Annual Precipitation for the Pacific Northwest Coastal Region. Mean annual contours for Washington and Oregon are from the Pacific Northwest River Basin Commission (PNRBC, 1970) and "normal" annual contours are from U.S. Department of Commerce (1977C) for California.

that at sea level, the sustained (over one minute) wind speed of a North Pacific cyclone exceeds 55 miles per hour every year, 76 every 5 years, 83 every 10 years, 92 every 25 years, 100 every 50 years, and 108 every 100 years (Quayle and Fulbright, 1975). The peak gusts (less than 20 seconds) are 1.4 times the sustained speed. The highest gusts ever measured in the Northwest reached 150 miles per hour in 1966 off Oregon. The annual peak speed of 55 miles per hour can tear down chimneys, fences, and electrical wires; uproot trees; and raise waves over 25 feet. Besides creating rough seas, the cyclone also produces the so-called "storm surge." As the low-pressure center passes over, it sucks the sea surface upward, thereby raising the local sea level a few feet. This often leads to flooding and shore erosion, especially during high tides.

All this lasts, however, for just six months out of the year. As the sun creeps northward during spring, the entire global circulation system follows it, including the tropical thunderstorms, the subtropical highs, the temperate lows, and the polar fronts. In the North Pacific, the Aleutian Low shrinks and retreats to the northern Bering Sea and eastern Siberia, and the traveling cyclones are confined to the Alaskan coast, seldom straying as far south as Vancouver Island. At the same time, the North Pacific High expands northward until it fills most of the Gulf of Alaska.

With these new conditions, the weather changes drastically. First, the violent, sporadic southwest winds are replaced by the steady northwest winds along the eastern margin of the high. Since the high is centered off San Francisco, its influence strengthens from Vancouver Island to central California. While the average monthly wind speed off central Washington peaks in winter (due to the cyclones) at 8.9 miles per hour in November and December, off Cape Blanco the same maximum of 8.9 miles per hour occurs surprisingly during the summer high, in June and July (Figure 9). In comparison, the winter average off Cape Blanco peaks in February at only 7.2 miles per hour. In other words, although the cyclones always bring the strongest absolute winds, these are always sporadic, and the steady circulation around the North Pacific High provides the greatest averages at least south of the central Oregon Coast. The direction of the summer winds also depends on location in relation to the high. The broad clockwise circulation brings moderate northwest winds off central Washington, strong north winds off Cape Blanco, and even stronger north-northeast winds off San Francisco.

The second summer peculiarity is the frequent fog. As the air subsides in the North Pacific High, it steadily warms until it reaches the ocean surface, which cools it considerably, especially in the nearshore where upwelling is frequent. At about 45° the moisture condenses out as layered or stratus clouds, and because they are cooler and denser than the overlying air, they hug the earth. At night the fog moves inland and settles into the hollows and valleys. Where it is thick the fog condenses on the evergreen needles and drips to the ground, thereby boosting the annual precipitation by 10%–20%. By midday, air temperatures rise and the fog evaporates. Cape Disappointment is one of the foggiest places in the U.S., averaging 2552 hours (106 days) of fog per year. Despite the fogs, the warm, subsiding air of the North Pacific High assures 12–18 days per month of clear or partly cloudy weather in summer.

Finally, with the cyclones now safely to the north, rainfall south of Vancouver Island comes to a near standstill. Along most of the coast, 80% of the precipitation falls from October to March, and only 5% in July and August (Proctor, et al., 1980) (Figure 7). During late July or August, a drought of usually one or two weeks occurs nearly every year. Though brief, this drought profoundly influences the Northwest landscape, controlling the growth and distribution of many plant species. Summer rain usually falls during brief showers, when marine air moves inland, warms, rises, and forms swelling cumulus clouds. On average, these develop into thunderheads about one day each month. On the whole, though, the drier summer air keeps rainfall to a minimum.

In contrast, throughout the east U.S. coast, rain falls about equally throughout the year; in the Gulf States, summer is the peak rainfall season. The cause is a simple interaction between the high interior temperatures and a major high-pressure system centered in the mid-Atlantic off Florida. The humid tropical air swings toward the northwest around the lower hub of the high, and passes over the entire Eastern Seaboard. When it encounters the 80°F temperatures common at this time of year, it explodes upward into towering thunderheads that deliver some 20 inches of rain throughout the summer, about 4 times the Northwest total. The peak monthly rainfall is 7 inches in Orlando, Florida in June; 4 inches in August in New Haven, Connecticut; and 3.5 inches in July in Beauceville, Quebec. In contrast, the annual minimum in North Bend, Oregon is just 0.5 inch in July.

OCEANOGRAPHY

Not only does the ocean offer its warmth and wetness to the wind, which carries its reach to plants and animals far inland, but within the anatomy, physiology, behavior, and distribution of nearly every marine organism lies a dramatic response to the prevailing rhythms of tides, waves, and currents.

As the wind drags across the turbulent sea, it pulls a current of water at the surface. The net result of the global air circulation described previously is a twin pattern of surface ocean currents. But because of the earth's rotation, the currents do not exactly follow the winds. The so-called "Coriolis effect" is the illusion, when viewed from the earth, of a curved trajectory in an object that is actually moving in a straight line relative to an observer at a fixed location outside the earth. Since this effect cannot be fully explained without the help of vector calculus, suffice to say that relative to the earth, any moving object veers to the right in the Northern Hemisphere and to the left in the Southern, and the veering increases with latitude. As a result, any surface ocean current in the Northern Hemisphere travels at an angle 45° to the right of the wind direction. This means that the water tends to travel in a tighter circle beneath the clockwise anticyclone, and a looser circle beneath the counterclockwise cyclone (Hare, 1966; Barry and Chorley, 1976).

The prevailing westerlies produce a more-or-less westerly ocean current at about 40° latitude called the North Pacific Drift. In the Gulf of Alaska this merges with the Subarctic Current, which travels at about 1–2 miles per day (Hare, 1966; Barry and Chorley, 1976). The Subarctic Current reaches shore near Vancouver Island and in the summer breaks into the southward-flowing California Current and the northward Alaska Current (Figure 11). The northerly winds on the east hub of the North Pacific High drag the California Current along at about 4 miles per day, and the cyclonic storms maintain the Alaska Current at about 8 miles per day (Figure 12).

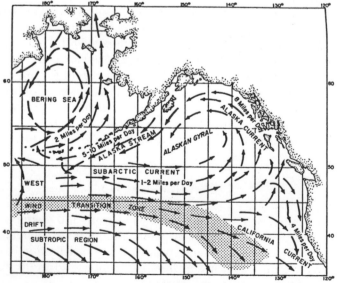

Figure 11. General Oceanic Circulation in the Northeast Pacific. A current speed of five miles per day is approximately 0.2 miles per hour or ten centimeters per second. (From U.S. Bureau of Land Management, 1974.)

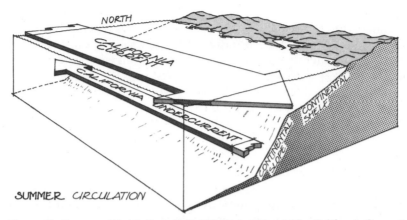

Figure 12. Summer Circulation off the Northwest Coast. The California Current, a broad, shallow surface current, drifts slowly southward over the continental shelf and slope during the summer. The California Undercurrent is a narrow, faster-moving current flowing northward at depths greater than 200 meters over the continental slope. This schematic diagram is not to scale. (From Parmenter and Bailey, 1985.)

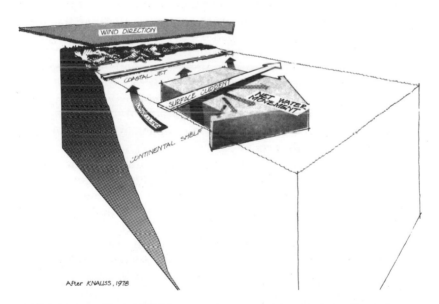

Figure 13. Offshore Water Transport and Upwelling. Wind blowing across the water sets up a spiral of water movement within the upper 20 to 40 meters of the surface. The result is a slow movement of this surface layer at right angles to the wind direction. Off Oregon, strong north winds in summer result in water moving seaward; deeper, nutrient-rich, high-salinity water flows shoreward and upwells into surface layers. A fast, narrow coastal jet develops along the coastline, moving in the direction of the wind. (From Parmenter and Bailey, 1985.)

    An important consequence of the California Current is the phenomenon of upwelling, whose repercussions reach throughout the coastal environment. Because of the Coriolis effect, the north winds of summer produce a surface current somewhat to the east of north. As this surface water moves offshore, it creates a lower pressure and sea level along the shoreline, and the deeper water rushes up to take its place (Figure 13). Water from as deep as 600 feet moves upward at speeds reaching 60 feet per day. Relative to the surface, the deep water is cold, high in salinity and nutrients, and low in oxygen; it emerges at the surface in a narrow band that hugs the shore from the surf zone out to about 10 miles, where it begins its return descent. Upwelling is most pronounced where the north winds are strongest along the central California coast, and around headlands, which themselves tend to divert the sea currents offshore (Huyer, 1983). On the Northwest Coast, upwelling seems to be most intense between capes Blanco and Mendocino, off the central Oregon Coast from Newport to Florence, and off Tillamook. At these locations temperatures in the surf zone average 43–45°F in the summer, while some 50 miles offshore, in the surf between capes Arago and Blanco, and along most of the Washington Coast they average a warm 55°F (Proctor, *et al.*, 1980). As mentioned above, the upwelled water often cools the overlying humid air enough to precipitate fog, which moves inland and eases the summer drought in the coastal forests. Moreover, the summer rise in nutrients causes a phytoplankton bloom that extends all the way up the food chain to seabirds, marine mammals, and humans (Proctor, *et al.*, 1980). Because of the upwelling, phytoplankton productivity in spring and summer is considerably higher on average along the nearshore than offshore. In fall and winter, nearshore productivity drops to levels comparable to the offshore.

    When the cyclones move to the south during winter, their powerful southwest winds reverse the California Current off Washington, Oregon, and northern California. This new Davidson Current travels northward at about 12–24 miles per day and buffers the region somewhat from cold temperatures (Figure 14). Nearshore winter temperatures average 47° off northern Oregon and Washington, 49°F off central Oregon, and between capes Blanco and Mendocino are actually warmer at 51° than in summer (Proctor, *et al.*, 1980).

    Since most of the Northwest rainwater evaporated from ouside the Northwest (the subtropical Pacific), the rate of runoff here exceeds the rate of evaporation, and surface nearshore waters are low in salinity. The voluminous Columbia and Fraser rivers are responsible for most of the freshwater over the continental shelf, especially off Washington. The southwest winds of winter push the

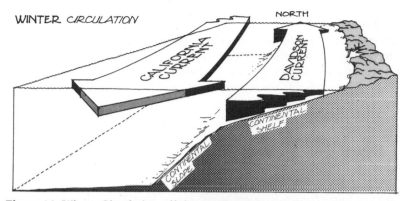

WINTER CIRCULATION

NORTH

Figure 14. Winter Circulation off the Northwest Coast. The fast-moving, relatively narrow Davidson Current flows northward at all depths over the continental shelf. The California Current, flowing slowly southward on the surface, is pushed offshore by the Davidson Current. This schematic diagram is not to scale. (From Parmenter and Bailey, 1985.)

Columbia "plume" fast against the Washington shore, where salinities fall below 30 parts per thousand as far north as Vancouver Island. As close as 100 miles offshore, however, they rise to at least 32 ppt. In contrast, surf zone salinities average 32.5 over Northern California and most of Oregon in winter. In the summer, the more northerly winds push the Columbia plume with its low salinities some 500 miles to the southwest. Summer nearshore salinities exceed 32 ppt along the Olympic peninsula and south of Newport in Oregon and California, but remain below 30 in much of the plume off the north Oregon Coast (Proctor, 1980).

In addition to the seasonal swings of currents, temperatures, and salinity, ocean waves play a premier role in the distribution and adaptation of shore organisms. Like currents, waves are caused by friction imposed on the sea surface by wind, but unlike currents, waves do not represent en masse horizontal movement of water, but rather a regular vertical oscillation that gives the illusion of forward movement. Wave height is determined by three factors: windspeed, wind duration, and the "fetch," or distance over which the wind acts. Wave heights on the Pacific Coast greatly exceed those on the Atlantic because of the larger size of the Pacific and the westerly winds that blow unremittingly from Japan to Oregon (Bascom, 1964; Anikouchine and Sternberg, 1981).

Oceanographers recognize two broad classes of wave. "Seas" are the chaotic turbulence immediately beneath a storm; as these distorted waves move out of the vicinity of the storm, they interact, modify each other, and develop into ordered, regular, and symmetrical wave trains known as "swells," and may travel under their own power several hundred miles from their origin. Most swells approach the Oregon and Washington coasts from the west and northwest, and originate in cyclonic storms in the Gulf of Alaska. In response to the prevailing winds, the local seas almost always approach from the southwest to south-southwest in winter and from the north and northwest in the summer.

The significant wave height, or average of the highest third of the waves, follows a regular seasonal pattern. In December, the roughest month, the significant sea height ranges from 3–9 feet 42% of the time, and from 19–23 feet 1.4% of the time. During the same month, the significant swell height ranges from 1–5 feet 56% of the time, and reaches a maximum of 23–25 feet 0.1% of the time (Proctor, *et al.*, 1980). When high seas occasionally meet high swells, they combine to produce colossal waves. In deep water off Oregon and Washington, the significant height of the resultant waves exceeds 39 feet every 5 years, 44 feet every 10 years, 52 feet every 25 years, 58 feet every 50 years, and 65 feet every 100 years (Proctor, *et al.*, 1980). Since the respective extreme wave heights average 1.8 times these values, we can expect at least a few 70-foot waves every 5 years, and a few 118-foot waves every century. Where on the continental shelf these appear, however, is anybody's guess. The maximum wave height ever measured off Oregon or Washington was 95 feet, although rocks have been tossed through the glass in the Tillamook Rock Lighthouse during winter storms, suggesting waves as high as 112 feet. In August, the calmest month, the significant sea height ranges from 1 to 3 feet 45% of the time, and 13–15 feet only 0.3% of the time; the swells are 1 to 5 feet 88% of the time.

As the waves reach land, they release their concealed energy on the shore and its inhabitants. But despite artistic appearances, over most of the coast they spend their power gradually as they interact with steadily shallower water, and at the same time they change size, shape, speed, and direction. In the process of shoaling, waves slow, steepen, and break as they drag over the shallow bottom, thus creating a surf zone whose width depends on the bottom slope. Waves slow down when the ratio of water depth to wavelength falls below 1:2, steepen when the ratio reaches 1:5, and break when the ratio of wave height to wavelength exceeds 1:7 (Proctor, *et al.*, 1980). A wave may break several times before its energy is completely dissipated. While the force of impact varies with the square of the wave velocity, the total energy of the wave (per unit area) varies with the square of its height. This means that a mussel feels the same slap from a 20-foot wave as it does from a 3-foot wave, as long as they are traveling at the same speed. But the important difference is that the 20-foot wave can, under the right conditions, lift and hurl a 600-pound rock or log into the mussel bed at 20 miles per hour, while the 3-foot wave throws the same rock only 3 miles per hour. Most of the damage to the inhabitants of a rocky shore is done not by the waves themselves but by the tossed and battered logs and boulders.

In addition to shoaling, waves also undergo refraction, diffraction, and reflection as they traverse shallow water. During refraction, a wave slows down in response to decreasing depth. Since the shore slope usually varies greatly along the length of a wave, the wave bends to align itself with the bottom contours. As a result, waves that approach a river mouth or cove diverge and sometimes fragment, distributing their energy over a broader area. Waves approaching a headland, on the other hand, converge like light rays in a magnifying glass, concentrating their energy on the point, as in the fisherman's dictum, "the points draw the waves." In the process of diffraction, a fragmented wave elongates as its energy spreads laterally along the crest. This allows the propagation of some wave energy behind an island, jetty, breakwater, or other barrier. A wave is reflected only if the bottom slope exceeds 1:20 or 5%; greater slopes reflect a greater fraction of wave energy (Bascom, 1964; Proctor, et al., 1980).

All these processes interact to create the complex but beautifully patterned textures clearly displayed at such places as Short Sands Cove, Seaside Cove, Hart's Cove, and Sunset Bay. Averaged over time, they sculpt an underlying pattern of habitats: broad gradients in energy, force, and direction of waves; in speed and direction of currents; and in size of sediments from sand to boulders. As we will see in the following, the marine biota responds to these gradients with intriguing variations in behavior, physiology, and distribution.

Tides

While the seas, swells, and global currents are powered ultimately by the rush of heat from equator to poles, tides rise and fall in response to the gravitational pull of the moon and sun. As the moon passes overhead, an object on the earth's surface experiences an infinitesimal weight loss as it is pulled slightly towards the center of the moon; the more massive the object, the greater the loss. Since the oceans are fluid and massive, they respond by rising conspicuously in great tidal bulges that follow the moon across the sky. Though virtually invisible at sea, when they hit shore the tides are usually magnified several times by local topography, creating wide gradients in exposure that dictate the distribution and life histories of many shore organisms.

As the earth rotates on its axis and the moon and earth hurtle along their orbits, the tide-generating forces drag across the earth in complex but predictable cycles. If we adopt Isaac Newton's brilliant equilibrium theory of tides, we can use our knowledge of these cycles to predict the number of tides per day, the relative heights of these tides, and broad shifts in tidal behavior from equator to poles. At the outset, we assume that the earth is covered with a uniformly deep ocean whose shape is in constant equilibrium with all tide-producing forces, and that the earth rotates freely beneath the tidal bulges without disturbing them in any way.

Two equal bulges, then, are always present on opposite sides of the earth. On the side closest to the moon, the bulge is a direct response to the pull of the moon; on the side opposite, the bulge is created because the moon pulls the rigid earth away from the ocean, and the ocean itself feels a weaker pull because it is farther away (this effect is often explained as "centrifugal force"). On the open ocean the moon's tidal bulges are about 13.9 inches above the average sea level. The sun's influence is similar but 46% weaker because of its greater distance from the earth; its bulges are only 6.3 inches and merge smoothly with the moon's (Bascom, 1964; Anikouchine and Sternberg, 1981).

So as the earth rotates, we might expect a point on its surface to experience four equal and alternating high and low tides: two high tides as it passes beneath the two bulges, and two low tides at 90° from each bulge. But this would be true only if the bulges were centered symmetrically on the equator, making them equally distant from a given line of latitude. Since the moon's orbital plane is tilted about 5° from the earth's, this happens only twice each lunar month, when the moon crosses the equator. The rest of the month, the moon veers north and south by at least 18.5°, and by as much as 28.5° every 18.6 years. Since the tidal bulges follow directly underneath, they move north and south by the same distance. So when the moon and bulges are at latitude 20°, for instance, one tidal bulge is centered on north latitude 20° and one directly opposite on south latitude 20°. These give rise to three broad latitudinal patterns. At north latitude 20°, a point on the earth's surface experiences an extreme high tide beneath the Northern Hemisphere bulge, but 12 hours later feels a weaker high because it passes beneath not the center of the southern bulge, but its northern fringe. For similar reasons, it also encounters two unequal low tides about 12 hours apart. This tidal pattern is known as "mixed." On the equator, a point passes symmetrically beneath the southern fringe of the northern bulge and the northern fringe of the southern, giving four equal tides each day. This is the "semidiurnal" (twice daily) pattern. Near the pole, the influence of the bulge of the opposite hemisphere fades out, leaving only one tide per day (the "diurnal" pattern) (Bascom, 1964; Anikouchine and Sternberg, 1981).

The equilibrium theory also predicts weekly and seasonal

cycles. When the moon, sun, and earth line up (at new and full moons), the sun's bulges complement the moon's, and the tidal ranges are 20% greater than average. In other words, since a high tide is above the mean tide level by the same amount that the next low tide is below that level, the highs are 10% higher and the lows 10% lower. These are known as "spring tides," not for the season, but because they jump so dramatically from one extreme to the other and back. In contrast, when the line connecting moon, earth, and sun forms a right angle (first and third quarters of the moon), the sun's bulges partly cancel out the moon's, making tidal ranges 20% less than average; these are the "neap tides" (Figure 15). Moreover, since the orbits of moon and earth are elliptical, the relative distances among earth, moon, and sun vary with the time of month and time of year. When the sun or moon is closer to the earth, the gravitational forces increase, the tidal bulges thicken, and the tides widen. The most extreme tides occur in late June and late December, when the earth reaches its closest approach to the sun. If at the same time the

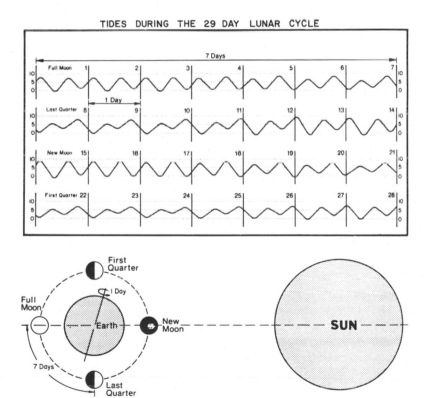

Figure 15. The Relationship Between Moon Phase and Tidal Signature for the Oregon Coast. Tidal ranges decrease slightly to the south, and increase slightly to the north. (From Hamilton, 1973.)

new or full moon is at its closest approach to the earth, then tidal ranges are more than 40% above average, and it's a long trudge to the surf at low tide. Of course, this is all an idealization. In reality, friction, inertia, the Coriolis effect, winds, currents, and atmospheric pressure combine to produce complex variations in the precise height and time of the tides (Fox, 1983; Bascom, 1964).

Centered at 44° latitude, the Northwest Coast is dominated by mixed tides, except for a few days twice each month when the moon passes over the equator to give semidiurnal tides. The usual sequence is higher high, lower low, lower high, and higher low, each separated by 6 hours and 12 minutes; as a result, the whole progression is repeated 50 minutes later each day. Over the years, the National Oceanic Survey has measured tidal heights at over 50 harbor stations on the Northwest Coast, and used Fourier analysis to compile the predictions published in the annual tide tables. In the tables, tidal heights are measured on a scale of feet and tenths of feet, and the level of the mean lower low tide is set arbitrarily at zero. At the Marine Science Center Dock on Yaquina Bay, the mean higher high water is 8.38 feet, the mean lower high water 6.86, and the mean higher low water 3.08 (Figure 16). Hence the mean difference between successive high tides is 1.52 feet, and low tides 3.08 feet, and the mean daily tidal range is 8.38 feet. The local mean sea level, defined as the mean water height calculated from hourly readings, is 4.51 feet. Although the most extreme tides ever measured here were minus 3.14 and plus 12.63, in a typical year tides range from about minus 2.5 feet during a June full moon to about 10 feet during a December new moon. Because of friction and inertia, tidal ranges decrease from north to south along the west coast, and spring tides occur about two to three days after a new or full moon.

Of course the best time to explore the shore whether out of curiosity or hunger is during minus tides, which comprise about a quarter of all low tides. Although the earth-sun distance is at a minimum in both June and December, the lowest tides are nevertheless in June because of the higher atmospheric pressure and greater incidence of easterly winds and currents. A drop in tide from zero to minus one exposes an additional 100 feet of ground on Clatsop Beach in Oregon, where razor clamming is de rigueur on early summer mornings.

Figure 16. Daily Tidal Variations and Terminology. A typical day's tide (for the Oregon coast) representative of the entire study area. Commonly used sea level descriptors are defined, and numerical values for Yaquina Bay, central to the study area, are given. (From Hamilton, 1973.)

Typical Days Tide

Tide Staff in ft. MLLW

14.5 Extreme High Tide — The highest projected tide that can occur. It is the sum of the highest predicted tide and the highest recorded storm surge. Such an event would be expected to have a very long recurrence interval. In some locations, the effect of a rain induced freshet must also be taken under consideration. The extreme high tide level is used by engineers for the design of harbor structures.

12.63 Highest Measured Tide — The highest tide actually observed on the tide staff.

10.3 Highest Predicted Tide — Highest tide predicted by the Tide Tables.

8.38 Mean Higher High Water — The average height of the higher high tides observed over a specific time interval. The intervals are related to the moon's many cycles which range from 28 days to 18.6 years. The time length chosen depends upon the refinement required. The datum plane of MHHW is used on National Ocean Survey charts to reference rocks awash and navigational clearances.

7.62 Mean High Water — The average of all observed high tides. The average is of both the higher high and of the lower high tide recorded each day over a specific time period. The datum of MHW is the boundary between upland and tideland. It is used on navigational charts to reference topographical features.

4.58 Mean Tide Level — Also called half-tide level. A level midway between mean high water and mean low water. The difference between mean tide level and local mean sea level reflects the asymmetry between local high and low tides.

4.51 Local Mean Sea Level — The average height of the water surface for all stages of the tide at a particular observation point. The level is usually determined from hourly height readings.

4.11 Mean Sea Level — A datum based upon observations taken over a number of years at various tide stations along the west coast of the United States and Canada. It is officially known as the **Sea Level Datum of 1929, 1947 adj**, and is the most common datum used by engineers. MSL is the reference for elevations on U.S. Geological Survey Quandrangles. The difference between MSL and Local MSL reflects numerous factors ranging from the location of the tide staff within an estuary to global weather patterns.

1.54 Mean Low Water — The average of all observed low tides. The average is of both the lower low and of the higher low tides recorded each day over a specific time period. The datum of MLW is the boundary between tideland and submerged land.

0.00 Mean Lower Low Water — The average height of the lower low tides observed over a specific time interval. The datum plane is used on Pacific coast nautical charts to reference soundings.

-2.9 Lowest Predicted Tide — The lowest tide predicted by the Tide Tables.

-3.14 Lowest Measured Tide — The lowest tide actually observed on the tide staff.

-3.5 Extreme Low Tide — The lowest estimated tide that can occur. Used by navigational and harbor interests.

Note: Specific elevations are based on six years of tide observations at the Oregon State University Marine Science Center Dock on Yaquina Bay. Values have been reduced by the National Ocean Survey (formerly the Coast and Geodetic Survey). The elevations differ from estuary to estuary and from different points within an estuary. The exception is MLLW which is zero by definition.

2

MARINE MAMMALS
AND SEABIRDS

*They say the sea is cold, but the sea contains
the hottest blood of all, and the wildest,
the most urgent.*

D. H. Lawrence, "Whales Weep Not"

As we walk the beaches and bluffs, it is difficult to envision how, some 3 billion years ago, the cold, gray oceans provided the first great arena of life. But it was here, in the deluged, volcanic childhood of the earth, where searing energy from volcanic heat and lightning by chance struck the proper combinations of methane, ammonia, and water vapor in the primeval atmosphere, producing the first organic molecules. Seventeen of the 19 phyla of animals on earth evolved, and still thrive, in the sea. Over the last 0.5 billion years, some of these abandoned the ocean and colonized land, where new selective forces catapulted them into new, advanced evolutionary trajectories, leaving their primitive ancestors in the sea. Later, a few of these land creatures re-entered the ocean, whose stable temperatures, buoyancy, and high productivity nurtured and gently reshaped their form and function over the ages.

In the following sections we explore some of these ocean newcomers, whose lives have captured the eye and imagination of people throughout history. Whales and seabirds are best seen from boat, but may be viewed from any headland, especially from Cape Alava in Washington; Ecola Point, Neahkahnie Mountain northmost turnoff, Cape Meares, Cape Lookout, Yaquina Head, Cape Arago, and Bandon in Oregon; and Trinidad Head in northern California. Seals and sea lions are easily seen at any bay outlet, and also at many locations on the outer coast, of which the best are Cape Alava in Washington; Strawberry Hill Wayside at Cape Perpetua, Simpson's Reef at Cape Arago (Plate 5), and the Sea Lion Caves in Oregon; and along Trinidad Head. Although sea otters are conspicuous at Monterey Bay, California, and in Alaskan waters, the only place to observe them on the Northwest Coast is along the outer Olympic Peninsula such as at Cape Alava and Sand Point.

MARINE MAMMALS

Evolution of Marine Mammals

WHALES

One of the most spectacular sights from the beaches of western North America is a 40-foot, 20-ton gray whale leaping bodily from the water. Even though most whale-watchers are aware that these awesome animals are not fish, but mammals, they often do not realize the significance of this fact. To say that whales are mammals implies that their evolutionary roots reach back to hairy animals that walked on dry land on four legs. That such an animal could develop into a whale is one of the most intriguing stories of evolution.

But it happened. Not once, but at least five times, did land mammals independently abandon the interior plains and forests and begin a slow exodus into rivers, estuaries, and seas. About 65 million years ago, the ancestor of whales entered the sea, around the same time as the ancestor of the sirenians (dugongs and manatees); 30 million years ago, the ancestors of the eared seals (e.g., Steller sea lions) and earless seals (e.g., harbor seals) independently entered the sea; and 5 million years ago the sea otters' ancestor moved from land to ocean.

What were the immediate land ancestors of whales, and did whales evolve from a single mammalian group, or from two or more separate forms? These two long-standing and baffling questions in whale evolution have recently been answered to the satisfaction of most paleontologists.

Several lines of biochemical evidence suggest that whales resemble modern cloven-hoofed ungulates, such as sheep, deer, camels, and pigs, more closely than any other group of terrestrial mammals. The evidence includes marked similarities in the structure of blood proteins, insulin, chromosomes, and tooth enamel, and in the anatomy of the uterus (Barnes, 1984). Hence we would expect to find the terrestrial progenitors of whales among the fossil ancestors of these animals. The modern ungulates evolved from an extinct order of terrestrial mammals called the Condylarthra, which is richly represented in the fossil record some 70 million years ago, and indeed within the Condylarthra is a family, the Mesonychidae, whose bones bear striking resemblance to those of the first fossil whales. The earliest known whale, the 50-million-year-old *Pakicetus inachus,* whose remains were unearthed from the Himalayan region of Pakistan in 1983, has a jawbone very similar to, and molars virtually identical to, those of mesonychids of roughly the same age uncovered in the same area. Yet it has an ear bone structure that shares with other early whales several peculiarities (although some-what more primitive) that appear to favor underwater hearing (Gingerich, *et al.,* 1983; Barnes 1984) (Figure 17).

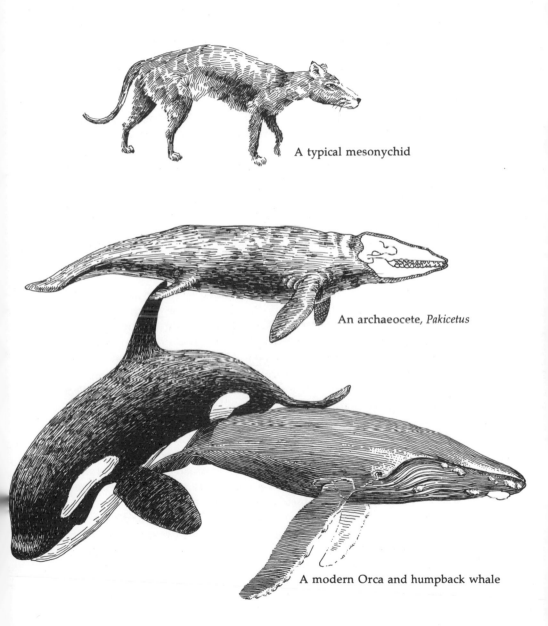

A typical mesonychid

An archaeocete, *Pakicetus*

A modern Orca and humpback whale

Figure 17. Artist's conception of whale ancestors. (Megahan)

But the first fossil whales, assigned to the suborder Archaeoceti, were already highly specialized for aquatic life. They had nostrils situated at the top of the snout, allowing efficient surface breathing; paddle-shaped front legs and a tail that undulated vertically (rather than horizontally, as in fish) for underwater locomotion; a long, streamlined body with shortened hind legs for reduced frictional drag while swimming; and several adaptations for underwater hearing, such as dense ear bones, air sacs between the ear and skull, and openings around the ear bones for fatty tissue (Barnes and Mitchell, 1978; Barnes, 1984). These attributes make for a vastly different animal from the mesonychids, and we have no fossils of any intermediate forms. Why should there be such a wide gap? Perhaps the initial changes were rapid and geologically isolated; if so, it would not be surprising if the later, better-adapted forms quickly outcompeted and extirpated the earlier, leaving just a short time interval for fossilization (Gaskin, 1982). In addition, the skeleton of a marine animal is rarely preserved intact, since its carcass usually remains in contact with water throughout the decay process, and the currents carry away the pieces as they decompose and separate (Gaskin, 1982). In any case, the improbable similarities in skull, jaw, and tooth morphology convince most paleontologists of the mesonychid ancestry of the archaeocetes.

So by 40–50 million years ago, we have a sudden abundance of archaeocete whales, from fossil digs throughout the world: India, Britain, North Africa, Australia, Antarctica, and the southeast United States (Barnes, 1984) (Figure 18). This suggests that the mesonychids took to the sea roughly 60–70 million years ago. Often, sudden appearances such as this are correlated with abrupt global changes in climate or geology (as in the pinnipeds, as discussed below). Were there any such changes 60–70 million years ago that might have promoted the evolution of whales? The most famous crisis in the history of the earth struck at the end of the Cretaceous period 65 million years ago: the mass extinction of most species of marine life and all of the dinosaurs, followed by an explosive diversification of mammals. As yet there has been no adequate explanation for these events, although several factors may have contributed, such as a cooling of the earth's climate as a result of an extended period of mountain building, predation of dinosaur eggs by mammals, and the collision of the earth with a giant meteor, leaving a suffocating pall of smoke encircling the globe. The semiaquatic mesonychids might have been unable to invade the sea successfully until their principal competitors, the highly adapted marine reptiles (e.g., ichthyosaurs, plesiosaurs, and mososaurs) had become extinct along with the rest of the dinosaurs.

Other less-dramatic events may have also played a role. In the

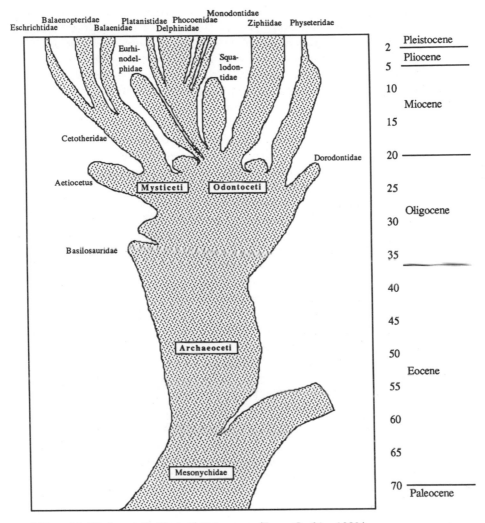

Figure 18. Phylogenetic Tree of Cetaceans. (From Gaskin, 1982.)

late Cretaceous (about 80 million years ago), the configuration of the continental masses was much different from today (Dott and Batten, 1981; Anikouchine and Sternberg, 1981). Africa and South America lay adjacent to each other, as well as northern Europe and North America. Between Africa and southern Europe and Asia was the Tethys Sea, a large, warm-water basin that extended southeastward to northern Australia and Southeast Asia. India was an island moving rapidly northward off the eastern coast of Africa, and would collide with the Asian continent, producing the Himalayas, in another 40 million years. About 75 million years ago, sea floor spreading opened up the South Atlantic Ocean between Africa and South America, pushing Africa closer towards southern Asia, thereby constricting the western margin of Tethys so that, by 40 million years ago, it was not much larger than the present Mediterranean Sea. The earliest fossil whales were found in sediments laid down at the margins of this small western arm of Tethys, all roughly 45–50 million years ago; for example, *Pakicetus* and *Indocetus ramani* in northern India, *Protocetus atavus* in Egypt, and *Pappocetus lugardi* in southern Nigeria. Perhaps the shrinking of Tethys, coupled with changes in the tropical marine climate, increased productivity in the estuaries emptying into Tethys, and this in turn favored the invasion of the mesonychids (Gaskin, 1982).

The archaeocetes became extinct 25–30 million years ago, about the time the first seals and sea lions appeared, as well as the two modern suborders of whales: the mysticetes (or baleen whales; mystax=moustache) and the odontocetes (or toothed whales; odontos=tooth), who diversified very rapidly into some seven families, including four of the nine modern ones (Mitchell and Tedford, 1978) (Figure 19). Today, 76 species of whales are recognized, comprising 66 odontocetes (including dolphins, porpoises, the killer whale, and the sperm whale); and 10 mysticetes (including all the large whales, most of whom are near extinction). Mysticetes and odontocetes differ in spectacular ways, and these divergences have supported the view that modern whales evolved from two separate ancestors (Slijper, 1962; Yablokov, 1964). Most obviously, the mysticetes lost their teeth, and instead, great plates of baleen evolved from the curved transverse ridges in the roof of the mouth, functioning to strain their planktonic food from the water. Odontocetes retained their teeth, but lost the differentiation of tooth shape and function: incisors, canines, and molars are replaced by a set of near-identical teeth, all of which are sharpened for catching and holding their swimming prey. Moreover, in odontocetes the skull is asymmetrical, the bones in the lower jaw grow together, males are larger than females, femurs are absent, and the blowhole is unpaired; whereas in mysticetes, the skull is symmetrical, the lower jaw bones are separate, females are larger than males, femurs are present, and the blowhole is paired (Slijper, 1962; Yablokov, 1964).

But current opinion sees these differences as minor adaptive variations on the same underlying anatomy (Van Valen, 1968; Barnes and Mitchell, 1978; Gaskin, 1982; Barnes, 1984). For example, the asymmetry in the odontocete skull involves complex specializations for echolocation, and the separateness of the mysticete jaw bones allows greater flexibility in feeding (Gaskin, 1982). These and other attributes could have arisen rapidly in the marine environment. Moreover, the chromosomes of odontocetes and mysticetes

Figure 19. Orcas (*Orcinus orca*) and harbor porpoises (*Phocoena phocoena*). (Megahan)

are very similar in shape, and the protein associated with the DNA (the C-heterochromatin) is distributed nearly identically in the two groups; this distribution could not possibly have originated by chance twice (Kulu, 1972; Arnason, 1974). A fossil whale found near Ona Beach on the central Oregon Coast figures prominently in this debate, since it combines features of both mysticetes and archaeocetes (Emlong, 1966). Like mysticetes, *Aetiocetus cotylalveus* has loose lower jaw bones and several peculiarities in its air-sinus system, but like all archaeocetes and primitive odontocetes, its teeth are differentiated into shearing, catching, and chewing types. For these various reasons, most modern paleontologists believe that both mysticetes and odontocetes evolved from primitive archaeocetes, whose skull morphology is in many respects beautifully intermediate between mesonychids and all modern whales.

SEALS, SEA LIONS, AND WALRUSES

Some 36 million years ago, the world climate suddenly cooled, causing major shifts in the circulation of sea and air. Among the changes was the onset of strong upwelling currents along the coasts of North America and Europe, resulting in a tremendous increase in nutrient recycling and productivity. This sudden new superabundance of food was apparently the incentive for the pinniped ancestors to enter the marine environment. The fossil record shows that, unlike whales, pinnipeds are a biphyletic group, having been derived from two separate terrestrial carnivores that moved from land to ocean at about the same time, one in the Pacific, and the other in the Atlantic (Figure 20). The Pacific ancestor was a dog- or bear-like carnivore that evolved into the walruses (family Odobenidae) and sea lions/fur seals (family Otariidae), while the Atlantic ancestor was an otter-like carnivore that gave rise to the true seals (family Phocidae). The trait held in common by all these groups is the modification of all four limbs into flippers, derived from the webbed feet of their freshwater ancestors. But the bone structure of pinniped flippers is unique. To provide leverage, the proximal bones shortened, and to increase the surface area, the distal bones greatly elongated. Pinnipeds also share a specialized tooth morphology. The teeth of terrestrial mammals are differentiated for catching and holding, shearing, and grinding, but in pinnipeds, all the teeth behind the canines have converged to a similar shape, adapted entirely for catching and holding. Apparently because shearing and chewing underwater would allow food to float away, pinnipeds usually swallow their food whole, and have no need for such teeth.

But despite these and other superficial resemblances, the Atlantic and Pacific pinnipeds differ greatly in anatomy and locomotion both on land and in water. Sea lions and fur seals use their

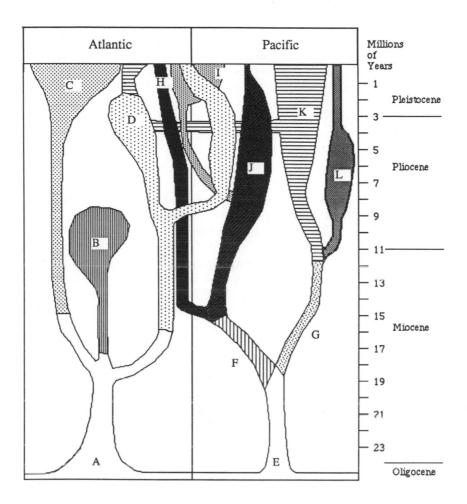

Figure 20. Phylogenetic Tree of Pinnipeds. (From Repenning, 1980.)

A   Enaliarctidae. Family ancestral to all Pacific-originated pinnipeds; derived from doglike land carnivore.

B   Desmatophocidae. Extinct sea lion-like family; primarily the genus Allodesmus.

C   Otariidae. Modern fur seals and sea lions.

D   Odobenidae. Modern and extinct walruses.

E   Phocidae. Family ancestral to all Atlantic-originated pinnipeds; derived from otterlike land carnivore.

F   Monachinae. Southern subfamily of the Phocidae.

G   Phocinae. Northern subfamily of the Phocidae.

H   Hawaiian monk seals—member of the Monachinae.

I   The Antarctic group of Monachinae: Leopard, crabeater, and elephant seals.

J   Caribbean and Mediterranean monk seals: members of the Monachinae.

K   Atlantic/Arctic Phocinae: Harp, harbor, and gray seals.

L   Paratethyan Phocinae: Ringed and Baikal seals.

forelimbs as paddles for underwater propulsion, "flying" through the water like penguins or murres. They usually turn their hind legs backwards for steering and equilibrium. Predictably, their greatest muscle mass lies in the front end of the body, where enlarged cervical and thoracic vertebrae provide solid muscle attachment. In contrast, the hind limbs of the true seals point permanently backwards to form a fish-like pseudotail. As a true seal swims, its hind end undulates from side to side, and the hind flippers stroke together, with the digits spread wide on the inward stroke to maximize the area exposed to water. The musculature of a true seal is concentrated in its hind end, and attached to enlarged lumbar vertebrae. The walrus is a slow and clumsy swimmer, and tends to rely more heavily on its hind flippers for propulsion.

On land, the wider rotation of the rear flippers allows the sea lions and fur seals to move about much more easily. All four flippers usually hold the body free of the ground, and the animal "walks" with alternate lifting of the flippers in much the same way as a terrestrial quadruped, or "gallops" by alternately lifting its upper and lower body. The heavy neck of sea lions and fur seals facilitates land movement by allowing them to balance on the front flippers while pulling the hind end forward; if not for this, they would be virtually immobile on land. In contrast, the skeletal attachment of the hind flipper of true seals blocks any forward rotation, and they can only hump and slide along, taking their weight alternately on the chest and pelvis. Some, such as the elephant seal, use the front flippers for partial support. The sea otter, in comparison, has accumulated few such specializations during its short history in the sea. Although its hind feet have developed into large, paddle-like flippers, its front paws are still typical of land mammals and are specialized for grooming and grasping, not swimming. When the otters float leisurely on their backs, they move by slow tail-wagging; when they dive for food, they propel themselves by paddling with their hind flipper-feet (Figure 21).

The oldest known pinniped fossil, *Enaliarctos mealsi*, was a strange beast with pinniped flippers but with a skull morphology somewhat intermediate between modern sea lions and the ancestors of bears. This animal entered the North Pacific at least 23 million years ago, and apparently evolved into all the North Pacific pinnipeds (Repenning, 1976, 1980). In addition to the flippers, *Enaliarctos* had a small tail and a long snout, and like the modern sea otter lacked several adaptations for marine life. Both, for example, have shearing and chewing teeth, and no specialization in skull shape for directional underwater hearing, or in the circulatory system for prolonged diving (Mitchell and Tedford, 1973; Repenning, 1980). Interestingly, fossils show that the Enaliarctidae had the

Figure 21. Sea otters in their typical foraging pose. (Megahan)

same geographical distribution as the sea otter: in the rich, cold, upwelling areas of the North Pacific coast from Japan to Southern California. Like the otter, *Enaliarctos* apparently could not disperse across the unproductive tropics to the Southern Hemisphere.

By 18 million years ago, the family Enaliarctidae had begun to diverge in new directions, and the different lines of descent are distinguished largely by their different modes of underwater hearing. About 17 million years ago, the Desmatophocidae appeared. This new group, represented primarily by the genus *Allodesmus*, lacked shearing and chewing teeth, had grown much larger than its enaliarctid ancestors, was sexually dimorphic (males were larger than females, indicating island breeding; see in the following), and had developed a primitive form of underwater hearing that involved the damping of low frequency sound. These adaptations probably freed them from a shallow coastal existence, and allowed them to range over deeper waters much as the modern sea lions. The desmatophocids dispersed throughout the North Pacific from Japan to Southern California from 15–12 million years ago, and probably dominated the region as a result of their adaptive superiority (Repenning, 1976, 1980).

By 14 million years ago, the first walruses evolved (family Odobenidae) from a group of enaliarctids that lost their shearing and chewing teeth. By far the most abundant form along the west coast of North America was the species *Imagotaria downsi*, which was the size of modern walruses, sexually dimorphic, and capable of underwater hearing (Repenning, 1976). These attributes undoubtedly allowed the animal to feed in the open ocean, placing it in direct competition with the desmatophocids. By 10 million years ago the desmatophocids disappeared, and *Imagotaria* diversified explosively into at least six new genera, as walruses dispersed into the Atlantic via the Central American Seaway (separating North and South America until roughly 5 million years ago), and became the only North Pacific pinniped to adapt to shallow water and feed on molluscs. In the Pacific the family eventually became extinct, but in the Atlantic evolved rapidly into the modern walrus *Odobenus,* which returned to the Pacific less than a million years ago via the Arctic Ocean and Bering Strait.

From 14–12 million years ago, the last remaining enaliarctids lost their shearing and chewing teeth and became the first otariids. Initially, they were small (about 50 pounds), the size of sea otters, and differed little from the enaliarctids apart from their teeth (Repenning, 1976). The prototype of the first otariids is considered to be the southern fur seal genus *Arctocephalus* (Repenning, 1976). After the walrus disappeared from the Pacific, however, the otariids became larger and sexually dimorphic. Probably during a period of global cooling 2–3 million years ago, the cooler, more productive tropical waters allowed otariids to disperse to the Southern Hemisphere, becoming the only North Pacific pinniped to do so. Nine species of otariids now live south of the equator, off Australia, New Zealand, and Cape Horn, and four species in the North Pacific (Repenning, 1980). Although the fur seals are considered a separate subfamily from sea lions because of their thick coat of fur, the skin parasites and fossil record of otariids show that the two fur seal genera, *Callorhinus* and *Arctocephalus,* are more distantly related to each other than *Arctocephalus* is to some sea lions (Repenning, 1976). The two common otariid species off the Northwest Coast are the Steller and California sea lions (*Eumetopias jubatus* and *Zalophus californianus*), both of whom are large, sexually dimorphic, island breeding, and pelagic (open ocean) feeding.

In sad contrast to this satisfying story of sea lion history, the evolutionary past of the North Atlantic pinnipeds, the true seals (family Phocidae), is only poorly known due to a lack of fossils. The best candidate for their land ancestor is *Potamotherium,* an otter-like animal similar in many ways to pinnipeds, and especially phocids. Peculiarities of its ear bones, for example, suggest the rudiments of underwater hearing, and the shape of the shoulder blade is similar to that of the harbor seal (Ray, 1976b). But *Potamotherium* is 22 million years old, while the earliest fossil seals are only about 15 million years old, and already highly adapted to marine life. Unfortunately,

Figure 22. Young male elephant seal and young harbor seal (*Phoca vitulina*) hauled out at Cape Arago. Summer 1986.

we have no fossils that link *Potamotherium* to the first Atlantic seals.

These early seals were already sufficiently advanced to belong to the two modern groups: the northern seals (subfamily Phocinae), and the southern seals (subfamily Monachinae); but the fossils are still scant, consisting primarily of a few dozen forelimb bones (Ray, 1976b). Later fossils are much more complete and diverse; some four to seven species from both groups appear by about 10 million years ago (Ray, 1976b). Initially, the monachines preferred the warm tropical waters of the Caribbean, while the phocines were centered in the cold waters of the North Atlantic. The monachines, however, soon dispersed widely. Some moved westward to the Pacific via the Central American Seaway, and after this was blocked by land masses some 3–5 million years ago, another group followed the new, warm Gulf Stream northward along the Atlantic seaboard and across the Atlantic to Europe; still others dispersed to the southern high latitudes, eventually giving rise to the five extant genera of antarctic seals. Among those who swam to the Pacific along the Central American Seaway (some 10 million years ago) was the ancestor of the elephant seal, probably *Prionodelphus* (Ray, 1976a). After the seaway closed, the ancestor became extinct on the Caribbean side, but on the Pacific side evolved into the elephant seal, *Mirounga*. The elephant seal soon split into two groups: one moved south along the west coast of South America to the Antarctic, and evolved into the modern *Mirounga leonina*, which dispersed throughout the subantarctic waters. The other moved north along the west coasts of Central and North America, and evolved into the modern *Mirounga angustirostris* (Ray 1976a). The northern elephant seal occasionally hauls out on Oregon beaches, notably on Shell Island off Cape Arago, but breeds on islands between central Baja California and the Farallons off San Francisco (Figure 22).

Figure 23. Harbor seal. (Megahan)

The phocines apparently spread rapidly through the North Atlantic and into the frigid Arctic, but never dispersed to the Southern Hemisphere. About 3 million years ago the Bering Strait opened up, allowing the phocine harbor seal *Phoca vitulina* to travel into the Pacific, where it rapidly dispersed in great numbers to all the coastal waters of the sea lions/fur seals. Today it is one of the most widespread pinnipeds, common in bays and near secluded outer beaches along the entire West Coast (Figures 23; 24).

Figure 24. Harbor seals (*Phoca vitulina*) at a favorite haul-out spot, Strawberry Hill Wayside, Cape Perpetua, Oregon. July, 1986.

THE SEA OTTER

A comparatively recent addition to the marine mammal fauna, the sea otter (*Enhydra lutris*) can be traced in the fossil record back at least two million years (Dawson and Krishtalka, 1984). It belongs to the family Mustelidae (badgers, otters, skunks, and weasels), and its closest land relative is considered to be the river otter (*Lutra canadensis*), although the fossil record is scanty and no intermediate forms have apparently been found. Like other members of the otter subfamily Lutrinae (i.e., the clawless African otters *Aonyx* and the giant Brazilian otters *Pteronura*) (Anderson and Jones, 1984), river and sea otters share several morphological attributes. These include their medium size, long and slender body, short legs, small eyes and external ear flaps, webbed digits, and long vibrissae growing from thick pads on the snout (Matthews, 1971).

The sea otter departs from its river counterpart, however, in several traits that adapt it to the marine environment (Kenyon, 1969, 1981, 1982). Unlike other members of the Carnivora, the sea otter lacks sharp, shearing teeth and instead has well-rounded teeth adapted to crushing the shells of crabs, urchins, and other invertebrates. The sea otter's hind feet are larger than those of the river otter, and broadly flattened into flippers that efficiently propel the animal as it lies on its back on the water surface. Propulsion is aided by the outer digits (little toes) of its hind feet, which are the longest digits. While the river otter's tail is thickened at the base and roughly round in cross section, that of the sea otter is nearly a uniform width and flattened horizontally, allowing it to be used as an efficient sculling oar. Because of this peculiar anatomy and the lack of any toughened pads on the hind feet except for a few small areas on the toes, the sea otter is extremely clumsy on land. Its ears are more similar to those of pinnipeds than river otters, being short, curled, and pointed downwards while diving apparently to exclude sea water.

Despite these adaptations, the sea otter is far less specialized to the marine habitat than the pinnipeds, being smaller, slower, less streamlined, and with poorer tolerance of diving anoxia and low temperatures. Unlike all other marine mammals, the sea otter lacks a subcutaneous layer of insulating fat, and instead relies on an extraordinarily thick pelage, which may reach 800 million fibers per animal, or twice the density of the northern fur seal. Fur, however, appears to be less efficient than blubber, since the sea otter metabolism is much more rapid than in any other marine mammal, and requires the animal to consume 20–25% of its weight each day.

Ancestors of the sea otter may have entered the rich upwelling region of the eastern North Pacific much as the otariids did many millions of years earlier, and eventually spread throughout the

Pacific Rim. As recently as the mid 1700's, the sea otter ranged from the northern islands of Japan and the Kuril Islands, the Commander and Aleutian islands, along the west coast of North America south to Morrow Hermoso Bay, Baja California and Mexico. Widespread hunting of the animal for its pelt, however, eliminated it from Baja California, Oregon, Washington, and British Columbia. In the 1970s, several hundred otters were captured from the Alaska populations and transplanted to British Columbia, Washington, and Oregon; the Oregon transplants disappeared by the early 1980s, but the others appear healthy.

Modifications Allowing Ocean Survival

It is a testimony to the great flexibility inherent in the mammalian body plan and its responsiveness to natural selection that whales and pinnipeds can have maintained their basic terrestrial form and functions, and yet become so thoroughly adapted to the sea. Here we consider some of the fascinating variations on the mammal theme that made oceanic life possible.

DIVING ADAPTATIONS

Despite being at home in the water, aquatic mammals have yet to free themselves from the necessity of breathing air, and like all other mammals will suffocate if trapped long enough below the surface. Nevertheless, for early aquatic mammals the need to interrupt breathing during prolonged underwater feeding runs must have been a strong selective force, and modern species demonstrate prodigious dive times. Sperm whales, for example, have been observed to dive over an hour, and many other species over a half-hour. But these are extremes, and both whales and pinnipeds seldom stay under for more than 10 minutes. Nevertheless, this is vastly superior to humans or any other terrestrial mammal.

Three main factors contribute to this unrivaled diving ability. First, marine mammals have a greater ability to store oxygen in the blood and muscles than land mammals, which hold it primarily in the lungs. Of the total amount of oxygen that a fin whale takes down with it, 42% is in the blood, 42% in the muscles, 9% in the lungs, and 7% in the tissue fluids (Slijper, 1979). In contrast, a human diver carries almost four times as much oxygen in the lungs and only a third as much in the muscle. Moreover, humans and terrestrial animals store much less oxygen per unit body weight overall because of the lower oxygen content of blood and muscles. The greater blood oxygen results primarily from a greater blood volume: whales have up to two to three times more blood per unit body weight than humans (Kanwisher and Ridgway, 1983). The greater muscle oxygen results from a greater concentration of a hemoglobin-like protein, "myoglobin," in the whale muscle tissue: whales have up to nine times more myoglobin than terrestrial mammals. In some whales, myoglobin is so abundant that it carries 50% more oxygen than the red blood cells (Kanwisher and Ridgway, 1983). In land mammals myoglobin is necessary in part because, when a muscle contracts, it presses against neighboring blood vessels, which reduces the local circulation and tends to cut off the oxygen supply. As this happens, the surrounding myoglobin releases more oxygen to the muscle cells, maintaining a steady supply. Thus its abundance in whales is not an innovation, but simply an enhancement of their mammalian inheritance.

Second, the muscles of marine mammals can function without oxygen longer than those of land mammals. In almost all animals, the metabolic pathways that provide the most energy for muscle contractions require oxygen. Other pathways exist, though, that provide less energy but do not demand oxygen. Fermentation, for example, liberates small amounts of energy from the conversion of sugars to lactic acid or alcohol. Marine mammals can prolong a dive if necessary by relying more on these alternate energy pathways. For unknown reasons, the resulting buildup of carbon dioxide and lactic acid in the animals' muscles and blood does not seem to cause them as much pain or injury as in land mammals.

Finally, marine mammals can make extremely economical use of their oxygen reserves during a dive. When researchers have prevented a dolphin from breathing by experimentally holding it underwater, the animal's heart rate dropped abruptly and the flow of blood and its contained oxygen shifted almost entirely to the animal's most important organs, the heart and brain. It is not known precisely how this is done, but whale circulatory anatomy provides some clues. For example, whales have massive networks of arteries and some veins called "retia mirabila" (or "wonderful nets"). The retia at the base of the whales' brain may help provide a steady flow of blood to the brain tissue to smooth out any fluctuations in the heart rate during diving (Harrison, 1972). Retia in other parts of the whales' body may help equalize local internal pressure differences that develop during fast up-or-down movements. Research on free dolphins in the sea, however, shows not only that heart rate remains constant during normal diving, but that the oxygen in the lungs is rapidly used up, forcing the animal to return to the surface or switch over to anaerobic metabolism (Kanwisher and Ridgway, 1983). This suggests that the reduced heart rate in restrained animals is not a normal diving response, but rather a high-stress reaction to the fear of drowning, and is probably used only in emergencies.

ADAPTATIONS TO COLD

Cold is a special problem for warm-blooded sea animals because water absorbs body heat about 20 times faster than does air. Several peculiarities in marine mammal metabolism and anatomy appear to be adaptations for heat conservation. First, like all other mammals, whales and pinnipeds use the heat generated from the burning of food during respiration to help maintain body temperature. But in whales, the basal metabolism is generally much higher than in terrestrial mammals of the same weight (Kanwisher and Ridgway, 1983), indicating the need for greater heat production in water than in air. Second, since a large body has a greater volume-to-surface ratio than a small one and therefore conserves heat more efficiently, the large size of many whales might be a heat-conserving adaptation. Fortunately, the bouyancy of the oceans facilitated this by reducing the need for a heavy supporting skeleton; when stranded on land, whales' massive bodies slowly collapse from a lack of skeletal support. The cold polar seas spurred the evolution of the largest animal ever to have lived, the blue whale, the largest of which reach 109 feet long and weigh 166 tons, as heavy as 38 average elephants.

Third, marine mammals are insulated from the chill waters by thick coats of fur, blubber, or both. The hairs of fur seals and sea otters grow in groups, consisting of a long stiff guard hair and several smaller underfur hairs crowded against it. When the animal dives, oil secretions and the fine tips of the fur fibers repel water, and the underfur traps air bubbles next to the skin, so that the water never penetrates to the skin. This rich, velvety coat is the reason for the commercial exploitation and near-extinction of fur seals and sea otters, and the total extirpation of sea otters in Oregon and Washington by 1906. A fundamental disadvantage of fur is that, for every 33 feet in depth, water pressure compresses the insulating layer of air to half its thickness. As a result the sea otter, the only marine mammal that relies solely on fur for warmth, feeds in shallow water near shore and grooms itself almost constantly. In pinnipeds and whales, a noncompressible layer of fat or "blubber," just beneath the skin, provides the necessary insulation. Whales indeed have lost virtually all body hair to minimize frictional drag while swimming, and rely totally on blubber, which may form a layer 20 inches thick in the bowhead whale. Seals generally have 3–4 inches of blubber, which amounts to one-third of the body weight of an adult elephant seal or walrus, and one-half the winter body weight of a ringed seal (Harrison, 1972).

Fourth, migration may be considered in part a behavioral adaptation to cold. Gray whales, for example, migrate each year from near-freezing arctic waters to tropical waters 77°F, in part because the baby gray whale is small and relatively blubberless, and requires warm water in the first weeks of life. After birth, the females with young are the last to leave the warm coastal waters, as they wait until their offspring grow large enough to endure the cold. Sperm whales, humpbacks, and other baleen whales migrate similar distances for apparently the same reasons. Besides providing insulation, blubber is used also as a food source during fasts in the often uncomfortably hot tropical seas. As it is digested, blubber releases about 40% less heat than the protein-rich foods the whales eat in cool arctic waters, and so helps them stay cooler during their interlude in the tropics (Harrison, 1972).

Finally, marine mammals have also evolved a specialized heat-conserving blood vessel anatomy. To prevent loss of heat from the blood that circulates through the flippers, tail flukes, and other extremities, the arteries, which carry warm blood to these appendages, are wrapped tightly by veins, which carry the colder de-oxygenated blood back to the heart. Some of the arterial heat that would otherwise flow into the sea is absorbed by the veins before it can reach the body surface, and is returned inside to warm the deep vital organs (Harrison, 1972).

Of course when the body temperature begins to exceed 99°F, an animal requires some mechanism for turning off the heat or radiating the excess out into its environment. Marine mammals lack the strategy of evaporative cooling provided in humans by sweat glands. Instead, the primary means of cooling in whales and phocids lies within the minute vessels just beneath the capillary bed. As the water warms, these vessels dilate to allow a greater flow of warm blood. The water bathing the skin may reach 77°F in the tropics, but is still cooler than the animals' blood and internal body, and cools the blood in the skin before it returns to the heart and body core. As a walrus cools off in this way, its body surface often turns a bright pink as the blood flows to the skin surface. When the water is sufficiently cold, the animals reverse the process by constricting these vessels, allowing just enough blood flow to prevent freezing (Harrison, 1972).

Unlike walruses and phocids, fur seals can dissipate heat only across the surface of their flippers, and can suffer from heat stress after exerting themselves. They often accelerate the cooling process by behavioral means, such as urinating on their flippers, panting like a dog, scooping sand on their backs, or occasionally going for a leisurely float at the water's surface.

SENSES

Like other mammals, marine mammals have highly developed senses of sight, hearing, and touch. But the primary sensory adaptations to an aquatic environment are those allowing low-light vision and directional underwater hearing. The eyes of pinnipeds are dark adapted by virtue of their large size and certain specializations of the retina. The retina contains only rods, thus preventing color vision, and as in cats, is lined with a reflective tapetum that doubles the intensity of incident light (Harris, 1972). But marine waters are too dark for this to be of much value, especially at the depths to which pinnipeds commonly dive. Hearing is a far more useful sense, because sound travels greater distances in water than in air. Nevertheless, the dependence on sound is problematic in some respects. Since the density of bone and tissues is similar to that of water, sound waves travel through body tissues of a submerged animal more readily than if the animal were in open air. In all land mammals (including aquatic ones) and the sea otter, when the animal is submerged, sound waves travel through all regions of the head to the inner ear, rather than through the ear canal. Hence to these animals, underwater sound appears to come from all directions. Whales and pinnipeds have evolved a great variety of complex specializations in skull morphology to permit directional hearing. Most of these involve the juxtaposition of tissues that differ in density and shape, and therefore in their ability to damp sound. In sea lions and walruses, for example, broad, flat areas on the skull tend to conduct sound more efficiently from some directions than others (Harrison, 1972). Moreover, all toothed whales and perhaps all pinnipeds have evolved the ability to echolocate, or use the echoes of their own vocalizations to judge the distance and direction of mute objects in their surroundings (see below). The fact that Atlantic pinnipeds, Pacific pinnipeds, and whales independently evolved different mechanisms for underwater hearing and echolocation indicates the supreme importance of these capabilities in the marine environment.

EVOLUTION OF POLYGYNY IN PINNIPEDS

Pinnipeds share several peculiar and entertaining reproductive traits that may be understood as behavioral adaptations to the marine environment. First, they breed seasonally on offshore islands, remote mainland beaches, or ice floes after an extended period of dispersed feeding (Figure 25). Second, they are extremely gregarious and site faithful, forming fantastically dense mating and pupping rookeries. Over 100 female sea lions may crowd together into a 100-square-yard area, returning year after year to give birth and mate at the place of their own birth. A female goes into estrus for just a few hours each year, and always just after giving birth in the rookery. Moreover, she delays implanting her newly conceived embryo in her uterine lining, so that pupping coincides with that of

Figure 25. California sea lions. (Megahan)

the other females the following year (the environmental signal for
implantation is unknown). Next to cave-dwelling bats, female pinnipeds are more gregarious than any other mammal.

Third, the males of many species are much larger and more
anatomically specialized than the females, and viciously aggressive
towards each other on the breeding grounds, defending small

territories from other males. Otariid males generally reach three to six times the size of females, and grow large canine teeth, protective patches of fur or skin on their upper body, and special structures for both visual and auditory threat displays. Male California sea lions, for example, have a pronounced forehead (sagittal) crest, and elephant seals an elongated "trunk" that amplifies their enraged bellows. Otariids are more sexually dimorphic, and display more intra-species aggression, than any other mammal.

Finally, as a result of male territorial defense, a single male will impregnate several females, and only a small fraction of the males (the largest and strongest) will breed each year; the rest congregate along the periphery of the territories, and occasionally attempt to copulate with passing females, rarely successfully. A territorial male northern fur seal (*Callorhinus ursinus*) may accumulate up to 100 females in its territory during the peak of breeding, impregnates typically 20–30 females per year, and sires roughly 80 young over its lifetime; an average female, however, gives birth to just three to four young in her lifetime (Bartholomew, 1970). This breeding system is a form of polygamy termed "polygyny" (poly=many, gyn=female). All the otariids are polygynous, but just two genera of phocids, the elephant seals (*Mirounga*) and the Atlantic or gray seal (*Halichoerus*). As mentioned previously, polygyny evolved early in otariids. The extinct sea lion *Allodesmus*, abundant in the North Pacific 12 million years ago, was sexually dimorphic, had enlarged canines, and growth zones on its teeth indicating seasonal fasting (Bartholomew, 1970; Repenning, 1976).

We can imagine how certain aspects of the pinniped physiology and environment should favor the evolution of poly-gyny (Emlen and Oring, 1977; Bartholomew, 1970; Trillmich and Trillmich, 1984; Pierotti and Pierotti, 1980). First of all, for polygyny to evolve in any species, the males must be able to defend the females economically. This can happen (1) if ecological circumstances force the females to congregate in a small area at the same time, so that a powerful male can defend them directly, or (2) if essential resources are clumped, so that a male can defend the area around the resources from other males, and mate with any female who enters. Second, other things being equal, heritable attributes of animals who leave the most offspring will tend to spread throughout a population in future generations. Thus, if polygynous males leave more offspring than monogamous ones, the polygynous will tend to replace the monogamous over evolutionary time. Contrary to intuition, a poly-gamous animal will not necessarily leave more offspring than a monogamous one. A polygamous parent must divide its energy among feeding, caring for young, and defending its harem or territory. If food is scarce or predation is intense, the young might not survive without considerable investment of time and effort by both parents. If so, then the energy wasted by a polygamous parent's fighting and vigilance might spell the doom of its young, and monogamous parents might leave more offspring in the long run. Moreover, the energy spent in securing and defending mates might detract seriously from a polygamous animal's own personal foraging. So as a rule, scarcity of food or a need for high parental investment in young will favor monogamy, while the reverse will open the door for polygamy.

How do pinnipeds fit in this scheme? As mentioned above, female pinnipeds are more densely clumped during the breeding season than virtually any other mammal. Several factors are responsible for this. First, the young are small and weak, and cannot survive in the water for several days after birth. Thus the mothers must haul out on land to give birth. Second, pinnipeds of all kinds and ages move about slowly and awkwardly on land, making them vulnerable to large terrestrial predators such as the cougar and wolf. Thus mainland pupping sites are generally out of the question, which leaves offshore islands that tend to be small and rugged, with but a few accessible flat areas for comfortable hauling out. Third, tropical pinnipeds need to immerse themselves frequently to stay cool, and thus congregate close to the water's edge when hauled out, leaving the rest of the island bare. Even California sea lions tend to stay close to the water when hauled out on their summer breeding rookeries. For the same reason, most sea lions prefer to haul out on the wind-exposed side of an island. Finally, pupping females prefer to haul out among other females rather than on perfectly suitable empty beaches nearby. This unusual gregariousness has yet to be explained adequately, but undoubtedly involves a homing attraction to the place of birth. So males clearly have ample opportunity to economically defend large numbers of females, by controlling either the females directly (as in elephant seals) or the piece of ground they are sprawled upon (as in sea lions).

But given this, should polygynous males leave more offspring than monogamous? Despite their initial helplessness in water, newborn pinnipeds generally need little parental care. Most otariids can move around and vocalize within seconds of birth, and a newborn northern fur seal is as capable as a three-week old domestic dog puppy (Bartholomew, 1970). Its mother suckles it more-or-less continuously its first four to five days, and then leaves it to forage, returning to nurse just once a week. Males are clearly unnecessary for rearing of the young, and not only do fathers invariably ignore the pups, but often inadvertently crush them during their blustering territorial charges. Thus they can devote themselves fully to the task of fighting and copulating.

Finally, since pinnipeds feed in the water, we might imagine that a male, who must remain situated in his territory or lose it, might run the risk of starvation as a result of his polygyny. But early on, pinnipeds evolved a large size and a thick layer of subcutaneous fat as adaptations for heat conservation in water, and these fortuitously permit them to survive comfortably for weeks without food. The lower metabolic rates of larger animals generally allow them to fast longer; bears, for example, can fast comfortably for months, whereas a shrew will starve within a few hours. In any case, cold is usually not a problem for most otariids while on land, and the blubber can be used as a food source instead of insulation.

We can test this model by showing that these various conditions are not met for the nonpolygynous or slightly polygynous pinnipeds. In the phocids that breed on ice floes, fasting does appear to be a major energy drain (Pierotti and Pierotti, 1980). Whereas pinnipeds can generally function easily in seawater of any temperature, a seal hauled-out on ice suffers from cold stress, which greatly limits the amount of time spent out of the water. As a result, not only do ice-breeding males fail to defend hauled out females, but females are often larger than males, presumably to conserve energy while they nurse the young on the ice floes until the pups are old enough to swim. This, however, is a much less extreme kind of polygyny than that of the sea lions. The abundant harbor seal (*Phoca vitulina*) is a familiar nonpolygamous pinniped in temperate waters. Interestingly, it is the only known pinniped that gives birth underwater (Pierotti and Pierotti, 1980). This might prevent females from forming dense pupping aggregations that can be easily defended by males. Moreover, harbor seals are much smaller than sea lions, which undoubtedly inhibits their ability to fast. Male harbor seals reach about five feet and 240 pounds while male Steller sea lions grow to 13 feet and a full ton.

The sexual dimorphism of otariids appears to influence their geographic distribution (Bartholomew, 1970). For example, the California sea lion breeds on offshore rocks from the California Channel Islands south, around the tip of Baja California to the Sea of Cortez. But after the end of the breeding season in mid-July, the adult and many subadult males migrate northward to overwinter as far north as British Columbia; in the winter these males are the most abundant pinnipeds off Oregon and Washington (Barholomew, 1970; Maser, *et al.*, 1981). The females and young, however, remain within the breeding range. Similarly, Steller sea lions breed mainly in California north of the Channel Islands, but as far north as Washington. In winter, the males migrate north into British Columbia and Alaska, leaving the females and young south of Washington. This exodus into cold northern waters presumably is allowed by the larger size and more efficient heat conservation of the males. The more diffuse winter population probably experiences reduced competition, allowing the animals to make fuller use of the food available.

WHALE AND DOLPHIN COGNITION

As mammals, whales and dolphins have inherited a central nervous system with a highly organized brain, and a behavioral flexibility that allows them to react and adjust to a changing and unpredictable environment. A major reason for the recent mushrooming of interest in whales is the idea that, with their large, complex brains, they may be highly intelligent, perhaps even more so than humans. To the scientific community, however, this subject is replete with wishful thinking perpetuated by poorly documented anecdotes and hopeful anthropomorphism. Nevertheless, the dolphin mystique dies hard, and only recently has controlled behavioral research begun to redefine that mystique.

Perhaps the most impressive behavioral deviation from humans and other primates is the ability of toothed whales and perhaps some baleen whales to judge the size, direction, and distance of nearby objects by the use of sound. Echolocation is an obvious benefit in a medium often clouded with sediment and penetrated poorly by light, and its evolution in toothed whales during the Oligocene may have allowed them to outcompete, and eventually cause the extinction of, the more primitive archaeocete whales. Dolphins produce a great variety of vocalizations, some with frequencies as high as 220,000 hertz (the human ear is sensitive to about 40,000 hertz at the high end) (Popper, 1980). Like bats, dolphins use click sequences when echolocating, and the high frequencies permit the greatest discrimination because they are sharper, less spreading, and reflect back from smaller objects more readily. The proportion of dolphin cerebral cortex devoted to sound production greatly exceeds that for bats, and a dolphin not only discriminates fine differences in the frequency of incoming clicks, but also controls the wavelength and frequency of its own emitted click sequences, presumably to maximize the information content of its echo in response to the size and shape of the objects encountered. Thus a bottlenosed dolphin (*Tursiops gillii*) can detect a school of 4000 mackerel at an average maximum distance of 319 yards, and discriminate between steel ball bearings 2.5 and 2.0 inches in diameter (Gaskin, 1982); a harbor porpoise (*Phocoena phocoena*) can negotiate wires 0.5 mm in diameter without contact 90% of the time (Popper, 1980). Several studies indicate that at various distances bottlenosed dolphins can recognize any dense object occupying more than 2.5 degrees of arc (Gaskin, 1982). This means an object at least 0.5 foot long at a distance of 11 feet, and 2 feet long at a distance

of 46 ft. Vision is greatly superior to this in good lighting, making echolocation useful primarily at night or in turbid water, and then only at short or intermediate distances.

Although baleen whales commonly produce click sequences, there is no evidence that they can echolocate with anything close to the accuracy of toothed whales: blindfolded gray and humpback whales (*Eschrichtius robustus* and (*Megaptera novaeangliae*) fail to negotiate simple obstacle courses (Gaskin, 1982). Nevertheless, hearing must be an important sense for some of these animals; the number of nerve fibers in one portion of the auditory cranial nerve of the fin and humpback whales greatly exceeds that of humans, the bottlenosed dolphin, and many other toothed whales (Herman and Tavolga, 1980).

Though echolocation is a spectacular adaptation to the aquatic environment requiring impressive specialization in hearing, sound production, and brain organization, nevertheless it may involve nothing resembling human reasoning. Other whale behavior, however, seems to require some kind of conscious intellect. When feeding, humpback whales for instance often blow a cylinder of bubbles around a school of fish (Figure 26). The intimidated fish are reluctant to swim through the bubble net, and the whale glides through the trapped school with mouth agape. Killer whales (*Orcinus orca*) appear to feed cooperatively by forming a circle around a group of large prey such as sea lions or walruses, and then swim one by one through the bunched prey to feed; bottlenosed dolphins also encircle fish schools in this way (Norris and Dohl, 1980). Both dolphins and killer whales also appear to herd their prey against the shoreline, the water surface, or underwater formations by fanning into a crescent behind the prey school, and swimming against and around the school in crisscrossing patterns. When the mullet begin their nearshore migration along the west African coast, native fishermen slap sticks on the water surface to attract Atlantic humpbacked dolphins (*Sousa chinensis teuszii*) and bottlenosed dolphins, who herd the fish into the shallows and the waiting gill nets (Madsen and Herman, 1980). The dolphins feed on the free fish as they mill helplessly against the nets, without which the fish might find refuge in the shallows. An individual dolphin appears to announce its identity to schoolmates with a unique "signature" whistle (Herman and Tavolga, 1980). Individual sperm whales (*Physeter catodon*) also produce acoustically unique "click" sequences, and narwhales (*Monodon monoceros*) a pulsing pure tone. These are just a few of the most impressive and best-documented field data commonly used to sup-

Figure 26. Humpback whales (*Megaptera novaeangliae*) are occasionally seen off the Northwest Coast. (Megahan)

port the existence of intellect in whales; many other examples could be given, such as the dominance hierarchies and age/sex segregation in schools of toothed whales; and the pervasiveness of "play" behavior in dolphins, including body surfing on ocean waves and bow waves of boats.

Although one could explain such behavior by postulating whales' understanding of concepts such as "net," "surround," and "self," sceptics are quick to point out that in all such examples the whales might not have the slightest idea about what they are doing, and their behavior might simply be a combination of haphazard trial-and-error, conditioning, and mimicry. The humpback, for example, might have blown bubbles purely by accident once, was rewarded by an easier mouthful of fish, and continues now because it has connected the two events mentally without knowing the reason for the connection; widespread mimicry perhaps eventually established the behavior firmly in the humpback population. Moreover, there are many examples of a lack of insight in whales, such as mass strandings and failure of dolphins to escape from drowning in purse seines by a short leap out of the water and over the net.

Captive dolphins, however, have yielded evidence of such higher mental abilities as concept formation, symbolism, both vocal and motor mimicry, observational learning, and second-order learning or "learning to learn" (Herman, 1980b). And as a rule, tests of confined animals underestimate their capabilities because the animals have little freedom to demonstrate their full mental powers evolved in the natural environment. We may never observe, for example, the complex social interplay and lightning speed of a group of cooperatively hunting killer whales.

Memory, the foundation of all learning, appears about equally developed in dolphins, chimpanzees, and other primates. In one experiment, a computer-generated whistle was broadcast from an underwater speaker in a dolphin's tank, and after a delay, two additional whistles were played, one identical to the first. If the dolphin could identify the matching whistle, the trainer tossed it a fish. After learning the rules, the dolphin performed the task nearly flawlessly to delays of at least 100 seconds for over 300 distinct whistles and other sounds it had never heard before (Herman, 1980b).

Interestingly, when this experiment was repeated using visually distinct objects instead of sounds, the dolphin failed miserably. Surprisingly, its performance improved after it was taught to associate a distinct sound with each disk. After it learned to respond to the correct disk according to the sound played, the sounds were eliminated and the test repeated. Now the dolphin responded correctly 80% of the time even with delays up to 30 seconds (Herman, 1980b).

Apparently, the dolphin could match visual objects only by first "naming" them in its mind, and then perhaps comparing the remembered names mentally instead of the visual appearance of the objects. We humans use similar tricks all the time, for example in remembering a phone number: instead of memorizing the written appearance of the numbers, we remember the auditory cadence of their names. Continued experimentation showed that the dolphin could perform correctly with visual objects entirely without sound if the objects were in motion, and even if visually identical objects were moved in different ways. Primates, ironically, perform about equally in comparable memory tests, but in the reverse order; chimpanzees, for example, have trouble remembering sounds but remember fixed shapes and small objects easily.

These results are strong evidence that dolphin and primate perception and memory evolved in adaptive response to their respective environments. While most terrestrial habitats are flooded with sunlight at least periodically, light intensity in the ocean drops off sharply with increasing depth. Sound produced underwater, however, can travel great distances. Songs of humpback whales have been recorded 20 miles from their source, and 20-hertz "moans" of the fin whale (*Balaenoptera physalus*) were heard 100 miles away. Physical calculations suggest that at certain depths, the low fin whale moans travel up to 500 miles, and may allow long distance communication that perhaps functions to synchronize breeding or feeding in the vastly dispersed population. A whale's world may be dark, but it is filled with a symphony of sound; crashing breakers, grunting fish, barking seals and sea lions, whining and humming boat engines and the clicks, buzzes, whistles, and groans of other whales are everpresent. There must have been considerable pressure on the earliest whales to overcome the limitations of darkness by evolving abilities to perceive, discriminate, remember, and learn from sounds. Similarly, the lack of stationary objects in the pelagic environment and the importance of efficient chase and capture of fast-swimming fish perhaps explains the dolphin's superior recognition and memory of movement over form. In short, the dolphin perceives the world quite differently from primates.

These experiments also demonstrate the ability of dolphins to form concepts such as "same" and "different," and to use symbolism, as they do when replacing a form with a sound. Conceptualizing and naming are two prerequisites for understanding human language, and in perhaps the most intriguing experiments ever performed on captive dolphins, Louis Herman of the University of Hawaii recently showed that, with patient training, dolphins, like chimpanzees and gorillas, can be taught a set of skills resembling the rudiments of language (Herman, 1980b). Initially, two dolphins were taught to associate (1) a "verb" with a natural action such as bite, tail-touch, fin-touch, go over, go under, go through, and fetch; (2) a "noun" with an object in the tank, such as ball, pipe, hoop, person, fish, frisbee, gate, window, and panel; and (3) certain "modifiers" for left, right, top, and bottom. The words were then combined to form commands that the dolphins had never heard before, such as "frisbee bite," "hoop go-through," "ball question" (meaning "is there a ball in the tank?"), "ball fetch panel" (meaning "carry the ball to the panel"), and "surface hoop fetch bottom basket" (meaning "carry the hoop on the surface to the basket on the bottom:" to do this the animal had to ignore the hoop on the bottom and the basket on the surface). After the first week of testing, the dolphins followed 600–700 two-word instructions correctly about 80% of the time; most of the errors were not in actions but in objects, especially when there were more than 6–8 to choose from. About 50% of the time they correctly performed three-word commands, consisting of direct object-verb-indirect object. Although most mistakes were to the indirect object, the dolphins demonstrated a clear understanding of simple logic by distinguishing on first hearing between, say, "ball fetch hoop," meaning to carry the ball to the hoop, and "hoop fetch ball," meaning to carry the hoop to the ball.

Similar experiments have yielded equally impressive results with chimpanzees, gorillas, and California sea lions. The sea lions have built up a vocabulary of 20 words and understand some 500 2–4-word commands. Their memory, however, is somewhat inferior, since they respond poorly when told to manipulate an object they have not seen in the last 10–12 seconds (Bower, 1984).

Although these results are certainly tantalizing and dramatic, we should not conclude that dolphins routinely "speak" among themselves in the wild, as though they were humans in wet suits. We have no evidence that they communicate anything save the most concrete, immediate information, let alone via a natural "language." If dolphins consciously and intentionally passed information back and forth in the wild, we would expect them to do so in captivity, but a series of classic experiments suggests that we would be disappointed (Herman and Tavolga, 1980). In these studies two dolphins were placed in the same tank and separated by a partition that was visually opaque but acoustically transparent. Each had a pair of paddles and was separately taught to touch either the left or right paddle when cued by a light (flashing=left, steady=right). Then one was chosen to be the "sender" and the other the "receiver." The cue light was removed from the receiver's vision and presented only to the sender. Now, the dolphins were rewarded only if they both responded (each in its own compartment) to the proper paddle at roughly the same time. The receiver could have no idea which paddle was correct unless the sender gave it some kind of acoustic signal. In this experiment and subsequent lengthy variations, the dolphins failed to demonstrate any unequivocal communication of this simple (though unnatural) signal.

Though evidence of intentional communication is slim, that of mimicry is much more impressive in both captive and wild animals. Whereas many birds can mimic with voice but not with body, and many primates, notably chimpanzees, can mimic with body but not voice, the only nonhuman animals adept at both are whales and dolphins.

The most striking example of whale vocal mimicry in the wild is the song of the humpback whale (Herman and Tavolga, 1980), which is occasionally seen off the Northwest Coast during migration. Every winter the humpbacks, like the grays, congregate in the subtropical and tropical Pacific to mate and calve. Unlike the grays, the humpbacks consist of three separate breeding populations around the islands of the southwest Pacific (the Ryukyu, Mariana, and Bonin islands), the Hawaiian Islands, and off the coasts of Baja California and nearby mainland Mexico. As they migrate to the breeding areas, the mature males begin singing. A song lasts 8–20 minutes or longer, and consists of a great variety of moans, squeals, rattles, chirps, and so on, ordered into several repeated phrases. A whale may sing continuously for over 22 hours, pausing only to surface. At the beginning of the breeding season, the songs are short, simple, and variable from whale to whale, but as the season progresses, the whales lengthen and adjust their songs in response to each other. But no matter how diverse the singing, by season's end every song of nearly every whale is the same. Each year the whales arrive at a breeding area singing only fragments of the previous year's song, and each year they leave all singing the same long and complex song, slightly different from the previous year's. Apparently they mimic each other throughout courtship and mating until they reach some kind of consensus, although how and why they come to any agreement is a mystery. Most researchers hypothesize that singing improves a male's chances of finding a mate, and singing the "most popular" song improves his chances even more; why this should be true is unknown.

Although the humpback's vocal versatility shames that of the dolphin, captive dolphins often spontaneously mimic the sounds they hear, and some have learned to do so on command (Herman, 1980b). With little trouble they can closely mimic electronically generated click trains as well as pure tones and undulating sine wave tones 2–16 kHz. One pair of dolphins even learned to imitate a different remembered sound in response to different objects in their tank, in effect "naming" the objects. Whether dolphins mimic each other in the wild is unknown; perhaps the ability is simply a felicitous outgrowth of an overall vocal flexibility brought on by the need for accurate echolocation. Many well-documented examples show that dolphins are also adept at motor mimicry. Captive dolphins have been observed to imitate the distinctive sleeping, swimming, and grooming postures of fur seals, as well as the brushing and cleaning movements of human divers in the same tank (Herman, 1980b).

We may well wonder why the mental capabilities of whales and dolphins are so similar to those of humans and other primates, while their respective habitats and evolutionary histories are so drastically different. It is not difficult to imagine that human-like reasoning would be highly adaptive to virtually any mobile animal in any environment, and that once any heritable rudiments of such an ability appeared, they would spread rapidly by natural selection. Of course, the probability that these rudiments will ever appear depends on the species' genetic resources and the overall developmental flexibility.

In birds and especially mammals, most learning occurs before adulthood, after which an animal's behavior tends to freeze; in humans, for example, the ability to learn language plummets after about age 12. Perhaps our own intelligence derives largely from our developmental flexibility: because our bodily development has slowed relative to the time of sexual maturity, humans retain many childhood traits through adulthood, including overall body proportions and childlike playfulness, curiosity, and learning. Adult humans, with our short faces, large craniums, and large ratio of brain weight to body weight, resemble immature apes more closely than adults. Whether a similar process has occurred in whales and dolphins is yet unknown, but is unlikely since most whale calves are highly precocious and require little parental care. Nevertheless, the brain/body ratio of dolphins is quite high. The amount by which the brain/body ratio of a bird or mammal species exceeds the average for other species of its size and weight, or its "encephalization quotient" (E.Q. for short, in analogy to I.Q.), may be a rough measure of overall brain function. Humans have the highest yet measured E.Q., but immediately below us, and above the other primates, lies the bottlenosed dolphin and probably most other toothed whales (Jerison, 1973).

What any particular harbor porpoise is doing with its large brain as it glides over the waves off Cape Arago is anybody's guess, and may be substantially different from anything it demonstrates in an aquarium. But though the porpoise and its relatives perceive a vastly different world from us, they react to it in ways that are amazingly human. How much of the whale mind is accessible to the human mind? Charles Darwin's comment applies equally to whales:

"He who understands a baboon would do more toward metaphysics than Locke."

Gray Whales

The annual migration of the California gray whale has distinguished the west coast of North America as the only shoreline in the world where large whales are visible in abundance from land. A discussion of the natural history of this outstanding animal provides a good introduction to the lifestyles of the 20-odd whale species in Northwest waters. In one of the most magnificent wildlife spectacles on the Pacific, and the longest migration known for any mammal, these whales travel every year on a 12,000-mile round trip through 50° of latitude, from their rich feeding grounds off Alaska to their ancestral calving grounds on the shores of Mexico. The small human population on the Pacific coast has been a blessing to the California grays, saving them from the intensive whaling that destroyed two other populations of gray whales. The Atlantic gray whale, known from subfossils in both Europe and North America, disappeared about 300 years ago, the radiocarbon age of the youngest specimen (Mead and Mitchell, 1984). The Korean gray whale, which migrated in a mirror image of the California population from the Sea of Okhotsk to Korea and Japan, nearly disappeared around 1890, and the last published citing was a solitary whale in 1979; the population may now be extinct (Yablokov and Bogoslovskaya, 1984). Yankee whalemen nearly exterminated the California population over just three decades in the mid-19th century, but reduced harvest in the 1930s and 1940s allowed the population to return to its original size of about 17,000. As a result, the California gray whale is the only large whale species to have fully recovered from overkilling.

The gray whale is extremely unusual, and not only in its migratory behavior. It is the only member of its taxonomic family, and its evolution is something of a dilemma. On the one hand, its body structure is the most primitive of all surviving baleen whales, suggesting the unlikely possibility that it arose several million years ago and remained unchanged to the present (Barnes and McLeod, 1984). On the other, the only recognized gray whale fossil is just 50,000 to 120,000 years old, and the fossil record of the gray whale barnacle extends back about the same length of time. If gray whales arose early on, their remains should have turned up in the productive San Diego Formation of southern California and northern Baja California, where numerous fossils of right whales, rorquals, and other marine vertebrates have been unearthed from sediments laid down in a shallow bay only a few million years ago. But gray whales are unmistakably primitive. Their baleen plates are thickest and

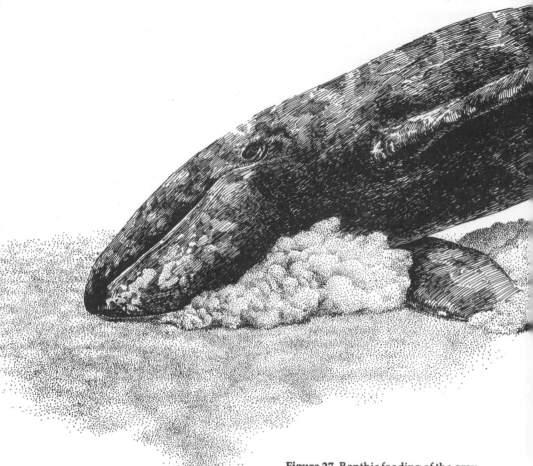

Figure 27. Benthic feeding of the gray whale (*Eschrichtius robustus*). (Megahan)

fewest of all baleen whales; the skull is small relative to the body; the neck vertebrae are unfused, allowing free head motion; the scapula is large; the mandible is nearly straight for the first two-thirds of its length; and the occipital bone is the smallest (relative to other skull bones) of all the baleen whales (Barnes and McLeod, 1984). With luck, new fossil discoveries will resolve this question soon.

To prepare for the migration, a typical gray whale spends four to six months each summer and fall feeding in the Bering and Chukchi seas, gaining 5.6 tons or about 25% of its body weight (Nerini, 1984). The gray whale's preferred feeding strategy is different from that of all other baleen whales, as it takes its prey not from the plankton but from the sea-bottom sediments. To feed, a whale dives to within a few inches of the bottom, turns on its right side, opens the right side of its mouth, and sucks in the sediments as it moves slowly forward (Figure 27). It then expels the sediments through its baleen, which filters out some of the prey organisms, creating a long stream of mud often visible around surfacing whales. The denser skin abrasions on the right side of the head suggest that most whales are right-handed while foraging. Perhaps because of this bottom-feeding strategy, gray whales seldom stray into waters deeper than about 230 feet, and remain well within sight of land through most of the migration.

Far and away the predominant prey items in gray whale stomachs are crustaceans of the amphipod (sand flea) order, and one or two species, usually including *Ampelisca macrocephala,* comprise 90% of the remains (Nerini, 1984; Blokhin, 1984). A whale spends more time and energy searching for a prey patch than it spends handling the prey, and we know neither how it finds the patch nor how much of the patch it consumes before moving on. *Ampelisca* and other members of its family live in sand tubes buried under about an inch of sediment at the sea bottom. They are extremely prolific, fast-growing opportunists that rapidly colonize disturbed ground, and multiply into dense colonies of up to 23,000 individuals per square yard. The richest aggregations lie within the Chirikov Basin, which comprises about 14,000 square miles between St. Lawrence Island and the Bering Strait, and here the gray whales congregate over most of the summer. *Ampelisca* thrives in disturbed areas, however, and the whale foraging probably stimulates its productivity.

By early October, the pregnant females abandon their arctic feeding grounds and form the vanguard of the southward migration (Braham, 1984). They leave first presumably because they must spend a month or two nursing their newborn calves in the warm Mexican waters before the calves are strong enough for the return trip. Next to leave are the barren adult females (usually in heat), followed by the adult males, immature females, and immature males (Rice and Wolman, 1971).

Unbelievable as it may seem, gray whales feed only sporadically during the migration. Whales stranded or killed along the migration route have empty or near-empty stomaches; mud plumes are seldom seen around migrating whales; and individuals lose as much as 30% of their weight before returning to the Arctic (Rice and Wolman, 1971). Apparently the bottom-feeding method is too time-consuming, or food resources too scarce.

The reasons for the migration itself are somewhat obscure, and we have no way of measuring the degree of conscious choice in the whales' movements. It is understandable that calving must occur in warm water because the small size of a calf gives it a large surface-to-volume ratio, preventing it from maintaining an optimal body temperature in the Arctic during the first few weeks of its life. But why the rest of the population should follow the pregnant females to Mexico is not obvious. The advancing pack ice may cut off the most preferred feeding grounds, but the whales hardly feed during migration, and the energy costs of migrating seem so great as to offset any gains from basking in the warm lagoons.

In any case, the population crosses Unimak Pass, Alaska, from late October to early January, and reaches Oregon about a month later traveling an average of 78 miles per day (Braham, 1984; Herzing and Mate, 1984). About 90% of the whales pass Oregon between December 19 and January 23, and reach their peak numbers the first week of January, when 29 whales pass within sight of the Yaquina Head Lighthouse every hour (Figure 28). Throughout the southward migration about 20% of the whales are less than a mile from Yaquina Head, and 50% between one and two miles (Herzing and Mate, 1984).

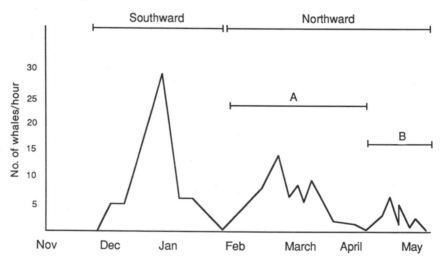

Figure 28. Gray Whale Migration Schedule at Newport, Oregon. (From Herzing and Mate, 1984).

In the breaks between storms, the whale spouts are clearly visible from nearly every headland along the west U.S. coast. During migration a typical whale surfaces 3 to 5 times at intervals of 13–15 seconds, then shows an arched tail stock and sometimes flukes as it dives, and three to five minutes later resurfaces about 100 yards away. The longest documented dive, of a radio tagged whale in Mexico, was 25.9 minutes. Occasionally a whale pokes its head repeatedly out of the water as though surveying the scene outside, but in most instances of this "spyhopping" behavior its eyes are either closed or underwater. The most dramatic behavior that whale watchers hope for is the breach, in which the whale leaps vertically out of the water. We may never know why a whale breaches or spy-hops, but scientists have proposed several utilitarian speculations, such as the idea that spyhopping cleans off the baleen or helps diges-tion, and breaching jars loose a few barnacles or skin lice or is the finale of a fish-feeding lunge. The proposal that breaching is a form of communication was discredited by the recent discovery that, at least in gray whales, it makes no detectable underwater sound. None of these notions has been demonstrated, and it is always possible that the benefits of a behavior, it they exist, are unobservable by anyone save the whale.

A less mystifying behavior is the act of copulation which, though inconspicuous, is observable throughout the migration. Heading south behind the late-pregnant females are the adult males and females in heat. At any given time, about half the females are pregnant. Since the sex ratio is 1:1, this means that there are two adults males for every female in heat. This lopsidedness has apparently led to the "mating triad," which consists of one female and two males migrating together. The few documented acts of copula-tion took place within mating triads and the males showed extraordinary cooperation and mutual aid. In one instance filmed for the television show NOVA, the act began as the cow swam more slowly. One bull then dove and rubbed his body against her genital area while the other pushed her down from above. This mutual stimulation continued until the cow turned on her back at the surface with her flippers extended, and the bulls responded by turning on their backs on either side of her, exposing their erect penises (Figure 29). Simultaneously, both bulls then turned toward her until one had

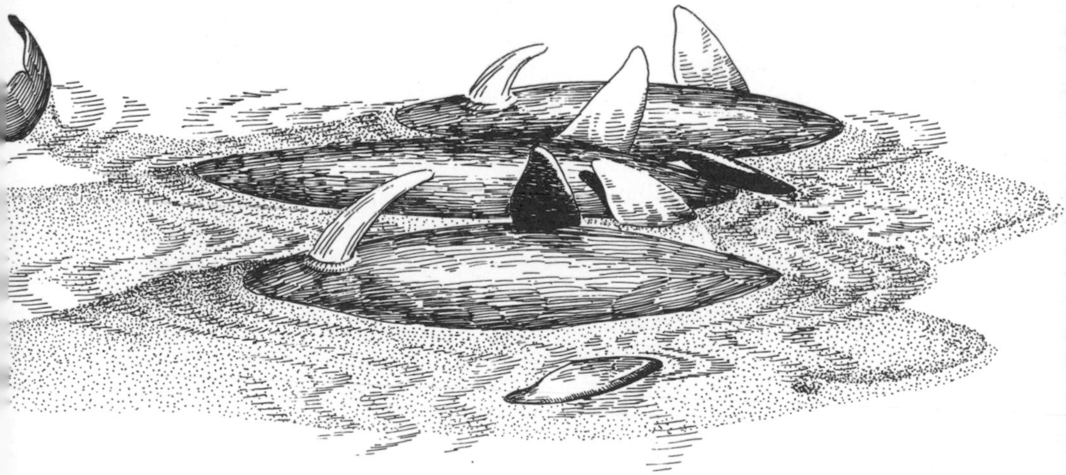

Figure 29. Artist's conception of mating gray whales (*Eschrichtius robustus*). (Megahan)

penetrated her genital slit with his penis. He and the cow then rotated 90° until they faced each other, and only a half-minute later they separated. Although prolonged stroking and rubbing with body and flippers is often observed in both pairs and triads, actual intercourse is seldom seen. Since most births occur between December 26 and March 1 and the gestation period is about 13.5 months, most conceptions must occur from November 11 to January 15, when the majority of whales are still heading south (Rice, et al., 1981). Nevertheless, triads and mating behavior persist at least through the northward migration off Oregon.

By mid-February almost all the whales have arrived at their calving areas in warm Mexican waters where they put on an entertaining show for tourists and researchers. Most calves are born in certain shallow lagoons on the west coast of Baja California: Scammon's Lagoon, San Ignacio Lagoon, Boca de Soledad, Guerrero Negro Lagoon, San Juanico Bight, and Bahia Almejas. A few determined individuals press on farther south around the peninsula and back up to the eastern shore of the Gulf, to Laguna Yavaros and Bahia Reforma of the mainland (Rice, et al., 1981). They prefer the shallow lagoons over the open ocean for giving birth presumably because of the shelter from heavy waves and predators such as killer whales, the ease of keeping track of the calves, and the necessity for the calves to stay near the surface until they learn the proper breathing and diving rhythms.

A newborn calf is 15–18 feet long and weighs about a quarter ton (Rice and Wolman, 1971; Rice, et al., 1981; Yablokov and Bogoslovskaya, 1984); it usually rides on top of its mother until its flukes and flippers harden. The nursing period lasts 6–8 months, during which the calf nearly doubles in length to 21–25 feet and gains 2–3 tons (Yablokov and Bogoslovskaya, 1984). To nurse a calf to this size while at the same time migrating 6000 miles, possibly feeding only sporadically, must be a prodigious feat for the mother. The average calf consumes 81 lbs. of milk per day (about 10 gallons) for a total of 5.5 tons (over 1300 gallons); the milk itself is extremely rich at 53% fat (Yablokov and Bogoslovskaya, 1984). Probably because of this energetic drain, 80% of the new mothers take the next year off to rest and feed before becoming pregnant again. The other 20% conceive again soon after giving birth, and go through the same ordeal all over again next year.

The adult males, females in heat, and immatures tend to congregate in "breeding aggregations" in the deeper water at the lagoon entrances, where most of the courtship and mating takes place. The cows and calves appear to avoid these aggregations, and stay well inside the lagoons in the shallow upper reaches (Jones and Swartz, 1984). If a cow/calf pair swims through the breeding whales, several males will often attack the mother at once, appearing to jockey for mating position with rough splashing and shows of flippers and flukes. These attacks are undoubtedly disruptive to the cow/calf relationship and may injure the calf. Normally a wide no-man's-land separates the nursing cows in the upper lagoons from all the other whales at the entrances.

Although the father forms no attachment to either mate or offspring, the cow/calf bond in gray whales is legendary. Early American whalers nicknamed the grays "devilfish" and "hard head" because the mothers often responded to the killing by ramming and stoving in the catcher boats, in several instances killing whalemen. Some crews preferred to kill calves to lure the mothers within harpoon range, while other avoided calves altogether for fear of attack by enraged mothers. This seemingly calculated and deliberate retaliation by the grays earned them the reputation as the most intelligent of the hunted whales. Their aggression, however, is apparently flexible and adaptive because the present population has never experienced severe human harrassment in the lagoons and is remarkably docile and gentle with the boatloads of tourists and fishermen. Since the winter of 1975–76, whale-watchers have reported increasing numbers of "friendly" or "curious" whales who seem attracted by the sounds of the boat motors, often rubbing against the engine or mouthing the propellor as it idles, and sometimes lolling at the surface while being rubbed and scratched by passengers. Many of these are calves whose mothers show no apprehension or hostility (Jones and Swartz, 1984).

By the time a calf is 3 weeks old, barnacles have already begun to settle on its skin (Yablokov and Bogoslovskaya, 1984; Mead and Mitchell, 1984). These belong to a single species, *Cryptolepas rhachianecti*, found only on gray whales. While in the warm lagoons, the adult barnacles on older whales release their larvae, which pupate and metamorphose into adults only when they come into contact with gray whale skin. Eventually they spread over the entire body, creating the mottled gray appearance that gives the whale its name. Also present are three species of skin parasites sometimes visible as dirty orange patches. These are the amphipod crustaceans *Cyamus ceti*, *C. scammoni*, and *C. kessleri*, which crawl about in the barnacle clusters, around the blowhole, in the throat grooves, around the eyes and ears, in wounds, and other protected places. Probably because of the time spent in warm, enriched coastal waters, gray whales suffer from more skin parasites than any other whale.

By late winter and spring, the balmy Mexican interlude draws to a close, and in two phases the whales filter out of the lagoons for their return trip north. At the intensively-studied San Ignacio Lagoon, the single whales depart from mid-February to mid-March, and the cow/calf pairs from mid-March to mid-May (Jones and Swartz, 1984). The first to leave are the newly pregnant females, presumably because they need to fatten up as much as possible before next year's marathon calving and nursing duty. But if this is the reason, then why they even bother to come to the lagoons instead of turning back immediately after conceiving is a mystery. Next are the adult males with any females not yet pregnant, and the immatures (other than calves). This group passes Yaquina Head, Oregon, in peak numbers (14 per hour) in mid-March, traveling at roughly 40 miles per day, nearly half the speed of the southward migration (Herzing and Mate, 1984). They also stay closer to shore: 40% are less than a mile from shore and 50% between 1–2 miles.

The cows remain with their offspring in the lagoons an extra 1–1.5 months possibly to nurse the calves to the proper size and strength for the trip. Before leaving, they behave in a curious manner that observers prone to anthropomorphism might interpret as celebration. Mothers and calves gather in large groups (up to 40 individuals) to splash, roll, dive, blow bubbles, and rub against each other with flippers, flukes, head, and body. A single group may remain intact from a few minutes to over 3 hours, and different groups form and reform repeatedly (Jones and Swartz, 1984). After leaving the lagoons, the cow/calf pairs travel much closer to shore than any other group. They reach Yaquina Head in peak numbers (6 per hour) in early May, and 97% pass within 0.5 mile from shore, just beyond the surf zone (Herzing and Mate, 1984). Shallow water may be necessary for the calf to learn breathing rhythms or possibly feeding skills.

The closer northward passage allows more intimate observation, especially from low, jutting headlands such as Cape Lookout, Oregon, from which a whale's entire body may be visible beneath the water surface. Although it is impossible to tell a whale's sex in the field, its rough age is often apparent. Calves through the first summer are shorter than 26 feet, while yearlings range from 26 to 31 feet (Sumich, 1982). A gray whale reaches 36 feet after 3 years, and becomes sexually mature at 8–12 years, when females average 39 feet and males 38 feet. Growth usually stops for both sexes at 43 feet, although the largest grays measured were a 49-foot female and a 47-foot male. The oldest were respectively 45 and 42 years as shown by growth layers in ear plugs, and the heaviest were 37 tons for a pregnant female and 18 tons for a male (Yablokov and Bogoslovskaya, 1984).

In recent years increasing numbers of grays have remained along the migration route all summer long instead of returning to the arctic feeding grounds, prompting speculation that the population has outgrown its traditional food supply and expanded southward, but this could easily reflect more careful observation. At least 100 whales and probably more than 150 summer off Oregon, and 35–50 off Vancouver Island; the Washington numbers are unknown (Sumich, 1982). Most of the Oregon whales are cow/calf pairs and immatures, some of whom appear small and undernourished; they fail to go the full distance probably because of their greater energy demands. Throughout the range of the gray whale, its benthic (sea bottom) food is distributed in disjunct patches (with the largest and richest patches in the Bering Sea) over which the whales congregate in large feeding aggregations. Along the migration route the food patches are apparently smaller, but they support small summering whale populations at several locations: the west coast of Vancouver Island; off California near Point St. George, the Klamath River mouth, Big Lagoon, and the Farallon Islands; and off Oregon in scattered locations mostly near river mouths (Sumich, 1982). Since estuarine sediments contain more organic remains than those offshore, it is no surprise that the whales near river mouths trail mud plumes more often, indicating normal bottom feeding in these richer areas.

Around headlands and elsewhere, however, their feeding is surprisingly atypical. A group of summering whales near Bamfield Marine Station on Vancouver Island feeds preferentially in the kelp beds around the headlands (Darling, 1984; Murison, et al., 1984). Fecal analysis and direct observation indicates that their primary food is *Holmesimysis sculpta*, a mysid crustacean or "opposum shrimp" that forms large swarms under cover of the seaweeds, and is also sought after by several fish species. Since the mysids and kelp beds occupy rocky sea floor, the whales most likely forego the bottom and instead suck or gulp the prey directly from the water column. Summering whales also frequent Oregon headlands. For 3 weeks in June and July, 1985, the same two young whales, identified by skin pigmentation, dove and surfaced erratically in the kelp beds off Cape Arago, Oregon, and may have been feeding in a similar manner. A third feeding method, probably rare and opportunistic, is pelagic feeding, often in deep water, on small schooling fish and plankton such as crab larvae. Researchers observe this type of foraging sporadically in the lagoons, and suspect it for the few summering grays sighted as far as 48 miles off Oregon, in water up to 1.7 mile deep (Sumich, 1982).

SEABIRD ECOLOGY

Like the marine mammals, seabirds also evolved from terrestrial ancestors, and since embarking on an oceanic existence have accumulated a variety of adaptations to problems of diving, food acquisition, locomotion, and heat conservation. Seabirds, however, are far more diverse than marine mammals, probably because birds have crossed over from land to ocean many more times than mammals. The independence from the ocean granted by the power of flight undoubtedly eased this crossover: unlike mammals, most seabirds are not forced to swim between feeding and breeding grounds (although some are, e.g., penguins). Worldwide, seabird species number 260–285, while pinnipeds number 33 species, and whales and dolphins about 76 (Nelson, 1979; Gaskin, 1982). Fossil evidence shows that nearly all groups of seabirds originated in the Indo-Pacific Oceans at about the same time as the whales, about 60 million years ago (Nelson, 1979).

True or "primary" seabirds obtain their food entirely from the ocean while swimming, flying, or diving, but not wading (Ashmole, 1971). These comprise four orders (Nelson, 1979):
1. *Sphenisciformes* (penguins);
2. *Procellariiformes*, or tubenoses (petrels, diving petrels, shearwaters, and albatrosses);
3. *Pelicaniformes* (pelicans, gannets and boobies, tropic birds, frigate birds, cormorants, and darters);
4. *Charadriiformes* (gulls, terns, skuas, skimmers, and auks).

The secondary seabirds, not discussed in this chapter, are those who obtain their food in the proper manner, but only seasonally from the ocean, such as loons, grebes, phalaropes, and seaducks (e.g., eiders, scoters, and mergansers); and those wading birds who forage primarily along the coast, including sandpipers, plovers, and oystercatchers.

Primary seabirds fall into two groups according to their degree of independence from land (Ashmole, 1971; Nelson, 1979; Boaden and Seed, 1985). Those who seldom stray outside the shallow continental shelf waters, such as pelicans, cormorants, auks, and most gulls and terns, are the "neritic" species. The "oceanic" species, including albatrosses, shearwaters, and petrels, spend the majority of their time on the open ocean, returning to land only to nest.

The primary seabirds and a few of the secondary (especially loons and grebes) include some of the most primitive avian species. Perhaps because of the monotonous uniformity of the ocean and the lack of competition and predation, seabirds have felt little pressure to specialize and diversify so have changed little since entering the marine realm. Another consequence of the relative scarcity of predators is the extremely low adult mortality rates and long lifespans of most seabirds. Annual mortality averages about 20%, but falls as low as 3% in some albatrosses (Lack, 1954); banded birds live typically 20–30 years, and one, a Laysan albatross (*Diomedea immutabilis*), lived a documented 53 years (Nelson, 1979). In contrast, 40–70% of adult passerines (songbirds) die each year (Boaden and Seed, 1985).

Distribution and Abundance

Worldwide, seabird abundance reflects ocean productivity, as birds tend to congregate, often in immense numbers, where prey are concentrated near the surface. At any given latitude, this is usually in upwelling areas and at the boundaries between water masses, since currents in both cases bring nutrients, plankton, and fish to the surface (Ashmole, 1971). As mentioned above, the Northwest Coast is a region of major upwelling in spring and summer, and because of this seabirds are extremely abundant. Over 40,000 birds breed along the Washington outer coast; over 400,000 off Oregon; and nearly 700,000 off California, of which 280,000 nest between the Oregon border and Cape Mendocino (Varoujean and Pitman, 1980; Sowls, 1980). Between capes Flattery and Mendocino, these constitute just 12–13 species in all, of which the most abundant are the common murre (*Uria aalge*, 28%) and rhinoceros auklet (*Cerorhinca monocerata*, 26%) in Washington (Varoujean, 1979); the common murre (59%) and Leach's storm petrel (*Oceanodroma leucorhoa*, 31%) in Oregon (Varoujean and Pitman, 1980); and the common murre (88%) and Leach's storm petrel (6.0%) between the Oregon border and Cape Mendocino (Sowls, 1980). Surprisingly, western gulls (*Larus occidentalis*) constitute only 1–2% of all breeding seabirds off the Northwest.

Abundance, however, is highly variable over time and space, as birds actively seek out transitory patches of locally abundant prey, often within strong upwelling currents. In addition to the breeders, some 15 species migrate through Northwest waters at various times of year (Figures 30, 31). Migratory movements, usually motivated by scarcity of food, may be divided into four classes (Nelson, 1979). *True migrations* are regular, seasonal, and often long-distance excursions between traditional breeding and feeding grounds. The most impressive are the transequatorial journeys of the Arctic tern (*Sterna paradisaea*), parasitic jaeger (*Stercorarius parasiticus*), long-tailed jaeger (*S. longicaudus*), Wilson's storm petrel (*Oceanites oceanicus*), Leach's storm petrel (*Oceanodroma leucorhoa*), and several shearwaters (Nelson, 1979). The Arctic tern migrates each year from its nesting grounds in the arctic tundra to "wintering" grounds in the austral

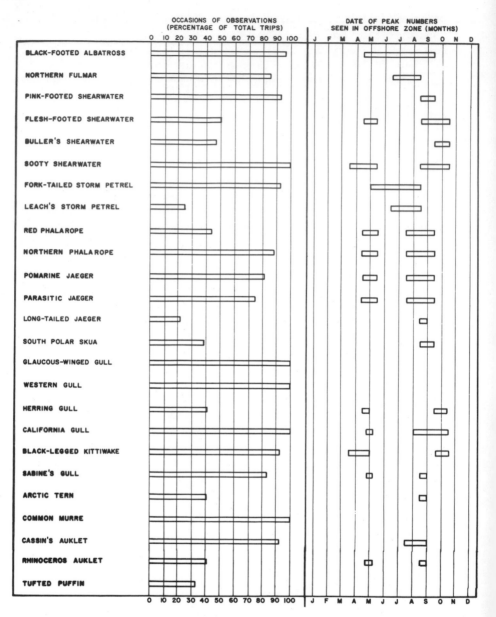

Figure 30. Sea Bird Frequency of Observation for 42 Trips off Westport, Washington. (After Wahl, 1975.)

summer, as far south as the Antarctic pack ice. Many of these marathon migrations seem senseless, because the birds pass over several perfectly good feeding sites along the way. In these cases, perhaps the innate, species-specific migratory behavior evolved

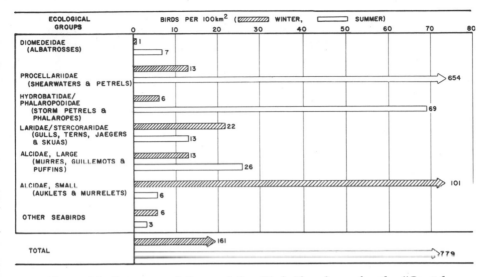

Figure 31. Summary of Seasonal Sea Bird Abundance for the "Coastal Domain." (After Sanger, 1972.)

during a time when different geologic and climatic conditions necessitated long-distance movements, and the rigid behavior has been passed along unchanged regardless of the new conditions. *Dispersal movements,* unlike true migrations, are less predictable or regular movements outside the breeding season, to any local patch of abundant prey. Cormorants (family Phalacrocoracidae) and murres, for example, move about more-or-less haphazardly throughout the winter as they search for transitory prey patches. *Nomadism,* primarily in albatrosses, shearwaters, and petrels, is a predictable, long-distance migration, but unlike true migrations, is not directed to a fixed wintering site. Rather, movement and feeding are continuous, along a broad arc or figure-8 pattern, beginning and ending at the nesting ground. *Foraging movements during nesting* are regular movements back and forth between feeding areas and hungry chicks. These vary greatly among species in frequency and distance from the nest. Oceanic seabirds such as shearwaters and petrels may forage up to 600 miles from their nests, while the neritic species commonly stay within a much shorter radius.

Adaptations

SEAWATER

The life of a modern seabird is made more comfortable than its ancestors' by a variety of anatomical and physiological specializations. Most coastal birds eliminate excess salt from their body fluids through nasal glands, located in or over the eye orbits (Nelson, 1979). These kidney-like organs discharge concentrated salt water into the nasal cavity, allowing seabirds to use the saline body fluids of their prey, and perhaps seawater as well. Nasal glands are larger and more highly developed in oceanic species than in most neritic and secondary seabirds, and the bills of some species have ridges that direct the fluid to the tip, presumably to prevent the bird from swallowing it again. Tubenoses (order Procellariiformes) are named for the pair of tubular projections on their bills that apparently shelter the nostrils from salt spray on stormy days.

FOOD ACQUISITION

The enormous variability in bill morphology of seabirds for the most part reflects differences in preferred prey. Auks that feed on soft-bodied organisms have a bill wide at the base and a smooth palate; fish-eating auks have a narrower bill with a grooved palate; plankton-feeding auks have horny papillae on the palate and a thicker tongue (Nelson, 1979). Pelicans trap fish in a pouch-like mandible that distends, like a plastic bag, as it fills with water; anyone who has tried to catch fish in a bucket will understand the usefulness of this distensibility. Rhinoceros auklets and tufted puffins (*Fratercula*) have teeth-like structures on the surface of their tongues that enable them to hold and carry several fish at the same time, while they continue to catch more (Nelson, 1979). Cassin's auklets (*Ptychoramphus aleuticus*) have a special pouch beneath the tongue that enables them to store and carry larger amounts of food from feeding grounds to nest, where they regurgitate it for their young. Tubenoses can transport their food long distances by converting it in the stomach to a concentrated oil with a high caloric content per unit weight, allowing them to forage over greater distances while feeding nestlings.

LOCOMOTION

Seabirds vary greatly in diving and swimming abilities, but since the laws of physics prevent a bird from excelling in both aerial and underwater flight, adaptations for speed and agility underwater generally pre-empt the possibility of soaring. Long, narrow wings allow albatrosses, shearwaters, and frigatebirds (family Fregatidae) to float effortlessly on the wind for days or weeks at a time, but commit them to a life above water. The small wings of fish-eating auks (e.g., common murres), diving petrels (*Pelecanoides* spp.), and penguins are used for underwater propulsion, but limit flight efficiency in most species and, when coupled with a large body, prevent it altogether in a few (e.g., penguins). The advantages of webbed or paddle-shaped feet in cormorants, murres, gulls, and others are obvious; in many species the feet and legs are set farther back on the body, allowing greater leverage in water, but barely interfering with the ability to cope with gravity on land. In contrast, sandpipers and other shorebirds have short legs set in the middle of the body for efficient running, or longer legs suitable for wading.

DIVING

Diving seabirds face the same problems in oxygen utilization and heat conservation as marine mammals, and have solved them in similar ways (Nelson, 1979). As in whales and pinnipeds, diving birds store large amounts of oxygen in myoglobin and in a larger blood volume than terrestrial relatives, and during long dives apparently slow their heart rate, switch to anaerobic respiration, and divert blood flow away from peripheral organ systems. But in addition, many seabirds store oxygen in a complex arrangement of air sacs that hold about half the oxygen carried down during a dive. Common murres have been observed surfacing with bottomfishes in water up to 200 feet deep, and have tangled themselves in fish nets set as deep as 600 feet off Newfoundland; their maximum observed dive time is 200 seconds, off the Oregon Coast (Hansell, 1983). While murres who have just dove for 105 seconds or less have about the same amount of lactic acid in their blood as nondivers, those who have just dove for over 2 minutes do have significantly more, indicating that they switch over to lactate fermentation as an energy source during long dives (Hansell, 1983).

Like sea otters, most seabirds conserve heat without the use of an insulating layer of fat, which would hinder flight. Instead, they depend on well-preened and oiled feathers, which in some species (e.g., penguins) resemble fur in density and in their short and narrow shape. The insulation of feathers hinges on their ability to retain air, which in turn requires the water-repellent properties of oil. In most birds of both ocean and land, a gland at the base of the tail secretes oil that is spread with the beak throughout the bird's feathers; seabirds preen in this manner several times a day (Nelson, 1979). Cormorants are not as well endowed with oil as other seabirds, so often stand for several minutes after dives with (probably cold) wings outstretched to dry. This wettability might be an adaptation, however, to allow deeper and longer dives by reducing buoyancy. Penguins in addition conserve heat with a layer of body fat that might be partly responsible for their flightlessness.

FEEDING BEHAVIOR

On a typical spring day from a lookout point at Ecola Park, Oregon, an observer can see some 20 bird species on the ocean surface and flying to and from the offshore rocks. Loons, grebes, cormorants, scoters, gulls, terns, murres, guillemots, puffins, and others forage in these mixed-species flocks or loose aggregations. Seabirds fall into roughly six classes according to their feeding behavior, and different behaviors appear specialized for capturing different prey types (Ashmole, 1971).

The seabirds best adapted to underwater foraging are wing- or foot-propelled underwater swimmers. These require speed and agility to catch their small fish prey, such as capelin, herring, and other bait fish. The shearwaters and murres use wings and sometimes feet for propulsion underwater, while the loons, grebes, cormorants, scoters and other diving ducks use feet only. The large size of these birds results from the relationship between size and swimming speed: speed increases with weight (and thus with the cube of length), whereas the water resistance increases with surface area (or with only the square of the length). Thus larger birds generally swim faster.

Less adapted to fish chasing are the plungers. Since these are usually buoyant and lack specializations for propulsion (e.g., small wings and streamlined body), they cannot dive from the water's surface as the previous seabirds can. Instead they plunge from the air into the water, using the momentum gained in the air to propel them forward underwater. Boobies and gannets (family Sulidae) are deep plungers, while tropicbirds, gulls and terns, and the brown pelican (*Pelecanus occidentalis*) are shallow or surface plungers. The shallow plungers eat small fish as well as more passive prey, such as crustaceans. The boobies and gannets may sometimes use their feet and wings to help them swim, but the main underwater function of these appendages is steering.

Seabirds that feed on small, passive prey such as zooplankton, crustaceans, and pteropods need no special swimming adaptations. These birds feed while settled on the surface by "surface seizing" or "surface filtering." Surface seizers, such as albatrosses, gadfly petrels (*Pterodroma* spp.), gulls, and phalaropes, simply grasp individual prey with the bill. They often sight food near the surface while in flight, then settle and immediately snatch the prey. Often this prey is a small bird, usually a sick or injured one, or a dead animal of any kind. Although the larger gulls are adapted for the capture of live prey, they have exploited the increased opportunities offered by man for scavenging. Some birds eat small surface organisms by "surface filtering," usually with the aid of a distensible throat pouch. Fulmars (*Fulmarus glacialis*) filter out their food by using their pouch to suck and expel water through a widespread system of extensions on the lower mandible, analogous to baleen whale feeding. When pelicans surface-feed on small shoaling fish, their throat pouch functions as a dip net.

Another group of birds feeds on small fish while flying at or near the sea surface. While in flight, "dipping" birds, including some terns and small petrels, use their bills to seize prey above or just below the surface. Storm petrels feed mainly by "pattering;" they use their feet and wings to position themselves at a constant height above the uneven water surface. This enables them to pick tiny organisms from the surface in quick succession. Gulls often use a combination of dipping and pattering as they hover in the sea breeze.

Still another group of birds are known for their habitual stealing of food from the bills of other birds and each other. The "pirates" or "kleptoparasites" (klepto = steal) include frigatebirds, jaegars and skuas (family Stercoraridae) and many gulls. Skuas (*Catharacta skua*) and large gulls can often be seen chasing and harrassing smaller birds in the air until the latter are sufficiently intimidated to disgorge or let go of their prey.

These diverse feeding methods may appear unrelated, but recent research suggests that they complement each other in ways that make mixed-species foraging highly efficient (Hoffmann, *et al.*, 1981). For example, the plunging of shearwaters and especially black-legged kittiwakes (*Rissa tridactyla*) is so conspicuous that it attracts other seabirds to their feeding area and a flock is created. Divers can see from a distance whether a kittiwake is feeding on a single fish or on a school, and approach only the latter. Thieving by gulls and kittiwakes tends to force puffins, murres, murrelets, and auklets to the less-exposed fringes of small flocks. And when these dive around the edges of the flock, they may help corral schools of fish and other prey towards the center of the flock and thus improve the flock's overall feeding success. Shearwaters, however, sometimes drive the fish schools deeper and out of reach of the rest of the flock when they dive by the hundreds into the middle of the schools.

A dozen seabird species, including northern fulmars, glaucous gulls (*Larus hyperboreus*), black-legged kittiwakes, short-tailed shearwaters (*Puffinus tenuirostris*), and horned puffins (*Fratercula corniculata*) take advantage of gray whales and other whales to help them feed (Harrison, 1979). As the whales rise to the surface, the startled fish and plankton above them flee toward the surface where they are seized by the birds. Also, when gray whales surface, they sometimes bring with them sediment and bottom-dwelling organisms stuck in their baleen and bristles. The whale shakes off this material and begins to dive, but before it disappears, the birds drop to the surface to attack the dislodged dregs. Short tailed shearwaters have been called "fin whale birds" by whalers due to their strategy of following gray, humpback, and fin whales.

Figure 32. An idealized seabird colony. (Megahan)

BREEDING ECOLOGY

The rigors of the marine environment have favored the evolution of several peculiarities in seabird breeding ecology, such as colonial nesting, nest-habitat specialization, monogamy, small clutch size, and late age of sexual maturity.

Nesting environment. Seabirds, especially oceanic species, nest on offshore islands and rocks that for the most part are quite small, averaging probably 20–30 yards in diameter along the Northwest Coast (Figure 32). Except for rare forays by bald eagles and other raptors, predators of adult birds are virtually nonexistent on these islands. As a result, most species nest in dense, conspicuous colonies, and competition, in the form of ritualized aggression, is often intense for good nest sites. About 98% of seabirds are colonial nesters, as compared to just 13% of all birds (Lack, 1968). Seabird populations have been observed to rise greatly after spreading onto new nesting areas (such as newly formed volcanic islands), indicating that nesting habitat limits population size in some cases.

Perhaps as a result of competition for nesting space, different species have evolved radically different nesting habitat preferences, thereby making maximum use of the available habitat (Sowls, 1980). Species who nest in burrows or rock crevices include the pigeon guillemot (*Cepphus columba*), horned and tufted puffins, fork-tailed storm petrel (*Oceanodroma furcata*), Leach's storm petrel, Kittlitz's murrelet (*Brachyramphus brevirostris*), ancient murrelet (*Synthliboramphus antiquus*), and rhinoceros and Cassin's auklets. With sharp claws and beak, these species excavate burrows in soil, kicking the earth out behind them. To avoid predation of eggs and young by gulls, the storm petrels feed young, mate, and brood only at night, and are seldom seen by humans.

Species nesting on the open surface may be divided into

1. those nesting on flat or gently sloping ground, including double-crested and Brandt's cormorants (*Phalacrocorax auritus* and *P. penicillatus*), gulls, and the black oystercatcher (*Haematopus bachmani*);
2. those nesting on ledges on cliff faces, such as the pelagic cormorant (*Phalacrocorax pelagicus*), common murre, and black-legged kittiwake; and
3. the single species that nests on tree branches, the marbled murrelet (*Brachyramphus marmoratus*).

Only a few marbled murrelet nests have been discovered, and they appear about equally distributed between tree branches and in burrows along lake margins.

Since some seabird nests seriously erode the soil, most islands evolve through a predictable series of geological stages and nesting communities (Sowls, 1980). Besides the burrowers, who obviously deplete their own habitat, several other species (pelicans, cormorants, gulls) cause further erosion by pulling out plants for nest building, and inadvertently killing vegetation with their excrement. A typical island begins with deep soil and often trees as wave erosion breaks off a piece of headland from the mainland. Burrowers are initially common, but gradually decline as they remove their habitat. As the soil thins and trees topple in the storms, surface nesters begin to dominate. Erosion by waves, rain, and wind continues, until the entire rock finally disappears beneath the swells.

Rock stacks at all these stages can be found along the West Coast. Obvious incipient islands include Point Sur at the north end of Big Sur, Trinidad Head itself, Pewetole Island just north of Trinidad Head, California, and Squaw Island at Cape Arago, Oregon (Sowls, 1980). These all support trees and deep soil, but as yet no nesting seabirds because of predator access at low tide. Pewetole Island, however, does support a few oystercatcher nests. The largest storm petrel colony in California is Little River Rock, a young, heavily vegetated but treeless island a few miles south of Trinidad Head. Double-crested cormorants have recently colonized, and burrowing habitat is noticeably declining (Sowls, 1980). Haystack Rock off Cannon Beach, Oregon, is also well vegetated but treeless, and supports a healthy population of tufted puffins. In 1911, ornithologists described numerous burrowing puffins, pigeon guillemots, Cassin's auklets, and Leach's storm petrels on Flatiron Rock north of Trinidad Head. Now, bare rock has replaced soil over most of the island, so fewer than 10 guillemots and puffins nest among over 10,000 murres, Brandt's cormorants, and western gulls (Sowls, 1980). Puffin Island, in the Chamisso Islands National Wildlife Refuge in Alaska, is seriously eroding as long, deep, horned puffin burrows collapse each year (Sowls, 1980).

Monogamy. Several features of the marine environment appear to favor monogamy (i.e., mating with the same partner each year) in seabirds. First, foraging for young is difficult, especially for oceanic seabirds nesting far from upwelling regions. Prey congregate and disappear unpredictably, often at great distances from the nesting island, and considerable foraging skill is necessary to avoid making long, unsuccessful trips. For this reason, older birds tend to raise offspring more successfully than younger. Hence a bird is taking a risk if mating with a stranger rather than with last year's mate, who already has at least a year of nurturing experience. Second, good nest sites are at a premium, and experienced birds are more likely to compete successfully for them, again favoring more skilled mates. Further, we would expect birds to avoid giving up a previously proven nest site, and indeed, in most species pairs return to the same nest year after year. Finally, if a different mate were chosen each year, the pair would likely end up nesting later than the rest of the colony due to a longer period of courtship, so latecomers would have poorer odds of winning a good nest site, or would waste more energy competing for a site already taken.

Small clutch size. Clearly, a bird wastes energy by producing more young than it is capable of incubating and feeding. Hence oceanic seabirds, who face longer foraging excursions and scarcer, less predictable prey populations, would be expected to lay fewer eggs than neritic species, whose nests already lie within upwelling regions. Indeed albatrosses, shearwaters, fulmars, and storm petrels all lay just one egg, while most neritic species lay more: alcids 1–2; pelicans 1–3; oystercatchers, western and glaucous-winged gulls 2–4; and cormorants usually 4–5 but up to 7 (Sowls, 1979) (Figure 33). In contrast, many terrestrial species lay 7–15 eggs, and often rear two broods per year.

Figure 33. Oystercatcher nest at South Cove, Cape Arago. Summer 1986.

Juvenile development. Probably because of the difficulty of raising young, most seabirds pass through a lengthy juvenile stage, typically 3–7 years (Ashmole, 1971). An adaptive rationale for this can easily be imagined: if a bird happened to mature earlier, say after one year (as in many passerines), it would have to endure the rigors of courtship and nesting competition, only to be faced with the prospect of feeding young perhaps before gaining enough experience to feed even itself. Such an individual might not only fail to rear any offspring, but die of starvation itself, as it expends energy courting and fighting and forfeits its hard-found food. Hence the improved success of an older, experienced bird might outweigh the lost time spent maturing. Similarly, most seabird young are nidicolous, or remain for a long period in the nest; this apparently gives them the time to develop the strength and size necessary to forage independently.

The common murre and other fish-feeding alcids stray from this pattern in an interesting way (Scott, 1973). The murre chick leaves the nest very soon after hatching, accompanies its father on the water until able to fly, and then strikes out on its own. During this time, the father stays close to his offspring and never flies. He, rather than the mother, plays the role of nurturer in this case perhaps because a single egg constitutes about 11% of a female's body weight, and she needs to rest for the next season; or perhaps because the father's larger size and weight make him a better predator.

Precociality of this sort might have evolved in response to the mediocre flight efficiency of murres (Scott, 1973). As mentioned previously, murres can feed on fish successfully because of their high wing loading (body weight/wing area), which endows them with speed and agility underwater but makes aerial flight laborious compared to that of other birds. Hence commuting back and forth between nest and feeding grounds becomes a major exertion. But with precocious young, the parent need not commute. Moreover, the pair can search for food at greater distances from the nest, can escape the possibly depleted waters immediately around the nest, and the chick can learn foraging skills while still safe with its parent. So those young who quickly leave the nest to follow the parent are more likely to survive and reproduce than those who stay.

A few independent patterns support this interpretation. Precocious alcids tend to feed farther offshore than the nonprecocious. All six precocious species forage more than 2 miles offshore on pelagic fish typically harder to catch than those closer to shore. The three species who feed in shallow nearshore waters are less precocious: their young stay in the nest the first 2–3 weeks. Finally, precocious species tend to have greater wing loading than nonprecocious: for example, 0.54 oz./in.^{2} in murres as compared to

0.31 oz./in.^{2} in pigeon guillemots (Scott, 1973).

Seasonality in breeding and mortality. A pronounced seasonality of breeding in temperate seabirds, coupled with high mortality during bad years and often in the fall, indicate that the quantity of available prey tends to limit the size of seabird populations. The breeding seasons of the common murre, pigeon guillemot, Brandt's cormorant, and pelagic cormorant overlap almost completely, and coincide nicely with the time of peak upwelling and plankton production in spring and early summer (Scott, 1973). In contrast, seabirds of the tropics, where productivity is patchy, irregular, and spread equally throughout the year, nest more-or-less the year around (Ashmole, 1971). The abundance of dead seabirds washed up on the beach, consisting mostly of newly hatched murres, usually peaks in late summer and fall as upwelling wanes and the summer productivity boom comes to an end.

Year-to-year variations in seabird mortality and breeding success usually mirror fluctuations in water temperature and the intensity of upwelling. During the El Nino of 1982 and 1983, upwelling weakened drastically as unseasonably warm northward currents upset the normal ocean conditions along the West Coast, and as a result, seabird populations suffered noticeably (Hodder and Graybill, 1985). At the University of Oregon pelagic cormorant colony at Cape Arago, Oregon, the frequency of successful nests dropped from a mean of 80% over seven previous years (1973, 1975–1978, 1980–1982) to 48% in the El Nino summer. Similarly, the mean number of chicks fledged per successful nest fell from a mean of 2.70 to 1.35. At the same time, at the pelagic cormorant colony at Coquille Point Rocks, Oregon, the birds abandoned 62% of the nests by August 8, 1983, leaving a total of only 38% successful. Through the 1982 and 1983 summers, unusually large numbers of dead seabirds washed up on the beaches of Oregon, Washington, and California. Along the 4.4-mile beach south of the Yaquina Bay outlet in Oregon, the number of dead adult murres ranged from 0.27/mi. to 5.63/m.i from April to August, 1983, significantly more than in the previous 5 years, when the numbers fell between 0.12/mi. and 3.42/mi. (Hodder and Graybill, 1985). Food scarcity also seems to affect the birds' reproductive behavior; during the El Nino summer several species showed less interest than usual in mating, building nests, and raising offspring.

THE ROLE OF MARINE MAMMALS AND SEABIRDS
IN THE MARINE ECOSYSTEM

Though penetrating the marine environment to different degrees, whales, pinnipeds, and seabirds are equally dependent on the productivity of the oceans. And as warm-blooded animals, they expend and consume large quantities of energy. What impact has this had on the marine food web? Although this kind of knowledge is extremely difficult and expensive to come by, it appears from preliminary rough estimates that, as consumers, marine mammals and seabirds exert as profound an effect on the oceans as terrestrial birds and mammals do on land.

A computer model of the energetic demands of the four most common Oregon seabirds suggests that they exact a heavy toll on small bait fish (Wiens and Scott, 1975). Each year, the sooty shearwater (*Puffinus griseus*), Leach's storm petrel, common murre, and Brandt's cormorant consume some 62,500 metric tons of fish, of which about 43% are anchovies, and the rest a mixture of Pacific herring, rockfish, smelt, sculpin, and cod. This amounts to as much as 22% of the annual production of pelagic fish, several times the annual troll catch of coho and chinook salmon by commercial fishermen (Wiens and Scott, 1975). Analysis of gut contents indicates that cormorants feed on bottom fish, storm petrels about equally on euphausiids and hydrozoans, shearwaters almost entirely on anchovies, and murres predominantly on herring, but also on anchovy, smelt, cod, and rockfish. During their peak migratory passage in autumn, shearwaters consume twice as much energy per day than the peak of any of the other species. Their total consumption of 24,000 metric tons of anchovies is seven times that of any other species during the fall, but over the entire year is roughly equivalent to that of the murres.

Anchovies spawn in water temperatures between 55°F and 63°F, and because the Columbia River plume usually exceeds 55°F in the summer (as compared to 45°F for surrounding seawater) they spawn in abundance in the river plume. At this time, the north winds push the plume south, close along the Oregon Coast, making the anchovies conveniently available to the murres at just about the time that parents and young begin to disperse from their nesting colonies (Wiens and Scott, 1975).

To prepare for their annual migration, gray whales consume tremendous amounts of sediment crustaceans. To gain enough blubber to make the trip, a typical whale must devour 0.4–1.3 tons of prey per day, for a total of 67–220 tons over the season (Nerini, 1984; Yablokov and Bogoslovskaya, 1984). In the Chirikov Basin of the

Bering Sea, the mean prey biomass of 0.72 tons per acre suggests that a whale must suck up about 0.5–1.8 acres of sea bottom every day, or from 75–270 acres over the season. This means that the minimum of 16,000 gray whales consume about 3%–27% of the total prey community each year. Of course the whales return much of these nutrients to the environment through their feces and their own deaths. Since the annual death rate of gray whales is about 9%, a total of 2000 whales, or 30,000 tons of whale corpses, return their energy and nutrients to the sea each year. This amounts to about 100 pounds of whale carcass per square mile per year throughout the gray whales' range. In comparison, close to the same weight of adult salmon die each year in the Northwest, but about two-thirds of these are eaten by humans, and do not return directly to the rivers, estuaries, and ocean.

These trends appear to hold worldwide. Based on very rough global estimates of whale abundance and weight-specific metabolic weights, researchers calculate that the 1–1.5 million sperm whales consume some 100 million tons of squid annually, and the 50–100 million small, toothed whales consume about 150–300 million tons of fish (Kanwisher and Ridgeway, 1983). Since pinnipeds haul out each year to breed, estimates of their populations are much more accurate; since many species have been held in captivity for long periods, we know much more about their caloric intake. Worldwide, pinnipeds probably consume some 50–60 million tons of fish each year. In comparison, the entire catch of the world fishery amounts to roughly 60 million tons.

Even though these are gross estimates, and we are far from a clear understanding of such large scale dynamics of nutrient and energy flow, the conclusion is inescapable that these highly adapted warm-blooded animals exert a profound effect on the marine food web. This raises several questions: Do whale, pinniped, and seabird populations tend to be limited by total food abundance, availability, or, especially in seabirds and pinnipeds, by breeding habitat? To what extent do these animals compete with fish for food? To what extent do they deplete fishery stocks? We already know that direct feeding by seabirds and marine mammals on salmonids and other commercial fish is very light, but their consumption of the prey of salmon and other commercial species is heavy. How does this consumption affect the commercial stocks? Needless to say, the answers are well concealed at present, and the large scale, ecosystem-wide research necessary to reveal them remains in the future.

Plate 1. Cape Falcon, Oswald West State Park, Oregon. June, 1984.

Plate 2. Neahkahnie Mountain, Oswald West State Park, Oregon, June, 1984.

Plate 3. Layers of uplifted sedimentary rock on the beach near Kalaloch, Washington. July, 1984.

Plate 4. Storm waves eroding the foredune at Gearhart, Oregon, December 1982.

Plate 5. Male California sea lion at North Cove, Cape Arago. August, 1984.

Plate 6. Beach at Cape Perpetua, Oregon.

Plate 7. The ochre sea star (*Pisaster ochraceus*) attacking its preferred prey, the California mussel (*Mytilus californianus*). Haystack Rock, Oregon. June, 1983.

Plate 8. Necanicum estuary, Gearhart, Oregon.

Plate 9. Fresh bear tracks in the dunes near Tahkenitch, Oregon. August, 1984.

Plate 10. A typical dune landscape, consisting of foredune, deflation plain shrubfields, beachgrass hummocks, a remnant forested island, and surviving active sand, as seen from the Oregon Dunes Overlook. August, 1984.

Plate 11. Retention ridge at Tahkenitch, Oregon. July, 1984.

Plate 12. Foredune at Gearhart, Oregon. January, 1984.

Plate 13. Parallel ridges at Gearhart, Oregon. January, 1984.

Plate 14. American beachgrass (*Ammophila arenaria*) outcompetes native pioneer species such as seashore lupine (*Lupinus littoralis*) and American glehnia (*Glehnia leiocarpa*). Tahkenitch, Oregon. August, 1984.

Plate 15. Dune advance created Threemile Lake, south of Tahkenitch, Oregon. August, 1984.

Plate 16. The pitcher plant (*Darlingtonia californica*), a carnivorous plant of bogs in the dunes and Klamath Mountains. Darlingtonia State Wayside, Oregon. August, 1984.

Plate 17. Largest known western redcedar (*Thuja plicata*) between Forks and Kalaloch, Washington. July, 1984.

Plate 18. A colonnade of western hemlock (*Tsuga heterophylla*) and Sitka spruce (*Picea sitchensis*) that originated on a nurse log. Hoh rain forest, Olympic National Park. July, 1984.

Plate 19. Gin Ridge, Gearhart, Oregon. June, 1983.

3

THE SEASHORE

Not hammer-strokes, but dance of the water sings the
pebbles into perfection.

   Rabindranath Tagore, Stray Birds *(1916), 126.*

While the creatures of the open ocean enjoy a largely stable and comfortable environment, shore inhabitants are doubly punished by perpetual wave battering and the twice-daily exposure to the elements during low tides. The prevailing westerlies and powerful cyclonic storms commonly raise up seas and swells over 10 feet on the Pacific Northwest Coast. Winds and waves not only release tremendous energy as they break against the shoreline, but also throw massive drift logs and rocks square against the beds of mussels and barnacles, grind larger boulders cruelly against each other, and scour all surfaces with sand and gravel. Low tides are an aggravation because nearly all intertidal species evolved recently from the subtidal sea bottom, and find it difficult or impossible to feed or respire when exposed to the open air and its drought, stinging rainfall, and extremes of temperature; most species function as well or better in an aquarium than in nature.

Why, then, do we find such a colorful diversity of life forms here? Why would an organism migrate from the comfortable subtidal up into the zone of waves and wind? Apparently, the answer is that, over evolutionary time, most intertidal species moved upwards to escape voracious and extremely efficient predators and competitors in deeper waters. In other words, for most species the zone between high and low tides is a high-stress refuge from natural enemies that are not as completely adapted to that zone's rigors. In some cases, however, the predators have adjusted to pursue their prey all the way to the upper intertidal, where the balance hangs on the slightly greater desiccation tolerance of the prey, now ironically exposed to a variety of terrestrial consumers such as shorebirds, forest mammals, and humans.

Rocky shores are wonderfully easy to study: they are thoroughly accessible; their inhabitants are predominantly sessile (fixed in one plane) or slow-moving and hence easy to count, measure, and map; and whole populations can be easily moved or manipulated so experimental controls are exceptionally easy to create. After decades of such experimentation ecologists now under-

Figure 34. Idealized rocky intertidal community. (Megahan)

stand the rocky intertidal more completely than nearly any other ecosystem. Some of the surprising strategies evolved by these plants and animals for protection from exposure and wave battering are dealt with in this chapter, as are their predators and competitors and their often striking effects on the shore community.

ENVIRONMENT AND DIVERSITY

Over the millenia, the west coast of North America has accumulated an impressively large number of species as compared to the east coast and other shorelines at similar latitudes (Stehli *et al.*, 1967; Goldman and Talbot, 1976; Paine, 1984). Some of the finest examples of biotic diversity on the Northwest Coast can be found at Point of the Arches and Rialto Beach in Washington; Ecola Point, Otter Rock, Cape Perpetua, Sunset Bay, and Cape Arago North Cove in Oregon; and various locations at Trinidad Head in northern California. This abundance is in part responsible for the greater scientific interest in west coast intertidal communities, and the early appearance of many western seashore guides, including E. F. Ricketts' classic 1939 work of natural history, *Between Pacific Tides.*

Several complementary factors account for this preeminent diversity. First, the west coast of North America contains long, continuous expanses of intertidal rock interspersed with small sandy beaches, as opposed to the reverse situation on the east coast. This is because the West Coast is primarily a leading-edge coast (see Chapter 1), and as the Pacific Plate grinds downward beneath the continent, large sections of sea floor sedimentary rock are uplifted into the intertidal zone and beyond. Other things being equal, rocky shores support more species than sandy beaches because rock is more stable and provides firmer support than sand. And large rocky expanses are more favorable than isolated fragments because they offer greater potential for broader dispersal and reduce the likelihood that a local disturbance will eliminate an entire species. Second, the Pacific Ocean is 300 million years old, which is sufficient time for the evolution of a virtually unlimited number of species. Since there is no reason to believe that rocky, shallow subtidal and intertidal habitats did not exist continuously throughout the life of the Pacific, these subhabitats are probably as old as the Pacific itself. In contrast, the Atlantic is about 200 million years old, a somewhat shorter period that may have contributed slightly to its lower diversity. Third, the prevailing westerlies lavish the West Coast with a comfortable maritime climate. Yearly variation in sea temperature is only about 11–23°F, while at the same latitude in New England the summers are hot and the winters frigid. This wide variation is produced not only by seasonal swings in the continental air masses, but also by the equal influences of the cold Labrador Current and the warm Gulf Stream. At the same time that the Labrador Current brings devastating ice floes to the New England shoreline, the same latitude on the West Coast is experiencing day temperatures rarely below freezing and often into the 50s. And in July, when coast temperatures south of Cape Cod are commonly in the 80s and 90s, the entire shoreline north of San Diego averages a cool 75°F or lower. This climatic uniformity also results in a noticeably greater north-south faunal uniformity on the West Coast; most of the dominant species on Vancouver Island are also present on the California shore. And finally, the heavy waves themselves may help maintain diversity by regularly ripping loose organisms that dominate space, thereby providing a perpetual supply of free surface for competitively inferior species that may otherwise have been crowded out of existence. During extremely violent storms, however, high seas can denude large segments of the rocky intertidal, and in the process cause a local extinction. On the West Coast, however, this is not likely to be permanent, because the large expanses of rocky habitat virtually guarantee that the lost species has survived intact somewhere nearby and can reseed into the devastated area when conditions improve.

ADAPTATIONS TO THE SEASHORE

Adaptations to Desiccation

The animals best adapted to desiccation stress are those with hard, nonporous body parts that can seal off the warm air outside. These include acorn barnacles, mussels, chitons, limpets, and snails. When the tide falls these animals usually seal in a small amount of water that bathes their gills and soft body parts, allowing limited respiration and protection from the heat. Many shore crabs also hold a small amount of water in their gill chambers during periods of exposure. Some limpets (e.g., *Collisella scabra*) tend to return to the same spot each day after foraging, eventually wearing a "home scar" into the rock, which protects them somewhat from the wind and sun (Haven, 1971). Of course desiccation stress is most acute at the highest shore levels, whose inhabitants may receive only occasional wave spray for the entire 2 weeks between successive spring high tides. Predictably, many limpets, barnacles, and littorine snails common at these heights can often survive several days or weeks in the laboratory out of the water at room temperature. Even the edible mussel *Mytilus edulis* can survive in 40°F air for days (Levinton, 1982).

Less adapted to desiccation stress are soft-bodied animals such as anemones, fish, and polychaete worms. These dry out or suffocate much more quickly, and rather than standing firm in the wind and sun, they either move in and out with the tides, seeking out moist shaded spots in crevices, under rocks and dense seaweeds, and among mussels; or settle in permanent tidepools. In the aggregating anemone *Anthopleura elegantissima,* the habit of reproducing asexually, by longitudinal fission, helps to conserve water. Repeated divisions convert a single individual into a tight clump of hundreds, all genetically identical and of the same sex and color pattern. Close pressing-together in these clones greatly reduces the amount of body surface exposed to the air.

With most of their functioning tissues wide open to the environment, seaweeds are less tolerant of desiccation than most shore organisms, and their presence or absence at a particular site often indicates the degree of desiccation stress. Filmy, delicate algae such as *Ulva* and *Enteromorpha* often survive well through the spring and early summer, only to turn brown and burn out during August low tides. Nevertheless, some species appear biochemically adapted to drought; *Porphyra,* for instance, can dry out to a cellophane-like consistency and revive fully when wetted. Many species coat themselves with a film of slimy mucus that restricts water loss to the thick cell walls rather than the cell contents.

Adaptations to Strong Water Movement

Of all shore organisms, those most vulnerable to wave-shock are the inhabitants of exposed sandy beaches. Here, battering storm waves can excavate the entire habitat in a matter of hours, and the few large species capable of surviving long enough to reproduce are fast, efficient burrowers such as the mole crab *Emerita analoga* and the razor clam *Siliqua patula.* A razor clam unearthed by a wave and lying flat on its side requires only a few seconds to rebury itself. Young sand dollars, *Dendraster excentricus,* anchor themselves in an unusual way. They selectively consume the heaviest grains of sand (usually iron oxides) and store them in a special area of the gut, where they function as a "weight belt" that helps to bury the animal's front end (Chia, 1973). Extremely small size may be another adaptation to the instability of sand; a great abundance of minute worm-shaped polychaetes, crustaceans, hydroids, and gastropods inhabit the spaces between sand grains larger than themselves.

While burrowing is about the only viable strategy on sandy beaches, several options are open to plants and animals of the rocks (leading in part to the greater diversity). The majority of organisms hold on to the rocks with impressive tenacity. The large seaweeds attach themselves with tough, disc-shaped extensions of the thallus called "holdfasts." Barnacles, tubeworms, and oysters cement themselves permanently to the rock. Mussels excrete a glue-like substance to produce "byssal threads" that hold tightly to the rock; these can be detached and repositioned to allow the mussel to move as much as several inches per day. The strong muscular foot of snails and limpets attaches temporarily to the rock with the help of mucus, an adhesive glycoprotein. Mucus production is energetically costly, and some limpets (such as *Collisella scabra*) recoup some of the cost by farming their algal prey in their mucus trails (Connor and Quinn, 1984). Seastars and sea urchins (Figure 35) have suction tube feet powered by a central hydraulic system, and the fins of some tidepool fish are highly specialized as suction cups.

Figure 35. The red sea urchin (*Strongylocentrotus franciscanus*) and purple sea urchins (*S. purpuratus*) in a low intertidal pool at North Cove, Cape Arago, Oregon. Summer, 1986.

Other miscellaneous adaptations include burrowing into sedimentary rock by piddock clams and into virtually all rock types by sea urchins; streamlined body contours and surface textures such as the low, conical form of limpets and the slippery mucus of seaweeds; the formation of dense aggregations to reduce surface area as in mussels and sea anemones; the flexibility of seaweed stipes; the thick, protective shells of mussels, barnacles, limpets, and others; and the use of crevices and other refuges by mobile species. Many of these devices also protect against desiccation and wide swings in air temperature.

Adaptations to High Light Intensity

While turbid waters provide shade during high tides, on clear days throughout the year low tides expose shore plants to visible and ultraviolet rays intense enough to break apart their chlorophyll molecules. *Ulva* and *Codium* solve this problem by housing their chlorophyll in chloroplasts that retreat to the cell interior at high light intensities (Boaden and Seed, 1985). Other species produce masking compounds such as polyphenol granules and brightly colored pigments (Boaden and Seed, 1985).

Life Cycles

One of the great advantages of the marine habitat is the opportunity to exploit the buoyancy of the water as a means of dispersal; longer dispersal distances mean reduced probabilities of extinction and of competition with parents. About 70% of all shore invertebrates and nearly all intertidal plants release larvae (animals) or spores (algae) into the water column, where they may swim or passively drift as plankton for weeks before settling down and metamorphosing into adults (Thorson, 1964). A barnacle, for instance, can extend its long, snake-like penis several body diameters to impregnate nearby individuals (although barnacles possess both male and female sex organs and are capable of self-fertilization, cross-fertilization is the rule). After the fertilized eggs develop internally for several weeks, the young larvae are released into the sea usually in time for the spring bloom of their food source, the phytoplankton. The well-developed swimming and sensory abilities of the larvae eventually enable them to select a favorable settling site on the shore bottom, usually a spot where adult barnacles have recently broken off (Knight-Jones, 1953). Barnacles are examples of "planktotrophic" (plankton-feeding) larvae, which are generally produced in large numbers and spend several days to weeks in the plankton. At the other extreme are "lecithotrophic" (egg-feeding) larvae, which are usually produced in small numbers, feed on stored yolk, and remain in the plankton only a few hours to days (e.g., the polychaete worm *Spirorbis spirorbis*) (Levinton, 1982). Lecithotropy is probably favored where larval predation is high, or where larval food is scarce in the water column.

Some larvae reduce predation by developing on or near the parent. The snail *Nucella* deposits its eggs in yellowish, vase-shaped capsules that adhere to rocks or shells; the larvae metamorphose within the capsules and emerge as tiny juvenile snails (Morris, *et al.*, 1980). The brooding anemone *Epiactis prolifera* has an intriguing sex life apparently unique in animals, but somewhat common in mustards, roses, and other plants. Individuals begin life as females, but as they age they develop testes, which become fully functional by the time the pedal disk reaches about an inch in diameter. As a result, the population consists of a large number of young females and a small number of older hermaphrodites, which release sperm into the water column. After a period of larval development, the mother discharges her embryos through her mouth, and carries them with her cilia across her oral disk and down her column to its base, where they are attached with mucus. Soon the larvae develop tentacles and become miniature anemones; after a few months they are old and large enough (4 mm) to live independently, and migrate away from their mother (Morris, et al., 1980).

Most marine algae have extremely complex life cycles that alternate between two forms, the asexual sporophyte and the sexual gametophyte. In some species the two forms are impossible to distinguish in the field (e.g., the sea lettuce *Ulva*), and in others nearly unrecognizable as the same species. Seaweeds in the brown algal order Laminariales, for instance, alternate between the large, conspicuous vegetative stalk and a microscopic filamentous gametophyte (Scagel, et al., 1982). Although multitudes of spores are usually produced, average dispersal distances are probably small. Some species, such as the sea palm *Postelsia palmaeformis*, release spores only at low tide, and the dispersal distance seldom exceeds a few feet (see below).

Feeding Methods

The enormous abundance of planktonic larvae, coupled with the availability of stable attachment sites in the rocky intertidal, have allowed the evolution of filter-feeding as a highly efficient foraging method. Barnacles, mussels, oysters, tubeworms, bryozoans, and ascidians have all independently evolved some kind of filtering system that collects larvae and other organic particles directly from the plankton. Barnacles gather food with their setae, mussels with gills, tubeworms and bryozoans with tentacular crowns, and ascidians with pharyngeal baskets (Boaden and Seed, 1985). These are all sessile species that save energy by relying on the water currents to supply them with a perpetual food source and to flush away their wastes.

Because of its stable attachment, lighted (shallow) water, and turbulent, nutrient-rich currents, the rocky shore is excellent habitat for large, sessile algae (seaweeds) and their consumers. Limpets and chitons are the primary herbivores in the upper and mid intertidal, scraping the rock surfaces clean of algae with file-like radulas that extend like a tongue from their mouths. Sea urchins feed voraciously on the low intertidal seaweeds with the "Aristotle's lantern," a complex system of teeth, each of which grows out rapidly enough in the laboratory to be renewed every 75 days (Morris, *et al.*, 1980).

Predators take a variety of forms; seastars, whelks, and crabs are the most significant. Seastars, such as the common and familiar ochre seastar *Pisaster ochraceus*, use a bizarre feeding method that apparently evolved in response to the thick, protective shells of their prey. The seastar turns its stomach inside-out, extrudes it through its mouth, inserts it into any opening between the prey's shells, and then envelops and digests the soft tissues within (MacGinitie and MacGinitie, 1949). To open a mussel, its favorite prey, the ochre seastar humps over the animal and pulls the valves apart with its suction tube feet. Although the mussel is stronger in the short run, the seastar's hydraulic system has much greater endurance and almost always wins out eventually. Whelks of the genus *Nucella* feed heavily on mussels and barnacles by first softening the prey's shell with the enzyme carbonic anhydrase (secreted from a boring organ on the sole of the foot), then drilling a hole with the radula, and extending proboscis and radula through the hole to feed on the soft tissues (Morris, *et al.*, 1980). Cancer crabs such as the Dungeness *Cancer magister*, the Oregon cancer crab *Cancer oregonensis*, and the red crab *Cancer productus* prey on barnacles; small clams, oysters, and mussels; polychaete worms; and other animals, using their strong claws to crush or chip away the prey's shell and tear the meat into bite-sized chunks (Morris, *et al.*, 1980).

Prey Defenses

Many anatomical and behavioral peculiarities of shore organisms can be understood as adaptations to avoid or survive attacks by these predators. Structural protections are ubiquitous, and include spines (urchins); thick shells (mussels and barnacles); tough exoskeletons (crabs); a woody or leathery texture in seaweeds (*Lessoniopsis littoralis, Pterygophora californica, Macrocystis integrifolia*); and the incorporation of hard calcium carbonate in the cell wall of coralline red algae (*Bossiella, Corallina, Lithothamnium*). Perhaps the most common behavioral defense, practiced by littorines, turban snails, limpets, and many others, is simply running away. If an ochre seastar is placed in a pool containing littorines and turban snails, they move quickly above the water line and then stop (Feder, 1963, 1972). The snail sprints at a pace of 3 inches per minute, almost four times its normal speed. Before limpets run, they must be touched by the tube foot of a seastar, if touched by anything else, they usually just clamp down harder. The sunflower star *Pycnopodia helianthoides* can outrun its predator seastar, the sun star *Solaster dawsoni* (Carefoot,

1977). The sun star, in turn, runs from other members of its own species, which sometimes practice cannibalism (Carefoot, 1977). A scallop (e.g., *Chlamys rubida*) rapidly opens and shuts its shell valves to propel itself away from predatory seastars such as the mottled star *Evasterias troschellii* (Feder, 1963). Animals frequenting sloping ledges or rock faces, such as the pill bug *Ligia pallasii* and black turban snail *Tegula funebralis,* often loosen their grasp and tumble down to safety when touched. Animals that violently twist or jump out of harm's way include the cockle *Clinocardium nuttallii,* the California sea cucumber *Parastichopus californicus,* and the abalone *Haliotis kamtschatkana* (Feder, 1972). Tubeworms simply hide by pulling into their protective tubes, and virtually all animals of sandy shores burrow into the sand to escape both predators and waves.

One of the most intriguing prey strategies is the ability to cast off arms and legs, or "autotomy," as a diversion during escape, one must assume in hopes of finding a safe place to grow them back. All crabs in the Pacific Northwest can do this, and some (e.g., the porcelain crab *Petrolisthes eriomerus*) have claws that continue to pinch viciously after broken off. The sunflower star also may cast off a few of its arms when provoked (Carefoot, 1977).

All seastars and sea urchins grow small protrusions with sharp jaws and poison sacks on their upper body surfaces. These "pedicillariae" not only bite and sting potential predators, but also prevent larvae from settling or growing on the body surface. The red and purple sea urchins deter their respective predators, the sun-flower star and the leather star *Dermasterias imbricata,* in this way (Rosenthal and Chess, 1972; Carefoot, 1977).

All sea anemones use a similar strategy. With numerous stinging cells (nematocysts) in their tentacles and elsewhere, they immobilize their prey as well as discourage most predators. One predator that is not discouraged, the nudibranch *Aeolidia papillosa,* feeds selectively on the aggregating anemone (Carefoot, 1977). The nudibranch somehow prevents the nematocysts from firing, and eats the entire anemone, nematocysts and all (Carefoot, 1977). The nudibranch then shunts the unfired nematocysts from its gut to spe-cial storage sacs in the tips of its fingerlike dorsal appendages. If an appendage happens to be torn off, perhaps by a predator, the nematocysts inside promptly explode. Many nudibranchs also protect themselves from fish and other enemies by secreting various acids and poisons through the skin; probably as a warning to their predators, most are brightly colored. A similar strategy is that of some scallops (e.g., *Chlamys hastata hericia*) which can repel potential predators by cultivating distasteful sponges on their shells (Bloom, 1975).

A few seaweeds use variations on the poison theme.

Desmarestia, for example, contains sulfuric acid, and is responsible for the low-tide rotten egg smell where seaweeds are abundant. Several species of brown algae resist grazers with phenolic compounds, including *Pelvetiopsis limitata*, *Pelvetia fastigiata*, and *Fucus distichus* (Steinberg, 1985). Interestingly, phenolic-rich species tend to be small and restricted to the intertidal, while phenolic-poor species tend to be large forms common in the subtidal, such as *Nereocystis luetkeana*, *Postelsia palmaeformis*, *Egregia menziesii*, and *Laminaria dentigera*. Perhaps this is because the more benign conditions in the subtidal allow plants to grow easily to large sizes as a defense against grazers, making chemical protection unnecessary. Or alternatively, since most of the phenolic-rich species belong to the order Laminariales, perhaps this trait arose just once in the common ancestor, and was passed along to descendents regardless of the environment (Steinberg, 1985).

Another common prey strategy is rapid growth to sizes too large for predators to handle. The acorn barnacle *Semibalanus cariosus* reaches a size refuge from whelks after 1–2 years' growth (Connell, 1970). By this time their shells are too thick for the whelks to bore into during a single tidal cycle, and they usually quit to avoid drying. Mussels also reach size refuges from both snails and seastars.

INTERTIDAL COMMUNITY STRUCTURE

The distribution of organisms in space and time, or their "community structure," often exhibits regular and predictable patterns. The explanation of these patterns has been a long-standing goal of ecology, and because of the great ease of observation and experimentation on rocky shores, their community structure is a particularly venerable problem in the annals of ecological research. Since the turn of the century, ecologists have been searching, describing, and manipulating the seashore biota in hopes of uncovering the underlying reasons for various patterns. In this process the rocky intertidal and especially that of the Pacific Coast has probably contributed as much to ecological theory as most terrestrial ecosystems.

Over the years, several generalizations have crystallized out of the volumes of research, many of which apply not just to seashores, but apparently to a wide variety of terrestrial communities as well.

1. Where physical conditions are harsh, abundance and biomass are low, and abiotic factors (climate, waves, currents) control the distribution of organisms.
2. Where physical conditions are less harsh, abundance and biomass increase, and competition among species limits their mutual boundaries.

3. Where physical conditions are benign, productivity rises, grazers and predators become commonplace, and their foraging largely creates the distributional patterns.
4. By luck, some populations may escape physical disturbances, predators, and competitors, and become locally or temporarily abundant outside their normal range or habitat.
5. Moderate disturbances (removal of organisms) reduce competition, allow species to coexist, and thereby maintain species diversity; severe disturbances eliminate entire species and thereby reduce diversity; where competition is intense, lack of disturbance allows dominant species to eliminate their competitors, again reducing diversity. Disturbances may result from predation or from physical factors such as desiccation or log battering.

I now explore whether these rules adequately explain an important aspect of shore community structure, namely community zonation.

Zonation

The most noticeable attribute of rocky shore communities, and probably the most debated, is their almost universal layout as distinct, ordered, horizontal bands. This zonation is similar to that of forest communities on mountain slopes, but differs greatly in the remarkably abrupt transitions from one zone to the next, especially on steep, homogeneous shore slopes. Ecologists have described a few major zones, whose sequence is remarkably constant worldwide, even though the absolute elevation of each varies considerably (Stephenson and Stephenson, 1949, 1972; Ricketts, E. F., 1985).

The supralittoral or spray zone lies above the direct influence of the tides, but still within the influence of wave spray. Its only obvious inhabitants are terrestrial birds, insects, salt-tolerant lichens, and maritime land plants such as the sea thrift *Armeria maritima* on rocks and the American searocket *Cakile edentula* on sand. The supralittoral fringe extends from the upper limits of tidal submersion (about 7 feet above mean lower low water) down to the first appearance of barnacles. This is a transitional zone of mostly bare rock, but with a predictable collection of littorine snails (especially *Littorina keenae*), the black-encrusting marine lichen *Verrucaria*, the crevice-inhabiting pill bug *Ligia*, the limpet *Collisella digitalis*, occasionally the green algae *Enteromorpha* and *Cladophora*, and the red alga *Porphyra*. On sand the beach hoppers *Traskorchestia* and

Megalorchestia live in burrows and feed on rotting debris at the high tide line.

The midlittoral zone extends from the upper limit of barnacles down to the first appearance of the brown alga *Laminaria,* and on most shores can be divided into three subzones. The uppermost is dominated by the acorn barnacle *Balanus glandula,* the snail *Littorina scutulata,* the black turban snail *Tegula funebralis,* and several limpets. The rock crab *Pachygrapsus crassipes* is locally abundant under rocks. In wave-sheltered areas the barnacles are mostly replaced by seaweeds, especially the rockweed *Pelvetia,* but also by various brown algae in the *Fucus* genus and the green alga *Enteromorpha.* The middle segment of the midlittoral is dominated on wave-exposed shores by dense colonies of the California mussel *Mytilus californianus,* along with the goose barnacle *Pollicipes polymerus,* the snail *Nucella emarginata,* and the ochre seastar *Pisaster ochraceus.* Less common are acorn barnacles, the rock crab *Hemigrapsus nudus,* the hermit crab *Pagurus hemphilli,* and many other species. In sheltered areas, the mussels and barnacles usually give way to a variety of seaweeds. The lowest portion of the midlittoral usually lacks mussel beds, and instead houses abundant algae, usually the brown alga *Hedophyllum* and various coralline red algae that form colorful crusts on the rock surfaces. Among the animals, the aggregating anemone *Anthopleura elegantissima* is often conspicuous, and forms dense, soft beds on moderately exposed shores.

The infralittoral fringe contains the greatest number of species, and extends from the upper limit of the laminarians down to the level of the extreme low spring tide (about −2 feet), beyond which is the subtidal zone. Dense jungles of laminarians usually dominate the infralittoral fringe, but in most locations they share space with beds of sea urchins (*Strongylocentrotus*), green anemones (*Anthopleura xanthogrammica*), seastars (*Pycnopodia, Solaster, Leptasterias, Henricia,* and others), and the surfgrass *Phyllospadix scouleri* with all its animal associates.

As the total hours of submergence per month rises from the upper to lower shore, the overall stress suffered by a typical organism decreases, and both species diversity and biomass increase. At the bottom, the infralittoral fringe is exposed only during the few spring tides each month, and normally remains submerged for days at a time; as a result it is quite hospitable, and in contrast to the other zones, most of its dominant species live also in the subtidal. The rocky subtidal itself is somewhat mysterious, having been observed only by scuba divers willing to risk the waves and currents. Its biota apparently differs substantially from the intertidal, whose solitary forms (e.g., barnacles and mussels) are here replaced by colonial organisms such as sponges and ascidians, which form extensive and colorful sheets, runners, and mounds. The subtidal is also home of the highly productive and diverse giant kelp forests, especially common off pre-settlement California (Foster and Schiel, 1985).

We can apply the community-structuring rules fairly easily to explain zonation. Since intertidal organisms evolved recently from the marine subtidal, any species will experience greater stress at the upper part of its distribution. Thus, we can predict that physical factors should not set the lower limits of a species, but rather biological factors such as predation and competition. The upper limits, on the other hand, should be set by physical factors if the species is high on the shore; the lower its position, the greater the influence of predation and competition. In other words, as mentioned above, each species escapes predation or competition by moving upwards, until it reaches a refuge where its tolerances of physical factors (primarily desiccation) exceed those of its enemy. The different bands are produced by different tolerances of predator, competitor, and prey to those factors. But how well do these predictions hold up for individual species?

PHYSICAL FACTORS SET THE UPPER LIMITS

A few casual observations offer convincing evidence that the lack of water kills organisms that settle above the normal zone for their species. First, zones of many species, especially barnacles, limpets, and others of the high intertidal, expand upwards on wave-exposed shores. This is clearly because wave spray maintains wetness of areas that usually dry out at low tides on sheltered shores. Indeed, the height of the infralittoral zone and fringe are indicators of the degree of wave exposure. Second, zones are usually higher on north-facing slopes. This could be due to decreased light intensity, more uniform and cooler temperatures, less severe desiccation, or a combination of these; in most cases experimentation (see the following) points to desiccation as the principal reason. Third, large and semipermanent tidepools high in the intertidal often house species not normally found at these levels, such as the green anemone, purple sea urchin, and some seaweeds. Fourth, the high-shore limpets, if carefully tracked, are seen to move upwards in the fall and winter, and back down in the spring and summer (Frank, 1965). In unusually dry summers, those in the upper areas dry up and die in greater numbers than those farther down. In severely cold winters, heavy frosts often exfoliate rocks and carry off the limpets (Frank, 1965). Fifth, where drainage is slow (as on gradually-sloping shores), evaporation is slow and zones again expand upwards. Finally, many organisms grow higher on the shore when protected among or beneath larger organisms, such as seaweeds and mussels.

Protected in their own tight clumps, aggregating anemones (*Anthopleura elegantissima*) survive higher on the shore than solitary green anemones (*A. xanthogrammica*).

Experimental manipulations directly demonstrate the importance of drought (Connell, 1972). If a barnacle-covered rock is moved above the usual limit, the barnacles dry out and die unless regularly wetted with seawater. If a permanent stream of seawater is rigged or a tidepool built in the infralittoral zone, seaweeds extend upward into the water. If the south face of a rock is shaded or regularly watered, its barnacles and seaweeds move upwards. If barnacles are grown in an aquarium, we find that those characteristically of higher levels survive desiccation better than those of lower levels, and that since larvae are less tolerant than adults, the adults themselves live lower than their own tolerance would indicate. In limpets, higher species again are more tolerant, but most species live lower on the shore than they need to; apparently they simply move down when stressed. So it appears that sessile species might be eliminated by death of larvae that settle above the adults, while mobile species avoid the upper levels altogether.

There is at least one counter-example to this tendency. On wharf pilings in New Zealand, the limpet *Collisella scabra* lives at higher levels than the limpet *Collisella paradigitalis*. If *C. scabra* are removed, *C. paradigitalis* individuals move upwards in response, and appear to function normally at this new higher level (Choat, 1977). This experiment indicates that competition limits the upper distribution of *C. paradigitalis*. In this case, the limpets have apparently become so well adapted to the upper shore that it no longer represents a serious stress, but instead allows at least the *C. scabra* population to grow large enough to dominate space, and perhaps also their shared algal food. Although both these limpets are also abundant on our shores, competition between them has not yet been demonstrated here.

PREDATION AND COMPETITION SET THE LOWER LIMITS

If we culture intertidal organisms in an aquarium or measure them in the field, we discover that many species grow faster and produce more spores or gametes when continually submerged in the laboratory and towards the lower margins of their distribution in the field. This is apparently due to greater humidity in algae and longer feeding times in barnacles, limpets, and mussels (Connell, 1972). So for most species studied, physical factors apparently fail to set their lower limits. Moreover, although competition and predation are more difficult to casually observe than physical factors, if we look carefully, we can find circumstantial evidence of a greater importance of competition and predation at lower shore levels.

Where the barnacle *Balanus glandula,* for example, lives in abundance with the smaller barnacle *Chthamalus dalli* (usually only towards the lower regions of the *Chthamalus* zone), we can often observe a single *Balanus* overgrowing or undercutting a *Chthamalus,* and a pair or trio of *Balanus* growing into and crushing an individual *Chthamalus,* suggesting competition for space. Also, many intertidal predators, such as the seastars and predatory snails *Nucella,* are restricted to the midlittoral or infralittoral fringe; none are abundant in the supralittoral fringe or zone.

However, the only way to demonstrate that competition or predation sets a species' lower limit is by experimental manipulation. As the above limpet study suggests, we can document competition and predation by removing the supposed competitor or predator or at least building a cage to exclude it, and noting whether another species responds favorably, as by faster growth, increased reproduction, decreased mortality, or expansion into the removed species' habitat. This has been done in several classic experiments over the last 30 years, with spectacular success.

First, consider predation. On most wave-swept rocky shores, the ochre seastar *Pisaster ochraceus* lives in the lower midlittoral zone, where individuals often crowd together when exposed to conserve moisture. During high tides, they separate and migrate upward to forage on their preferred prey, the California mussel *Mytilus californianus* (Figure 36; Plate 7). At Tatoosh Island and Mukkaw Bay, Washington, when the seastars were experimentally removed from

Figure 36. The ochre seastar (*Pisaster ochraceus*) feeding on the California mussel (*Mytilus californianus*). (Kellerman)

several locations, the mussels migrated downward at a rate of 3–4 feet in three years, and stabilized at their new lower level, maintained perhaps by predation by the channeled whelk *Nucella lamellosa*, common near their new lower boundary (Paine, 1974). The downward migration results both from adults being crowded down from above, and the settlement and growth of larvae. Not only mussels, but the barnacle *Balanus glandula* also expands downward into the new seastar-free zone. This is an undisputable demonstration that seastar foraging sets the lower limit of both the mussel and barnacle, whose precise lower boundaries are determined by the desiccation tolerance of the stars.

On San Juan Island, Washington, the barnacle *Balanus glandula* occupies a narrow band in the upper midlittoral zone. Its primary predators are the three whelk species *Nucella emarginata, N. canaliculata,* and *N. lamellosa,* which drill through the shells of adults to reach the soft tissues inside (Connell, 1970). The barnacle larvae settle throughout the intertidal zone in spring and summer, but grow fastest in the lower midlittoral or infralittoral fringe. Why, then, do adults live only in the upper midlittoral? If we protect the settled larvae with experimental cages that exclude the whelks and other predators, the barnacles survive to adulthood throughout the intertidal zone (Connell, 1970). Moreover, in sheltered bays the whelks are scarce, and again the barnacles occupy the entire width of the shore. Their lower boundaries in whelk-free areas seldom lie beneath the extreme low tide level, possibly because the larvae persistently swim to the water surface before settling; predation by seastars might also keep the adults out of the subtidal. Outside the cages, the whelks eliminate lower level barnacles by autumn, and in autumn and winter migrate upwards to feed on the barnacles of the middle levels, which usually disappear by the following spring. This leaves a distinct band of adult barnacles at the top of the shore, safe from the whelks due to the whelks' lower desiccation tolerance (Connell, 1970).

But the remarkable abruptness of the lower level of the barnacle zone requires an explanation. A typical *Nucella* requires about 8 hours to dispatch an adult barnacle: 5 hours to drill, and 3 hours to ingest. Since the operation exposes the animal to desiccation, however, it must be done underwater. The whelks usually retreat into moist crevices during daytime low tides on clear days, and move upwards to forage as the tide rolls in. But the length of time available for foraging depends on how far up the whelk travels before it chooses a barnacle to drill. If it stops below the level of the higher of the two daily low tides, then it has about 12–20 hours to feed before being exposed by the next lower low tide, enough time to consume two barnacles. If it stops above the higher low tide, on the other hand, it has only 5–6 hours before being exposed again, not enough for even a single barnacle. Hence, the level of the higher low tide represents an abrupt physiological barrier to the whelk's foraging, and therefore an abrupt spatial boundary to the barnacle (Connell, 1970).

Such boundaries can also result from intense interspecific competition, usually for living space. For example, on wave-exposed shores in Washington, the edible mussel *Mytilus edulis* occupies a narrow band above the California mussel *Mytilus californianus*. If California mussels are experimentally cleared from the rocks, edible mussels will migrate down and recruit into the freed space. The California mussels, however, grow faster, to larger sizes, develop a thicker shell, and attach themselves to the rocks more securely than the edibles, and as a result they not only block any movement of the latter, but also overgrow and crush any edible mussels that settle among them. This happens often, since the edible mussel grows more rapidly, and can colonize bare space where waves or drift logs have torn off clumps of the California mussel (Suchanek, 1978). On calm shores, the edible mussel usually wins out. Here, the slower currents allow sand and clay to accumulate on the mussels, and the edible mussel is better able to migrate out from under the sediment to avoid suffocation (Figure 37; Harger, 1968).

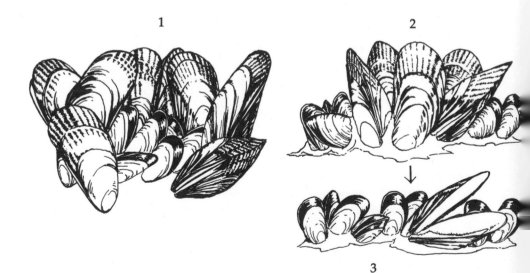

Figure 37. Disturbance and Mussel Survival. 1 The California mussel (*Mytilus californianus*) and edible mussel (*Mytilus edulis*) often occur sympatrically. **2** Siltation occurs in quiet water. **3** The interior mobility of the California mussel often prevents survival, leaving the edible mussel. (Kellerman)

The seaweed *Gastroclonium coulteri* is dominant in many areas in California and Oregon from about the mean level of the lower of the 2 daily low tides to about two feet above this level. If *G. coulteri* is taken out of its zone and replanted higher on the shore it will survive and grow there throughout most of the year. In March and April, however, low tides occur during the day, and days are often warm, clear, and windy (Hodgson, 1980). Under these conditions, the plants simply dry up and die. If *G. coulteri* is transplanted lower in the intertidal, it survives throughout the year in shallow areas lacking its competitors, namely *Prionitis lanceolata* and the surfgrass *Phyllospadix scouleri*. If transplanted in the deeper lower intertidal areas where its competitors thrive, *G. coulteri* dies within a month. Further, if all the surfgrass and *P. lanceolata* are removed from an area, the *G. coulteri* becomes more dominant below the lower boundary of its zone (Hodgson, 1980). These results show that physical stresses set the upward boundary of *G. coulteri*, while competition sets the lower.

Despite the appealing clarity of these studies, predation and competition apparently do not set the lower limits of all intertidal species. The snail *Littorina keenae* lives high on the shore and holds on to the rocks only weakly; if transplanted downward, strong waves pull it loose (Ricketts, 1985). Of course, if the composition of the rocks changes at lower levels, their physical properties may set the lower limits of several species. Where rocks emerge from a sandy beach, for example, the lower shore might be sand, a drastically different habitat. Moreover, on such a beach the waves and currents scour the lower rocks with sand, killing newly settled larvae, spores, and sporelings sometimes several feet above the level of the sand surface. So sand may set lower limits obviously by burial, or much less recognizably by scouring. If submerged continuously, some shore seaweeds (e.g., *Fucus spiralis* and *Pelvetia canaliculata*) and snails (e.g., *Littorine saxatilis*) die within a few days (Connell, 1972). In nature, however, most of these are never constantly submerged, so some other factor must be blocking their downward migration. Finally, settling larvae might systematically avoid the lower levels; as mentioned above, larvae of some species swim to the surface before settling, thereby eliminating any possibility of colonizing the subtidal. On the whole, however, these experiments demonstrate that predation and competition are powerful enough to define the lower limits of at least the dominant species at their zone levels, mussels and certain barnacles and seaweeds, and it seems reasonable to expect future research to demonstrate the same trend for others.

Horizontal Distribution

So far, we have been indulging in a little one-dimensional oversimplification by considering distributional patterns only along the vertical gradient. Are shore communities patterned along a horizontal gradient as well, and do the community structure rules apply equally well to this second dimension? For convenience, we should distinguish two scales of horizontal distribution: latitudinal and local.

LATITUDINAL

On Northwest shores, latitudinal variation is largely nonexistent. Nearly all the dominant organisms, including the California mussel *Mytilus californianus*, the gooseneck barnacle *Pollicipes polymerus*, the acorn barnacle *Balanus glandula*, the ochre seastar *Pisaster ochraceus*, the high-shore limpet *Collisella digitalis*, and both the aggregating and green anemone *Anthopleura elegantissima* and *A. xanthogrammica* live in suitable habitat from at least Alaska to Baja California, and some beyond; the green anemone, for instance, ranges from Unalaska to Panama, an unbelievable 26 degrees of latitude. A few species find their northern or southern boundary within the region, but such examples are rare. For instance, the limpet *Littorina keenae* and the rock crab *Pachygrapsus crassipes* reach no farther north than Cape Arago, and the limpet *Littorina sitkana* no farther south than Cape Arago (Ricketts, 1985). Cape Arago appears to be the main migratory barrier in the region (such as it is), possibly because of warmer temperatures to the south and the difficulty of dispersing past 52 miles of sandy beaches to or from the nearest rocky shore to the north.

As noted above, the biotic uniformity results from the comfortable uniformity in climate. In the summer, the cool upwelled waters off California neutralize the low latitude heat, and the morning fogs keep the air cool and humid during the early low tides. In the winter, the warm Japan Current soothes the coast of British Columbia and Alaska, maintaining temperatures nearly as high as those at Point Conception, California. An anemone transplanted from Cape Mendocino to Flattery would probably not feel much of a difference.

LOCAL

While broad latitudinal breaks are missing, abrupt horizontal shifts in species abundance are often found within any particular locale; as we scan across a given shore level, we might see a bed of mussels give way to a sparse patch of barnacles, followed by a cover of algae, a bed of urchins or anemones, and another patch of mussels. To predict such shifts based on the community structure rules, we first must identify a gradient in the intensity of some environmental force, and that gradient must constitute a good, overall measure of physiological stress to shore organisms. In other words, stress is low at one extreme of the gradient, but increases smoothly to the other extreme. Then we postulate that physical factors dominate at the high-stress end, competition in intermediate areas, and predation at the benign end. The trouble is that, in contrast to length of air exposure along the vertical gradient, there is no horizontally varying factor that tends to stress most or all organisms at one extreme and not at the other. We might imagine, for example, that heavy wave-shock aggravates all organisms about equally, so that predation dominates in protected coves, while battering forces control the community on exposed headlands. This is true to some extent; log battering can severely abrade headlands, leaving various-sized patches of bare rock and therefore openings for colonizing algae and barnacles. But for several species, the stress gradient runs in precisely the reverse direction. The luxuriant stands of large seaweeds common in exposed areas, for example, owe their existence to the wave spray that keeps them wet at low tide; they virtually disappear from calm shores, as in Puget Sound. The California mussel *Mytilus californianus*, as well as many hydroids and associated arthropods, have difficulty surviving in still water because the absence of cleansing currents allows them to silt up and die. These and many other species thrive in heavy surf, and despite occasional log battering, usually reach sufficient numbers to compete for space and feed a variety of predators and grazers.

So we might be tempted to amend our rule and say that, *for those species* that are stressed by heavy waves, wave battering dominates on exposed shores and biological forces on protected shores; and the reverse for the other species. But in order to test this prediction we need to know which species belong to which group, but to learn this one would need to discover the very community patterns we were trying to predict. It is difficult to imagine any *horizontally varying* physical variable, such as nutrient concentration, light intensity, temperature, turbidity, and so on, that, in analogy to the vertically varying length of tidal exposure, reaches sufficiently extreme levels on Northwest shores to unseat competition and predation. So it appears that most horizontal community variation is due not to a single factor or simple community-wide effect, but rather to a variety of forces working separately on each species or population. I will now sketch how the most important of these, namely habitat selection (by both larvae and adults), wave exposure and other physical gradients, predation, competition, and symbiosis, produce local patchiness in seashore biota.

Physical gradients. In probably the majority of shore species, larvae and spores disperse and settle over a much wider range of physical conditions than they are capable of surviving. While mobile species can move after settling to more congenial habitat, most sessile juveniles eventually die from excessive wave exposure, heat or cold, and desiccation, leaving the few who happened to settle within their tolerance ranges as the new adult population. This may appear a suicidal way of doing business, and perhaps generalized dispersal is a maladaptive trait. On the other hand, perhaps it is an adaptation to avoid competition between parents and offspring, or perhaps most species with highly specialized dispersal have gone extinct due to their greater vulnerability to local disasters.

In any case, these important physical conditions are usually correlated with various attributes of the rocks themselves, so that knowledge of shore physiognomy is to a great extent a knowledge of shore biota. Rock size explains by far the greatest amount of horizontal community variation. Small particles (i.e. sand) house a radically different community from that of cobbles, cobbles from boulders, and boulders from solid sheets of bedrock. Rock type also makes a difference; communities of sedimentary rock (e.g., piddock clams) differ somewhat from those of basalt. A shore marked by a large distribution of rock sizes and types contains an enormous variety of microhabitats and species. Different points on a boulder's surface experience different degrees of shading, heat and cold, and wave-shock, depending on the compass direction the surface faces and whether the point lies on the top, bottom, or side. Species of the upper surface resemble those of the adjacent bedrock, while those of the underside and lower regions often require shade and dampness; these include sponges, bryozoans, ascidians, hydroids, and tubeworms. When the surf lifts boulders and grinds them together, the surface organisms are often killed or torn off. Thus small boulders, which are rolled more frequently, support young communities of opportunistic algae and barnacles, while the older mussel beds and large gastropods are mostly restricted to bedrock or large boulders. Caves and crevices offer damp, sheltered havens for species that may survive nowhere else on the shore. Light intensity, humidity, sediment size, and water circulation differ in inner, middle, and outer reaches of most crevices, resulting in a distinct zonation of their inhabitants: mostly transient littorine snails, insects, and crabs occupy the outer region; a diverse and abundant population of mites, clams, and isopods the middle; and a few polychaete worms the inmost depths (Kensler, 1967). Some shade-loving seaweeds (e.g., *Rhodochorton purpureum*) are common in caves (Waaland, 1977).

Within any particular microhabitat, water movement is a

common cause of death of both juveniles and adults, and shapes shore communities in several ways: through direct physical force; increased oxygenation, turbidity, and wave spray; and a greater supply of larvae, spores, and planktonic food. Since the combined effects of these factors tend to harm some species and benefit others, communities on exposed headlands often differ greatly from those in protected coves. In Washington, the dominant organisms of highly exposed shores (e.g., Tatoosh and Waadah islands) are the sea palm *Postelsia palmaeformis;* the seaweeds *Laminaria setchellii, Lessoniopsis littoralis,* and *Hedophyllum sessile;* the California mussel *Mytilus californianus;* the gooseneck barnacle *Pollicipes polymerus;* the green anemone *Anthopleura xanthogrammica;* and several acorn barnacles. The California mussel/gooseneck barnacle community is an indicator of heavy wave-shock all along the Northwest Coast. Dominant organisms on moderately exposed shores (e.g., Shi Shi Beach and Portage Head) include the aggregating anemone *Anthopleura elegantissima,* the seaweeds *Fucus distichus* and *Gigartina papillata,* and acorn barnacles. On protected sites (e.g., Colin's Cove and Turn Rock on San Juan Island) *Fucus, Gigartina* and barnacles are the common inhabitants (Dayton, 1971).

The aggregating anemone appears intolerant of both wave-shock and desiccation; hence its restriction to moderately exposed shores. Aggregating anemones cover only 10% of the exposed side of a surge channel at Shi Shi Beach, but over 80% of the protected side; on San Juan Island the anemone lives only on the west side, at a few locales open to wave splash (Dayton, 1971). If anemones are experimentally transplanted to the fully protected east side of the island, they survive until March, when the low tides fall during the day, and then turn brown and die (Dayton, 1971). As previously noted, the California mussel is more sensitive to siltation on calm shores, and most of the large algae to desiccation; hence their restriction to more turbulent shores.

Old mussel beds are often highly vulnerable to wave-shock. After a layer of mussels colonizes bare rock, later mussels settle preferentially on the byssal threads and shells of the first individuals rather than on the rock itself. After several generations of such colonization, the bed becomes top heavy because it is held to the rock entirely by the bottom layer of mussels. If a log, rock, or ochre seastar tears off a small clump, normal waves and currents are usually strong enough to eat away at the newly exposed byssal threads of the remaining mussels, greatly enlarging the original opening. Beds of sea palms and barnacles are similarly unstable for the same reasons. After such a disturbance, a great variety of larvae and spores settle on the newly exposed rock, so a succession of algal and barnacle communities develops over time into a new mussel bed (details following). Hence, on most exposed headlands, where log and rock battering are common, a patchy mosaic of mussel beds, bare rock from recent disturbances, and a variety of algal and barnacle communities on sites disturbed at various times in the past are found (Paine and Levin, 1981).

Water currents on exposed shores often contain a greater abundance of larvae, spores, and planktonic food, which alone may explain the faster growth and denser settlement of some species on the outer coast, such as two European species of barnacle and one limpet (Connell, 1972). Nutrient abundance may partly explain why over 90% of the razor clam (*Siliqua patula*) population lives on the wide sandy beaches between Tillamook Head, Oregon, and Lead-better Point, Washington (Lewin, 1978; Lewin, *et al.*, 1979a and 1979b). Their staple food, the microscopic diatoms *Chaetoceros armatum* and *Asterionella socialis*, require waterborne silicon, an element common in the volcanic rocks of the Cascades and Rockies, and washed to sea by the Columbia River. If the sandy habitat alone were the reason, we would expect far more razors on other long sandy beaches, such as those between the outlet of Coos Bay and Sea Lion Point, Oregon.

Behavior and patchiness. While wave-shock and other abiotic forces can influence shore patchiness by bodily removing or killing organisms, the organisms themselves often augment the patchiness by staying within, or congregating in, optimum or favorable microhabitats; in a sense, by avoiding these selective forces in the first place.

In sessile species, such as barnacles, the site of larval settlement is supremely important because the immobile adult cannot reverse a bad youthful decision; larval choice *is* adult choice. Larvae of both sessile and mobile species usually demonstrate remarkable sensory abilities and exacting discrimination about future home-sites. Many larvae perceive and respond to a surprising variety of chemical and tactile cues on or near the settling surface, such as texture (pits and crevices are often preferred); inclination; contour; light-reflecting properties; various biotic factors such as bacterial films, adults of the same species, and certain other species; and the current regime. Most or all of these cues are indicators of the probability of adult survival. Pits and crevices protect from log battering and desiccation; inclination and contour determine exposure to sunlight, which in turn contributes to desiccation; the presence of adults is probably the best indicator of favorable physical conditions; and the current regime controls food availability, turbidity, and probability of sand burial. Barnacles, tubeworms, oysters, the inkeeper worm *Urechis caupo*, and the sand dollar *Dendraster excentricus* preferentially settle among their own kind; the sessile species often space themselves out just enough to leave room for growth to adulthood. In many of these species, the "scent" of species-specific chemicals induces settling. Some barnacle larvae, for example, recognize certain quinone-tanned proteins in the adult shell (Boaden and Seed, 1985). In the laboratory, sand dollar larvae preferentially settle in sand collected from adult sand dollar beds rather than clean sand, and thereby avoid juvenile predators such as *Leptochelia dubia* (a tube-building worm) and other micropredators, who are killed or injured by adult sand dollars as they burrow in to and rework the sediment (Highsmith, 1982). But as noted previously, such gregariousness in mussels and barnacles can be detrimental on waveswept shores, as it often results in an unstable community prone to wave tear. Serpulid worms, spirorbids, bryozoans, and mussels settle preferentially on certain algae, possibly recognized by specific chemicals exuded by the plants, and only later move down to the rock surface. This might be an adaptation to avoid the abrasive radulas of limpets as they graze the rocks for algae, or in the case of the mussel, to prevent adults from preying on their own larvae. Several sea slugs and the lined chiton *Tonicella* respond favorably to their primary foods (Barnes and Gonor, 1973). Small (approx. ½ inch) settled juveniles of both aggregating anemones *Anthopleura elegantissima* and green anemones *A. xanthogrammica* often reach great densities in mussel beds while adjacent rocks remain bare; up to 49 individuals per square yard in Mukkaw Bay, Washington, and 35 per square yard at Cape Arago (Sebens, 1981). It is possible that the larvae prefer to settle on the mussel byssal threads or shells, or that they settle haphazardly and survive only among the mussels. In any case, the beds certainly appear to offer better living conditions than most other habitats, due to the protection from waves and desiccation and the abundance of small food items, such as juvenile mussels, certain gastropods, annelid worms, and a variety of minute crustaceans.

Not only larvae, but adults of mobile species also exercise a certain prejudice in choosing homesites. Territoriality; homing behavior (in limpets); and responses to light, currents, air, and other species all tend to clump and segregate species along horizontal gradients.

At Mission Point on the central California coast, the limpets *Collisella digitalis* and *C. scabra* occupy slightly different habitats, with *C. scabra* favoring horizontal surfaces and *C. digitalis* frequenting vertical rock faces, overhangs, and only those horizontal surfaces covered with barnacles or algae (Haven, 1971). Individuals of *Collisella digitalis* clump together more often, usually reach greatest abundance in wave-exposed areas, range to higher shore levels, and occupy tidepools less often than *C. scabra*. If *C. digitalis* is transplanted to bare, level surfaces, it moves into crevices within a day or two, and returns to vertical faces or overhangs within about a week. In contrast, if *C. scabra* is transplanted from vertical to horizontal rocks, it remains in the open. Can limpet behavior alone explain these differences? After feeding excursions during high tides and after dark, *C. scabra* almost always returns to precisely the same spot on the rock, where it stays until the next mealtime. This homing behavior forces its shell to grow to a precise fit to the surface contours in the animal's homesite. While tightly fitted in its homesite, *C. scabra* retains water more efficiently and is more resistant to desiccation. *Collisella digitalis*, on the other hand, homes only rarely, and its shell margin, though ribbed and crenulated, is far less irregular than that of *C. scabra*. So on the basis of homing alone, we would expect *C. scabra* to tolerate desiccation-prone habitats better than *C. digitalis*. This difference clearly explains why *C. scabra* is more abundant on bare, level surfaces exposed directly to the sun, and why *C. digitalis* persists in such areas only when algae and barnacles are there to slow the drainage. It also explains the greater incidence of clumping in *C. digitalis* and its greater abundance where refreshed by wave spray (Haven, 1971).

But why then should *C. digitalis* reach higher shore levels, and only seldom submerge itself in tidepools? Behavior, again, provides part of the answer. Because *C. digitalis* does not home, it is free to move about opportunistically in response to tides, weather, and feeding conditions. Hence it can move upward during the winter, when heavier surf and wave spray more consistently wet the upper shore levels. *C. scabra*, however, is confined for life to a small region around its homesite. If it is to survive the calm water of summer, the homesite must be lower on the shore than would be necessary if winter conditions persisted year around; i.e., lower than *C. digitalis* is free to forage. But this explanation still fails to account for the scarcity of *C. digitalis* submerged in tidepools. One possible reason is a greater ability of *C. digitalis* to respire out of water. Both species expand their vascularized mantle fold to use as an extra respiratory surface during low tides, but *C. digitalis* might have evolved biochemical mechanisms that give it the edge over *C. scabra* (Haven, 1971).

If *C. scabra* can survive perfectly well on vertical surfaces, why is it is so scarce in such habitats? If we experimentally cage the two limpets together, we find that *C. scabra* grows much more slowly, and young individuals reach a maximum size far smaller than those in nearby control plots. Moreover, the drop in growth rate is proportional to the abundance of algal food. Hence, *C. digitalis* apparently competes more efficiently for food than *C. scabra*, enough so to eliminate the latter from the former's optimal habitat (Haven, 1973).

These insights point towards a plausible evolutionary story. We can easily imagine that, perhaps several centuries in the past, a single nonhoming ancestral limpet species occupied well-shaded vertical rock faces and crevices in exposed surfaces. Some individuals evolved homing behavior, and thereby restricted themselves to a small home range, while others continued to forage more widely, gaining a competitive edge in damp, comfortable habitats. Some of the homing individuals escaped competition by settling or migrating to dry, sunny surfaces, and their homing allowed them to survive there, safe from their competitor. In their separate habitats, the two groups became sufficiently isolated to evolve eventually into separate species. Of course, the real story is probably much more complicated than this, but the experiments support at least these broad generalities.

A similar process might explain the differing habitat preferences of the two littorine snails *Littorina scutulata* and *L. sitkana* in Puget Sound and the Strait of Georgia (Carefoot, 1977). *L. scutulata* adheres more tightly to rocks than *L. sitkana*, and is more common on wave-exposed shores. Since *L. scutulata* is wrenched loose by the same waves, it prefers calm water and damp, protected crevices. Moreover, *L. scutulata* deposits its eggs in sticky masses on the shore where they hatch in 7–8 days into free-swimming larvae that disperse widely in the surf. Eggs of *L. sitkana*, on the other hand, develop over a much longer period of time directly into miniature snails, without any pelagic stage. Since the eggs lay exposed longer, they experience a greater risk of desiccation, and hence are usually laid in moist, shaded depressions. Although these snails have apparently never been transplanted to see how they respond, we can probably assume that they actively seek out their respective habitats. Moreover, caging experiments show that *L. scutulata* and a third species, *L. keenae*, compete for food where they overlap. Since *L. scutulata* and *L. sitkana* also overlap in moderately exposed shores, it is likely that they too compete, and that, as in the limpets, over evolutionary time this competition has favored their habitat differentiation, and perhaps also their reproductive differences.

Three crabs in Coos Bay, Oregon, also compete through direct aggression, creating patchy distributions (Daly, 1981). The purple shore crab *Hemigrapsus nudus*, the yellow shore crab *Hemigrapsus oregonensis*, and the red crab *Cancer productus* all take refuge from waves and predators under rocks and boulders. But boulder size makes a big difference: the smaller the rock, the better the chance that waves will roll it and crush the crabs underneath. So the crabs apparently fight for the largest rocks, with the largest crabs generally winning by more forceful pushing and shoving and perhaps more convincing brandishing of claws. *C. productus* reaches 6 inches in width, *H. nudus* over 2 inches, and *H. oregonensis* over 1 inch. On beaches supporting both shore crab species, *H. nudus* dominates under the largest boulders, leaving *H. oregonensis* to the cobbles. Where just one of these species lives more-or-less alone, the distributions are nearly identical, with larger boulders greatly preferred by both (Daly, 1981). Where all three crabs share the beach, *C. productus* easily displaces *H. nudus* from the larger rocks. We might therefore predict that the greater mortality suffered by *H. oregonensis* should have consigned it to extinction. But the small size of this species gives it a definite reproductive advantage over the others; *H. oregonensis* reaches maturity earlier and has higher reproductive rates that apparently compensate for the greater mortality.

The owl limpet *Lottia gigantea* provides another striking example of aggression, competition, and patchiness (Stimson 1970, 1973; Wright 1982). Like other limpets, this species grazes on algal films on the rock surface. But unlike the others, *Lottia* aggressively defends its territory against intruders (Stimson, 1970). If barnacles settle, *Lottia* rasps them off with its radula; if sea anemones, mussels, other limpets, and even other *Lottia* settle or move in from nearby, *Lottia* dislodges or bulldozes them away with its shell. In this way, *Lottia* maintains a territory about a square foot in area; by selective grazing, it cultivates a verdant algal film at least a millimeter thick. In spring and summer, these patches of green are visible up to 50 feet away. If *Lottia* is transplanted, it establishes another territory the same size within about 3 weeks, while smaller limpets invade the old territory and quickly graze away the algal film so painstakingly protected. Like the limpet *Collisella scabra*, some *Lottia*, though not all, return each day to a specific homesite on the rock, whose surface contours direct the limpet's shell growth to a tight fit.

In the aggregating anemone *Anthopleura elegantissima*, aggressive encounters between individuals of the same species, for no obvious purpose, maintain strict boundaries between adjacent clumps. The violence is done by large, stinging nematocysts packed inside knob-like swellings just outside the ring of tentacles. During normal asexual reproduction, two neighboring clones expand until their margins eventually meet. When peripheral anemones in adjacent clones touch tentacles, they sting each other repeatedly with their nematocysts, and the injured tissues eventually die and slough off. After such an encounter, the combatants draw away from each other, creating an anemone-free zone as wide as 2–3 inches. This boundary normally remains stable for several years, and provides settling space for opportunistic algae and barnacles. The neighboring anemones seldom die as a result of their hostilities, but the large energy expenditure required apparently reduces their growth rates and inhibits gonad development (Francis, 1973, 1979).

Although such within-species aggression appears senseless at first sight, its spread through a population by natural selection can be easily understood. Imagine an ancestral anemone population in which a few individuals have recently evolved the aggressive response. These few will easily outcompete the passive, defenseless members for scarce rock space, and as a result will reproduce more successfully both sexually and asexually, passing the trait on to future generations. But why should they leave their clonemates alone, and attack only genetically *different* individuals? Perhaps because of the protection from desiccation and waves offered by the tightly clumped lifestyle: any anemone blindly attacking all surrounding individuals would soon find itself alone, and wide open to the dry wind at low tide.

A kind of infighting also structures to some degree the lower intertidal seaweed communities, although a zoologist might be loathe to call this aggression. As in forest plant species, we can generally divide seaweeds into three groups: large, usually perennial "canopy" species; fast-reproducing, usually annual "fugitive" species that quickly colonize bare rock but succumb to competition with the canopy species; and "obligate understory" species that survive only under the damp shade of the canopy (Dayton, 1975a). At Tatoosh, Waadah, and San Juan islands, Washington, common canopy species include *Hedophyllum sessile, Lessoniopsis littoralis, Laminaria setchellii,* and *Nereocystis luetkeana.* Common understory species are *Corallina officinalis, C. vancouveriensis, Bossiella* sp., *Calliarthron regenerans,* and *Serraticardia macmillani.* Some of the more familiar of the 33 fugitive species are *Porphyra perforata, Gigartina papillata, Iridaea cordata, Endocladia muricata,* and *Rhodomela larix.* The canopy species outcompete the fugitives in three ways: the large blades overshade them; the blades of at least *Lessoniopsis* whiplash them; and fast, vegetative growth of the holdfast buries or displaces them. Ironically, many of the understory species not only compete among themselves, but also suffer from the aggressive holdfast growth of the canopy, even though they depend on the canopy for shade. The dominant canopy species on the Washington outer coast, *Hedophyllum sessile, Laminaria setchellii,* and *Lessoniopsis littoralis,* also compete among themselves. On wave-exposed shores, *Lessoniopsis* and *Laminaria* outcompete and tend to eliminate *Hedophyllum sessile,* as well as a large variety of fugitive species. On moderately exposed shores, however, *Hedophyllum* wins the battle, possibly due to superior desiccation tolerance (Dayton, 1975a). On calm shores, severe summer drought eliminates all three. Interestingly, if *Lessoniopsis* and *Laminaria* are removed from exposed rocks, the *Hedophyllum* that eventually dominates grows faster than the *Hedophyllum* that naturally prevails on moderately exposed shores. Apparently, competition with *Laminaria* and *Lessoniopsis* forces

Hedophyllum out of its optimal high-surf habitat, and into a higher-stress refuge (Dayton, 1975a).

Many sessile animals, especially acorn barnacles and California mussels, gain a competitive edge with a similar kind of aggressive growth. As barnacles grow, the sharp edges at the base of their shells can undercut and detach smaller barnacles, juvenile anemones and other sessile animals, and small seaweeds such as filamentous red and green algae. Two growing barnacles can crush smaller barnacles between them, and single individuals can overgrow and smother smaller ones. If dense beds of the barnacle *Semibalanus cariosus* are experimentally scraped off rocks on San Juan Island, adjacent aggregating anemones spread onto the cleared areas, by both immigration and asexual division (Dayton, 1971). The California mussel *Mytilus californianus* competitively dominates virtually all other plants and animals in the middle intertidal of rocky shores. By virtue of its large size, thick shells, strong attachment threads, and mobility, it easily crushes, smothers, and overgrows most organisms. If mussel beds are removed experimentally or by log battering, a great variety of ephemeral algae and barnacles settle into the bare rock. If all ochre seastars (*Pisaster ochraceus*) are removed from shores on Tatoosh and Waadah islands in Washington, the California mussels that spread downwards obliterate the beds of anemones in their path (Paine, 1974).

Predation and grazing. Mussels, barnacles, and anemones as well, may come to dominate space not only by overwhelming growth, but also by consuming the larvae of competitors. Both mussels and barnacles feed on plankton; mussels by pumping a stream of water through their gills and filtering organs, and barnacles by a net-like use of their modified legs. Any member of the plankton unlucky enough to contact the tentacles of an anemone will be killed or immobilized by stinging nematocysts. Hence, planktonic larvae generally fail to settle in dense beds of mussels, barnacles, and anemones, including the larvae of these animals themselves. If small patches of aggregating anemones are removed from the rocks at Shi Shi Beach in May, diatoms and the green alga *Enteromorpha* (*E. linza* and *E. intestinalis*) quickly colonize the bared space, followed by the barnacle *Balanus glandula* in July (Dayton, 1971).

Predation and grazing of adults can also create striking horizontal patterns. As might be predicted, the distribution of specialist predators usually coincides with that of their preferred prey. Sponges, hydroids, and bryozoans each support their own group of nudibranch predators; the snail *Nucella emarginata* seldom strays from its barnacle prey; the limpet *Notoacmaea insessa* lives only on the fronds of the feather boa kelp *Egregia menziesii*, in sheltered depressions that it grazes into the fronds; and the limpet *Notoacmaea paleacea* lives solely on the blades of surfgrass *Phyllospadix*, feeding on both epiphytic algae and the surfgrass itself (Morris, *et al.*, 1980).

Predators and grazers may also influence the distribution of their prey. The sea urchins *Strongylocentrotus purpuratus* and *S. franciscanus* graze voraciously on large brown kelps of the subtidal and lower intertidal, usually preferring *Macrocystis* over others. In areas of abundant urchins, large seaweeds are usually sparse or absent. When all urchins were removed from shallow tidepools in Mukkaw Bay, Washington, a great variety of opportunistic algae sprang up, and over time a verdant jungle of large seaweeds emerged, with the canopy species *Hedophyllum sessile* eventually dominating. In neighboring control pools left untouched, the surviving algae were primarily calcareous species, protected from grazing by the hard calcium carbonate in their cell walls (Paine and Vadas, 1969). Sea otters (*Enhydra lutris*) prey heavily on urchins, and in Monterey Bay, California, a recent resurgence in the sea otter population brought a new abundance of kelp and associated fish where they were once rarer (Morris, *et al.*, 1980; VanBlaricom and Estes, 1988). In general, wherever grazing is severe in the infralittoral and lower midlittoral, both crustose and erect calcareous red algae thrive in comparison to the more tender greens and browns.

In the high midlittoral, several species of grazing limpets, especially *Collisella digitalis*, heavily influence the distribution of both filamentous algae and barnacles. With their hard, file-like radulas they scrape the rocks clean of newly settled spores and larvae. If, in May, all limpets are removed from an area, or a cage is built to exclude them, by August abundant barnacles (especially *Balanus glandula*) appear in grooves and depressions, and the gray rock will have turned a verdant green as filamentous red algae, especially *Bangia* and *Urospora*, grow unchecked (Cubit, 1975). The combined rasping activities of dozens of limpets per square yard probably shave ½ inch of rock from the surface every 20 years or so.

Recently, ecologists have discovered that predation by shorebirds, such as the black oystercatcher *Haematopus bachmani*, surfbird *Aphriza virgata*, and black turnstone *Arenaria melanocephala* causes considerable patchiness in rocky intertidal communities. We might predict, for example, that the Farallon Islands off San Francisco should have a rich and diverse rocky intertidal community because of their long-standing freedom from any human disruptions whatsoever. On the contrary; human absence has allowed totally unrestrained and rampant foraging by oystercatchers and other birds, and as a result, populations of limpets, barnacles, and other species have been decimated, and the shore is disappointingly bare (Frank, 1982).

In general, where shorebird foraging is severe, the preferred prey species show an extremely patchy distribution, with organisms congregating in inaccessible habitats. The kind of prey preferred depends on the bill shape and behavioral repertoire of the bird. Oystercatchers use a hammering motion with their stout bills to dislodge limpets and mussels from the rocks, and to open mussel shells. They also have been observed to thrust their bills into the opening between the mussel shells as the mussels feed in shallow water. Oystercatchers usually carry their dislodged prey to the top of a special boulder or rock outcrop to feed, leaving shells scattered about for biologists to identify. Surfbirds tug upwards with their stout bills to wrench loose mussels, gooseneck barnacles, and sometimes acorn barnacles; they consume their prey on the spot, usually swallowing the barnacle shells whole. Black turnstones use two techniques: hammering with their chisel-shaped bills to dislodge compressed prey, such as limpets and a wider size range of acorn barnacles than the surfbirds; and pushing aside algae and surfgrass to expose the mobile arthropods taking shelter beneath (Marsh, 1983).

In the fall and winter of 1980–1981 in Middle Cove of Cape Arago, oystercatchers consumed an average of 1.8 limpets per square yard of intertidal, at a mean feeding rate of one limpet per oystercatcher every 3 minutes; nearly all prey exceeded 10–14 mm in length (Frank, 1982). This may seem insignificant, but the number taken was averaged over the entire shore area, of which 90% was free of limpets; over the total upper shore limpet habitat, the birds consumed perhaps 10–20 limpets per square yard. As a result, limpet abundances declined precipitously. In August, researchers counted over 300 *Notoacmaea persona* over 0.79 in. long per hour of search time; the following March they counted only two. Similarly, large *N. scutum* fell from 500 to 13, and *Collisella pelta* from 231 to 109 (Frank, 1982). The survivors, almost without exception, were found on steep cliffs or high on the sides of boulders; large *N. persona* showed an especially patchy distribution, with large individuals almost exclusively on a few boulders greater than 6 feet in height. These results indicate that, as soon as a limpet reaches 10–14 mm in length, it will not survive the winter unless it happens to occupy a high, steep surface. This is understandable, since oystercatchers stand upright as they feed, and cannot climb steep rock faces or float on the water surface. Oystercatcher predation also affects algal growth indirectly: by the end of the winter, gently sloping surfaces support rich algal growths, while the vertical cliffs are usually barren. In spring and summer of 1981, oystercatchers apparently left Middle Cove to nest, and unhindered limpet movements during foraging tended to randomize the population once again (Frank, 1982). Surfbirds and black turnstones also prey on limpets heavily enough to control their distribution. But because these birds have shorter bills than oystercatchers, limpets in crevices, even on horizontal surfaces, usually escape their foraging (Marsh, 1985). So a close inspection of limpet size and distribution on a rocky shore often betrays not only the intensity of shorebird foraging, but whether just surfbirds and black turnstones, or both oystercatchers and other species, are the primary plunderers.

Sanderlings and their prey. On sandy beaches, the vast majority of prey biomass lies hidden beneath the surface, and their responses to predation are largely invisible to the casual naturalist. But their most conspicuous predators, the shorebirds, show patterns of behavior that conform neatly to the patterns of behavior and distribution of their prey.

A beach would not be a beach without the legions of sanderlings, the gray-white or brown shorebirds that endlessly chase the receding waves, only to flee the oncoming surge, usually hopping, running, pecking in the sand like a frantic wind-up toy, but always nimbly escaping a drenching in the cold seawater. This of course is foraging behavior, for the sanderlings prey on the small burrowing crustaceans in the upper sandy intertidal. This behavior is more complicated than it looks, and involves desperate avoidance tactics by the birds' prey, the crustaceans, and shrewd search strategies by the sanderlings.

Sanderlings spend the winter months doing little besides feeding along the Pacific and Atlantic coasts, as far north as Vancouver Island. In Northern California (especially Bodega Bay) Myers and coworkers (1979, 1980) found that Bodega Bay sanderlings feed on the isopods *Excirolana linguifrons* and *E. kincaidii*, and the mole crab *Emerita analoga*. Not all prey, however, are equally likely to be caught. The density, size, and depth of the prey, and the penetrability of the substrate (mostly sand) in which they burrow all control the ease and success of capture.

Prey density is important because the prey leave no marks on the sand surface after they burrow, and the birds thus have no visual clues as to where to peck in the sand. Accordingly, they find their prey purely by chance, and the more prey in a given area, the more the birds will catch. Prey density usually varies from none to 1200 per square yard. In the spring, though, widespread reproduction may raise the density to 4000 per square yard, so abundant that it takes a sanderling longer to ingest a prey item than to find it (Myers, et al., 1980).

Understandably, larger prey items are easier to find. Prey with body area 25 square millimeters are caught 80% of the time, and 20 square millimeters 40% of the time. Prey size varies seasonally with their reproductive cycle; average prey size in the spring is comparatively small. Since sanderlings will not eat prey more than 0.6 in. long, the adult female sand crabs, which may reach 2 in. in length, are immune to the birds. The isopods, though, do not reach a size refuge; the oldest only reach about 0.3 in. long (Myers, *et al.*, 1980).

Deeper prey are caught less often because sanderlings rarely insert their bills in the sand more than 1 inch. A sanderling in effect digs a hole: the bird jabs its bill into the sand, opens it at the bottom and withdraws it open, thus widening the opening, then repeats this 5–10 times, making the opening progressively wider and deeper. Prey resting less than 0.4 in. deep have a 60% chance of being caught; prey more than 0.4 inch have less than a 30% chance. Penetrability of the sand controls the depth of a bird's probing. Since a bird cannot jab its bill as deep into compact sand as loose sand, it leaves behind more prey in compact sand (Myers, *et al.*, 1980).

From the prey's point of view, then, the best strategy is to burrow deep in compact sand, stay small, and stay away from other prey items. Luckily for the sanderlings, however, the prey's lifestyle makes these objectives unattainable. To reproduce, both isopods and sand crabs require internal fertilization. This means that prey must often be at close quarters in the breeding season, thus raising their chances of being caught. Adult females are generally larger than adult males because larger females can produce larger broods. Females thus generally sustain greater risks until they reach a size refuge.

The prey's feeding behavior also raises their risk in several interesting ways. Both isopods and sand crabs feed on plankton and detritus suspended in seawater. To feed, they must wait until close to high tide when the surf begins to wash over their burrowing sites. The sand crabs then extend their feeding antennae, and the isopods climb out of their holes, swim around eating the plankton, then quickly burrow back into the sand before the wave recedes. The wave wash, however, removes some of the surface sand, bringing the prey closer to the surface and easier to catch. When a wave recedes, it leaves the sand with a temporary surface sheen, which quickly disappears, leaving the sand merely wet. "Surface-sheen" sand is looser and much easier for a bird's bill to penetrate than wet sand.

Now it is clear why a sanderling must feed at water's edge, and why it runs quickly after the receding waves. The faster a sanderling can follow a wave, the looser and more penetrable the sand is underfoot, and the more likely that the bird will be able to catch a prey item before it has started to burrow back into the sand after a feeding foray, or at least, before it has burrowed back very deeply.

Commensalism. Although I have so far considered only the effects of negative interactions (competition, grazing, and predation) on intertidal community structure, positive interactions between populations control the distributions of species at least as powerfully. Commensalism, a relationship in which one population benefits while the other is largely unaffected, is ubiquitous on the seashore, as organisms seek out other organisms for living space.

A bed of California mussels and its inhabitants is a classic example of commensalism. As a habitat, a mussel bed offers several advantages. First, the mussels shelter the spaces between and under them from waves, currents, predators, and high temperatures during low tides. Second, the shell surfaces greatly increase the amount of stable surface area for attachment by barnacles and other sessile species. Third, the abundant red algae growing on the shells and sheltered rock spaces among them serve as food for grazing animals. And finally, the waste products of the mussels themselves sustain abundant deposit-feeders. The byssal threads often filter and trap these wastes and other miscellaneous detrital particles that settle out of the slower currents through the beds. The result is a diverse community of animals, including barnacles, nematode worms (Sabellids, Serpulids, Nereids, and Syllids), limpets, anemones such as the piling anemone *Metridium senile* and juvenile aggregating and green anemones (*Anthopleura elegantissima* and *A. xanthogrammica*), rock snails, tunicates, and bryozoans. Ten square inches of a mussel bed appears to contain upwards of 5000 individual animals of some 22 different species, of which about 600 are mussels. If such a community is experimentally scraped off the rock, many of these species fail to re-inhabit the cleared space until after a second generation of mussels appears, which takes about 2 years. Mussel beds clearly enhance the shore diversity, and are truly forests in miniature.

The same comforts are offered by other dense assemblages, such as beds of large seaweeds, surfgrass, large acorn and goose barnacles, aggregating anemones, and oysters in estuaries. Each of these has its own collection of smaller plants and animals exploiting the cool shade, dampness, shelter from surf, and other luxuries in the small interstitial spaces. As mentioned above, if the large canopy seaweeds *Hedophyllum*, *Laminaria*, and *Lessoniopsis* are experimentally removed, a variety of obligate understory species, such as *Corallina* and *Bossiella* die from exposure soon thereafter (Dayton, 1975a). If the acorn barnacle *Semibalanus cariosus* is removed from areas on the west shore of San Juan Island, neighboring aggregating anemones colonize the cleared space over the fall and winter, but die back severely in the summer. In contrast, nearby anemones clumped around the bases of large intact *S. cariosus* are protected from the wind, and show very little mortality (Dayton, 1971). The anemones, in turn, protect the predatory snail *Nucella* from desiccation, thus increasing its efficiency of barnacle consumption (Dayton, 1971). The subtidal kelp forests are famous for their diversity of understory species, many of which are endemic to the community. The same is true of surfgrass forests worldwide; since eelgrass is abundant in Northwest estuaries, we will consider these in the next chapter.

Escapes. A common pattern in shore community structure involves patchy distributions within a single population: entire populations dominated by individuals of the same age are often found, and these often consist of extremely large organisms who have escaped predation and are isolated from the main distribution of the species. These dominant age classes usually arise through an interaction between biological and physical factors. Despite the uniformity of the Northwest climate, the currents and temperatures of air and ocean can vary from one year to the next (as demonstrated by the El Nino current of the winter of 1982–1983). Occasionally, the North Pacific High dominates for several weeks at a time off Washington and Oregon, even in the fall and winter. The resulting north winds cause strong upwelling currents and abnormally high nutrient concentrations. Any pelagic larvae lucky enough to be released into these waters thrive on the higher productivity of the phytoplankton and its zooplankton consumers. Hence these larval species tend to settle out in abnormally high numbers (augmented sometimes by natural population cycles), and the result is an enormous population of juveniles in the sand or on the rock surface. Since adults of different species release larvae at different times of the year, different species will benefit in this way depending on the season. Normally, mussels and barnacles that settle in the infralittoral or lower midlittoral succumb to predation by whelks and seastars before reaching maturity. But if these settle out abundantly enough, they swamp their predators' ability to consume them all. This might also happen during bad years in which the predator population collapses while the prey persists unharmed. As a result, a few prey patches might survive long enough to reach a size too large to be eaten. From then on, they live in comparative safety, dominated by large organisms all of the same age. Hence, where predation is severe, as at lower shore levels, the populations of preferred prey tend to show dominant age classes. In contrast, where predation is less severe, mixed-age distributions can prevail because juvenile survival is not contingent on a favorable year; even in a small crop, some youngsters can survive predation each year.

    For example, on San Juan Island, when the acorn barnacle *Semibalanus cariosus* settles in the lower intertidal, virtually all juveniles are eaten by the whelk *Nucella lamellosa* during a normal year. If the *Nucella* suffer heavy mortality during a bad year, or if the barnacles recruit in abundance during a good year, a few of the young survive. If they persist 2 years, they reach a permanent size refuge from *Nucella* (Connell, 1972). The ochre seastar *Pisaster ochraceus*, on the other hand, is large enough to eat *S. cariosus* of all sizes, but only at the lower levels of the *S. cariosus* zone.

Similarly, *Nucella* consumes all newly settled *Balanus glandula* at lower shore levels within a year. Since this species is too small to reach a size refuge, it never forms dominant age classes at lower levels. If protective cages are built around the juvenile barnacles, however, over several years they develop mixed-aged distributions at the lower shore levels, similar to those normally formed at intermediate levels where predation is less severe (Connell, 1972). The California mussel normally fails to recruit into the infralittoral and often the lower midlittoral because of predation by the ochre seastar. But scuba divers have discovered small patches of large individuals in water as deep as 100 feet (Paine, 1974). Here the mussels reach up to a foot in length, and survive apparently because their major predator can no longer handle them; it is difficult to imagine an ochre seastar successfully opening a mussel larger than about 6 inches.

If grazing limpets are experimentally removed from certain British shores, dense populations of fugitive algae quickly colonize. Eventually new limpets reinhabit the area, but not before many of the seaweeds have grown too large for the limpets to consume. These new limpets graze away all the smaller algae, and prevent any new algal recruitment for a few months or years. During this time, the algal population consists entirely of a few large, dominant age classes. But sooner or later, these die, and healthy limpet grazing again prevents any algal recruitment at all (Connell, 1972).

At high shore levels, where predation is light, sporadic escapes from physical forces sometimes create the same pattern. On Bodega Head, for example, the upper intertidal population of *Collisella scabra* consisted mainly of four-year-olds in 1966, presumably because of a good recruitment year followed by three bad ones. Over the next four years, the population declined steadily as individuals died of desiccation, log battering, and other causes, and virtually no juveniles settled in (Sutherland, 1970). Other species that routinely form populations of large, old individuals include the ochre seastar (Dayton, 1971), the purple urchin (Dayton, 1971), and the whelk *Nucella lamellosa* (Connell, 1970); whether these are local escapes from predators or the elements remains to be seen.

Disturbance Maintains Diversity

We have already seen how a few voracious and aggressive predators and competitors can eliminate other species from some shore zones and habitats, and thereby set their local population boundaries. Obviously, these dominant species may be prevented from doing this by any physical or biological disturbances that keep their numbers sufficiently low. In this way, regular disturbances can actually maintain a diversity of species. In general, as the community-structuring rules assert, we would expect that small disturbances should have little effect and thus allow competitive or predatory exclusion; severe disturbances should eliminate large numbers of all species; but intermediate disturbances should both reduce competition by thinning out the competitors, and inhibit predatory exclusion by aggravating the predators. In other words, we predict few species in highly disturbed and undisturbed areas, and a maximum number of species in moderately disturbed areas.

These patterns are vividly displayed in the outer-coast mussel beds. As has been noted, the California mussel *Mytilus californianus* dominates in the midlittoral of exposed rocky shores by virtue of its ability to overgrow, smother, and crush most seaweeds, barnacles, and other organisms too large to fit in the small spaces between the bases of adjacent shells. These unfortunates can coexist with the mussels only where drift logs, seastars, and waves have torn off sections of the mussel bed and exposed the rock surface. Within two to three years, however, the neighboring mussels migrate or recruit into the cleared space, and force the intruders out once again.

In Mukkaw Bay, Washington, and probably all along the Northwest shores, the regular consumption of mussels by the ochre seastar *Pisaster ochraceus* opens rock space for a variety of species that otherwise would succumb to the competitive talents of the mussels. The seastar also provides food for some of its neighbors; the mussels loosened by its foraging often fall into the waiting tentacles of sea anemones beneath (Dayton, 1973b). Where the seastars forage in the lower midlittoral, some 20–30 species of algae and animals coexist (Paine, 1974). Especially abundant are the acorn barnacles *Semibalanus cariosus, Balanus glandula,* and *Chthamalus fissus;* the coralline alga *Corallina vancouveriensis;* and the limpet *Collisella digitalis.* Usually accompanying these are the algae *Endocladia muricata, Lithothamnium, Hedophyllum sessile, Ulva, Porphyra, Rhodomela larix, Gigartina papillata,* and others; the gooseneck barnacle *Pollicipes polymerus;* the sponge *Halichondria panicea;* the green anemone *Anthopleura xanthogrammica;* the purple urchin *Strongylocentrotus purpuratus;* and various limpets, whelks, and chitons. Moreover, about 10% of the rock space is unoccupied. If the seastars are experimentally removed, the mussels spread aggressively over the lower midlittoral, and over the next 3 years eliminate virtually all these species, leaving just a few traces of open space (Paine, 1974).

One of the mussel bed competitors, the sea palm *Postelsia palmaeformis* (Figure 38), is an annual seaweed that needs to recolonize the shore each year in order to maintain a population. This might appear impossible in the mussel beds, but the sea palm succeeds by exploiting wave force and seastars in an especially intriguing way. This unusual plant is a survivor par excellance of the roughest surf conditions, indeed cannot live in quiet water, and actually thrives on disaster. Its adaptiveness to exposed shores is granted mostly by a surprising ability to remove competitors by smothering them, or collaborating with the waves to rip them off the rocks (Dayton, 1973a; Paine, 1979).

Figure 38. The sea palm (*Postelsia palmaeformis*) at Cape Perpetua. July, 1986.

To recruit into a mussel bed for the first time, a sea palm needs bare rock space provided by either log battering or seastar foraging. Abundant spores, perhaps from adult plants torn loose and drifting nearby, quickly settle onto any cleared spaces. Microscopic gametophytes soon spring up, which rapidly produce a tightly clumped population of sporophytes on the bare rock. While these are growing to maturity, a variety of other algae and barnacles settle in and begin to encroach on the sea palms. If the barnacles continue to proliferate undisturbed, their sharp shell bases begin to grow into and undercut the sea palms and other algae. The palms respond to this challenge at low tides, when their spores, produced in special areas on the fronds, are released and flow down grooves in the drooping fronds. They drip onto the substrate in enormous numbers, and attach immediately not only directly to the rock, but also to the barnacle shells and fronds of algae all growing beneath. The spores develop into gametophytes that quickly produce the fast-growing sporophyte phase, often directly on top of the algal and barnacle competitors (Dayton, 1973a).

The sea palms attached to algae are unstable in the surf-swept rocky areas, and by the time they reach a height of about 4 inches, they and the attached algae are wrenched loose by waves, again exposing bare rock which is quickly colonized by more sea palm sporophytes (Figure 39). Barnacles are more securely attached and cannot be immediately ripped free; however, a few sea palms grow over and smother them, and eventually the sea palms and their adhering barnacle corpses wash away, again exposing more rock for sea palm colonization. But what about the mussels, the competitive dominants? These generally fail to crowd out the sea palms because their larvae rarely settle on bare rock; they prefer to settle and attach to algae, barnacles, or the byssal threads of adult mussels, and only later may move to the rock surface. When the sea palms rip the algae and barnacles free, they ruthlessly remove important settling space for the mussels, thereby severely inhibiting their encroachment (Dayton, 1973a).

Sea palms, then, appear to sacrifice a few individuals to the pounding surf to kill their competitors and ensure the survival of the whole patch. It should be emphasized, though, that this kind of behavior is unusual. Most annual seaweeds dependent on such unpredictable, transient habitats rely on long-distance spore disper-sal for their survival. Examples are the fast-growing, opportunistic algae that first colonize the bare rock in the mussel beds. Such species are called "fugitives" because they must constantly move from place to place; intense competition prevents them from surviving long in one place. Their success, then, requires quick growth to reproductive maturity, and production of large numbers of

Figure 39. Sea palm (*Postelsia palmaeformis*) dynamics. 1 Open space. **2** *Postelsia* colonizes. **3** Sporophyte releases spores. **4** New generation appears on barnacles and algae. **5** Some *Postelsia* is torn loose by waves. **6** Some competitors are eliminated with *Postelsia*, and new space is opened. (Kellerman)

spores capable of traveling long distances. The greater the spore number and distance traveled, the greater their probability of finding another disturbed, open habitat, and the cycle repeats itself. The marine environment is especially favorable to this lifestyle, because currents can can carry waterborne spores great distances.

The sea palm, however, releases spores only when it is high and dry at low tides, so they rarely settle more than 2–3 yards from the adult. In a sense, instead of constantly moving, the sea palm is constantly maintaining beneath it an otherwise unpredictable, transient habitat, and so does not require reliable long-distance dispersal. This dispersal is only needed to colonize a newly exposed patch for the first time, which can happen when a spore-bearing adult plant or frond is torn loose by waves and carried along in the longshore transport currents.

There are limits, though, to a sea palm's love of calamity. While the plant thrives in places where predictable, moderate local disturbances ("disasters") are common, it perishes in the wake of rare, unpredictable, large-scale disturbances ("catastrophes"), which send it to the line of rotting corpses at the high tide line. Specifically, sea palm patches persist only in sites that experience a disturbance about every two years that removes roughly 5–20% of the mussel beds. They do not persist in areas where disturbances are much less frequent and more destructive. Of course, neither do they occur in areas of slight disturbance, say, less than 5%: here their ripping ability is denied and they succumb to mussel and barnacle competition. In other words, we find no sea palms in sites of recent catastrophes, but wherever they persist, we can expect disaster (Paine, 1979).

In calm waters, such as along the eastern shore of San Juan Island, the mussels die out, leaving acorn barnacles to struggle among themselves for rock space. Above reach of the ochre seastar, the large barnacle *Semibalanus cariosus* can competitively eliminate both *Balanus glandula* and *Chthamalus dalli* by overgrowing and smothering, or crushing the smaller individuals between adjacent *Semibalanus*. In most areas, however, log battering and predation by the whelk *Nucella* and the limpet *Collisella* maintain enough open space to prevent this (Dayton, 1971). As we would predict, where these depredations are severe, they not only decimate the *Semibalanus* but virtually all other organisms as well; where they are moderate, they tend to allow coexistence of the three barnacle species. At Eagle Point on the south shore of San Juan Island, if cages are built in early spring to exclude the seastars, limpets, and whelks, barnacle populations fluctuate in a predictable sequence. First, *Balanus glandula* overgrows and excludes virtually all the smaller *Chthamalus* by April or May, when it reaches a peak in dominance, occupying 25–100% of the rock space. *Semibalanus*, in the meantime, grows more slowly, but catches up to *Balanus* usually by June or July. After this time, *Balanus* declines as it is crushed or overgrown by the larger *Semibalanus*, and the latter comes to occupy virtually 100% of the space usually by the end of the summer, but at the latest by autumn of the following year. On the other hand, if just the seastars are excluded, and either limpets or whelks are allowed to forage (but not both), the three barnacles tend to coexist at least until October, each occupying 5–25% of the space between tide levels two and four feet (Dayton, 1971). If all three predators are allowed free rein, however, all barnacles disappear from most areas; those that recruit in are routinely eaten in a few months. As mentioned previously, however, in nature predators inevitably experience a bad year from time to time, and their reduced foraging gives *Semibalanus* enough time to reach a size refuge from the whelks. As a result, single-age classes of *Semibalanus* dominate in many areas in the midlittoral above reach of seastars on San Juan Island, even though limpets and whelks continue to remove youngsters of all species (Dayton, 1971).

On the outer coast, where *Semibalanus* is rare, *Balanus* and *Chthamalus* interact with predators in a similar way. Where seastars, whelks, and limpets are all excluded from cages built in May at Shi Shi Beach and Portage Head, *Balanus* usually dominates by October, especially above a shore level of 4 feet (Dayton, 1971). But if just the seastars and limpets are excluded and the whelks are allowed free movement, *Balanus* disappears usually by July, and *Chthamalus* expands over 5–30% of the rock space (Dayton, 1971). This is apparently because the whelks prey much more heavily on the *Balanus*, due probably to its larger size, and so maintain free space for the otherwise inferior *Chthamalus*. In nature, however, both limpets and whelks feed heavily on barnacles, greatly reducing the density of both species, and in general preventing any competitive monopolization by either (Dayton, 1971; Connell, 1970).

As noted earlier, the dominant herbivores of the upper intertidal, the limpets, graze heavily enough to reduce both diversity and biomass of the small and tender algae. Similarly in the subtidal and lower intertidal, severe grazing by sea urchins, especially the purple urchin *Strongylocentrotus purpuratus*, drastically reduces the diversity of neighboring seaweeds. In Mukkaw Bay, Washington, tidepools densely populated with urchins contain fewer than about 10 species; primarily the grazing-resistant calcareous forms *Corallina vancouveriensis*, *C. officinalis*, *Bossiella*, *Calliarthron tuberculosum*, and *Lithothamnium*; but also the small fleshy *Polysiphonia* and *Ulva rigida* (Paine and Vadas, 1969). When all urchins were experimentally removed in the summers of 1964–66, 6–12 new algal species appeared within about a year in the average pool, and over 20 new species across all pools (Paine and Vadas, 1969). In the intertidal, the new canopy species included *Odonthalia floccosa*, *Desmarestia herbacea*, *Costaria costata*, *Alaria nana*, *Hedophyllum sessile*, and *Nereocystis luetkeana*; but, over time, *Hedophyllum* tended to outcompete and eliminate the others, dominating 50–80% of the space. In subtidal areas *Laminaria setchellii*, *L. groenlandica*, and *L. complanata* predominated. Taking shelter beneath these were a greater and more unpredictable variety of obligate understory species, including *Spongomorpha*, *Codium fragile*, *Gigartina papillata*, *Delesseria decipiens*, *Prionitis lyallii*, *Bryopsis*, *Rhodymenia*, *Laurencia*, *Opuntiella*, and *Pterosiphonia* (Paine and Vadas, 1969).

Along most of the West Coast, urchins and large fleshy

seaweeds tend to be mutually exclusive, with patches of one or the other but not both. Ecologists have yet to uncover the reasons urchins vary in numbers from place to place, but predators, including humans, may eliminate them in some areas, and thereby enhance the local abundance and diversity of seaweeds. For example, the sunflower star *Pycnopodia helianthoides* and the green anemone *Anthopleura xanthogrammica* prey heavily enough on urchins to clear them from large areas (Dayton, 1975a), while local populations of the sea otter *Enhydra lutris* in Monterey Bay, California and off the Olympic Peninsula, Washington, consume enough urchins to keep the seaweed jungles dense and healthy (Morris, *et al.,* 1980). Urchins are not the only consumers of the large fleshy seaweeds; the chiton *Katharina tunicata* and other gastropods also make their mark, which in turn are sought by the large seastars of the subtidal. In consuming the herbivores, these and other predators, more abundant in the benign lower zones, might be responsible for the vivid, dense stands of large brown algae that mark the upper boundary of the infralittoral fringe (or "laminarian zone") at most locales.

In contrast, for those species that successfully resist grazing, such as the coralline red algae, the attacks by urchins, limpets, and other herbivores are usually sufficiently mild to actually maintain species diversity by reducing competition (Paine, 1984). Underneath the lower intertidal *Hedophyllum* canopy at Tatoosh Island, Washington, is a colorful community of coralline algae. Some form hard, orange and crimson crusts over the rocks, such as *Pseudolithophyllum lichenare, P. whidbeyense, Lithothamnium phymatodeum,* and *Lithophyllum impressum;* while others grow erect from a crust-like base, such as *Bossiella.* These compete among themselves for space by overgrowth and smothering, but with unpredictable outcomes. *Pseudolithophyllum lichenare,* for example, has a thicker, more grazer-resistant crust that can push over the erect corallines. But its thickness is exploited for living space by parasites such as boring sponges and other burrowing invertebrates (including the worm *Dodecaceria fewkesi* and the clam *Hiatella arctica).* The thinner crust of *Lithothamnium* grows more rapidly over its competitors, but is more vulnerable to grazing. Similarly, the erect species can overshade the crustose, but are more easily grazed and bulldozed by other holdfasts. As a result, in some cases no competitive winner emerges after as much as two years, but when one does it differs from place to place, depending on the activities of grazers and parasites and the amount of space initially occupied by neighboring crusts (Paine, 1984).

Considering interactions among just these five coralline species, although *Pseudolithophyllum lichenare* wins virtually all of its non-stalemated bouts, the others fare less successfully. *Lithophyllum* excludes *Lithothamnium* 60% of the time (while the reverse occurs 40%); *Pseudolithophyllum whidbeyense* excludes *Lithothamnium* 70% of the time, and *Lithophyllum* only 30% of the time. Overall, *Lithophyllum* wins about 61%, *Pseudolithophyllum whidbeyense* 45%, *Lithothamnium* 29%, and *Bossiella* wins none (Paine, 1984). So the outcome varies considerably in pairwise matches of *Lithothamnium, P. whidbeyense,* and *Lithophyllum.* In contrast, when grazers are experimentally excluded in the field, these reversals tend to disappear, and a clear winner emerges: *Lithothamnium* excludes both *Lithophyllum* and *P. whidbeyense* virtually 100% of the time. Nevertheless, the outcome still remains uncertain between *P. whidbeyense* and *Lithophyllum:* the latter now wins 70% of the time instead of 30%. This uncertainty might reflect the variation in rock texture; *Lithophyllum* tends to escape overgrowth where it occupies small rises above *P. whidbeyense.* If this topographic variation is eliminated by growing the algae on glass plates in the laboratory, then *P. whidbeyense* excludes *Lithophyllum* virtually 100% of the time, and a clear competitive hierarchy appears, ordered from inferior to superior as follows: *Bossiella, Lithophyllum, P. whidbeyense, Lithothamnium,* and *P. lichenare* (Paine, 1894). These results show that, without grazers, the thick-crusted *P. lichenare* would tend to overgrow, and eventually eliminate, the rest. But with grazers, although each competitive bout usually leads to exclusion, different bouts have different winners, so that diversity is maintained on a large scale. Physical disturbances, such as log battering, of course also clear space, and might be even more important than grazing for such overall losers as *Bossiella.*

In permanent tidepools on San Juan Island, a variety of unpredictable disturbances, including waves, wave-thrown rocks and logs, excessive heat, and sudden invasions of predators and herbivores, all combine to preserve variety over a large scale where more predictable forces (such as tidal exposure and competition) simultaneously push toward uniformity on a small scale (Dethier, 1984). Without disturbances, a single species usually dominates depending on the tidal height of the pool, and eventually occupies 20–50% of the pool bottom. From low to high pools, these dominants are (Dethier, 1984):

1. the surfgrass *Phyllospadix scouleri,*
2. various articulated coralline algae,
3. the California mussel on exposed shores,
4. the aggregating anemone on more-protected shores,
5. the red alga *Rhodomela larix,* and
6. green algae in the genus *Cladophora.*

Since air exposure is not a problem in a tidepool, the upper limits of these species are probably set by other stresses in the higher pools, such as higher temperatures, greater stagnation, and scarcity of food. Once one of these dominants colonizes a pool, it spreads rapidly by enhanced recruitment, and in the case of the plants, by aggressive vegetative growth (expansion of holdfasts in the algae, and rhizomatous growth in the surfgrass).

But this dominance is overthrown by disturbances: primarily summer heat stress in the high intertidal, and winter log or wave damage in the lower. On average, a disturbance serious enough to kill some of the dominant organisms hits a pool every two to five years, and a dominant requires anywhere from three months to over two years to recover to its original level, as long as some of its population remains; if not, the slow recruitment of spores or larvae from long distances may boost the time to over three years (Dethier, 1984). In the meantime, the whole gamut of other intertidal species may invade and run rampant in the pool. So disturbances occur at about the right frequencies to offset the length of time necessary for dominants to re-establish themselves, and for every pool monopolized by a single species, we can usually find another at the same level with a variety of competitively inferior species taking advantage of space opened up by a recent disturbance.

SUCCESSION

Now I change the focus from spatial patterns in shore communities to predictable temporal patterns. For example, after log battering opens new rock space in the mussel beds on Tatoosh and Waadah Islands, Washington, organisms invade the surface in a highly predictable sequence:
1. filamentous red and green algae;
2. foliose and coralline algae;
3. the acorn barnacles *Balanus glandula, Chthamalus dalli,* and *Semibalanus cariosus;*
4. the gooseneck barnacle *Pollicipes polymerus* and the acorn barnacle *Semibalanus cariosus;* and finally
5. the California mussel *Mytilus californianus* on gently sloping inclines, or often the sea palm *Postelsia palmaeformis* on steeper surfaces (Dayton, 1971, 1973).

In the beds of surfgrass *Phyllospadix scouleri* at Squaw Island at Cape Arago and Boiler Bay, Oregon, the green alga *Ulva* colonizes bared rock by May. By October, the *Ulva* gives way to several other algae, most commonly *Rhodomela larix, Cryptosiphonia woodii,* and *Odonthalia floccosa.* Over several months or years, the surfgrass replaces these, occupying up to 80% of the canopy (Turner, 1983b). On the boulder field at Ellwood Beach, California, *Ulva* again colonizes cleared surfaces within about a month. Usually by the fall or winter of the first year, several perennial red algae take over, including *Gelidium coulteri, Gigartina leptorhynchos, Rhodoglossum affine,* and *Gigartina canaliculata.* Over 2–3 years, *G. canaliculata* gradually dominates, eventually occupying 60–90% of the space (Sousa, 1980a). Such predictable sequences, leading to an internally stable end point, are called "succession."

Ecologists have observed succession of one form or another in virtually every ecosystem studied, and for decades have searched for the reasons why these same sequences recur time after time. The classical hypothesis, that of facilitation and inhibition (Clements, 1916; Odum, 1969), proposes that species early in succession modify the environment in a way that simultaneously inhibits their own survival and facilitates the invasion or survival of later species. Moreover, later species tend to competitively inhibit or exclude the earlier, with the final community comprising the overall competitive dominants. In other words, a community occupying a fixed interval in the successional sequence fails to appear sooner because it requires the earlier communities to prepare its environment; and persists only temporarily because either it inhibits its own survival or the later species competitively exclude it. This scenario works tolerably well in highly stressed terrestrial habitats such as salt marshes and sand dunes (as I shall deal with), but with a few exceptions the concept of facilitation misses the mark in the rocky intertidal.

As a rule, mid- and late-successional species in the marine environment (including all those listed above) can and do colonize bare rock in the absence of the earlier species. Mussels, for example, settle preferentially on adult byssal threads, algae, and hydroids, but these are not necessary; any rough surface will do. Nevertheless, the earlier species generally appear first because they possess certain opportunistic life history traits, including year-round production of spores or larvae that disperse long distances, rapid settlement, and rapid growth to adulthood. Later successional species, on the other hand, generally release propagules only at certain times of year, and grow more slowly (Sousa, 1980a). So although the opportunists are the first to make an appearance, many of the later species usually have also settled in alongside, but due to their slower growth, have been swamped by the opportunists. Not only do the earlier species fail to facilitate, but in most cases they actually inhibit the later species as well, by overshading, shielding the site from additional spore settlement, and growing tough, unyielding holdfasts. Indeed at many sites, some kind of disturbance, biological or physical, is necessary to remove some of the opportunists before the later species can begin to assert themselves. Often, the reason for the faster growth of the opportunists, namely their thinner, more delicate blades, also results in their early demise by making them much more vulnerable to grazers, heavy waves, and drought. For example, at Ellwood Beach, California, the rock crab *Pachygrapsus crassipes* passes over the later-successional algae during its grazing forays, instead seeking out *Ulva* and other more tender colonizing green algae. As a result of this predation preference and their greater susceptibility to desiccation, these opportunists die out within a few months after they first appear, allowing the tougher, middle-successional red algae to take over. Where the grazers are excluded by cages, the *Ulva* persists indefinitely (Sousa, 1980a).

Similarly, at Boiler Bay, Squaw Island, and probably the length of the outer Oregon and Washington coasts, the algal cover drops dramatically in the fall, most likely because of shorter days, lower temperatures due to nighttime low tides, heavier surf, more voluminous freshwater input from rains, and greater sand scour (Turner, 1983a). The colonizing *Ulva* in the lower surfgrass beds quite likely suffers more than the later algae, and its death probably allows *Cryptosiphonia* and *Rhodomela* to encroach upon and eventually dominate the next successional stage.

In concordance with the classical model of succession, however, some of the middle species and probably most of the eventual dominants secure their living space by direct competition, rather than passive expansion into cleared areas, even though they fail to appear early due to slow growth rates. So for example, as noted earlier, the mid-successional acorn barnacles competitively exclude earlier algae by undercutting their holdfasts. And the large barnacle *Semibalanus cariosus* excludes other acorn barnacles before being excluded itself (on exposed shores) by the dominant California mussel. At Ellwood Beach, *Gigartina canaliculata* eventually dominates the algal canopy because it shades and whiplashes *Ulva* and the mid-successional red algae, and expands into cleared areas by vegetative propagation from its holdfast (Sousa, 1980a). The surfgrass eventually dominates in its lower intertidal zone through aggressive vegetative spreading and overshading of virtually all other plants.

Though facilitation is probably the exception in marine succession, the single verified example of obligate facilitation, discovered just recently, appears to be the key to success for the only flowering plant on wave-swept shores, the surfgrass *Phyllospadix scouleri* (Turner, 1983b). While surfgrass spreads into nearby open spaces by rhizomal growth, it disperses over long distances only by releasing large seeds into the surf. But unlike the miniscule pelagic spores of benthic algae, the settling surfgrass seeds cannot attach themselves to the rocks with an adherent holdfast. So how do they defend themselves from the heavy waves of their preferred habitat? Surfgrass seeds are about 6 mm wide and U-shaped, with numerous, fine, angular barbs inside the U. This curious morphology allows them to attach, like a beggar's tick, to any rough object small enough to fit inside the U. At Boiler Bay and Squaw Island, Oregon, the only suitable attachment sites appear to be several erect, mostly coralline, algae, with a central axis about 1 millimeter in diameter and bushy side branches (Turner, 1983b). These include *Bossiella plumosa*, *Corallina vancouveriensis*, *Odonthalia floccosa*, and *Rhodomela larix* (Turner, 1983b). All the attached seeds censussed in 1980 and 1981 were attached to the branches of these corals and two similarly shaped species, but none were attached to the blade-like algae such as *Egregia menziesii*, *Iridaea heterocarpa*, and *Dilsea californica*, even though these were common (Turner, 1983b). Moreover, these algal species also protect the germinated seedlings from desiccation, as proved by seeds which were attached to experimental nets placed in cleared areas, upon which the seedlings turned white and died during the morning low tides of the spring. In contrast, about 10% of the algal-attached seedlings survive the first seven months after germination (Turner, 1983b). A seed produces first leaves and then roots, which eventually anchor the plant to crevices in the rock; once anchored, the plant invades neighboring space vegetatively, producing new roots and shoots along a spreading rhizome.

So unlike the California mussel and other competitive dominants, newly recruiting surfgrass requires the presence of certain earlier facilitative species before it can take its place in the successional parade. This is not surprising, given predictions by ecological theorists (Connell and Slayter, 1977) that we should expect more facilitation in harsh than in mild environments. Under severe conditions, a recruiting youngster is less likely to survive the rigors alone, and is more likely to require the protection from the elements offered by dense stands of other organisms. Heavy surf can certainly be viewed as a major stress, especially for a vascular plant whose recent ancestors probably lived on dry land, and whose only defense is a slow rooting system much better suited to soil than bare rock.

The closest relative of surfgrass, the eelgrass *Zostera*, lives in calm water, usually rooted in the sand and mud of estuaries. Interestingly, its seeds are barbless. *Phyllospadix* is thought to have evolved from *Zostera*, and it is easy to imagine an evolutionary scenario. In an estuarine population of eelgrass near an exposed rocky shore, some individuals by chance produced barbed seeds. Currents carried some of these genetically different seeds out the bay and to the outer beaches, where, instead of dying in the surf as a normal eelgrass seed would, they anchored upon certain kinds of seaweeds. Some germinated, survived, and produced barbed seeds that continued to colonize new locations on the outer coast. Now isolated from its ancestral eelgrass, this new form gradually developed the attributes of surfgrass. This scenario is of course speculation, but it would be interesting to experiment with eelgrass transplants to see whether the absence of seed attachment, death of seedlings, or some other factor prevents its survival on waveswept shores.

Over the long run, any successional sequence eventually is shunted back to the beginning by one of the many possible perturbations that rock the shore. Since the precise time and location that any disturbance strikes are largely unpredictable, the typical intertidal habitat is an array of small pockets of determinism in a larger arena of chance; succession marches on here as it is struck down there, producing a mosaic of communities: young stages occupy heavily-disturbed areas, while older occupy more sheltered havens. But even in the protected coves, shore creatures are subject to the whims of the weather—a low-tide drought or heavy rain occasionally wipe out whole populations. Though safer from their deeper-water enemies, these plants and animals nevertheless remain at the mercy of hostile chance in this unique wave-washed world.

4

ESTUARIES

There is no joy but calm.
Alfred, Lord Tennyson, The Lotus-Eaters *(1842)*

FUNDAMENTALS

The shore is a collection of stark alternatives as organisms choose sides in the conflict between land and sea. While on the outer coast the confrontation has come to blows as the ocean lashes furiously and violently against the beach and headlands, in the estuary the meeting is polite and civilized, as though the quarrel had lapsed, at least for the time being, into a drowsy and serene companionship.

As the tide rises, seawater gently floods the coastal rivers and their tributaries, creating the transitional habitat known as the estuary. The seaward boundary of an estuary is defined as the line that connects the headlands at its mouth. The estuary extends landward through a zone of mixing of fresh and salt water to the point where the salinity has dropped to 0.5 ppt, beyond which the water is considered fresh. An estuary is thus a region of mixing of fresh river and sea water, whose salinity rises and falls with the tides (Figure 40, Plate 8).

Two fundamental themes underly and unify the ecology of nearly all estuaries on earth. The natural estuarine habitat appears to be nearly the most productive and most variable environment known. Superimposed on these characteristics is the supreme value of large estuaries to humans as easily traversed corridors for shipping and commerce. From the Nile Delta region to London (Thames River) and New York (Hudson River), large cities have always flourished near river mouths, and estuaries have across history played a crucial role in the development of civilization.

A walk across the mudflats bounding upper Tillamook Bay during a summer morning low tide reveals several unique features of the bay shore and water. First, most of the bay is extremely shallow, and except in a few deep channels, water currents are sluggish. Second, except during severe storms, there are no waves. The absence of any vigorous water movement in Tillamook and other enclosed and protected bays creates a safe and comfortable "low energy" sanctuary in which estuarine plants and animals thrive.

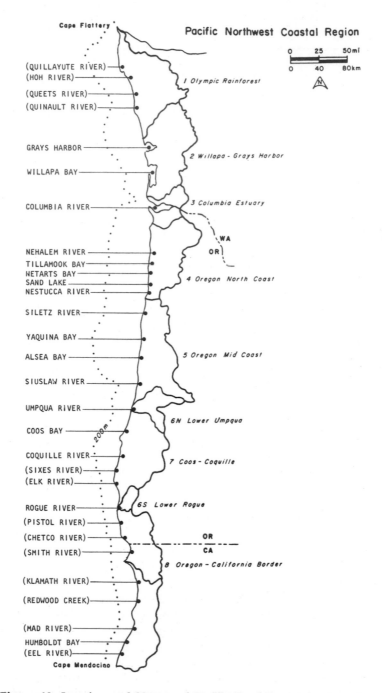

Figure 40. Location and Names of Pacific Northwest Estuaries. Those in parentheses are smaller than 2.0 km² (0.7 mi²) in area. (From Proctor *et al.*, 1980.)

Many estuarine species cannot survive in swift, uprooting currents heavy, crushing sea waves. Hence they remain in the sheltered haven between the two extremes.

Moreover, rivers are often choked with decaying bits of plant and animal matter and fine sediments eroded from upstream banks. The bay waters are calm enough to permit these materials to sink and settle on the bottom. As they accumulate along the bay margins, they eventually form broad expanses of dirty, clay-like mudflats, composed of particles much finer and organically richer than the coarse white sands of the outer wave-swept beaches. Thanks to the calm bay waters, enough fine bits of decaying organic material settle out to account for 10% of the sediment weight of a typical estuarine mudflat. A tremendous abundance of burrowing animals exploit this detritus as a rich and nutritious food source. Most are deposit-feeding worms, who make their living by swallowing the sediments, digesting the edible material, and voiding the undigestible mud and sand. These creatures in turn serve as an inexhaustible food base for predatory animals, mainly birds and fish. Shorebirds, some waterfowl, and any number of fish feed on the abundant burrowers, while the wading birds feed on the fish. Sooner or later, algae and rooted plants invade the stable mudflats and well-lit shallows, creating richly productive salt marshes and eelgrass beds. These die back each winter, whereupon the tides distribute their ample detritus over the sediments to fuel once again the detrital food web. The rich mudflats, in short, sustain nearly the entire arena of estuarine life. Since the shelter afforded by the enclosed bay is largely responsible for the enriched sediments and stable living conditions, estuarine productivity is largely attributable to the lack of vigorous water movement. Thus, as long as a bay is well protected from ocean breakers but open to the tides, it need not have a large freshwater input to be highly productive. In other words, it need not be an estuary. Protected bays and sounds with little freshwater input, such as Tomales Bay in California, are often equally or more productive than true estuaries. In general, any marine habitat falls somewhere on a spectrum from exposed to sheltered depending on the force of the waves. Productivity tends to increase with degree of shelter, since organisms can devote more energy to growth and less to just holding on. Estuaries are just one habitat at the extreme sheltered end of the spectrum.

Nevertheless, estuarine inhabitants endure their share of pain and grief. The twice daily rise and fall of the tides creates stresses to which few species have adapted. Estuarine creatures must endure not only all the same chemical fluctuations faced by the mussels and barnacles of the outer coast, but also additional fluctuations in salinity and temperature. At low tide, freshwater from the river often dominates the upper reaches of an estuary, only to be flooded with sea water at high tide. The salinity at one point may vary from nearly zero to 33 ppt within a six-hour period. Such radical changes present severe problems of water balance to estuarine animals and nutrient uptake to plants.

Since river water undergoes wider seasonal temperature fluctuations than the ocean, any organism in an estuary with a large freshwater input will feel those ups and downs. In midsummer, when stream water is warmest, temperature at one location may vary from 70°F at low tide to 45°F during the high-tide surge of cold seawater, again presenting difficult challenges to metabolism. And of course, all the usual stresses of the intertidal zone, such as fluctuating water, oxygen, food availability, and light intensity are also present. But since the tidal water is often felt at all depths, the variations in salinity and temperature occur throughout the estuary, not just in the intertidal.

Very few marine species have had the evolutionary wherewithal to adapt to these severe stresses. The number of marine species greatly exceeds the number of estuarine species. Those few that have adapted are immensely abundant and productive due to both the ample food supply and wave shelter in the estuary. Their talents for survival are generously rewarded.

Throughout history, estuaries have also rewarded the human species, and the Northwest is no exception. The three main industries of the region—forestry, fisheries, and agriculture—all rely on and affect the estuaries. Every large river-mouth town is heavily dependent on one or more of these industries. Logs are stored in and shipped through the large estuaries, especially Grays Harbor and Coos Bay, and the dairy industry would not exist if not for the diking and filling of estuarine salt marshes for pasture, notably around Tillamook and Coos bays. The high estuarine productivity supports the lucrative fish and shellfish industries by providing spawning, rearing, and feeding habitat for over half of all commercial fish. Salmon migrate through estuaries from the ocean to spawning grounds and back again. Flatfish and crabs use estuaries during the productive spring and summer, and of course clams and oysters remain year around. Estuaries, in short, offer something for everyone.

Formation of Estuaries

An estuary can be divided into four subhabitats: the riverine, bay, slough, and marine (Bottom, *et al.*, 1979). The riverine subhabitat is the region of lowest salinity farthest upstream, and is usually dominated by deep river channels, swift and abrasive currents, and coarse sediments. The bay is of course the large, sheltered central body of water of variable salinity, usually fringed by broad expanses of mud and sand flats, salt marshes, and eelgrass beds. Sloughs are small creeks that flow into the bay. Though dominated by tidewater, they are removed from strong currents of any kind, and hence are the most sheltered areas of the estuary. With their mud-flats, salt marshes, and eelgrass beds, they often represent a com-plete microcosm of the entire estuary. The marine subhabitat is roughly the estuary mouth. This is a turbulent, high-energy and high-salinity zone trampled by crushing waves and tearing river and tidal currents. The sediments here are coarse, clean marine sands.

As a rule, the biomass and productivity of estuarine biota rises as water movement slows. Productivity is lowest in the riverine and marine sections and highest in the sheltered bay and slough. But each estuary is unique, and different estuaries have widely different relative acreages of the four subhabitats. All estuaries by definition have riverine and marine sections, but some, like the Quinault, Rogue, and Chetco, have virtually no bay at all. How then, is the stupendously productive estuarine bay created? There are essen-tially four ways, and hence four kinds of estuary: the drowned river, bar-built, fjord, and tectonic estuary (Lauff, et al., 1967).

All Northwest estuaries are young, having developed as the last glacial ice age retreated 10,000 to 12,000 years ago (McKee, 1972). As the glaciers melted into the ocean, the sea rose some 400 feet and flooded the river valleys, creating drowned river estuaries, as well as marine sounds and embayments (such as Puget Sound), nearshore islands (such as the San Juan archipelago), and a variety of other coastal irregularities. Drowned river estuaries take the shape of the river's lower drainage pattern, and are usually funnel-shaped as the channel widens and deepens toward the mouth, triangular in cross-section, and often deep (up to 100 feet), though usually much wider than deep. Their naturally deep channels make drowned river estuaries the most useful for shipping and commerce. Where the coastal terrain is low and flat, the sea inundated a large expanse of land, forming a broad estuarine bay. This is the most common and best studied type of estuary, and the prime example is Chesapeake Bay in Maryland. Most West Coast estuaries are drowned river valleys of which the best examples are the Columbia, Coos, Tillamook, Umpqua, and Yaquina estuaries.

Often the tidal flow in these drowned river estuaries is so great that it is felt much farther upstream than it actually reaches. In the Columbia, for example, seawater only extends upstream about 23 miles to Puget Island (Proctor, et al., 1980). But the tidal flow is so voluminous that it reverses the freshwater river flow as far as 50 miles upstream, and beyond this forces the freshwater to rise and fall

all the way to Bonneville Dam, 140 miles upstream, resulting in the creation of freshwater intertidal flats. The sea has truly invaded the Columbia valley.

Bar-built estuaries form over shallow and gently sloping continental shelves, as for instance off southern Washington. In these areas waves build offshore sandbars that can easily rise above sea level to form barrier islands and sandspits. These enlarge and coalesce until they extend between headlands in a chain, thereby enclosing a marine bay that may or may not receive freshwater input. The tides are usually strong enough to maintain one or two inlets, which allow freshwater discharge and ample, refreshing tidal flow through the entire shallow bay. The sandspits successfully shelter the bay from waves, and allow the formation of mudflats, eelgrass beds, and salt marshes in the tranquil peripheral pockets. Elsewhere the beaches are usually clean and sandy.

In some cases tidal and river flow are too weak to maintain an inlet, and the sandbar seals off the estuary, creating a stagnant lagoon or "blind estuary." This is usually only a temporary summer phenomenon, when river levels are lowest. The gushing river flows of winter are almost always great enough to break through the sandbar and reawaken the estuary.

The largest bar-built estuary in America is Pamlico Sound in North Carolina. The only examples on the West Coast are Willapa Bay, Grays Harbor, Humboldt Bay, Netarts Bay, and Sand Lake. Willapa Bay, with only a small freshwater inflow, may be the most productive estuary on the west coast of North America.

During the last ice age, glaciers gouged out coastal valleys above about 39° latitude and usually on the west side of continents. The ocean-exposed end of such a valley is a fjord. As the glaciers melted, they dropped their load of gouged material at the mouth of the fjord, forming a shallow sill. The sill acts as a barrier restricting tidal flow at the fjord bottom, often leading to prolonged periods of stagnation. Fjords are usually steep-walled, U-shaped in cross-section, and deep (up to 1200 feet). The famous fjords of Norway are more spectacular than ours, which are the only type of estuary from Puget Sound northward.

The tectonic estuary is a catch-all classification for estuaries not quite filling the definition of the other categories. Whenever faulting, folding, or local sinking of the earth brings the ocean into new contact with freshwater, a tectonic estuary is formed. None exist along the Northwest Coast, and San Francisco Bay, predictably created by faulting, is the only major example on the West Coast.

Although the drowned river is only one of four types of estuary, all estuaries (indeed the entire shoreline) have been inundated by the rising sea since the latest ice age. In this sense, all estuaries are drowned, even though some might not possess a drownable river. And although this drowning may have created or enlarged estuarine bays of every type, it is only temporary. As a river levels out into a bay, its currents slow and drop their load of sediment. Once the sea level stabilizes or begins to fall, estuarine bays will slowly fill up with riverborne clay and sand, from the margins inward. Salt marshes will spread thickly across the mudflats, followed perhaps by shrubs and trees, until a narrow river channel is all that remains of the once deep and wide bay. In this way, geological processes will eventually bring the rising sea to equilibrium with the land, at least until the sea begins to rise once again. Ironically, the very conditions that make the bay so productive, namely slow currents and sedimentation, ultimately force its demise.

FLOW RATIO AND GRADIENT

Nearly all estuarine bays share three fundamental features: wave protection, high productivity, and highly variable salinity. But just about every other imaginable attribute varies widely from one estuary to the next, including the fresh/seawater mixing pattern, the upstream distance of seawater penetration, the fraction of bay area exposed at low tide, the total size of the bay, the depth, current speeds, and so on. These are all important from an ecological point of view, since bay size and intertidal area help determine the acreages of salt marsh and eelgrass beds and hence total productivity, and current speeds and salinity largely control the distribution of animals in an estuary. Of course, all these variables are ultimately controlled by the topography of the watershed and tidal basin. However, the control is often exerted in two wonderfully simple and measurable ways.

The first is the ratio of freshwater flow to tidal flow through the estuary (Proctor, et al., 1980). The freshwater flow is called the "runoff" or "discharge," and the average volume of seawater that flows in and out of an estuary during a single tidal cycle is the "tidal prism." The ratio of runoff per tidal cycle to tidal prism is the "flow ratio." If the flow ratio is greater than one, then the estuary is "river-dominated" and the mixing of fresh and salt water is orderly and predictable. Since freshwater is less dense and viscous than seawater, it tends to float on top of the latter. If the runoff is greater than the tidal prism, then the freshwater simply glides seaward on top of the seawater, while the seawater inches landward underneath. Fluctuations in salinity and temperature occur as high tides force the low-lying "salt wedge" several miles upstream, and low tides and high peak river flows drive it downstream and sometimes out of the estuary. All the mixing in this "two-layered" estuary occurs within a narrow band at the interface of the two water layers (Figure 41). A river-dominated estuary is often fresh near the mouth, espe-

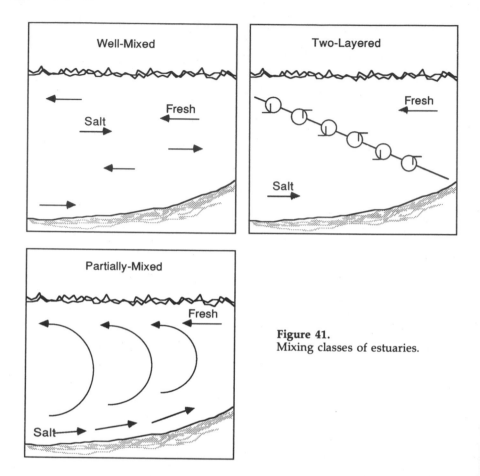

Figure 41.
Mixing classes of estuaries.

cially during the high flows of winter. Nearly all Northwest drowned river estuaries are two-layered during peak river flows.

At the other extreme is the tide-dominated estuary, whose flow ratio is under 0.1. In this case, the commanding tidal flows collide head-on with the weak river currents, forcing turbulence that leads to thorough mixing of salt and fresh. In this "well-mixed" estuary, the difference in salinity between the water surface and bottom is only 3% or less (Figure 41). This estuary is usually small and bar-built, more saline higher upstream, and less variable than river-dominated estuaries because of smaller fluctuations in river flow.

Between these two extremes is the "partially mixed" estuary, whose flow ratio is around 0.25, and the difference between surface and bottom salinity is anywhere from 4 to 19%.

As with most classification systems, this one is not a perfect description of the real world. Although each estuary tends to remain in one of these three mixing classes most of the time, nearly all

Northwest estuaries prefer to jump around from one category to the next with the changing seasons. In winter the flow ratio rises as drenching rains bring surging streamflows. The flood of freshwater spreads out over the surface of the more saline, denser estuary, and simply shoves the previously well-mixed body of bay water out to sea. Eventually the strong surface flow stabilizes, and allows the deep salt wedge to slide in and out with the tides. From late spring to early winter, slackened rainfall starves the rivers, and some of the highest tides of the year wrest turbulent control of the estuary, keeping the flow ratio low and the estuary partially to well mixed.

An important concept related to flow ratios is the flushing time of an estuary, equal to the expected length of time that a molecule of water remains in the estuary before being flushed out to sea (McLusky, 1981). Probably the best estimate of flushing time is figured by dividing the total volume of the estuary by the total volume of tidal and river flow through it per day. As flushing time shortens, the estuary becomes less vulnerable to pollution, because sewage and toxic wastes have less time to do their damage. Unfortunately, estuarine circulation is more complex than this, and often swirling eddies exist which, like a revolving door, trap stray particles and send them spinning in endless circles as the rest of the bay fills and flushes on schedule.

The second phenomenon that colors an estuary's personality is its "gradient," equal to the drop in elevation per mile experienced by a river as it flows from source to mouth (Bottom, 1979; Proctor, et al., 1980). The gradient largely determines the tidal prism, current speed, and sedimentation rates of an estuary.

In controlling the tidal prism, the gradient effectively controls the size of an estuary. A low gradient invites the tidewater to flood a broad expanse of flat coastal lowlands, often forming a large shallow bay with extensive tidelands, as in Willapa Bay and Grays Harbor. Eelgrass thrives in the well-lit shallows, and the greater the intertidal acreage, the greater the potential salt marsh acreage. As the gradient levels out, river currents slow down and drop their load of sediments. As currents slacken, progressively finer sediment particles sink and settle to the bottom, starting with the coarser pebbles and sands, and finishing with the finer silts and clays (Figure 42). Conversely, as currents accelerate, they scoop progressively larger sediment particles off the bottom and into the water column.

At the river's headwaters, where the gradient is steepest (more than 25 feet/mile), currents are swift enough (over 10 feet/second) to erode away all sand, gravel, and pebbles, leaving only cobble and boulders more than about 6 inches in diameter (Proctor, et al., 1980). Farther downstream the river bed begins to level, and the slackening currents drop out pebbles and gravel. Eventually the river reaches a

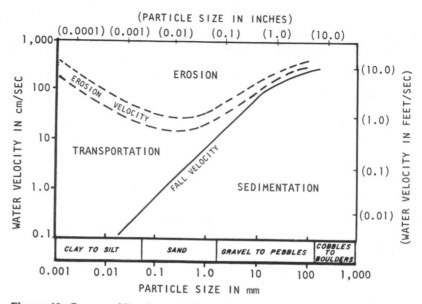

Figure 42. Curves of Erosion and Deposition for Uniform Material. Erosion velocity is shown as a band. Particle types (names), from clay to boulders, are based on size. (From Morisawa, 1968, and Shepard, 1963.)

zone where about as much fine sediments are being eroded away as coarse sediments from upstream are being deposited. The gradient in this zone lies somewhere between 5 and 25 feet/mile, and the currents are about 1 foot/second, slow enough to deposit sand and gravel.

By the time the river reaches the estuary, the gradient has dropped to near zero, but the currents may still be strong depending on how much momentum they gathered on the way down, which in turn depends on the total gradient, from source to mouth. In most estuaries strong currents in the riverine and marine sections still prevent the finest clays and silts from settling anywhere except two specific regions (McLusky, 1981; Proctor, *et al.*, 1980). The first is in the middle reaches of the estuary, where the landward flow of the deep salt wedge counteracts the seaward flow of the river, creating a net flow near zero. This spot is called the "turbidity maximum." Here enough sediments drop out to form numerous shoals and sandflats. These often hinder the passage of ships, and in the larger estuaries (such as Grays Harbor) necessitate regular dredging, which may do severe ecological harm (see Chapter 7). The second region of clay and silt deposit is along the upper intertidal, where tidewater often comes to a near stop during high slack tide. Here the broad mudflats and shallows develop, and welcome the invasion of eelgrass, salt marsh plants, benthic algae, and deposit-feeding invertebrates.

So, happily, the situation is not very complicated. High-gradient-estuaries tend to be small, with only a modest complement of tidelands. Their currents are swifter and more abrasive on the average, and may prevent not only the accumulation of rich clays and silt, but also the establishment of rooted plants and other biota. Low-gradient-estuaries on the other hand, especially those with moderate river flows, can be immense and marvelously productive. Bar-built estuaries take the easy route by forming essentially over the ocean, thereby granting themselves a naturally low gradient.

The Northwest Coast's estuaries have done us a favor by conveniently falling into three groups according to gradient (Bottom, 1979). In two areas, steep mountains border the sea and have produced the highest-gradient estuaries in the region. These are the Olympics in northern Washington and the Klamaths, which straddle the Oregon/California border. These estuaries, which include the smallest in the region, are sometimes blind in the summer due to vanishing, low streamflows. The erosion-resistant rock formations in the Klamaths have also reduced estuarine sedimentation. The bar-built Humboldt Bay is anomalous, having scorned the mountains and formed over the ocean on recent alluvial deposits. Its low gradient naturally makes it large and fertile.

The smallest gradients in the region produced the largest estuaries, namely Columbia, Willapa Bay, and Grays Harbor. The last two are truly gems and Willapa is the Hope Diamond of west coast estuaries. The immense freshwater flow (indeed the largest in western North America) of the Columbia makes it quite barren. While Willapa is highly saline, with rich eelgrass beds, marshes, and a thriving oyster industry, the Columbia is fresh, with little intertidal or marshes, and no eelgrass or oysters.

Along the rest of the Coast Range from the Necanicum River to the Rogue lie estuaries intermediate in gradient and size. Since the Coast Range is composed primarily of soft, erodable sandstone and shales, sedimentation in these estuaries (and in Willapa and Grays) is rapid, and in some cases has triggered the formation of immense sand dunes, which themselves have a fascinating history described in the next chapter.

Causes of high productivity. Having described the nature of the estuarine environment, I now proceed to those who call it home.

Estuarine producers fall into three categories: large plants firmly attached to a solid object, microscopic plants likewise attached, and unattached, free-floating plants. Attached plants are termed "benthic," and may be rooted in the sediments (as in eelgrass and salt marsh plants); nonrooting but firmly attached to rocks, logs, piers, and so on with a strong holdfast (as in seaweeds); or leading a sedentary life interstitially among the sand grains (microscopic diatoms). The unattached plants, or phytoplankton, float passively in the well-lit surface waters.

As mentioned above, the wave protection afforded by estuarine bays permits survival of benthic plants and animals that would be torn, battered, or uprooted on the violent outer coast. Some of the plants, notably seaweeds and eelgrass, produce up to 6–8 pounds of new living tissue (dry weight) per square yard every year (Odum, 1961; Phillips and Thayer, 1977; Phillips, 1984). This phenomenal amount exceeds the average production of U.S. corn or wheat fields by 3–4 times (Odum, 1961), and is about double the productivity of young Coast Range forests (Proctor, *et al.*, 1980). Although ensuring survival, wave protection alone cannot account for such high productivity. Rapid growth demands rapid nutrient uptake, which in turn requires one of two conditions: either a steady inflow of new nutrients from external sources (e.g., tidewater and rivers), or rapid recycling of used nutrients from within.

It turns out estuaries are blessed with both these virtues. As noted in the preceding chapters, nutrients tend to sink to the sea bottom as feces and dead plant and animal matter. In the deep sea, water movement is only at the surface, and hence dooms the lost nutrients to an average of over a thousand years of biological uselessness on the ocean bottom before they manage to reappear at the surface in upwelling currents (Pomeroy, 1980). In the shelf waters, winter storms and summer upwelling stir up the water from surface to bottom year around, maintaining ample nutrients in the upper productive levels, and none remain on the bottom longer than a few weeks or months. Luckily for the estuaries, these nutrient-fortified waters bathe, nourish, and refresh them twice each day during high tides.

This is especially advantageous to the benthic plants. As any aquatic plant rapidly photosynthesizes, it begins to deplete the closely surrounding water of carbon dioxide and nutrients. If nutrient levels remained low, productivity would drop. But large benthic plants are much better off than phytoplankton, because they are held in one place as the tidewater flows over them, rinsing away the envelope of barren water and replenishing the nutrient supply (Mann, 1982). Phytoplankton, on the other hand, must always move with the current, never against, because they have no motive powers of their own and nothing to hold onto. As a result, they remain trapped within their own empty cocoon, where their productivity can be as low as a tenth that of the larger seaweeds. Tides in general benefit both plants and animals by removing wastes and scattering food and nutrients throughout the estuary. Organisms need not expend energy moving around to search for food and to escape their own wastes, and instead can settle down into a sedentary existence, let the tides do all their work, and use the energy they save for growth and reproduction. Low-gradient-estuaries, with their greater tidal prism, are much better off in this respect. The tides are thus an "energy subsidy" to estuaries because the energy provided by their gentle currents is just about optimal (Odum, 1971, 1974). If it were much greater it would be destructive, and if much smaller, nearly useless.

Despite all this refreshing effervescence in estuaries, nutrients still manage to sink into the bottom sediments. But estuaries, because of their shallow, well-lit waters and naturally abundant rooted plants, bacteria, and burrowing animals, remedy this situation much more quickly and profitably than the outer coast or offshore waters. The deep roots of eelgrass and salt marsh plants simply absorb the sediment nutrients and convert them immediately into new living tissue. Bacteria also absorb the nutrients, and are eaten by burrowing deposit-feeders whose feces are colonized by more bacteria, continuing the cycle. Most of the rooted plants die each year, and the tides distribute their abundant detritus over the mudflats, where it decomposes into the sediments and feeds the burrowing animals.

The brisk and vigorous biological activity in the surface sediments not only converts otherwise lost nutrients into living organisms, but also pumps those nutrients steadily back into the water column, where they nourish the phytoplankton. Eelgrass, for instance, absorbs sediment phosphate through its roots, but leaks about as much out of its leaves as it incorporates into its tissues (Pomeroy, 1980). The plant thus extracts phosphate from the sediment and pumps it into the water. Sediment bacteria also secrete dissolved phosphorus and nitrogen as waste products, and the benthic animals that consume them expel the same nutrients into the water when they defecate at the sediment surface. Of course, strong currents can scoop the sediments up into the water column, where they liberate much of their nutrients. In shallow coastal waters, nutrients regenerated from the sediments satisfy up to 100% of the phytoplankton's needs, while in the offshore waters they satisfy less than 50%. In short, the shelter and comfort afforded by estuarine bay attract organisms in an abundance so great that few estuarine nutrients go to waste.

Several other miscellaneous ingredients combine to further promote the productivity of estuaries. Phosphorus, heavy metals, and other nutrients in rivers can attach chemically to fine particles of sediment and detritus (Nixon, 1982). As these accumulate in the calm estuarine waters, they build up a soil rich in nutrients for the bacteria and all benthic plants. Phosphorus is so plentiful in some estuarine sediments that it alone could satisfy the phosphorus requirements of the plants for the next 500 years (Pomeroy, 1965). Just 0.02 cubic inch of these sediments could replace all the phosphorus in the water. As a result, growth is usually limited by available nitrogen, not phosphorus.

The shape and orientation of the plant leaves contributes to salt marsh productivity. Since their leaves are narrow and stand straight up, the rushes, sedges, and grasses of the marshes cast minimal shadows on each other, maximize the leaf surface exposed to the sun over the entire day, and avoid exposure to direct, overheating sunlight (Keefe, 1972).

The benefits of leaf orientation can be measured in marshes by comparing leaf surface area to ground surface area beneath. If the ratio of leaf surface to ground is high, then production per square yard of ground is high, providing the leaf shadows of neighboring plants do not stifle each other's productivity. As plant density rises, mutual shading begins to limit production. Generally, horizontal leaves cast the largest shadow. The horizontal leaves of most cultivated crops prevent the leaf surface-to-ground ratio from exceeding 3 or 4, because intolerable shading begins to prevent photosynthesis. In contrast, the narrow, vertical leaves of salt marsh plants permit growth so dense that the leaf surface-to-ground ratio reaches 10–20 before mutual shading begins (Keefe, 1972). This allows them to capture three times as much incident sunlight as crop plants.

Of course, the fact that estuaries are an aquatic environment has a major influence on their productivity. As long as the water movement is enough to keep the plants refreshed, aquatic environments are generally more productive per square yard than terrestrial. Besides being bathed at least periodically by nutrient-rich water year around, coastal plants also experience less temperature variation than those on land. The relatively constant seawater temperatures buffer the estuarine plants against seasonal extremes in air temperatures, allowing them to produce more in spring and fall then terrestrial plants. Benthic diatoms, in particular, grow at a near-constant rate throughout the year (Odum, 1971). In the comfortably maritime climate of the Northwest, however, the benefits are small because the air temperatures stay close to the ocean temperature anyway, allowing many evergreen terrestrial plants to grow nearly year round, and the productivity of young Coast Range forests to approach that of the salt marshes.

PRODUCERS

Phytoplankton

As noted, their drifting lifestyle makes phytoplankton less productive than many submerged benthic plants, especially seaweeds. Three other factors also limit their productivity. First, riverborne sediments often cloud the estuarine waters, blocking the sunlight. Second, the tides sometimes flush the plankton out of the estuary before they get a chance to contribute. Third, the salt wedge in two-layered estuaries acts as a barrier preventing the sediment nutrients from reaching the lighted surface waters (McLusky, 1981).

The wide variability in sediment input and tidal prism in Northwest estuaries creates large differences in phytoplankton productivity from one estuary to the next. In Netarts Bay, the small river input has kept the waters clear enough to allow some five pounds per square yard of annual phytoplankton net productivity. In other estuaries this drops to as low as a tenth of a pound per square yard every year (Gaumer, *et al.*, 1983).

However, even if the production of these tiny drifting plants is low per square yard of bay water, other considerations make their productivity perhaps more important than any other estuarine plant. First, the total acreage occupied by seaweeds, eelgrass, salt marsh, and benthic diatoms is often small compared to the bay that houses the phytoplankton. Hence, even though small per square yard, the total phytoplankton productivity over the entire bay may be large, and perhaps exceed the total productivity of the other plants. Only a few estuaries have been studied enough to give any idea of total productivities. In the Newport River estuary in North Carolina, phytoplankton production accounts for about 50% of the total productivity (Peterson and Peterson, 1979), and in Grays Harbor, somewhere between 10% and 25% (Thom, 1981).

Even if they were unproductive, phytoplankton are nevertheless indispensable. They are the primary food of zooplankton, and zooplankton are the main food of young fish, including salmon and many other commercially valuable species. Most of these fish species spend their plankton-eating stages in sheltered estuary shallows. Clearly, the second most important industry in the Northwest Coast depends indirectly on the productivity of estuarine phytoplankton. With that in mind, it is surprising how little research has been done on these tiny yet ubiquitous bits of trapped sunlight.

Benthic Microalgae

As fine sediments accumulate along the bayshores, they form broad, shallow mudflats often laying exposed to air at low tide. A variety of microscopic algae take advantage of the wave-shelter and sunlight offered by the flats. Benthic diatoms are usually the most numerous, and form a dirty brown surface scum, while benthic dinoflagellates, filamentous green algae, and blue-green algae occasionally tint the surface with bright greens. These also grow in better lighted open areas in salt marshes, much like the shrub layer in a forest. In Grays Harbor, all the benthic microalgae combined produce about two lbs/yd^2/yr (Thom, 1981), and in Yaquina Bay 0.5–1.2 lbs/yd^2/yr (Riznyk and Phinney, 1972).

A variety of comforts keep these algae humming throughout the year (Amspoker and McIntyre, 1978). First, the sediment bacteria continuously recycle nitrogen, phosphorus, and other nutrients, maintaining a steady supply. Second, the diatoms bind themselves to sand grains with a sugar compound that probably helps protect them from the rigors of summer drying and fluctuating salinity. Third, the sands themselves probably provide warmth during winter. And fourth, believe it or not, are the intriguing behavioral adaptations of the type of diatoms that build sediment tubes in which they move up and down apparently at will. During the day, these mobile forms creep up to the lighted surface, and when the water or air temperature becomes too hot or cold, they retreat down their tubes as much as 6 inches into the sheltering sediment. If the surface of a stable mudflat is watched after it has been uncovered on a sunny day, a gradual change from brown to green or yellow occurs as the diatoms migrate to the surface.

In many estuaries, benthic microalgae production varies with the tides. In summer, productivity is highest during high tides when the algae are water-cooled. In winter, productivity often peaks during low tides, when sunlight warms the flats. This keeps the production steady at a constant rate throughout the year (Odum, 1971).

In Yaquina Bay and probably in general, sediment size controls the vitality of the benthic microalgae (Riznyk and Phinney, 1972). The finer sediments at Sally's Bend contain more organic material, including sawdust from upstream wood processing mills, than the coarse sandflats at Southbeach. Because of this and their higher sediment surface area, the fine Sally's Bend flats contain more bacteria and detritus-feeding nematodes, amphipods, copepods, and others. The result is bad news for the fine-sediment diatoms. Bacterial respiration depletes their supply of oxygen and nutrients, and the abundant animals consume them. Productivity thus plummets from 1.2 lbs/yd²/yr in the sandflats at Southbeach to 0.0–0.5 lbs/yd²/yr in the mudflats at Sally's Bend (Riznyk and Phinney, 1972).

Eelgrass

Especially in winter, strong currents can shift and scatter the estuarine sediments. Any sediment plant must be able to hold on, and the minute diatoms succeed by gluing themselves to the sediment grains. The larger algae, or seaweeds, are out of luck, and usually only survive attached to rocks, mussels, oysters, logs, piers, and other fixed objects. Rooted plants, however, can embrace the sediments with a grip unapproached by seaweeds, and often take over where the seaweeds leave off.

Worldwide, 12 genera of flowering plants have, like the whales, forsaken their terrestrial origins and returned to the sea, to live side by side once again with the relatives of their remote algal ancestors (Mann, 1982). Two of these grow in our waters. Surfgrass (*Phyllospadix scouleri*) prefers the lower intertidal of the outer rocky coast. Eelgrass (*Zostera marina*) is common only in sheltered bays, sounds, and sloughs, where it often forms dense, tangled underwater jungles. Both are only rarely exposed by low tides, and produce their pale yellow flowers underwater, where the pollen is released and carried by currents and waves to other plants. Their seeds are also dispersed by currents, making these and other coastal plants the most widely distributed in the world (Phillips and Thayer, 1977; Phillips, 1984). Currents, migratory birds, and ships have dispersed eelgrass throughout the Atlantic and Pacific coasts, from the Tropic of Cancer to the Arctic Circle. Individuals from different regions often differ strikingly in temperature and salinity tolerances, suggesting that eelgrass may actually be an assortment of many separately adapted species or subspecies.

Although eelgrass seeds come to rest in a wide range of coastal habitats in Northwest waters, they germinate and survive only where conditions are comfortable. First, the currents must remain at around a foot per second (Proctor, et al., 1980). If swifter currents or heavy waves persist for several days, they simply tear the leaves loose or uproot the entire plant. If more sluggish currents persist, then the slow replenishment of nutrients across the leaf blades leads to poor growth or death (Phillips and Thayer, 1977). Second, though it is shade-tolerant, eelgrass requires water clear enough to allow penetration of at least 1% of the incident light (Phillips and Thayer, 1977). How deep the light penetrates depends on the angle of the sun (which in turn depends on season and latitude), and on the sediment content of the water. In La Jolla, California, where the sun is high, eelgrass grows as deep as 50 feet, while in Alaska, it is usually no deeper than 10 feet (Proctor, *et al.*, 1980). Although winter storm waves can make shallow waters murky, human activities are more often to blame. Dredging kicks up dense clouds of sediments, and is the major threat to eelgrass in Grays Harbor and other bays. Sewage and industrial effluents can trigger blooms of phytoplankton, which intercept sunlight at the surface. Erosion of upstream lands by agriculture or logging can fill estuaries with clouds of mud. Largely because of turbidity, the densest meadows of native eelgrass, *Zostera marina*, lie from minus one to plus three feet above mean lower low water. The uncommon (but spreading) introduced eelgrass *Zostera japonica*, grows above plus three feet, and abundantly only around plus five feet.

Eelgrass tolerates all salinities from fresh- to seawater. Like many other marine plants, it survives seawater with the help of salt glands on the leaves that remove sodium and chloride from the cell sap (Phillips and Thayer, 1977).

Where conditions are right, eelgrass spreads over vast expanses of shallow estuarine bottoms. Each shoot sends out an underground stem, or rhizome, which sprouts roots and aerial stems every few inches. These proliferate into dense, spreading mats of above- and below-ground vegetation. Above-ground production is about 1 lb/yd^2/yr, but may reach 6 lbs/yd^2/yr in especially dense beds (Proctor, *et al.*, 1980).

This productivity is assisted by the abundant anaerobic bacteria in the eelgrass sediments, which pull nitrogen out of the air and change it into a chemical form the eelgrass roots can absorb and use (Proctor, *et al.*, 1980). This may make eelgrass independent of water-borne nitrogen, which often limits productivity in coastal waters.

Eelgrass blades also provide an attachment surface and a source of nutrients for several species of macroalgae, especially *Smithora naiadum* and *Monostoma zostericola*. In yet another example of the efficient nutrient recycling in estuaries, these algae absorb the abundant phosphorus and nitrates that leak from the surface of eelgrass leaves (Proctor, *et al.*, 1980). As a result, they grow luxuriantly, and may even approach the eelgrass itself in biomass and productivity. Though eelgrass is perennial, about three-fourths of the aerial production dies each year and decomposes into the sediments, leaving somewhat sparser beds for the winter (Phillips and Thayer, 1977).

With about 24 square miles of eelgrass, Willapa Bay contains more than all the rest of the Northwest Coast's bays combined (Phillips and Thayer, 1977). Grays Harbor contains 8.7, Oregon's bays a total of 7.8, and Humboldt Bay 5.9 square miles. In a North Carolina estuary, eelgrass covers a sixth of the bottom and contributes 64% of the total productivity (Peterson and Peterson, 1979).

The strategy of rhizomatous reproduction can make eelgrass beds dense enough to influence the overall water circulation, sedimentation, and biology of an estuary. The leaves act as a baffle retarding currents and forcing them to drop their load of organic particles and fine sediments. The thick, interlacing mat of roots and rhizomes reduces erosion by binding the sediments. And the leaves themselves not only give off abundant oxygen but also offer a stable, three-dimensional surface where previously there were only shifting sediments. In short, eelgrass creates an environment that can satisfy the needs of a wide variety of animals, not to mention a few plants. As will be seen in more detail in the following, the eelgrass ecosystem is nearly self-contained, with its own abundant producers, consumers, and decomposers. In short, the eelgrass beds support a greater diversity of animal species than any other estuarine habitat. The expansive eelgrass meadows of Willapa Bay are the raison d'etre of the Willapa National Wildlife Refuge, and feed several thousand brant (*Branta bernicla*) each year. Without these lush meadows our estuaries would be truly destitute.

Benthic Macroalgae

These large, attached algae are roughly "seaweeds," and unlike flowering plants, have no roots. They gain a precarious foothold on solid objects by means of a tough holdfast, and in general colonize rocky shores while flowering plants colonize soft, sedimenting shores. Although exposed bedrock and boulders are rare in Northwest estuaries, seaweeds nevertheless can be abundant. They manage to attach to and grow on a variety of solid objects, including floating docks and piers, mussel and oyster shells, leaves of eelgrass and salt marsh plants, and old storm logs now immobile. They can also grow on intertidal mudflats, as long as the flats either contain small pebbles (about an inch upwards) or are extremely sheltered. Where rock does occur, seaweed beds can become as expansive and commanding as the eelgrass meadows. Some species are unharmed by separation from their substrate, and apparently live comfortably just drifting freely in the water currents.

Algae evolved in the ocean, and many seaweed species cannot tolerate freshwater. As a result, seaweed diversity is usually greatest near the estuary mouth, but progressively fewer species survive as salinity steadily declines upstream. The most widespread species in Grays Harbor are *Enteromorpha intestinalis* and *Fucus distichus* spp. *edentatus* (Thom, 1981). Species that begin life attached to rocks, shells, waterlogged sticks, and so on, but often end up free-floating include *Ulva fenestrata, Polysiphonia hendryi* var. *deliquescens,* and a variety of *Enteromorpha* species, including *E. clathrata* var. *crinita, E. flexuosa,* and *E. prolifera. Vaucheria longicaulis* and other *Vaucheria* form nearly black, felt-like mats on sand, especially near freshwater seepage. *Rhizoclonium riparium* is also a mat-former on sand. Kelp beds flourish in deeper, high salinity channels over bedrock and boulders. These are essentially the same as in the outer rocky sub-tidal. As noted earler, *Smithora naiadum* and *Monostoma zostericola* are abundant in eelgrass beds.

Seaweed production varies widely in response to salinity, turbidity, and seasonal changes in nutrients, sunlight, and tempera-ture. Annual productivity is usually limited by nitrogen. Growth rates skyrocket in the spring and summer, but 80–90% of the annual production dies each winter, decomposing into the water column and sediments, where it feeds the abundant detritivores (Thom, 1981). In Grays Harbor, *Fucus distichus* ssp. *edentatus* produces 7.2 pounds dry weight per square yard each year, *Enteromorpha clathrata* var. *crinita* 5.3 lbs/yd^2/yr, and *E. intestinalis* 3.4 lbs/yd^2/yr; these are the highest seaweed values recorded in the Harbor (Thom, 1981).

Salt Marshes

Of all the flowering plant species worldwide, there is a small group that can survive nowhere on earth except along the fringes of sheltered marine and estuarine bays. These and a few more cosmopolitan species join ranks in the salt marshes, the verdant grassy fields that blanket the rich estuarine tidal flats. While eelgrass has successfully returned to the sea, the salt marsh plants, though on the verge, have not quite crossed the line, and stand hesitantly at water's edge as though contemplating whether to take the plunge. The most venturesome among them can withstand no more than 18 continuous hours submerged beneath tidewater, while most of the rest die if inundated longer than about 6 hours at a time (Jefferson, 1973; Eilers, 1975). On the other hand, an hour-long inundation banishes all terrestrial plants, and if saline enough, the tidewater also cold-shoulders cattails, bulrush, sedges, and other freshwater marsh flora, leaving the salt marsh plants to themselves. Hence, salt marshes occupy just the narrow band of mudflats between about mean sea level (4 feet above mean lower low water), and the extreme high tide line. Below this band the plants drown in the seawater, and above it they succumb to aggressive competition by terrestrial and freshwater marsh vegetation.

Salt marshes are thus a strictly tidal phenomenon. Tidewater inundates the lowest reaches twice daily, and the highest only a few times a year during winter storms. In eliminating the salt marsh com-petitors, the tides maintain the status quo in much the same way as other selectively destructive forces in other habitats. The ochre seastar of the outer coast, for example, favors barnacles by consuming the competitively dominant mussels; the sea otter preserves the seaweeds from the voracious urchins.

Since salt marshes are a product of the tides, it follows that their size depends on the acreage of sheltered tidelands in an estuary. This is roughly true, except that farmers have diked and drained some of our best marshes for use as pastureland. In general, estuaries with a low gradient and high tidal prism have the most extensive salt marshes. In the Umpqua estuary, for example, only 22% of the bay area is intertidal and only 5% is salt marsh, while at Sandlake over 75% is intertidal and the salt marsh acreage actually exceeds the estuary size by about 30% (Akins and Jefferson, 1973). Oregon currently has roughly 11 square miles of salt marsh. This is about a sixth of the total estuarine acreage, and a third of the total tideflat acreage.

The crucial process creating tidelands is of course sedimentation. As riverborne silts and clays accumulate, they eventually break the estuary surface and become intertidal flats. Surprisingly, it has been suggested that roughly half of all salt marshes in Oregon (and probably a similar amount in Washington and Northern California) owe their existence to the logging and farming industries (Dicken, *et al.*, 1961). Construction of logging roads and clearing of the land for timber and farming exposes the soil to the elements and accelerates erosion. The rivers and streams fill with silts and clays that eventually run aground in the quiet bays, forming the broad mudflats that welcome the salt marshes. Many of the Northwest Coast's salt marshes are less than 200 years old, and 2–3 feet beneath many of them lie sawed logs and a layer of bark chips dating from around the turn of the century.

Sedimentation is rapid and obvious in nine of the region's estuaries: Grays, Willapa, Nehalem, Tillamook, Alsea, Umpqua, Coos, Coquille, and Humboldt (Akins and Jefferson, 1973) (Figure 43). Silts and clays pour into these low-gradient-estuaries at rates ranging from 72,000 tons per year in Coos Bay to roughly a million in Grays Harbor, allowing a striking expansion of salt marshes over the last century. The Tillamook Burn, triggered by sparks from logging machinery, sent huge quantities of topsoil into Tillamook and Nehalem Bays, which contain the best examples on the Oregon Coast of fast and aggressive salt marsh invasion. Encroachment of mudflats and marshes has shrunk Tillamook and Humboldt bays to 40% and 55% of their respective original sizes (Dicken, *et al.*, 1961). In the upper Tillamook Bay, salt marshes have spread across the mudflats at a rate of 14 feet per year from 1867 to 1939, and about 9 feet per year since then for a total of roughly a quarter of a mile. In Nehalem Bay, the rate of expansion was 18 feet per year from 1875 to

1939, and 27 feet per year since then, for a total of nearly one-half mile. In contrast, the steep gradient and erosion-resistant watershed of the Rogue and other Klamath and Olympic estuaries has kept sedimentation and marshes to a minimum.

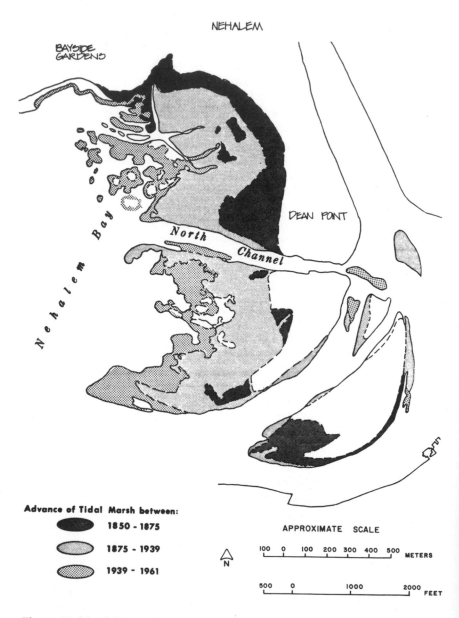

Figure 43. Marsh Expansion in Nehalem Bay, Oregon, Over 100 Years. (From Johannessen, 1964.)

Unfortunately, however, the effects of the agriculture industry are not entirely positive. In Coos and Humboldt estuaries farmers have diked and drained or filled nearly all the salt marshes. Currently, over the Northwest Coast as a whole, the rate of salt marsh destruction in this manner exceeds the rate of natural expansion, so the marshes are steadily shrinking as they are slowly replaced by cow pasture.

But the plants at the vanguard of the salt marsh invasion usually remain unharmed, and these newborn marshes have revealed some fascinating stories about their own creation. As the gentle tides scatter sediments over the estuary bottom, the shallows steadily rise until they emerge as sand- or mudflats at low tide. When the flats reach an elevation of about 4 feet above mean lower low water (about the level of the higher low tide), tidal inundation drops abruptly, and permits a few robust pioneer plants to colonize. The tidal currents carry rhizome fragments of these species to the flats, where they settle down and sprout roots and stems. The underground stems, or rhizomes, grow rapidly, radiating outward at all angles like spokes on a wheel, sprouting new roots and stems every few inches. Soon a dense circular colony arises, which continues to enlarge around the circumference. Since all the plants in this colony arose ultimately from the same individual, they are all genetically identical and collectively constitute a "clone" (Johannessen, 1964; Jefferson, 1973; Eilers, 1975).

The composition of these pioneering clones depends on salinity and the size of the sediment particles. On sandbars, the first pioneer is usually salicornia (*Salicornia virginica*), whose example is soon followed by sand spurry (*Spergularia canadensis*) and three-square rush (*Scirpus americanus*) (Jefferson 1973; Akins and Jefferson, 1973). On flats composed of finer clays and silts, the initial colonizers are seaside arrowgrass (*Triglochin maritimum*), the spike rush *Eleocharis parvula*, and the sand spurry *Spergularia marina*. These constitute the "low silt marsh." Where freshwater runoff regularly dilutes the seawater, the commonest pioneers are bulrush (*Scirpus validus*) and Lyngbyei's sedge (*Carex lyngbyei*). These "bulrush and sedge" marshes flourish on silt or sand, usually along sloughs or on delta islands in the upper estuary. As the salinity drops upstream, the sedge disappears.

The presence of these pioneers alters their environment in some fundamental ways. The dense growth of stems and leaves retards the tidal currents, forcing them to drop their load of fine sediments. This raises the circular clones until they stand upon small circular islands. Tidewater inundates the islands less frequently, and instead flows more often between them than over them. As the colonies enlarge, they eventually coalesce, and tend to restrict most of the tidal flow to the narrow network of creeks between them. The flow is often strong enough to cut sharp vertical banks several inches deep. In some places, the coalescing clones isolate bare spots called "salt pans." In hot weather the water in the pans often evaporates, leaving salt crystals on the surface that are sought out and consumed by band-tailed pigeons and other animals. Heavy rain can dilute the water in the pans, resulting in salinity fluctuations wide enough to eliminate most organisms. The only conspicuous biota of the salt pans are a few specialized macroalgae and diatoms, which may color the surface a dirty green.

Meanwhile, the pioneers continue to trap sediments. As the marsh surface rises, the frequency of inundation steadily falls, the circular clones tend to die out in the center, and the pioneers are gradually replaced by a variety of less water-loving marsh plants (Eilers, 1975). On the sand flats, these are most commonly salt grass, jaumea, and seaside plantain, with lesser numbers of the sand spurries *Spergularia canadensis* and *S. macrotheca*, alkali grass (*Puccinellia maritima*), Lyngbyei's sedge, and milkwort (*Glaux maritima*) (Akins and Jefferson, 1973; Jefferson, 1973). Often the fringes of the pioneer clones survive in the lowest reaches. These plants collectively constitute the "low sand marsh." On fine clays and silts, Lyngbyei's sedge usually invades soon after the pioneers, forming circular clones of its own. The dense growths of almost exclusively Lyngbyei's sedge are the "sedge marshes" (Akins and Jefferson, 1973; Jefferson, 1973).

The sedge, bulrush and sedge, low silt, and low sand marshes are all, more broadly, "low marshes," and share several attributes. They lie within reach of nearly all high tides, and are inundated twice almost every day. Each fall the aboveground vegetation dies down and floats out into the estuary with the tides, where bacteria decompose it (Eilers, 1975). With a steady sediment supply, however, this can change suddenly as the low marshes are transformed into "high marshes."

The marsh surface continues to rise slowly until it reaches the mean higher high water level, where the accretion rate abruptly jumps. The change is so sudden that the low and high marshes are often separated by a steep rise several inches high (Eilers, 1975). The main cause of this is the sudden drop in the duration and frequency of the tides. Since few tides reach above mean higher high water, the marsh litter can no longer float into the estuary, and instead stays put and decomposes where it falls. And decomposition itself is slow for two reasons. First, enough tidewater still flows over the marsh soil to prevent oxygen from penetrating, thereby eliminating the abundant earthworms, fungi, insects, and other decomposers of well-aerated terrestrial soils (Eilers, 1975). Second, some high marsh plants (e.g.,

Juncus balticus and *Agrostis alba*) are themselves more resistant to decay. As a result, thick layers of slowly rotting plant matter soon blanket the marsh, which in turn is covered by the normal high tide flotsam and jetsam, creating the sudden rise in elevation.

This steep transitional zone is occupied by the "immature high marsh," or "middle marsh," dominated about equally by both tufted hair grass (*Deschampsia caespitosa*) and salt grass (*Distichlis spicata*) (Jefferson, 1973; Eilers, 1975). The pioneering seaside arrowgrass is often also present, as well as salicornia and Lyngbyei's sedge. The vegetation slows the tidal currents enough to maintain a soil rich in fine silts and clays, even though the marsh may have originated on sand. Salt pans and deep tidal creeks often scar the surface.

If the marsh surface continues to rise, it eventually reaches a level untouched by all but the most extreme high tides. At this point, roughly 10 feet, accretion slows and the surface levels out for two reasons (Eilers, 1975). First, the lack of tidal inundation keeps the soil dry enough to allow oxygen to penetrate, which welcomes abundant earthworms and other terrestrial decomposers. Second, many of the commoner plants, such as Pacific silverweed (*Potentilla pacifica*) and water parsely (*Oenanthe sarmentosa*), decay rapidly and have little chance to build up a thick sod (Eilers, 1975). The most abundant plants of this "mature high marsh" are tufted hair grass, salt rush (*Juncus lesueurii*), and creeping bentgrass (*Agrostis tenuis* var. *palustris*) although scattered remnants of earlier populations usually survive. At the highest elevations, the creek channels fade away to just shallow depressions, and masses of drift logs invite the settlement of several terrestrial species. Among these are gum plant, *Aster subspicatus*, Pacific silverweed, water parsely, and salt bush (*Atriplex patula* var. *hastata*). Often seedlings of Sitka spruce (*Picea sitchensis*, sometimes called "tideland spruce") appear on the logs, where they may escape the tides. Although we might suppose that the mature high marsh must eventually dry up and give way to upland forest, nowhere has this yet happened. Either the high marsh is a true climax community, or else our exceptionally youthful salt marshes are simply not quite ripe for forest.

An odd community that fits nowhere in this scheme is the "intertidal gravel marsh," a sparse collection of spike rushes (*Eleocharis palustris*, *E. montevidensis*, and *E. parvula*) and a few forbs (Jefferson, 1973). In Oregon these grow only on the gravel flats of the Rogue and Chetco estuaries, where the steep gradient maintains currents too swift to deposit fine clay and silt. The tidewater that inundates these plants is so fresh that they should perhaps be considered a freshwater marsh. In any case, the intertidal gravel marsh appears stable: simultaneously both pioneer and climax.

Starting at water's edge, there lies a clear zonation from bare

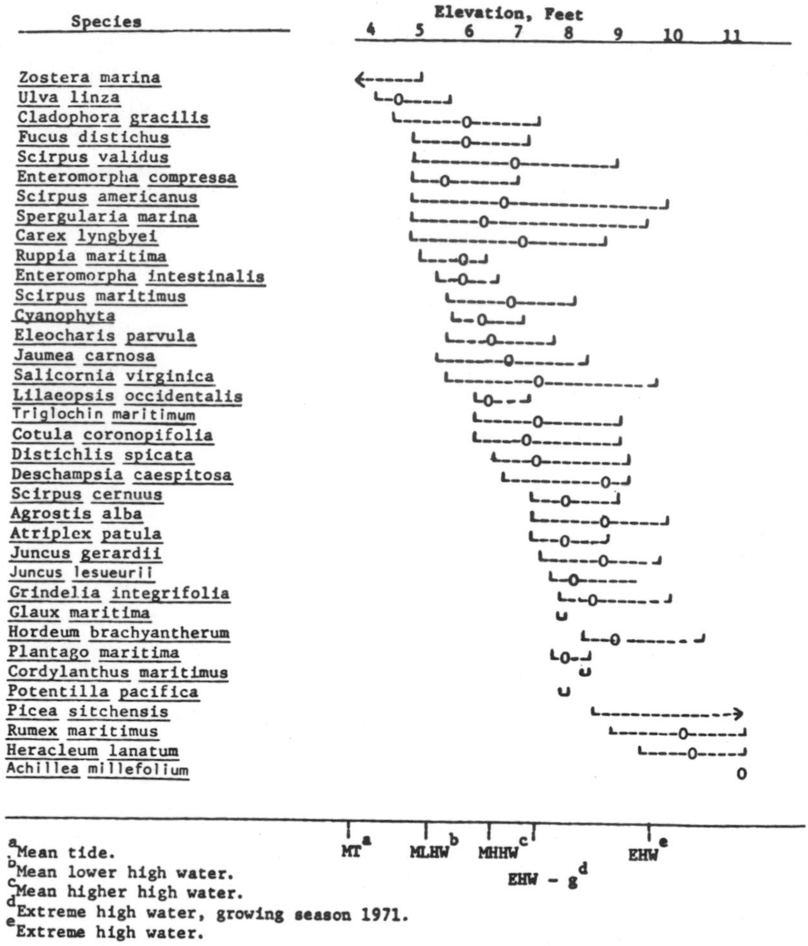
Species
Elevation, Feet
4 5 6 7 8 9 10 11
Zostera marina
Ulva linza
Cladophora gracilis
Fucus distichus
Scirpus validus
Enteromorpha compressa
Scirpus americanus
Spergularia marina
Carex lyngbyei
Ruppia maritima
Enteromorpha intestinalis
Scirpus maritimus
Cyanophyta
Eleocharis parvula
Jaumea carnosa
Salicornia virginica
Lilaeopsis occidentalis
Triglochin maritimum
Cotula coronopifolia
Distichlis spicata
Deschampsia caespitosa
Scirpus cernuus
Agrostis alba
Atriplex patula
Juncus gerardii
Juncus lesueurii
Grindelia integrifolia
Glaux maritima
Hordeum brachyantherum
Plantago maritima
Cordylanthus maritimus
Potentilla pacifica
Picea sitchensis
Rumex maritimus
Heracleum lanatum
Achillea millefolium
MT[a]
MLHW[b]
MHHW[c]
EHW[e]
EHW - g[d]
[a]Mean tide.
[b]Mean lower high water.
[c]Mean higher high water.
[d]Extreme high water, growing season 1971.
[e]Extreme high water.

Figure 44. Ranges of Oregon Salt Marsh Plants Relative to Mean Lower Low Water. (Directly from Jefferson, 1974.)

mudflats to low marshes, through the abrupt rise of the immature high marsh and on the the level, mature high marsh that culminates in spruce-covered drift logs (Figure 44). It is important to realize that this is not necessarily a consecutive series of successional stages. Most of the pioneers are perennials that manage to persist until the very end, while many of the latecomers have spread by rhizomes down to the lower levels. Hence what is often seen is a tangled hodge-podge of old and new, of early and late. Nevertheless, we can be sure of at least two trends. First, the regular and prolonged tidal inundation at the lower levels creates stresses that only a few species can tolerate. As elevation rises, the tides and their discomfort abate. As a result, species diversity is lowest in the low marshes, and steadily rises until it reaches a peak in the high marsh (Eilers, 1979). Monocultures of only two or three species often blanket the low marshes, while often eight or ten species coexist in the high marsh. Second, whenever an army of circular clones spread over the mudflats, we can be sure that upstream erosion has triggered an aggressive expansion of the salt marshes (Johannessen, 1964) (Figure 45).

ADAPTATIONS OF SALT MARSH PLANTS

Formidable obstacles block the evolutionary movement of most plants from land to tidewater. The successful species of the salt marshes, however, have vaulted these hurdles with a variety of minor adjustments in physiology and anatomy. Seawater harrasses terrestrial plants with the inescapable process of osmosis, whereby water flows across a membrane toward the higher solute concentration. Equally threatening is the companion process, diffusion, whereby dissolved salts flow spontaneously from a region of high concentration to a region of low concentration. A salt marsh plant, periodically submerged by a potent saline solution, faces at least three challenges:

1. how to absorb water from such a solution;
2. how to maintain its internal salt levels within comfortable limits; and
3. how to absorb enough essential nutrients from a solution rich in toxic salts.

Salt marsh plants meet the first challenge simply by absorbing enough salts from the tidewater to keep their internal levels above the external (Queen, 1975). This strategy ensures that water will flow spontaneously into the plant. But a plant will not function if it freely assimilates the salts in the same proportions that exist in seawater. So nearly all salt-tolerant plants use mechanisms to exclude the bad and attract the good. These involve a variety of complicated chemical interactions in the cell membrane, including selective ion pumps and specialized carrier molecules that bind some ions and not others. As a result, the internal fluids differ greatly from the external. The ratio of sodium to potassium inside the cell, for example, is much smaller than in seawater. These mechanisms operate with varying success in all organisms, and have simply been modified or upgraded in salt marsh plants.

Nevertheless, such control can never be absolute, so some of the more toxic and abundant elements in seawater (such as sodium) inevitably manage to accumulate to dangerous levels in the tissues of some salt marsh plants. Many of these plants owe their survival to a curious assortment of anatomical organs that evolved to eliminate these unwanted salts. These organs, known as "salt glands," are found on the leaves and stems of most salt-tolerant plants, including

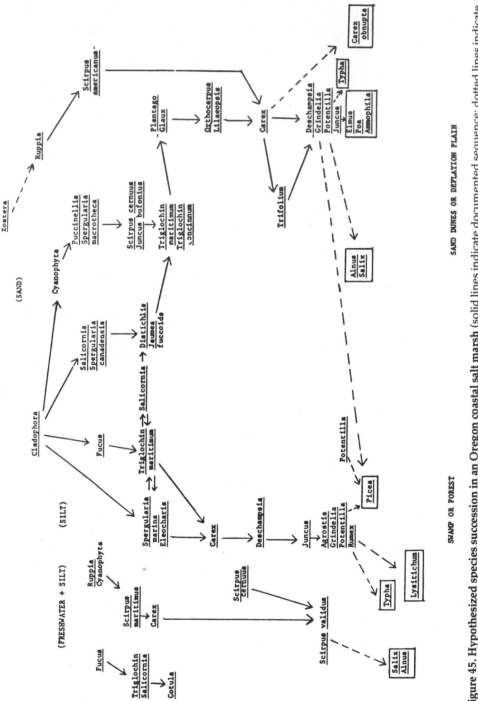

Figure 45. Hypothesized species succession in an Oregon coastal salt marsh (solid lines indicate documented sequence; dotted lines indicate possible but unobserved succession.) (From Jefferson, 1974).

salt grass, eelgrass, and cordgrass (*Spartina alterniflora*, the dominant plant of East Coast salt marshes) (Proctor, *et al.*, 1980). In salt bush and other plants of the *Atriplex* genus, the glands take the form of tiny hairs that periodically swell with salts, mostly sodium and chloride, and then burst to exude their contents out over the leaf surface. When these salty teardrops dry, they leave tiny white deposits clearly visible on the leaves of salt bush, salt grass, and many others.

Another common strategy involves the transfer of salts to safe locations inside the plant rather than their extrusion to the outside. Salicornia and jaumea, for example, have evolved columns of water-storing cells in leaves and stems that create an overall fleshiness known as "succulence." These plants dispose of sodium and other unwanted salts in these water-swollen cells, where the water dilutes them and their toxic effects. The salty tissues of salicornia are easily tasted when one of its jointed, leafless stems is bitten. Recently botanists have surmised that specialized compartments inside individual cells may also function as disposal sites for salts, even in nonsucculent plants (Queen, 1975).

Clearly, plants of the salt marshes battle the tidewater with a formidable armory of defenses. But if transplanted to a greenhouse, virtually every species grows much better in freshwater than in seawater! Apparently these plants have no requirement for seawater per se, but, with their array of adaptations, simply tolerate it much better than any other species. In the process of adapting, however, they have lost the strength to compete outside the salt marsh, and as a result have consigned themselves indefinitely to this unique tide-washed environment.

SALT MARSH PRODUCTIVITY

The tides command all facets of salt marsh existence, controlling succession, composition, species diversity, and export of litter. It remains to be seen how they influence productivity.

Two broad and simple trends have emerged from two decades of research on salt marshes of the East Coast and Europe. First, marsh plants tend to be taller and more productive along the water's edge, and shorter and less productive with increasing elevation and distance from the water. Streamside productivity at Sapelo Island, Georgia, averages 7.4 lbs/yd²/yr, and levee productivity 3.7 lbs/yd²/yr (Mann, 1982). Second, the distance between the level of the mean high tide and mean low tide often varies within an estuary, but as it widens, the salt marsh productivity rises. What these two trends add up to is an overall positive and constructive role for the tides: the greater their influence (within limits), the greater the productivity.

One explanation for this is simple. Marsh productivity is

limited by the supply of nitrogen, and tidewater contains abundant quantities of this essential nutrient. Submergence by the tidewater nourishes the plants and boosts their productivity. It is true that symbiotic bacteria in the roots of many marsh plants can fix nitrogen, and thereby liberate them from their dependence on waterborne sources of this nutrient. But this can be expensive, because the plants must sustain the bacteria with a steady supply of photosynthetic energy (about a pound of carbohydrate for every 0.001 pound of fixed nitrogen) (Mann, 1982). Hence dissolved nitrogen is much cheaper, and when inundated by the tides, marsh plants can dispense with the bacteria, absorb the nitrogen directly from the water, and use the energy gained for growth and reproduction.

Unfortunately, however, the situation is not this clear-cut on the West Coast, where research is scanty and the role of the tides is vague and somewhat controversial. In Nehalem Bay, productivity tends to increase as the marsh surface rises. The low marshes average about 2.2, the middle marsh 2.6, and the high marsh 3.1 lbs/yd^2/yr (Eilers, 1975). The pioneering seaside arrowgrass clones are the least productive at 0.41 lb/yd^2/yr, and the high marsh aster/Pacific silverweed/water parsely grouping is highest at 5.2 lbs/yd^2/yr. The most productive species is Lyngbyei's sedge, whose low streambank clones sprout roughly 2.4 lbs/yd^2/yr. In Grays Harbor the pattern is similar; the low silt marsh produces about 3.1 lbs/yd^2/yr, the low sand 4.0, the sedge 2.1, the immature high 4.5. In Coos Bay, however, the reverse trend appears, and productivity seems to peak in the low marsh. Of all species measured, the low-lying bulrush stand in North Slough is the most productive at 2.1 lbs/yd^2/yr, and other high marsh communities produce about half this amount (Hoffnagle and Olson, 1974).

Furthermore, productivity of Northwest salt marshes seems unaffected by tidal range. In Puget Sound, the tidal range is nearly double that of Nehalem Bay (10 feet versus 5.9 feet), yet the salt marshes appear about equally fertile. Lyngbyei's sedge, for example, manufactures about 2.6 lbs/yd^2/yr in the Nisqually estuary, and 2.4 lbs/yd^2/yr in the Nehalem (Proctor, et al., 1980).

Apparently, the tidal influence in Northwest estuaries is neither here nor there, and at least in Grays Harbor and Nehalem, some other factors are involved. If looked at more closely, these productivity values reveal that the more northerly marshes are more fertile; Grays Harbor appears to be roughly twice as productive as Coos Bay. Research has shown that this trend applies to the entire West Coast from southern California to Puget Sound: productivity tends to increase with latitude. The reason may be related not to nitrogen but to salinity (Mann, 1982). As mentioned, high salinities aggravate and fatigue marsh plants by interfering with a balanced nutrient uptake, thereby stunting growth and reducing productivity. Since the roots absorb most of the nutrients, soil salinity is critical, while tidewater salinity is almost irrelevant. So productivity tends to drop as soil salinity rises.

But what controls soil salinity? In the low marshes the soil is of course about as saline as the tidewater, but in the seldom-submerged high marshes, soil salinity is controlled not by inundation but by rainfall. In wet climates, rain dilutes the salt and promotes higher productivity, while in dry climates evaporation actually concentrates the salt, thereby stifling productivity (Ranwell, 1972). So on the basis of soil salinity alone, higher marshes should be more fertile than low marshes in wet climates, and the reverse in hot, dry climates. On the West Coast, this pattern may well explain both the confusion about marsh elevation versus productivity and the general rise in productivity with latitude.

THE FATE OF ESTUARINE PRODUCTION

The high plant productivity made possible by the sheltered and enriched estuarine waters sustains a large community of consumers, from the myriad of single-celled forms through an abundance of worms, shrimp, crabs, mussels, oysters, clams, and other invertebrates, and finally to fish, birds, and humans.

As far as the consumers are concerned, estuarine plants fall into just two groups: the rooted (flowering) plants, and all the rest. The rooted plants are special because their evolutionary history includes a prolonged period on dry land, during which they evolved a variety of tough, fibrous, supporting tissues. Many of these tissues contain carbohydrates that higher animals cannot digest, such as lignin and cellulose. On the other hand, though algae contain cellulose and similar substances, they are generally more nutritious and digestible than the rooted plants. Hence, while consumers can eat the phytoplankton, diatoms, and seaweeds directly, they have little use for intact eelgrass and salt marsh plants. As a rule, only about 10% of eelgrass and salt marsh production is grazed directly (Phillips and Thayer, 1977; Pomeroy, 1980). The most abundant grazers of salt marsh plants are insects, which digest the plants with the help of microorganisms in their gut.

The other 90%, however, is by no means wasted. Each fall, nearly all the above-ground vegetation dies and is colonized by a rich community of decomposers. Fungi usually appear first and extend their fine hyphal filaments inside the detritus. Bacterial growths develop later, and tend to stay on the outer surface, even on top of the fungi (Peterson and Peterson, 1979). Both contain enzymes that digest cellulose and other tough structural material. Not only do the decomposers break down and incorporate the carbohydrates, fats, and proteins of the plant into their own tissues with supreme efficiency, but they also scavenge dissolved food and nutrients from the water. As a result, while the larger consumers cannot digest the dead plants any easier than they can the live ones, they certainly have no trouble digesting the outer coating of nutritious, energy-rich bacteria and fungi. A clean particle of *Spartina* detritus contains only about 6% protein, whereas a bacteria-covered particle is 24% protein (McLusky, 1981).

Hence, when a lugworm eats a piece of detritus, it digests and absorbs the bacteria and fungi, and passes out the plant matter virtually unchanged in its feces. As soon as the clean feces see the light of day, they are colonized by a new wave of decomposers. The cycle continues as the lugworm or another detritus feeder now eats the newly enriched feces, and again digests off the bacteria while leaving the rest intact. In this way the detritus recycles repeatedly through the consumer community, steadily shrinking as its nutrient values disappear first into the bacteria and then into the tissues of the larger consumers. The continual processing also breaks the detritus into progressively smaller particles, creating progressively greater surface area for an increasing complement of bacteria, thereby growing steadily more valuable as a food source. In this way the decomposers act as an indispensable intermediary between the plants and the consumers. Nearly all large populations of estuarine invertebrates feed on the fine detritus and its associated bacteria (Peterson and Peterson, 1979). Surprisingly, not only does the biomass of the bacteria approach that of the entire fauna of the coastal waters, but the productivity is much greater, providing ample indication of the overwhelming importance of these minute creatures (Mann, 1982).

The calm waters of sheltered bays allow not only the fine sediment to sink to the bottom, but the small detritus particles as well, making the mudflats richer in food than the water column. Organic material makes up about 10% of the sediment weight (Proctor, *et al.*, 1980), and is usually a mixture of algae, root, and leaf particles, feces and corpses of planktonic and burrowing animals, and often wood chips, sawdust, and bark, especially near wood processing mills and log rafts. Rich blooms of bacteria blanket all of these, and a single square yard of mud may contain thousands of detritus-feeding worms and bivalves. Since fine sediments have a greater surface area, they invite a richer population of bacteria and fungi, and in general support a greater biomass of consumers than coarse sands (Peterson and Peterson, 1979). The concentration of decomposers in the sediments make nutrients more rapidly available to the benthic (especially rooted) plants than to the phytoplankton, which depend on the slower release of nutrients into the water column.

It is natural to wonder which of the estuarine producers contributes the most organic material to the consumers, and is thereby most responsible for their continued survival. The amount of work necessary to answer this question, however, is enormous and expensive, and has seldom been attempted. In Grays Harbor, it appears that the rivers bring in from four to eight times the organic material contributed from all the producers combined, while ocean input is negligible (Thom, 1981). Here is a direct, positive linkage between two ecosystems. The rivers of course flow through lush forests of spruce and hemlock, where great masses of dead logs, branches, leaves, and twigs pile up on and in the soil and streams. As the fungi and bacteria of the streams decompose this superabundance of litter, they send a flood of organic nutrients into the water currents, which wash them and all the bits and pieces of wood and leaves eventually into the estuary, where they settle in the calm waters. Hence, in Grays Harbor, the forests feed the estuary, and the salt marshes, eelgrass beds, and other estuarine producers are comparatively insignificant, despite all the attention given in the past to the detrital food webs of marshes and eelgrass.

Of course, this may not be true for all Northwest estuaries, especially those with a richer complement of producers and a smaller runoff than Grays Harbor. But when surveying only the salt marshes and eelgrass, we find that the same trend holds. For each estuary, the salt marsh acreage and runoff is known. If we assume the marshes produce 2.5 lbs/yd^2/yr, and the rivers all contain the same amount of organic material as the Chehalis, about 200 lbs/acre-foot of water (Thom, 1981), then the food input of river versus salt marsh for each estuary can be compared. On the average, each year the rivers contribute more than a hundred times the total amount of organic material produced by the salt marshes. The ratio varies from about 1 at Sandlake to over 800 for the Necanicum. If an eelgrass productivity of 6 lbs/yd^2 is included, the rivers still contribute a total of 40 times the productivity of rooted plants. Of course, there are other producers besides these, and in any case some big assumptions have been made. Unfortunately, we simply have no reliable measurements of total productivity of the various producer categories in any but a few West Coast estuaries, and the necessary research may be several years away.

In any case, the estuarine plants can be valuable in a variety of ways, and several factors make productivity by no means a good measure of a producer's importance. First, we simply have little knowledge about how much production is actually consumed. Some may become buried too deep in the sediments to be used, and some may wash out to the open ocean and sink to the abyssal depths or at least vanish from the estuarine scene. Second, consumers differ greatly in their diet. Oysters and some snails for example feed almost exclusively on algae, and brant and widgeon graze almost entirely on eelgrass. So even though algae or eelgrass may be unproductive in some estuaries, they still are indispensable for some animals, and therefore "important." Third, rooted plants are inherently less nutritious than algae. When eating wood debris, eelgrass or marsh plants, a consumer must absorb the energy and nutrients from an intermediary, the bacteria and fungi. The energy flow from the plant is necessarily wasteful because some must go to support the decomposers. When eating algae, however, the consumer has all the profits to itself. Unfortunately, we as yet have no exact knowledge of the relative food values of rooted plants and algae. And fourth, the annual gain in weight of a plant's leaves and stems does not precisely equal its productivity. When bright sunlight and plentiful carbon dioxide favor photosynthesis, plants often fix the carbon dioxide automatically even when they have insufficient nutrients for growth. If nutrients are scarce, the plant simply releases the fixed carbon dioxide back into the water, where bacteria can absorb it and thereby make it available to the larger consumers (Mann, 1982). This carbon is called "dissolved organic material" (DOM) to distinguish it from large bits of detritus, or "particulate organic material" (POM). The amount of DOM released by eelgrass adds 12–20% to its productivity (Phillips and Thayer, 1977), and seaweeds up to 40% (Mann, 1982). Moreover, the biomass of plant roots often exceeds that of the leaves and stems, and of course the roots also grow and may account for over 40% of salt marsh detritus. Unfortunately, we have no way to measure root growth accurately. Until we know more about DOM and root production, our knowledge of total aerial productivities may have little meaning.

Despite all this, a few broad and meaningful seasonal trends emerge. In spring and summer, plentiful nutrients and long sunny days trigger rapid growth in all estuarine producers. During this time, river flows are lowest and most of the waterborne organic material is algal, from either planktonic or benthic species. The period from April to July spans 70–100% of all salt marsh production, but the plants stay put until the fall (Hoffnagle and Olson, 1974). In September, the river flow remains low, but colder water and fewer daylight hours bring most plant growth to an end. By October, nearly all salt marsh plants have died down aboveground and offer their detritus as the predominant food material in the water. On the average, the low marshes contribute 100% of their annual production to the adjacent estuary, the immature high marsh about 50%, and the high marsh 5% (Eilers, 1975). As much as 75% of the annual marsh production is flushed into the estuary; the rest enriches the upper marsh soil. Sporadic storm tides may sometimes sweep away the detritus from the mature high marsh. Since decomposition is slow, most marsh detritus will not completely rot until the following April. By December and January, drenching rainfall floods the rivers and wind waves tear loose the dead eelgrass, sometimes roots and all. Throughout the winter eelgrass and river organics contribute about equally to the potential food supply (Thom, 1981).

Clearly, the seasonal replacement of organics and the slow decomposition of detritus can maintain the food supply at a steady level throughout the year, allowing the consumers to feed and grow throughout the year. This is in contrast to the deep waters of the ocean, where zooplankton and fish are at the mercy of the boom and bust cycle of the phytoplankton (Hoffnagle and Olson, 1974).

ESTUARINE CONSUMERS

On a typical summer day little of the animal world is seen on the bayshore other than a scattered horde of screaming gulls, a great blue heron standing frozen in the shallows, and perhaps a few crows croaking and strutting in the tidal debris. But in the estuary as in most of nature, the visible is but a shallow footprint of a larger and more elusive truth. By far the greatest animal biomass rests hidden in the cold and muddy sand, and to admire its complexities binoculars must be traded for boots, shovel, and magnifying devices.

The estuarine environment arranges its consumers into several categories. Those living in or on the bottom sediments are "benthos," composed of the infauna, epifauna, and mobile epibenthos. The infauna, including the abundant worms, shrimp, and clams, live buried beneath the surface. The epifauna, mainly barnacles, mussels, and oysters, live attached to a solid object at or above the surface. The mobile epibenthos include snails, crabs, seastars, and other animals that glide or crawl along the bottom. Animals free of the bottom, or "nekton," include the passively drifting zooplankton and the actively swimming fishes and birds. In addition to these are the terrestrial consumers, which care little for the water and usually move in at low tide to graze and scavenge. Among the invertebrates are the flies, leaf hoppers, bees, wasps, ants, and spiders, which live mainly in the salt marshes, and are often eaten by salmon and other fish and hawked in mid-air by swallows. The vertebrates include a variety of amphibians, birds, reptiles, and mammals. Shrews, voles, and mice dine on the marsh plants and are in turn sought after by the red fox, coyote, and other carnivores. Deer and elk often graze the marshes in the early morning, and raccoons (*Procyon lotor*), skunk (*Mephitus*), and river otter (*Lutra canadensis*) raven the invertebrates of the marshes and tideflats.

Infauna

The bare sediment surface offers no protection from waves, currents, predators, or widely fluctuating salinities. To escape these rigors, the vast majority of estuarine animals simply burrow underground. One of the great advantages of a burrowing lifestyle is its freedom from extremes in salinity and temperature. The only water felt by a creature of the infauna is the "interstitial" water, or the water between the mud particles. But the bulk of the sediments prevents the interstitial water from mixing well with the overlying tidewater. Hence the water column swings from warm to cool and fresh to marine with the tides and runoff, while the sediments remain about constant (Peterson and Peterson, 1979). Since the high salinity salt wedge lies on top of the sediments, the interstitial salinity tends to hold steady near that of the salt wedge, permitting infaunal animals to move farther into an estuary than many fishes (McLusky, 1981). In short, the sediments buffer the infauna from the worst punishments an estuary can inflict.

This freedom, however, is bought at a price. A member of the infauna depends heavily and inescapably on the size of the sediment grains. Its feeding method, distribution, abundance, and overall lifestyle hinge on the relative amounts of fine clays and coarse sands in its burrows.

Mudflats differ from sandflats in several notable ways. The low energy environment of the mudflat permits the buildup of fine particles of detritus, which invite rich blooms of bacteria. Added to this is the greater surface area of the fine clays and silts, to which the bacteria can attach. The result is a much richer bacterial flora on mudflats (McLusky, 1981). The lively bacterial metabolism eventually exhausts the oxygen supply of the mudflat, and at deeper levels the aerobic bacteria are replaced by anaerobic bacteria. Oxygen usually penetrates no deeper than about 12-inches before it is used up by the aerobic microbes (Peterson and Peterson, 1979). The anaerobic substratum boundary is marked either by the presence of a layer of black sand or the smell of rotten eggs. Anaerobic bacteria release hydrogen sulfide as waste, which is responsible for the fetid odor. If iron is present, it reacts to form the black iron sulfide (Proctor, *et al.*, 1980). Another problem of mudflats is the tendency of the fine clays to stick together, which further restricts the penetration of aerated water even more.

In contrast, sand grains are large, and the spaces between them are wide enough to permit a rapid exchange between the interstitial water and the overlying river and tides. Also, the high-energy environment of the sandflat prevents the accumulation of minute organic particles, and bacteria are less abundant. Hence, the greater the sand content of an intertidal flat, the greater the depth of the surface oxygen-rich layer and the lesser its protection from severe fluctuations of the overlying water.

At the mercy of this environment are the members of the infauna. The smallest are the little-studied "microfauna." These microscopic creatures, primarily forameniferans, ciliates, and other protozoa, feed on bacteria. The "meiofauna" comprise all the animals about the size of the mud particles, primarily free-living nematodes. Their distribution depends strikingly on the mud content of the sediments. The mud meiofauna tend to have large stocky bodies, and must remain in the upper half-inch of the sediments, where oxygen is plentiful (Peterson and Peterson, 1979). The sand meiofauna often have long, worm-shaped bodies that slither smoothly among the sand grains. Thanks to the more thorough circulation of oxygen through the sands, these forms survive to much deeper levels than those in the muds. Since the oxygen crowds the mud meiofauna at the surface, the shrimp and larger worms can feed on them much more efficiently than on the loosely scattered sand meiofauna, which are thus a poor food source and comparatively safe from predation. The mud meiofauna feed primarily on the ample detritus, bacteria, and microfauna, while the sand meiofauna consume benthic diatoms or each other (McLusky, 1981). In many estuaries the meiofauna account for roughly a third of the productivity of all herbivores and detritivores, or about 100 pounds per acre each year (McLusky, 1981). Shrimp, worms, and other consumers prey so heavily on them, however, that the biomass at any given time seldom exceeds about 10% this value.

The final category of infauna is the "macrofauna," containing the largest animals. In order of abundance, the vast majority are polychaete worms, clams, and shrimp. As a rule, the worms and shrimp are deposit feeders and mine immense quantities of sediments for the valuable nuggets of detritus, diatoms, micro-, and meiofauna. Most clams are suspension feeders, and filter out particles of detritus and plankton from the water column. Some clams also deposit-feed on the surface sediments, and some worms and shrimp actively search out and devour small animals in the fashion of a true predator.

Perhaps the most abundant large mudflat worm on the Northwest Coast is the lugworm *Abarenicola pacifica*, which sometimes numbers 50, and occasionally 100 individuals under a square yard of sediments (Rudy and Rudy, 1983). Little piles of coiled muddy feces betray its presence, for like so many other infauna, the lugworm satisfies its hunger by swallowing mud. All members of the lugworm family sharpen their feeding efficiency by constructing J- or U-shaped burrows in which the animal resides roughly upside-down, with the tail end near the surface. At the other end of the J, the head swallows the sediments, and new sediments constantly fall inward from above as the old are consumed. In this way the dirty mud moves from the head through the lugworm's digestive tract, and finishes as clean fecal castings on the surface (MacGinitie and MacGinitie, 1949). Often the worm adopts a "gardening" strategy whereby bacteria and microfauna colonize the feces, enriching it with nitrogen. If the worm happens to reingest its feces, it absorbs the microbes, and in the course of a day processes and recycles large quantities of mud and sand. To avoid suffocating in the stagnant interstitial water, the lugworm maintains a constant current of water through the burrow with successive dilations and contractions of its body segments. Another surprising adaptation is the unusual gills, which protrude as several pairs of bushy tufts along the worm's midsection, where they lay fully exposed to the current. This intriguing existence typifies the infaunal lifestyle. Buried in the mud, the animal escapes waves and predators, avoids drying out, and lies bathed in its own food supply. The only discomfort is the lack of oxygen, and the lugworm's solution is the stream of water and external gills.

One of the most abundant shrimp of Northwest estuarine mudflats is the ghost shrimp *Callianassa californiensis,* especially common in Willapa, Necanicum, Tillamook, Netarts, Yaquina, Alsea, Umpqua, and Coos estuaries (Figure 46). Unlike the lugworm, the ghost shrimp has five pairs of legs, each of which performs a different function during digging, walking, and feeding (MacGinitie and MacGinitie, 1949). In digging a burrow, the claws of the first and second legs loosen the silt, then the third legs and the mouth parts simultaneously sweep the silt into a "mud basket" formed by the mouth parts. When the basket fills, the shrimp backs out and empties its load of sediments. After digging several inches downward in this way, the shrimp hollows out a rounded space wide enough to turn around in, and from this time on it never leaves the burrow. To unload its mud and sand, the shrimp walks forward to the burrow opening, and emerges just far enough to push the load out onto the surface. It then backs down to the turnaround and continues building other tunnels in various directions. Its first priority is to dig at least one more tunnel open to the surface, so that it can prevent suffocation by maintaining a current of clean water through the burrows. Whenever the animal pauses briefly to rest or clean itself, its fan-shaped abdominal appendages ("swimmerets") beat slowly to keep the water circulating, at least when the tide is in. When the low tides expose the flats, the shrimp probably slows all its activities. If the overlying water is too warm or too fresh, the animal seems to stop this circulation, and in any case can survive without oxygen up to 6 days (Rudy and Rudy, 1983).

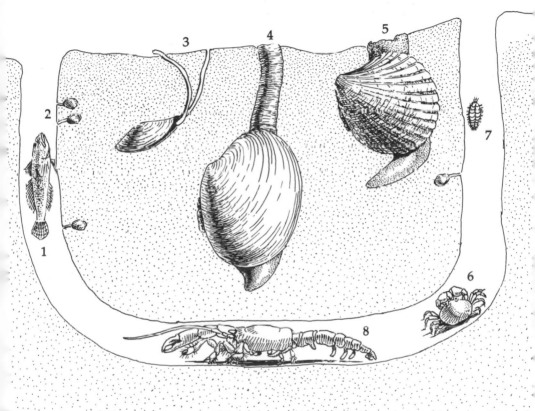

Figure 46. The ghost shrimp (*Callianassa californiensis*) and other tideflat animals. 1 The goby *Clevelandia ios*. **2** The clam *Cryptomya californica*. **3** The clam *Macoma*. **4** The butter clam *Saxidomus*. **5** The heart cockle *Clinocardium*. **6** A pinnotheria crab. **7** The scale worm *Hesperonoe complanata*. **8** The ghost shrimp. (Megahan)

The ghost shrimp is condemned to a life of near-constant digging simply to gather enough food to survive on. Like other detritus feeders, it swallows fine sediments and detritus, and digests off the thick coating of nitrogen-rich bacteria. To collect the mud, the second and third legs scoop it loose and sift through it with their hairy fringes, until just the finest particles remain. The hairs on the mouth parts sweep these up, sort through them some more, and then spoon them into the mouth. The coarser grains discarded earlier eventually pile up, and when enough material accumulates for a load the shrimp gathers it up and shoves it out the burrow (MacGinitie and MacGinitie, 1949). Eventually the animal builds a mound of sediments around the entrance of its burrow, and in a dense shrimp bed these volcanolike mounds cover the surface by the millions. In a year, a colony of 3000 shrimp will heap over 700 cubic feet of sand on the surface (MacGinitie and MacGinitie, 1949).

The permanent network of well irrigated tunnels always attracts several other species, which reap all the benefits of the burrows but need not expend any digging energy themselves (MacGinitie and MacGinitie, 1949). The clam *Cryptomya californica* digs deep into the ghost shrimp beds, and opens its siphons into the burrows, where they filter out any detrital particles in the water current (Figure 46). The scale worm *Hesperonoe complanata,* three species of pea crabs, and a goby fish *Clevelandia ios* scavenge any large detrital particles discarded by the shrimp. When the goby finds a piece of meat too big to swallow, it shows astonishing resourcefulness by offering it to the pea crabs. The crabs snatch it up with delight and begin tearing it to pieces, but the goby watches over them intently until the morsel shrinks to a manageable size, and then darts in and seizes it (MacGinitie and MacGinitie, 1949). Meanwhile, the indifferent ghost shrimp continues its endless digging and sorting, oblivious to the freeloaders.

These and other houseguests also invade the tunnels of at least two other common Northwest burrowers. The blue mud shrimp, though different in appearance (light blue-green instead of transparent pink) mirrors the ghost shrimp in habits and habitat. Since low oxygen kills the mud shrimp more easily, it digs its burrows only half as deep as the ghost shrimp (about 18 inches), and often plugs the entrances at low tide (Rudy and Rudy, 1983). The aptly named "fat innkeeper" is a worm-like burrower famous for its motley collection of guests, nearly the same group as those of the ghost shrimp. The innkeeper ranges as far north as Humboldt Bay, and like the lugworm, constructs a U-shaped burrow well irrigated by contractions of its body wall (Kozloff, 1983). Its feeding method, however, is spectacularly different. With its own mucus, the innkeeper spins a slimy net across the entrance of the burrow, which traps any particles in the water current. When the net fills, the animal consumes it together with the trapped mud and detritus. Surprisingly, the net is so efficient that it catches particles as small as 1/25,000 inch, which includes individual bacteria (MacGinitie and MacGinitie, 1949). The innkeeper consumes only the finest particles, and leaves the coarser ones for its hungry guests.

Although most of our 16-odd species of clams can survive deep enough on the outer coast to escape the breakers, nearly all grow and reproduce best in the sheltered waters of the estuaries. The reason is simply their weak and sluggish powers of digging. Heavy surf can wrench a clam out of its hole, and to survive, the animal must dig back in before the next crushing breaker. Only one clam on the Northwest coast is quick enough. This is the razor clam (*Siliqua patula*) whose speed and strength easily win the blue ribbon. From lying flat on the sand surface, a razor can completely bury itself in a few seconds, and thereby escape most of the heavy winter storm waves. In contrast, adult softshell (*Mya arenaria*), gaper (*Tresus* spp.), butter (*Saxidomus* spp.), geoduck (*Panopea generosa*), piddock (e.g., *Penitella* spp.), bentnose (*Macoma nasuta*), and other bay clams have little or no digging power at all, and thrive best in the tranquil, wave-sheltered estuarine sediments (Figure 46).

Unlike the worms and shrimp, nearly all clams depend for food on whatever tidbits they can filter out of the water column, mostly phytoplankton and small detritus particles. In essence the feeding method resembles the fat innkeeper's, because the main ingredients are a mucus net and a current of water. The current flows through a pair of hose-like "siphons," in one and out the other. In some clams, such as the bentnose, the siphons are separate, while in others, such as the gaper and razor, the siphons are fused together to form the "neck" (a misnomer, since the siphons are actually the rear end of the beast). When feeding, a clam secretes a sheet of mucus over the gills. Pumped by hair-like cilia on the gills, the water current flows through one siphon, and must filter through the mucus before it enters the gills, and finally flows back out through the other siphon. The mucus-net strains out even the finest waterborne particles, and when it fills up, other cilia carry it in food-laden strings to the mouth. This same pumping mechanism also brings oxygen to the gills (MacGinitie and MacGinitie, 1949).

The abundant and widespread bent-nosed clam employs a feeding method intriguing in its flexibility. The bright orange siphons of the bent-nose are entirely separate, and the inhalant siphon can either inhale a current of water (suspension-feed) or it can suck in the film of bacteria, detritus, and diatoms on the sediment surface much like a vacuum cleaner (deposit-feed) (McLusky, 1981). How the clam decides to feed apparently depends on tides and sediments. Living as it does in the middle intertidal, the bent-nose can suspension-feed only when submerged by the tides. Predictably, the amount of time it spends deposit-feeding rises with the organic content of the sediments. When the animal exhausts the surface food supply, it simply withdraws the siphon and re-extends it to new feeding grounds a few inches away. By feeding in whatever manner is most profitable at the moment, the clam protects itself from the wide fluctuations of the estuarine habitat. Perhaps this ability to roll with the punches is what has allowed the bent-nose to spread in abundance to nearly every kind of mudflat on the Northwest Coast.

Benthic Epifauna

These sessile species, primarily barnacles, mussels, and oysters, resemble the seaweeds in their need for a solid, stable attachment surface, and they often blanket jetty boulders and rock outcrops with a thick crust of densely packed shells. Their lack of burrowing powers obliges them to adjust in other ways to the adversities inflicted by the tides and currents. Foremost is the ability to shut their shell parts tight enough to seal out uncomfortably warm or fresh water. As has already been pointed out, this is a common adaptation of intertidal animals in or out of the estuary.

The supreme success of mussels and barnacles stems in part from their ability to create a snug and stable environment where there was none before. For example, oysters (species of *Crassostrea* and *Ostrea*) can easily colonize bits of shells and rocks scattered over the shifting sediments. The shells of these pioneers provide attachment space for more oysters, and as these invade, the colony becomes steadily denser, until a continuous bed of oysters hides the sediments. The bed is usually so dense (often a few hundred individuals per square yard) that it slows currents as effectively as eelgrass and salt marshes. This protects the interior oysters in the same way as the surrounding forest protects a single tree from heavy wind. Of course currents are already slow throughout most of a protected bay, so a bed of oysters fixed securely to a stable foundation of bedrock probably has little need for this baffle effect. In any case, oysters appear perfectly adapted to estuaries, and fossils show that they have formed dense beds in estuaries long before humans even existed (Hedgpeth, 1966).

The only native oyster on the West Coast, *Ostrea lurida*, grows commonly in Puget Sound and San Francisco Bay, but is hard to find elsewhere. The commercially valuable Pacific oyster (*Crassostrea gigas*), grown in Willapa and Tillamook estuaries, reproduces poorly here possibly because turbidity prevents survival of the larvae (Morris, *et al.*, 1980). Hence oyster growers must periodically import young Pacific oysters from Japan and elsewhere. Luckily, conditions are usually fine for growth and fattening.

Like eelgrass, mussels and oysters often form beds so dense and massive that they influence the biological and physical character of the entire estuary. These animals suspension-feed in the same way as their relatives, the clams, and a large bed can filter out immense quantities of plankton and suspended detritus. A bed of oysters filters about 62,500 gallons of seawater per square yard, and retains about 11% of the food material or roughly 2150 kilocalories per square yard, of which typically 60% passes through the gut undigested (Bernard, 1974). In this way, a dense bed of mussels or oysters recycles nutrients rapidly, and helps to maintain the high productivity of the estuary.

Distribution of the Infauna and Epifauna

Clearly, the burrowing animals, and to a lesser extent the animals living fixed to the surface, depend heavily on the estuary bottom for attachment space, concealment, shelter, and feeding. Hence it is no surprise that the nature of the bottom, primarily the size of the sediment particles, largely determines where in an estuary a benthic animal lives and how it feeds.

And the patterns turn out to be quite simple. As a rule, wherever deposit-feeders are abundant, suspension-feeders are rare, and vice-versa (Peterson and Peterson, 1979). This happens for two reasons. First, deposit-feeders are much more abundant in muddy tideflats and bottoms than sandy ones, because the finer sediments offer more surface area for bacterial attachment and some of the fine particles themselves are bits of detritus. Hence the mudflats contain a richer food supply for the deposit-feeders, and the organic content of the sediments largely controls their biomass and productivity. As has been seen, the finest sediments predominate in the quietest reaches of an estuary, notably in salt marshes, sloughs, eelgrass beds, and gently sloping intertidal flats in the sheltered bay, and in these habitats we find the most abundant mud-swallowers. In contrast, coarse sands tend to predominate in the high-energy marine and riverine sections of an estuary, as well as deep channels exposed to strong currents in the bay. The lack of food in these habitats prevents proliferation of the deposit-feeders.

Second, the direct activities of deposit feeders can decimate entire populations of suspension-feeders. The ghost shrimp and other burrowing deposit feeders dump enormous quantities of sediments on the surface, creating a loose, fluffy layer of silt on the surface. Even gentle waves and currents can easily sweep these muds and sands into the water, where they swirl in thick, murky clouds above the deposit-feeding populations. Unfortunately, these waterborne sediments clog the siphons and mucus-nets of clams, mussels, oysters, and other suspension-feeders, leading to suffocation or starvation (Peterson and Peterson, 1979). The result is a dearth of oysters, gaper clams, and other species anywhere near the dense beds of ghost shrimp and other deposit-feeders. Predictably, suspension-feeders are found in greatest abundance in the coarser sediment flats. The war between these two is fiercest in the commercial oyster beds of Willapa and Tillamook bays. Here, the abundant ghost shrimp could decimate the oysters if the oyster farmers failed to soak the mudflats every few years with the pesticide Sevin, which kills virtually all animals wherever it falls. Oystermen in Tillamook Bay had been spraying Sevin illegally for over 10 years before they were caught in 1982, triggering a flood of criticism from conservation groups and scientists (Oregon Journal, 19 July 1982 p. 4 c. 1). Sevin remains illegal in Oregon estuaries until its impacts are more fully researched.

The distribution of infauna also depends on the adult deposit-feeders themselves. Deposit-feeders generally assimilate all digestible material in the muds they swallow, including juvenile members of the infauna (Peterson and Peterson, 1979). Hence especially dense beds of deposit-feeders can exclude many potential newcomers by simply eating them soon after they settle in the sediments. As a result, whoever gets to the mudflats first has the best chance to prevail in the long run.

Mobile Epibenthos

A diversity of estuarine animals crawl or glide along the bottom, including isopods, amphipods, crabs, shrimp, snails, sand dollars, and seastars. Unlike the immobile species dealt with earlier, the fastest among these can escape uncomfortably warm or fresh water by literally running away. Most, however, have little chance of surviving unless concealed from fish, birds, and other predators, and hence prefer to hide under logs, rocks, and in beds of mussels, oysters, eelgrass, and seaweed. Only seldom does a crab or other crustacean stray out onto the bare mudflat.

This diverse collection of animals contains about equal numbers of species of detritus-feeders, predators, and herbivores (Peterson and Peterson, 1979). Isopods and amphipods, small crustaceans often camouflaged with the same color patterns as the seaweeds on which they live, for the most part feed on detritus. Unlike the deposit-feeders, they search out masses of decaying material and ingest it directly. One of the most common and conspicuous isopods, the rock louse (*Ligia pallasii*), lives on cliffs 5–20 feet above the tide, often along freshwater seeps, and scavenges primarily on plant material (Rudy and Rudy, 1983). Most Northwest amphipods also scavenge on all kinds of detritus, and often hide in the rotting debris at high tide line. In South Slough of Coos Bay, the beach hopper *Megalorchestia pugettensis* forages in abundance in the debris, and is partial to seaweeds, wet cardboard, and the bodies of other arthropods (Rudy and Rudy, 1983).

Unlike most of our estuarine crabs, which are more common on the protected outer coast, the hairy shore crab *Hemigrapsus oregonensis* prefers muddy bottoms of quiet bays. It is primarily a vegetarian, and uses its claws to scrape algae (*Ulva* or *Enteromorpha*) off the rocks (Rudy and Rudy, 1983). Like other crabs, it finds the right food not just by taste, but by sight and touch as well (Rudy and Rudy, 1983).

The seasonal migration of the well-known Dungeness crab (*Cancer magister*) typifies the lifestyle of many crabs. In the summer, the Dungeness invade the shallow waters of estuaries and the outer coast to feed during the most productive time of year. They prefer to eat small clams and crustaceans, though they also scavenge when necessary. As the food supply drops in fall and winter, the crabs move offshore to deep waters, where their feeding and other activities slow down. While in the shallows, the adults molt, leaving scattered piles of "skeletons" that convince many beachcombers that some horrible disaster has struck. Just before the female molts, the male clasps her tightly, face-to-face, and over a period of several days helps her off with her old skin. Now that her exterior has softened, he can fertilize her, and she produces over a million eggs (Ricketts, *et al.*, 1985; Figure 47). In winter, egg-carrying females move into shallow waters, where the eggs hatch into free-swimming larvae. While feeding on a variety of phyto- and zooplankton, the larvae scatter to deeper waters. After about 3 months, they begin to creep back toward the shore, and often hitch a ride with *Velella velella,* the "by the wind sailor" (Rudy and Rudy, 1983). Once in the shallows, they settle to the bottom and develop into juvenile crabs, where their life of hunting and scavenging has begun. To escape predators, the crabs burrow beneath the sand and mud, and those who end up in the estuaries often hide in beds of eelgrass and seaweeds. As they grow older they steadily move to deeper waters. In 2 or 3 years, the crabs have become adults, and settle once again into the seasonal migration between deep and shallow waters. If unmolested, a Dungeness crab lives an average of 8 years (Rudy and Rudy, 1983).

Many of the outer coast snails also live in the estuaries. On rocks, herbivorous limpets, black turban snail, and periwinkles, and the predatory dogwinkles are found. Among the scavengers on sandflats are the purple olive snail and the basket shell, who may also

Figure 47. Mating Dungeness crabs. (Megahan)

prey on live polychaete worms and other animals. The basket shell, the wide chink shell, and others often prefer to hide in the beds of eelgrass and seaweeds.

Zooplankton

Most of the zooplankton in an estuary are simply the larvae of the multitudes of estuarine and shore invertebrates, and destined not to remain in the water column longer than a few months. The permanent members, mostly copepods, come and go with the seasons. In most estuaries in the Northern Hemisphere, seasonal fluctuations in temperature, sunlight, river flow, and upwelling force seasonal changes in waterborne nutrients. The result is a shift in phytoplankton, from diatoms in winter and spring to dinoflagellates in summer and early fall. Since they feed on the phytoplankton, the zooplankton follow this rhythm closely. The genus *Acartia,* for example, switches from *A. clausi* in the spring to *A. tonsa* in the summer (Hedgpeth, 1966).

Zooplankton produce on the order of 3–4 pounds per acre per year, but this is limited by the phytoplankton productivity, which is usually low in estuaries with a high runoff and turbid waters (McLusky, 1981). Of course, zooplankton are an indispensable source of food for young fish.

Fish

As we walk along the shallow bayshore in summer, our approach sends countless small fish darting from the shallows to deeper water. If we could have followed one of these from egg to adult, we would discover that, although it spends much of its adult life in the ocean, its chances of surviving to adulthood would have been nil if not for the estuary.

For several reasons, a protected bay provides indispensable nursery grounds for dozens of fish species on the Northwest Coast (Peterson and Peterson, 1979). First, females can lay eggs in beds of eelgrass, mussels, and oysters, and other locales where waves are not likely to batter and scatter them. Second, juveniles can gorge themselves on the high productivity of estuaries. Third, predatory fish are reluctant to enter the shallows, and so the youngsters can wedge themselves in right at the water's edge to escape their enemies, though they still keep a watchful eye out for beachcombers and other terrestrial predators. The beds of mussels and eelgrass also provide a sheltered haven from predators. As a result, roughly 80–90% of the world's commercial fish species depend on estuaries at some point in the life cycle (Phillips and Thayer, 1977), which amounts to some 69% of the 3 million tons landed each year in the U.S.A. (Mann, 1982).

The vast majority of estuarine-dependent fish are predators, and among the most successful and characteristic are the flatfish, or flounders, sole, and halibut (families Bothidae, Pleuronectidae, Soleidae, and Cynoglossidae). Flatfish are the chameleons of the fish world, and live camouflaged on the muddy or gravelly bottom of estuaries and the ocean. When they first hatch they look much like the typical fish, with eyes on opposite sides of the head, and they swim upright. After a few months, however, one eye creeps around to the opposite side by the other eye, and the fish turns on its side and heads down to the bottom, where it spends the rest of its life.

A flounder forages in a wonderfully efficient manner. After settling on the bottom, it momentarily shivers to scatter sand over its back, leaving only eyes and mouth exposed. It waits in hiding until a small fish, shrimp, crab, or other epibenthos wanders near, and then springs up and devours the prey. This quick dash is so powerful that, in shallow water, it may carry the fish some 2 feet into the air.

At least 9, and perhaps as many as 15, of the 20 species of flat-fish in the North Pacific frequent estuaries, and 3 of these depend heavily on protected bays during the first year of life (Hart, 1973). These are the English sole (*Parophrys vetulus*), starry flounder (*Platichthys stellatus*), and sand sole (*Psettichthys melanostictus*). In winter, each of these moves up from deeper water to spawn, and the eggs hatch into free-swimming pelagic larvae that move steadily into the estuaries. Six months after hatching (roughly midsummer) the larvae develop into the lopsided juveniles, and spend the next year in the estuary shallows, most of the time hiding in the eelgrass beds. As they grow, they move gradually out of the estuary to deeper water, English sole no deeper than 1800 feet, and starry flounder and sand sole no deeper than about 900 feet. They mature at 2 to 4 years, and adults sometimes migrate into the warm estuarine waters to feed in the summer.

Though among the most common, these flatfish are by no means the only fish in Northwest estuaries. In order of abundance, the dominant fish in Tillamook Bay are surf smelt (*Hypomesus pretiosus*), Pacific herring (*Clupea pallasi*), shiner perch (*Cymatogaster aggregata*), English sole, staghorn sculpin (*Leptocottus armatus*), and starry flounder. In Grays Harbor, these and another two species, northern anchovy (*Engraulis mordax*) and threespine stickleback (*Gasterosteus aculeatus*) are most abundant. All spawn in shallow water, spend the juvenile period in estuaries (usually in eelgrass), and as adults tend to migrate out to sea to rest during winter and back into the estuaries to feed during spring and summer.

Their life cycles, however, contain a few individual quirks. Herring eggs are covered by an adhesive material that makes them stick to nearly anything in a sheltered bay: eelgrass, marsh plants, mussels, oysters, rocks, pilings, waterlogged sticks, beer cans, and so on (Hart, 1973). In about 10 days, the eggs hatch into larvae that feed on invertebrate eggs, copepods, and diatoms in the eelgrass beds (Hart, 1973). The juveniles feed on zooplankton (copepods, euphausiids, and various larvae of crustaceans), and the adults on larger crustaceans and small fish.

In summer and fall, spawning surf smelt swim onto gravel beaches during the high tides of evening or early morning. Females burrow tail first 2–4 inches into the gravel and lay their eggs, which hatch in about 10 days (Hart, 1973; Washington Dept. of Ecol., 1977). To survive, eggs must remain moist yet well aerated, so they are laid in the intertidal in sediments no finer than coarse sand. Despite its name, the surf smelt prefers to spawn in sheltered bays and sloughs to avoid the heavy surf. Their food is primarily zooplankton, including copepods and the larvae of fish and crustaceans.

Like all surf perch, the shiner gives birth to live young. In spring or summer, copulation occurs after a complicated mating ritual by the male (Hart, 1973). But the female holds the sperm for 5–6 months (until late fall) before allowing them to fertilize her eggs. In the following summer, she gives birth to anywhere from 5 to 20 live young. Males are mature at birth, and females after 2 years. The young feed first on zooplankton and later on mussels and algae; adults eat a variety of benthic crustaceans (Hart, 1973; Simenstad, *et al.*, 1979).

In many West Coast estuaries, the Pacific staghorn sculpin (or "mudcat") is the most abundant and widely distributed fish, and provides hours of amusement to young anglers. Adults spawn from late winter to early spring, and eggs hatch in about 10 days (Washington Dept. of Ecol., 1977). Juveniles eat a variety of small epibenthic invertebrates, while adults eat the shore crabs *Hemigrapsus nudus* and *H. oregonensis* and other larger species. Sculpins move into deeper water as they age, and often migrate out of the estuary in winter.

The most famous and sought-after fish in the Northwest cannot be considered abundant estuarine species, but nevertheless depend heavily on estuaries during two critical stages in life. The salmon are divided into five species in the Pacific: pink (*Oncorhynchus gorbuscha*), chum (*O. keta*), coho (*O. kisutch*), sockeye (*O. nerka*), and chinook (*O. tshawytscha*). In addition to these, the rainbow trout (*Salmo gairdneri*), brown trout (*Salmo trutta*), and cutthroat trout (*S. clarki*) are well known for their amazing talent of returning unerringly, after years of ocean migration, to spawn in the same tributary in which they hatched (Figures 48, 49). Columbia River salmon may spawn as far inland as the Rockies, which they reach only after traversing raging rapids and hurling themselves up waterfalls with powerful thrusts of their meaty tail. Why is this remarkable "homing" ability necessary? First, it functions to bring males and females together at the same place. Second, it prevents spawning in inhospitable places, where eggs and juveniles might not survive. The creeks used are proven favorable by the spawners' own birth and survival there (Hasler, *et al.*, 1978).

Successful November spawning for the coho salmon requires fast-flowing, well-oxygenated, gravel-bottom streams with a minimum of predators and an abundance of food, mostly plankton and small insects. After a mating dance with her breeding partner, the female turns on her side and scoops out a nest in the gravel with her tail fin. She then lays her eggs, and after the male fertilizes them, she covers them with gravel. The exhausted parents then die and their bodies drift downstream (Proctor, *et al.*, 1980).

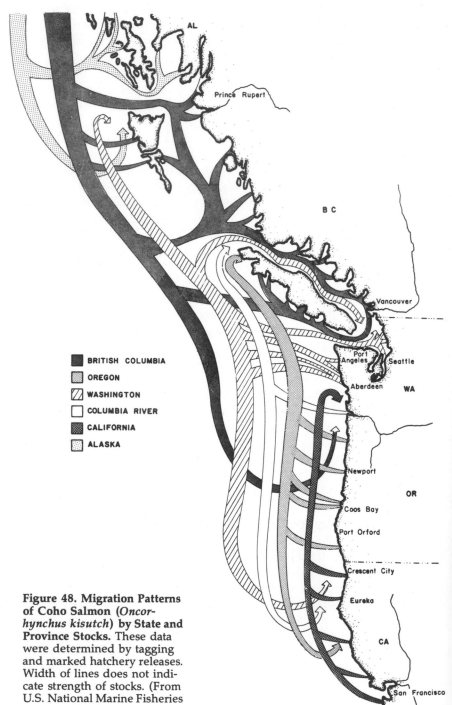

Figure 48. Migration Patterns of Coho Salmon (*Oncorhynchus kisutch*) by State and Province Stocks. These data were determined by tagging and marked hatchery releases. Width of lines does not indicate strength of stocks. (From U.S. National Marine Fisheries Service, 1976.)

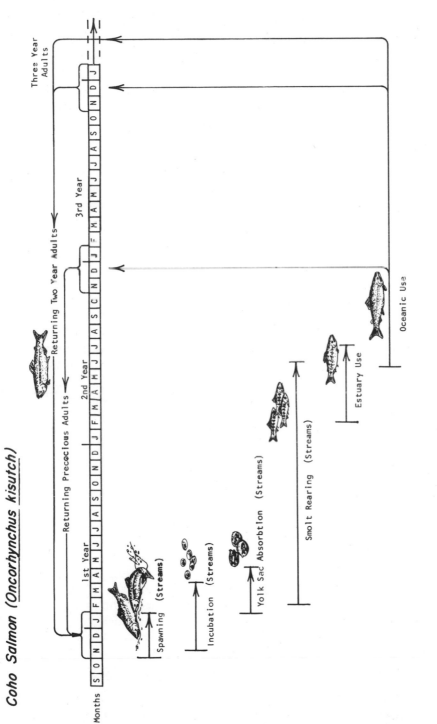

Figure 49. General Life Cycle and Migration Chart of Coho Salmon. (From Mahnken and Joyner, 1973.)

The eggs hatch 2 months later and the hatchlings remain under the gravel, protected from predators, and nourished by egg-yolk carbohydrates, proteins, vitamins, and minerals (Hasler, *et al.*, 1978). At this stage, the immobility of the young fish makes its survival dependent on a constant flow of clean, well-oxygenated water. If mud washes off a clearcut slope and buries the nest, the hatchlings suffocate. By the time the fish reach the age of four months, they have used up the yolk and must emerge from the nest to feed on plankton and small insects (Hasler, *et al.*, 1978). At this stage, the young coho are called "fry." The fry usually stake out feeding territories, thereby sharing the food supply equally. With their heads pointed upstream, they wait underneath an overhanging bank for prey to drift within reach, and occasionally fight intruders who stray into the territory. The fry themselves are preyed on by larger fish and birds. Only about 1 egg of every 30 survives and develops through the end of the fry stage. Body coloration, dark green with vertical black bars, blends in with the stream backgrounds but does little to conceal most fry from predators.

At about 18 months (in April or May) the surviving fry have grown to about 4 inches long and are ready to leave the stream of their birth. The new stage, the "smolt" stage, is triggered by the increasing day length in spring, which activates pituitary hormones (Hasler, *et al.*, 1978). These in turn alter the fishes' internal body functions, body shape, and behavior to prepare them for the long trip downstream to the ocean. The black stripes disappear and the smolt becomes silver. To ease their transition from fresh to salt water, the fish develop mechanisms to regulate the amounts of salts in their body fluids. They give up their territorial behavior, congregate in schools of thousands and begin to drift passively downstream (Hasler, *et al.*, 1978).

While in the ocean, the salmon feed on enough squid, plankton, and small fish to gain 11 pounds and 30 inches in length (Hasler, *et al.*, 1978). After 1.5 years, the fish undergo another series of radical physical changes to prepare them for their migration home. Instead of eating, they rely solely on accumulated body fats. When they reach the mouth of their home river, they usually stay offshore for a month while their water/salt regulatory systems readapt to freshwater. Increasing sex-hormone activity ripens the gonads, and as the coho pass through the estuary and head upstream, their sides flush bright red and their upper jaws become hooked. This distinctive new appearance enables spawning adults to recognize each other.

But how do the salmon find their way home after 3 years' and hundreds of miles of travel? The answer is that local differences in soil and vegetation of each drainage system give it a unique chemical composition and thus a distinct and persistent odor to the fish

(Hasler, et al., 1978). While blind fish can usually find their way home to spawn, fish with experimentally plugged nostrils cannot (Hasler, et al., 1978). Laboratory and hatchery fish can be made to recognize synthetic chemicals; after the fish are released, they return to whatever stream is scented with these chemicals. Before the juveniles begin their downstream migration, they must "memorize" the odor of their natal stream, and seek it out on their return trip.

A salmon is most vulnerable to the estuary's buffetings during its visit as a juvenile, when it must stay 1–4 months as it adjusts to seawater. A young salmon usually hugs the estuary shore to keep clear of predators during the day, and at night moves into deeper waters to forage under cover of darkness. As we walk along the shore, we can distinguish chinook from pink and chum salmon by their response to our approach: chinooks scatter, while pinks and chums school (Washington Dept. of Ecol., 1977). They usually prefer a gently sloping shore with mixed gravel and sand, but sometimes also hide in crevices on steeply sloped rocky shores. While in the estuary, the young salmon feed on small fish such as sand lance (Ammodytes hexapterus), eulachon (Thaleichthys pacificus), herring, rockfish, terrestrial insects, and a variety of crustaceans, including crab and barnacle larvae.

On its return trip the spawning adult uses the estuary as little more than a migration corridor, but some researchers have suggested that heavy pollution in some bays during salmon runs may mask the odor of the home stream, causing confusion and reduced spawning success (Hasler, et al. 1978).

To summarize, estuarine fish as a group follow some simple patterns. Especially when young, the vast majority avoid predators by hiding in the shallows or in eelgrass, seaweeds, rocks, and woody debris. Because of the greater plant productivity, abundance and diversity peak in summer when as many as 70 species may be present (Pinto, et al., 1972). While the adults prey on a variety of fish and crustaceans, most pass through a larval stage that feeds almost entirely on plankton. Hence the fish depend ultimately on the production of both phytoplankton and detritus.

Birds

Estuaries provide ideal feeding grounds for multitudes of often large and conspicuous birds. The abundant invertebrates, fish, eelgrass, and salt marsh plants provide a rich source of food, and the wide expanses of open ground and water offer few hiding places from approaching predators. Unlike the fish, who forage mainly in the deep channels, the birds feed in the intertidal and shallow subtidal; only a few specialized species can penetrate the depths. Since birds are not only abundant but also warm-blooded and have a high metabolic rate, they consume great quantities of food and exact a heavy toll on the mudflat invertebrates.

Estuarine birds fall into several categories according to their foraging strategy: the waders, the shallow-probing and surface-searching shorebirds, the deep-probing shorebirds, the aerial searchers, the floaters and divers, and the raptors (or birds of prey).

WADERS

These long-legged birds wade in the bay shallows year-around in search of fish. The largest and most impressive, the great blue heron (*Ardea herodias*), impersonates a stick as it stands frozen in the shallows. When a fish swims near, the heron inches its long neck downward almost imperceptibly, until its head is within about a foot of the fish, then suddenly jabs the prey with its sharp beak. Herons on the Fraser River delta near Vancouver, B.C. consume staghorn sculpin and starry flounder 67% of the time, but also shiner perch, penpoint gunnel, and shrimp (Simenstad, *et al.*, 1979). Other prey include frogs, salamanders, insects, and small mammals. This species nests in colonies in tall trees usually near water.

The smaller, more reclusive green heron (*Butorides striatus*) uses a more active technique, stepping briskly through the shallows or along the flat at water's edge, and making a quick strike as soon as it gets within reach of its prey.

The greater and lesser yellowlegs (*Tringa melanoleuca* and *T. flavipes*) are considered waders and not shorebirds because they feed primarily on fish, though also on crustaceans, insects, and their larvae. Yellowlegs nest in the muskegs and tundra of Alaska and Canada, and only show up along the West Coast during their spring and fall migrations. They usually migrate at night.

The remaining waders are the great white and snowy egrets (*Casmerodius albus* and *Egretta thula*), as a rule seldom seen in Northwest estuaries.

SHALLOW-PROBING AND SURFACE-SEARCHING SHOREBIRDS

The most diverse grouping of estuarine birds, the shorebirds, are those species that evolved to exploit the vast multitudes of infauna and epifauna of the estuaries and outer beaches (Figure 50). These small birds scamper over large mudflats by the thousands, pecking and jabbing constantly in the sand. The shorebirds fall into two foraging groups each composed mostly of sandpipers: those with short bills and those with long bills.

The short-billed shorebirds feed on whatever is abundant on or slightly beneath the ground surface. Presumably to avoid competition, each species has evolved its own specialty. Plovers and the smaller sandpipers feed mainly by sight, and therefore depend

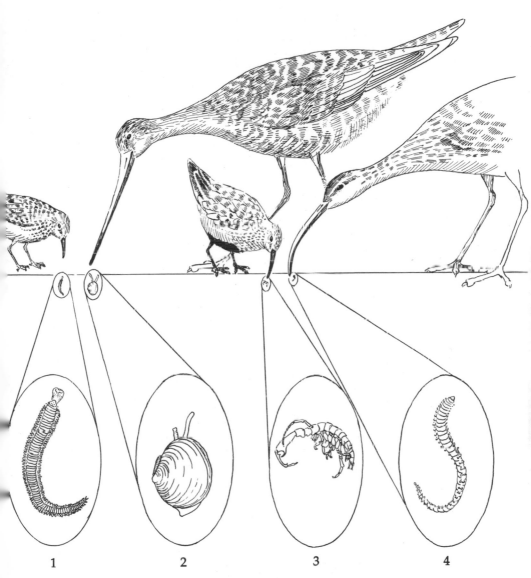

Figure 50. Shorebirds and prey. 1 Western sandpiper and *Eteone*. **2** Marbled godwit and *Macoma.* **3** Dunlin and *Corophium*. **4** Whimbrel and polychaete annelid. (Megahan)

heavily on the surface fauna, mostly insects and amphipods. Most of the others have highly enervated, sensitive bills and can feed by touch on polychaete worms and other animals beneath the sediment surface (Peterson and Peterson, 1979).

Black and ruddy turnstones (*Arenaria melanocephala* and *A. interpres*) feed on any rocks, pilings, and oyster beds surrounded by soft sediments. The mysterious Virginia and sora rails (*Rallus limicola* and *Porzana carolina*) hide in the salt marshes and venture out onto the mudflats only at low tide. The oystercatcher (*Haematopus bachmani*) is a heavy duty shorebird adapted to eat heavily shelled invertebrates, primarily mussels, limpets, barnacles, and chitons. If a mussel is firmly attached and feeding while underwater, the oyster-catcher jabs its bill between the slightly open shell valves, stabs the meat, and tears it out. If the mussels are attached loosely, the bird rips them from the rock, and with its strong, thick beak hammers the shell until it breaks. The bird then grips the meat inside and shakes it loose from the shell (McLusky, 1981).

Far and away the most abundant shorebirds in Grays Harbor are western sandpiper (*Calidris mauri*), dunlin (*Calidris alpina*), long-and short-billed dowitchers (*Limnodromus scolopaceus* and *L. griseus*), and knot (*Calidrus canutus*) (Herman and Bulger, 1981). Western sandpiper feeds primarily on polychaete annelids (24%, including *Streblospio benedicti* and *Eteone longa*); nematodes (13%); amphipods (9%, *Euhaustorius washingtonicus*); adult and larval insects (7%); and tanaids (2%) (U.S. Army Corps of Engineers, 1977). When high tides force them off the flats, they eat seeds of salt marsh plants sand spurry (*Spergularia marina*), seaside arrowgrass, and tufted hair grass. Dunlin feed primarily on the small infaunal crustaceans *Corophium* and *Anisogammarus confervicolous*. Although the dowitchers have long bills, they nevertheless rarely probe the full 3–4 inches, and usually take shallowly burrowed prey. One long-billed dowitcher in Grays Harbor had fed on *Corophium* and polychaetes, as well as the deep-lying clams *Macoma inconspicua* and *Mya arenaria*.

Most shorebirds breed in the Canadian tundra and over-winter on southern coasts, only passing through our beaches during the spring and fall migrations. While the fall migration spans several months, the spring lasts only 1–2 months. This is perhaps because the more abundant prey and lower tides of spring allow the birds to refuel more quickly and efficiently. The species that find the Oregon and Washington coasts mild enough for overwintering are the Virginia rail, oystercatcher, black-bellied plover (*Pluvialis squatarola*), snowy plover (*Charadrius alexandrinus*), killdeer (*C. vociferus*), spotted sandpiper (*Actitus macularia*), common snipe (*Gallinago gallinago*), surfbird (*Aphriza virgata*), black turnstone, rock sandpiper (*Calidris ptilocnemis*), dunlin, sanderling, least sandpiper (*Calidris minutilla*), and western sandpiper (Robbins, *et al.*, 1983).

Of over 195 square miles of sheltered coastal tideflats, just one small cove, a single square mile in size, sustains by far the most awe-some and spectacular congregation of spring-migrant shorebirds. This is Bowerman Basin, just west of Hoquiam in Grays Harbor (Herman and Bulger, 1981). At the peak of migration (April 23–24), an overwhelming 400,000 shorebirds sweep into Bowerman, which is roughly half the entire population of Grays Harbor. Grays Harbor itself hosts more spring shorebirds than any other estuary on the Pacific Coast south of Alaska, largely because of its strategic position as the northernmost large bay, where the birds must congregate in preparation for their long, barren trip to the northern breeding grounds. The 1000 miles between Alaska and Grays Harbor offer only a few small resting spots.

DEEP-PROBING SHOREBIRDS

The most common long-billed shorebirds on Northwest estuaries are the marbled godwit (*Limosa fedoa*), whimbrel (*Numenius phaeopus*), willet (*Catoptrophorus semipalmatus*), and long-billed curlew (*Numenius americanus*). Predictably, these usually take deeper, larger prey (Figure 51), since they feed more effectively when wading in shallow water than the short-billed species. They also tend to forage lower in the intertidal, dining primarily on the abundant ghost shrimp and blue mud shrimp, and less often on clams, lugworms, and other polychaetes (Recher, 1966; Washington Dept. of Ecol., 1977).

The willet is unusual because it often gives up probing with its long bill, and instead aggressively robs other birds of their food, mostly marbled godwits, sanderlings, and other small shorebirds. Its diet accordingly resembles that of the shallow probers (Peterson and Peterson, 1979).

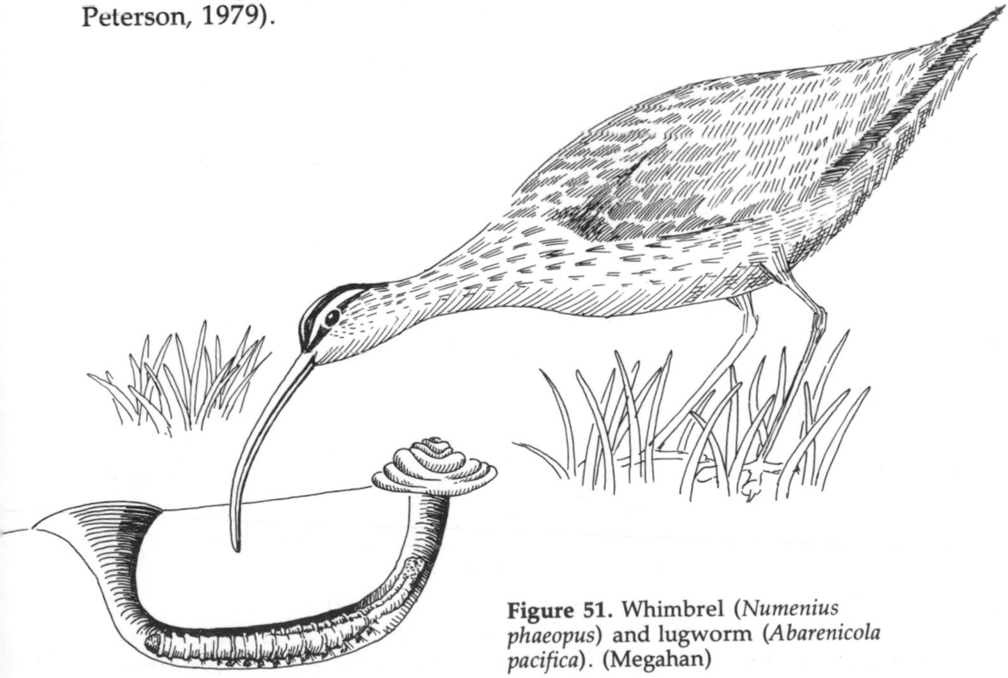

Figure 51. Whimbrel (*Numenius phaeopus*) and lugworm (*Abarenicola pacifica*). (Megahan)

AERIAL SEARCHERS

These birds, consisting mostly of gulls, terns, kingfishers, and brown pelicans, feed on fish they spot on the wing. The terns, pelicans, and most gulls also feed in the open ocean, using strategies outlined in Chapter 2.

Aside from the terns, kingfishers are the only small birds in the world that career headlong from air into water. The only Northwest species, the belted kingfisher (*Ceryle alcyon*), may dive from a perch, or it may hover in mid-air until it sights a fish and then takes a sudden dive. While rarely abundant at any one place, the kingfisher survives singly or in pairs along nearly any body of water, on the coast or inland. In estuaries they probably feed primarily on the shiner perch and staghorn sculpin, though they have also been seen eating crabs and other marine animals.

Kingfishers nest in tunnels dug with bill and feet into steep, sandy riverbanks or beach-facing bluffs. Those living near estuaries must of course dig their nests above the highest tides, which usually means nesting upstream from their feeding areas (Green, 1968).

The best feeding waters for aerial searchers have two attributes. First, they are shallow enough to force most fish near the surface. Second, they lie sheltered from any wind or waves that may ruffle the surface and obscure the view. Of course both these virtues obtain in most estuaries.

FLOATERS AND DIVERS

These birds paddle along on the water surface and either dive underwater for food, or stay on the surface tipping down and stretching their necks underwater. The vast majority are ducks that nest along tundra and only move into the Northwest when the lakes freeze in fall and winter.

On the Pacific Coast, 31 species of ducks, geese, and swans (collectively "waterfowl") migrate along a corridor known as the "Pacific Flyway," which extends from the shore to some 700 miles inland (U.S. Fish and Wildlife Service, 1979). The Pacific Flyway is actually an arbitrary collection of several smaller corridors, each of which connects a different series of lakes and marshes, and originates in a different nesting region. One such corridor is the shoreline itself, which would be next to worthless as a migration route without the estuaries, primarily San Francisco, Humboldt, Coos, Tillamook, Columbia, Willapa, and Grays.

Taking all species together, the coastal wetlands of Washington and Oregon (including Puget Sound) support about 4% of the Pacific Flyway's total waterfowl population in midwinter (U.S. Fish and Wildlife Service, 1979). This percentage is higher, however, for more northerly bay-loving species such as brant (*Branta bernicla,*

11%); canvasback (*Aythya valisineria,* 14%); scaups (*Aythya affinis* and *A. marila,* 18%); American widgeon (*Anas americana,* 18%); scoters (*Melanitta* spp., 67%); bufflehead (*Bucephala albeola,* 64%); goldeneyes (*B. clangula* and *B. islandica,* 58%); and mergansers (*Mergus merganser* and *M. serrator,* 18%) (U.S. Fish and Wildlife Service, 1979). Moreover, many birds wintering to the south stop along the coast on their way farther south. Aside from this, coastal wetlands are indispensable during extremes in temperature. When inland marshes freeze over or dry up, swarms of inland waterfowl often descend on the estuaries and dune lakes (U.S. Fish and Wildlife Service, 1979).

Thanks to Puget Sound and two large coastal estuaries, Washington supports about seven times as many wintering waterfowl as Oregon (350,000 as compared to 50,000 in an average winter) (U.S. Fish and Wildlife Service, 1979). Southern Oregon, however, has the honor of feeding and sheltering about 30 endangered Aleutian Canada geese (*Branta canadensis leucopareia*) on their way to wintering grounds in Northern California, where they join another thousand migrating in directly from the ocean.

Floaters and divers fall into three feeding groups: the fish eaters, benthic invertebrate eaters, and herbivores. Loons, grebes, cormorants, and mergansers make up the fish-eating group. The first three are nonwaterfowl who separately evolved the ability to float and dive, and though they often fish in shallow waters, they can dive much deeper than the waterfowl. Mergansers (red-breasted and common) have long and narrow bills with serrated edges adapted for gripping slippery fish. When several feed together, they sometimes coordinate their efforts and drive a school of fish into the shallows (Bellrose, 1976).

The benthic invertebrate eaters include the scaups (lesser and greater), scoters (surf, white-winged, and black), bufflehead, goldeneyes (common and Barrow's), oldsquaw (*Clangula hyemalis*), and to a lesser extent, the ruddy duck (*Oxyura jamaicensis*) and redhead (*Aythya americana*). All dive for food, the phenomenal oldsquaw as deep as 240 feet (Bellrose, 1976). The last two, however, usually plunge no deeper than about 10 feet, and often just dabble at the surface on marsh plants (Bellrose, 1976).

Clams dominate the diet of the deeper divers. In Humboldt Bay, a variety of clams make up about 50% of the scaup food (Yocum and Keller, 1961). Lesser scaups eat about three times as much plant material as greater, mostly eelgrass (Yocum and Keller, 1961). Surf and black scoters feed about equally on clams and mussels, while the white-winged scoter strongly prefers clams (Bellrose, 1976). Crustaceans and molluscs make up 80–90% of the estuarine diet of buffleheads. Barrow's goldeneye prefers molluscs (mussels and snails), while the common goldeneye and oldsquaw choose crustaceans.

Although the ruddy duck and redhead also feed on the benthos, their shallow dives commit them to a primarily vegetarian diet, mostly roots and seeds of marsh plants. Widgeon grass comprises about 70% of the food taken by ruddy ducks in Humboldt Bay (Yocum and Keller, 1961).

The remaining waterfowl are nondiving herbivores who occasionally eat benthic invertebrates and insects along with the plant seeds and roots. Most prefer freshwater and are not often seen in estuaries, including the mallard, gadwall (*Anas strepera*), northern shoveler (*Anas clypeata*), green-winged teal (*Anas crecca*), blue-winged teal (*Anas discors*), cinnamon teal (*Anas cyanoptera*), wood duck (*Aix sponsa*), and ring-necked duck (*Aythya collaris*). I will deal with these in Chapter 5. Nevertheless, some of the commonest waterfowl in our estuaries are herbivores, such as the Canada goose, American widgeon, pintail, canvasback, and brant.

For all these, the most important plant food in the estuary is eelgrass, which almost singlehandedly nourishes wintering brant, widgeon, and Canada geese. A brant or Canada goose eats about a square yard of eelgrass every day. These two species together consume nearly a fifth of the eelgrass standing crop in Izembek Lagoon in Alaska (McRoy, 1966). Eelgrass makes up 80% of the diet of brant and widgeon, and these two species are abundant enough to account for respectively 20% and 47% of the wintering waterfowl in Humboldt Bay (Yocum and Keller, 1961).

RAPTORS

An estuary's abundant fish and shorebirds are the main attractions for some 13 species of predatory hawks, eagles, osprey, and falcons, and about 9 owls. Most feed opportunistically on whatever small animals they can find and catch, and often range far from the coast and its estuaries.

The most common, the northern harrier (*Circus cyaneus*) glides low over the salt marshes in search of mice, voles, and other small animals, holding its wings slightly above the horizontal and often tilting from side to side. Like the kingfisher and other raptors, it often hovers in midair as it searches below for prey.

The osprey (*Pandion haliaetus*) soars or hovers up to 60 yards above the water, and when it spots a fish near the surface, plummets spectacularly to seize the prey with its talons. Osprey usually feed in the sheltered shallows of lakes and estuaries, where fish stay closer to the surface, and the smooth surface sharpens visibility. The adult builds its nest with a variety of sticks, stems, and softer lining material, usually on cliffs or in trees but also on the ground or even on abandoned buildings. The dune lakes and marshes between Florence and Coos Bay provide by far the best nesting habitat on the Northwest Coast outside Puget Sound, supporting about 20 osprey nests (Proctor, *et al.*, 1980). A few nests are also found near the Rogue and Humboldt estuaries.

When our biggest and most awesome raptor, the bald eagle (*Haliaeetus leucocephalus*) floats lazily over an estuary like a giant pterodactyl, it sends the gulls to the sky in a squawking, flapping panic. Though it can and does take live animals of many kinds, the eagle normally scavenges on dead or injured fish and birds, and the gulls take wing only to demonstrate their ability to flee, so any cripples left on the beach face a pair of crushing talons. Bald eagles also raid seabird colonies, taking guillemots, puffins, and cormorants, and seize benthic invertebrates such as crabs, sea urchins, and abalone (Simenstad, *et al.*, 1979). Their most commonly eaten estuarine fish are probably sculpin, herring, and spawned-out salmon.

Like brown pelicans, peregrine falcons, and many other top carnivores, bald eagles have been decimated by pesticides. Over the years DDT and DDE have accumulated in their tissues, and the disastrous results include nervous aggressive behavior (including egg eating), premature death, and the laying of eggs with embryos injured or missing and with shells too thin to support the weight of incubating adults (Welty and Baptista, 1988). Eagle populations plummeted in the 1960s and 1970s, and only recently have begun a slow rise as a result of the U.S. DDT ban in 1972. Nevertheless, the bald eagle is threatened in Washington and Oregon, and endangered in California under the federal Endangered Species Act.

Bald eagles mate for life, and build enormous nests out of sticks placed usually at the trunk and near the top of a large living tree such as Douglas fir or Sitka spruce. Probably the largest recorded bald eagle nest measured 9 feet across and 18 feet deep (near St. Petersburg, Florida) (Welty and Baptista, 1988). Eagles almost always build the nest within about 200 feet of the ocean, and remodel and reuse the same nest year after year (Washington Dept. of Ecol., 1977). Far and away the greatest number of eagle nests on the Pacific Coast lie along the shore of Alaska and British Columbia, and none are recorded south of Coos Bay, Oregon (Proctor, *et al.*, 1980). Researchers recently counted 250–300 nests in Western Washington, of which about half were on the San Juan Islands and in the northern section of the Olympic Peninsula (Washington Dept. of Ecol., 1977). During a typical year, eagles use only about half these nests (Washington Dept. of Ecol., 1977).

Another raptor nearly destroyed by DDT, the peregrine falcon (*Falco peregrinus*) is endangered nationwide. Ominously, it has never recovered from the pesticide and continues to dwindle in numbers throughout its range. The species includes three races, each of which nests in steep rocky cliffs in a different region of the United States. *Falco peregrinus anatum* nests in the continental interior west of the Rocky Mountains; *tundrius* in arctic tundra from Alaska to Greenland; and *pealei* along the coast from the Olympics to the Aleutians (Herman and Bulger, 1981; U.S. Fish and Wildlife Service, 1980).

All three races feed almost entirely on birds captured dramatically in mid-air, and travel to the larger estuaries primarily to feed on the abundant migrating shorebirds. Over a million shorebirds crowd into Grays Harbor in spring, followed by hungry peregrines who chase and kill western sandpipers, dunlin, dowitchers, and other species (Herman and Bulger, 1981). The presence of adult peregrine pairs at Grays Harbor in late April is intriguing because the races *pealei* and *anatum* are incubating and raising young far from the estuary this time of year. This leaves *tundrius,* but until recently we had no firm records of *tundrius* west of Wisconsin. Since this race nests somewhat later, in late May, it may have enough time to swing by Grays Harbor during the shorebird peak, on its way from South and Central America to its arctic breeding grounds.

EELGRASS AS AN ANIMAL HABITAT

Of course this colorful array of consumers is not found scattered randomly across an estuary. As noted, fishes and mobile epibenthos tend to avoid open spaces and cluster in structurally complex areas of an estuary, where they find shelter, concealment, and often an abundance of food; their predators usually follow. One such area is a bed of eelgrass, which deserves special attention for at least two reasons. First, the eelgrass community probably contains more species than any other habitat in the estuary, and is nearly self-sufficient, with its own producers, consumers, and decomposers (Phillips and Thayer, 1977) (Figure 52-table). Second, eelgrass is one of over 40 species of seagrasses spread over estuaries and seacoasts worldwide, and represents one of the most common coastal ecosystems (Phillips and Thayer, 1977). The same general categories of organisms interact in the same manner not only in the surfgrass beds of the outer coast, but in nearly all seagrass meadows from Alaska to Chile, from Oregon to the Mediterranean.

The categories include animals living on the leaves and stems, those crawling or gliding over the sediment surface, those burrowed beneath it, those swimming among the plants, and the birds and mammals, who migrate in and out with the tides and seasons (Phillips and Thayer, 1977; Proctor, *et al.*, 1980; Phillips, 1984; Figure 53).

Figure 52. Quantitative Relationships of Eelgrass System. Data are weights, given in tons. (From ACOE, 1976, after Phillips, 1974.)

	Willapa Low*	Willapa High**	% of total
Eelgrass	205,230	1,207,234	78%
Herbivorous Animals	8,551	50,302	3.3
Starfish	214	1,258	0.082
Small Fish	86	503	0.033
Plankton	599	3,521	0.23
Herring, etc.	60	352	0.023
Cod	52	302	0.020
Flatfish	43	252	0.016
Larger Predatory Crustaceans, Gastropods, etc.	430	25,151	1.6
Ducks, Brant, Geese	42,757	251,509	16

*If 17 grams/square foot organic matter produced annually.
**If 100 grams/square foot organic matter produced annually.

The leaf/stem fauna feed mainly on the algae attached to the grass leaves, but also on detritus and small animals. The leaf algae include single-celled diatoms as well as macroscopic algae visible to the naked eye as thin strands or sheets. As mentioned earlier, these may produce as much as the eelgrass itself. Many of the leaf/stem fauna depend so heavily on the grass that they survive only rarely elsewhere, mostly in seaweed meadows. The animals of the leaves and stems can be further divided into several groups.

(1) Those living in and on the algal coating comprise more species than any other grouping in the eelgrass beds. Because most are microscopic little is known of them; they apparently include a variety of herbivores, detritivores, bacteria, carnivorous protozoans, free-living nematodes, and some small polychaetes and crustaceans.

(2) Attached firmly to the leaf surface are predatory anemones, bryozoans, and jellyfish, who feed on small crustaceans, larval fish, and detritus. Sometimes barnacles, a variety of eggs (from herring, the channeled basket snail, and others), and young scallops and clams are also attached to the leaf.

(3) Snails, limpets, worms, starfish, and sea urchins glide slowly over the leaves, while small crustaceans cling and walk about on hooked appendages. Large and especially conspicuous are the various shrimps such as the grass shrimp. The skeleton shrimp and isopods of the genus *Idothea* have legs specially adapted for gripping the eelgrass blades. Though large, these animals constitute only a minor proportion of the animal biomass.

(4) Finally, several tube-dwelling polychaetes and amphipods live attached to the stems and roots, and feed mainly on detritus.

The second category comprises a variety of animals that glide or crawl over the bottom, including flatfish, crabs, shrimp, amphipods, sea slugs, snails, brittle stars, sea urchins, ribbon worms, polychaete worms, flatworms, nematodes, and rotifers. Among these, the Dungeness crab, English sole, and starry flounder are commercially valuable.

Animals of the third category, or infauna, usually account for the greatest faunal biomass of the eelgrass beds. In the muddy sediments, countless worms writhe about the eelgrass roots with clams, brittle stars, and crustaceans such as the ghost shrimp and the blue mud shrimp. Most filter-feed or deposit-feed on fine particles of eelgrass detritus. Since the grass slows currents, the sediments beneath it are finer and organically richer than in bare areas, and sustain denser populations of deposit-feeders. Among the more common clams, the gaper, softshell and cockles are much sought after by fish, the Dungeness crab, and of course humans.

The fourth category, the animals swimming among the leaves and stems, includes fish, shrimp (genus *Pandalus*), and crabs (genus *Pugettia, Cancer,* and *Pagurus*). Although they sometimes feed on detritus, most prefer to prey on the abundant detritivores of the eelgrass beds. Young fish depend heavily on eelgrass as a nursery area. Adults, moreover, also prefer to hunt and hide in eelgrass. In Tillamook Bay, more species of adult fish are found in eelgrass than in any other habitat. This amounts to 28 species, or 74% of all species in the bay. After an exhausting pursuit of prey or a sprint through waves and fast currents, many of these can rest their tired bodies on the eelgrass stems and leaves. Commercial fishermen take many animals in this category, including broken-back shrimp (*Heptacarpus*), coon-stripe shrimp (*Pandalus*), Dungeness crab, Pacific herring, English sole, striped seaperch (*Embiotoca lateralis*) and salmon.

The final category, the birds and mammals, feed primarily on the eelgrass itself. I have already dealt with the birds, including the herbivorous waterfowl and the great blue heron, who often stalks fish in the beds. Among the mammals, the river otter, raccoon, and others forage in the beds during low tides at night. Black-tailed deer occasionally wander far out over the mudflats at low tide, where they either feed on eelgrass and algae or take salt from the seawater. Harbor seals often chase schools of food fish (Pacific herring, northern anchovy, sculpin, and others) into the eelgrass beds.

Weighing each component of the eelgrass beds separately, we find that, of the total biomass, eelgrass itself accounts for about 78%, followed by the waterfowl (16%), the larger detritus-eating invertebrates, the herbivorous invertebrates, the carnivorous invertebrates, and the fishes (Proctor, *et al.*, 1980). The detritus-feeders predominate among the inverebrates largely because

Figure 53. An idealized eelgrass community. (Megahan)

eelgrass detritus often outweighs the live eelgrass itself. Since detritus and algae are more nutritious than the live eelgrass, the eelgrass-eating waterfowl and invertebrates may depend more heavily on the abundant algae growing on the leaf blades than on the grass itself.

In any case, live and dead eelgrass and its epiphytes are the most abundant and easily available nourishment in the beds, and feed most of the inhabitants either directly or indirectly. As new leaves and stems sprout up in the spring and summer, the meadows become lusher, and sustain denser populations of herbivores and microscopic leaf-inhabiting plants and animals. As the grass dies down above-ground in the fall and winter, its detritus proliferates and feeds a rising population of detritivores, suspension-feeders, and minute flagellates. Several species of the larger invertebrates breed in the fall and winter because the adults and their larvae feed on the temporarily-abundant flagellates. Clearly, the links in the food chain bind the eelgrass inhabitants tightly together.

Dredging is the main killer of eelgrass, and threatens some of the meadows in Grays Harbor and other estuaries. We may naturally wonder whether any of these animals would survive without the grass and its generous food and shelter. Conveniently, nature did an experiment when an epidemic destroyed 90–99% of all eelgrass along the north Atlantic in 1930–33. The resulting shifts in animal populations clearly indicate which species depend most heavily on the grass.

Among the waterfowl of the U.S., the brant population dropped 80% in the 1930s presumably due to starvation. However, the Atlantic brant feed more exclusively on eelgrass than the Pacific brant, who also enjoy surfgrass, salicornia, and a variety of green algae in the Ulvaceae family. So when eelgrass became scarce in Tomales Bay, California in 1940, the brant survived by feeding on the outer coast, where their diet was 51% surfgrass and only 47% eelgrass (Hedgpeth and Obreski, 1981).

Of the roughly 55 species of larger eelgrass-associated invertebrates in a lagoon in Massachusetts, only 36 survived after the grass disappeared in the 1930s (Proctor, et al., 1980). Among the losers were some burrowing polychaete worms, the edible mussel, the bay scallop and other clams, and several snails, arthropods, and bryozoans living on the leaves and stems. The survivors found alternative shelter in seaweed meadows. The clams disappeared most likely because they depend on eelgrass as a safe attachment site for their young, who remain until they grow large enough to settle into the mud and sand.

Surprisingly, the eelgrass losses left the fish populations largely unharmed, probably because of their mobility and the abundance of seaweeds, woody debris, and shallows in estuaries and the outer coast.

To summarize, eelgrass meadows are probably the most important submerged habitat in an estuary, supporting a greater diversity and abundance of animals and algae than that of most neighboring areas. The most heavily dependent animals are the sessile species, some of whom are specifically adapted for gripping or adhering to the leaves and stems, and others for consuming eelgrass detritus and algae. All animals benefit from the wave protection and concealment offered by the lush, leafy growth.

THE SALT MARSH AS AN ANIMAL HABITAT

Salt marshes feed and shelter animals in much the same ways as eelgrass (Figure 54). The tides, however, expose the marshes to the air at least twice every day, and force two basic differences in the faunal communities. First, aquatic species are less common and terrestrial species more common than in eelgrass. Second, more animals migrate in and out with the tides than in eelgrass beds.

Though mostly gone in the winter, insects predominate among the consumers of live salt marsh plants, and include carnivores, saprovores, and parasites as well as herbivores. The herbivores include the leafhoppers (Cicadellidae and Delphacidae), aphids (Aphididae) and leaf bugs (Miridae), which suck the plant juices, and the grasshoppers and crickets (Orthopterans), which chew the tissues. These tend to congregate in the salt grass, which they apparently prefer as a food source. Leafhoppers consume roughly 7% of salt grass production each year (Hoffnagle and Olson, 1974).

Spiders predominate among the carnivores, followed by beetles, dragonflies, and others. The beetles cluster in the tufted hair grass in the high marsh, while the dragonflies seize flying insects in mid-air throughout the marsh. Most of the Hymenopterans in the marsh are wasp-like parasites of other insects and spiders, while most of the two-winged flies (Dipterans) feed on dead animal matter. The most important decomposers, however, are not insects, but the abundant bacteria and fungi on the leaves and in the sediments, and the small burrowing amphipods. Most of these also inhabit the bare mudflats.

The only conspicuous permanent residents of Northwest marshes are a community of three snails and a slug, all under a quarter-inch in length: *Assiminea californica, Almagorda newcombiana, Ovatella myosotis,* and the sea slug *Alderia modesta* (Proctor, et al., 1980). Of these, only *Ovatella myosotis* is land-adapted with air-breathing lungs; the rest breathe water. Snails are found under driftwood and in other debris, in mud, and of course on marsh plants; they avoid most tides by remaining in the higher levels of the marsh. With the rasping action of their radulas they feed on algae and detritus, which is plentiful enough to sustain some 250 to 900 snails per square yard (Proctor, *et al.*, 1980). The sea slug *Alderia modesta* forages exclusively on a certain kind of algae, *Vaucheria*, and lives only on the proliferating mats of *Vaucheria* on the marsh surface (Rudy and Rudy, 1983; Kozloff, 1983).

The marsh creeks provide a completely different habitat, usually unvegetated and submerged. Although most of the tideflat species occur here, some suspension-feeders may be less common because the slower currents raise the likelihood of silting up. The most common clams are *Cryptomya californica*, *Macoma nasuta*, *Macoma inconspicua*, and *Mya arenaria*, which usually range from 14 to 170 individuals per square yard (MacDonald, 1969).

For the most part, the marsh vertebrates are highly mobile species who migrate into the marsh in response to changes in tides, daylight, seasons, and their own life cycles, usually in search of food and cover. The staghorn sculpin, shiner perch, and other fish move in only during higher tides to feed and hide from predators. During lower tides deer mice (*Peromyscus maniculatus*) often move out into the high marsh, while wandering shrews (*Sorex vagrans*) venture as far as the immature high marsh, both in search of beetles, amphipods, and other invertebrates (Hoffnagle and Olson, 1974). After sunset raccoons dig up the clams of the tidal creeks and nearby mudflats, often leaving their baby-like footprints and shell-laden feces on the sand or on a favorite log. Muskrats (*Ondatra zibethica*) tend to prefer the less-saline waters in upstream areas of the marsh (Hoffnagle and Olson, 1974).

Most of the birds migrate in and out with the seasons. Many shorebirds stop over during spring and fall migrations and roost in the marshes when the high tides cover their usual feeding grounds, sometimes foraging on seeds of marsh plants. Wintering waterfowl also feed heavily on seeds, although eelgrass tends to sustain the greatest burden of their feeding forays. The most common salt marsh waterfowl are primarily herbivores, such as the mallard, pintail, American widgeon, green-winged teal, canvasback, and ruddy duck. These occasionally become abundant enough to attract raptors, including the red-tailed hawk, rough-legged hawk (*Buteo lagopus*), bald eagle, and peregrine falcon. Only the northern harrier, however, seems to spend most of its hunting time over the marshes, where it glides low in search of deer mice, wandering shrews, and other small mammals.

The most conspicuous songbirds are probably the common crows (*Corvus brachyrhynchos*), who efficiently clean up the marsh by

Figure 54. Idealized salt marsh community. (Megahan)

devouring any washed-up animal carcass they encounter during their waddling strolls across the flats. Other common songbirds are the marsh wren (*Cistothorus palustris*), song sparrow (*Melospiza melodia*), and swallows (family Hirundinidae). The wren and sparrow nest in the marsh, and while the swallows and sparrow move in and out in response to feeding conditions, the wren seldom strays from the tall grasses and sedges of the high marsh. The swallows migrate in during spring, when they feed on the abundant flying insects of the marsh (Hoffnagle and Olson, 1974).

The salt marsh is essentially a transition zone between the upland forest and the bare tideflats, and as such feeds and shelters animals from both habitats. Only in the salt marsh do black-tailed deer, shiner perch, and least sandpipers share a common habitat all nibbling, gulping, and probing among the same tufts of arrowgrass.

EVOLUTION IN ESTUARIES

Ever since the first glimmerings of life pulsed and squirmed in the sea, the shorelines of the world have witnessed a slow but steady parade of plants and animals from ocean to land, an inevitable evolutionary march from sea swells and breakers to rivers and mountains that continues even to the present day. A marine animal faced with the prospect of invading land has two options. It may either liberate itself entirely from its aquatic existence through the development of lungs, or it may remain submerged but abandon its ocean home for a new life in the freshwater rivers and lakes. In other words, the evolution from sea to land is not necessarily a movement from water to air, but may instead be a migration from seawater to freshwater. Of course, no organism has any choice of its own in the matter, and can only leave its offspring to the random whims of evolution.

Obviously, unless a marine animal adapts to air, it can reach a river or lake only by way of an estuary. So, before it can adapt to freshwater it must first survive the estuary. For this reason estuaries, through the ages, have been avenues of evolution, gateways to a freshwater existence; nearly all river and lake animals can count among their ancestors a primitive form that lived in estuaries (Ingle, 1953). The only certain exceptions are some insects, pulmonate molluscs, and a few mammals, who became well adapted to air long before they returned to the aquatic environment.

But survival of the estuary is by no means an easy game. Estuaries are among the most variable environments on earth, and survival in the face of the wide daily swings in salinity and temperature requires a tough adaptability rare in aquatic animals.

The most formidable challenge facing a marine animal is the low salinity of the estuary. For this the processes of osmosis and diffusion can be blamed. The blood and body fluids of most animals contain about the same total concentration of dissolved salts as seawater. As a result, a marine animal placed in a tank of freshwater, where the salts in its internal fluids flow out of its body across its semipermeable membranes, water flows in, and the animal often swells up and dies. To prevent this, an estuarine inhabitant must somehow maintain a stable internal environment, even though its external milieu surges and swings in wild and sudden oscillations. Most successful organisms do one or more of the following: (1) secrete the water as fast as it enters (usually with enlarged kidneys); (2) take up salts; (3) develop an impermeable skin; or (4) simply flee the discomfort, by swimming away (as in fish), sealing off tightly with the shell (as in mussels and oysters), retreating into a burrow, or digging deeper (as in many worms).

Animals blessed with the liberating ability to control the salt content of their own blood and body fluids are called "osmoregulators," and use a variety of interesting stratagems to maintain a stable internal environment. As a rule, osmoregulators fall into two groups. In protozoa, many coelenterates, and other small organisms (including small algae), most cells lie in direct contact with the water, and all salts and water flow directly between the cell interior and the external medium. In the larger multicellular animals (including annelid worms, molluscs, crustaceans, echinoderms, and vertebrates), the outside water only touches a small proportion of the cells, and the body fluid acts as an intermediary that buffers any changes in the environment from the blood. In many of these animals, an impermeable skin allows greater control over the internal salt concentration, and the actual uptake and extrusion of salts is accomplished by a few specialized cells on the gills, body surface, gut, or excretory organs. Luckily, most marine invertebrates (whose body fluids contain about the same total concentration of dissolved salts as seawater) already absorb and extrude ions across their cell membranes, mainly to eliminate some of the more common sea salts and replace them with rarer but more useful ones. Hence, they are already suited to an invasion of the estuaries, and only need a few small changes to survive fresher water.

The simple, one-celled protozoan illustrates a basic method of maintaining the status quo. If some varieties are placed in fresher water than they prefer, they collect the inflowing water in small contractile vacuoles. When the vacuoles are full, they disgorge the water through a small pore in the cell membrane. Similarly, flatworms have a "flame cell" which rhythmically collects and expels water. As a rule, freshwater flatworms possess large and sophisticated flame cells, estuarine flatworms smaller ones, and marine flatworms apparently none at all.

The most conspicuous osmoregulators, the fishes, have successfully invaded every conceivable kind of freshwater river, stream, lake, and pond. The most widespread and successful modern fishes, the bony fishes (infraclass Teleostei), probably evolved in freshwater after their ancestors adapted gradually to the reduction in salts (Ingle, 1953). The breakthrough from salt to fresh may have been accomplished in an enormous bay, perhaps the size of the Gulf of California, on the margin of some unknown continent a few hundred million years ago. In this scenario, the bay at first opens into the ocean, and receives full-strength seawater and a variety of marine fish. Eventually, however, earthquakes, sedimentation, or some other geologic events seal off the mouth of the bay. Cut off from the ocean, the water, over several thousand years, gradually changes from saline to fresh. Unable to leave, most of the fish die out, but some evolve the means to maintain an internal salt and water balance. These survive to invade the freshwater streams, eventually evolving into the familiar bony fishes (including salmon, trout, bass, and countless others). Later, geological events open the bay once again to the ocean, allowing the bony fish to re-cross the osmotic barrier and return to the sea.

Freshwater bony fish use some predictable tricks to keep the water out and the salts in. Although the skin is impermeable, the gills and mouth constantly take in water. Large, well-developed kidneys remove the excess water from the blood and body fluids by secreting copious dilute urine. When bony fishes returned to seawater, their problems were reversed. Since their blood contained slightly less salt than seawater, water tended to flow out of their bodies. To replace it, they swallowed the seawater and secreted the excess salts through their gills. Since they have no need to secrete voluminous urine, they have smaller, less active kidneys than their freshwater relatives (Ingle, 1953).

Several species of bony fish, notably salmon and steelhead, pass with impunity from fresh to salt as juveniles, and back to fresh again during the adult spawning run. The ease of transition results simply from the ease in alternating from one osmoregulatory system to the other. While in the rivers and streams, the salmon excretes copious dilute urine; when in the ocean, the fish gulps water, eliminates the sea salts through its gills, and produces scant concentrated urine. The fish can hardly changeover from one phase to the other instantaneously however, and usually must first wait in or near the estuary for several weeks or months as its body makes the necessary adjustments. Surprisingly, over 170 species of North American fish can wander at will among salt, fresh, and mixed waters (Ingle, 1953).

Despite the triumph of the bony fishes, the variable and often low salinities of estuaries are a major stumbling block for colonization by marine animals. Although most sea creatures can control their salt intake to a modest degree, few can maintain their blood salts at a level much different from the surrounding medium. So as they migrate into the estuary, the salinity of their blood and body fluids drops to that of the surrounding water, and if it falls to 25% or below, their cells and tissues usually cease to function and they die. Hence starfish, sea urchins, sand dollars, and many other marine animals can penetrate an estuary upstream only as far as the 25 ppt salinity level. In the summer, when the salinity is greatest, they can temporarily move far upstream, where they may remain until the winter rain torrents force them back down.

In contrast, the osmoregulators penetrate upstream beyond the 25 ppt level, usually to 18 ppt but sometimes all the way to pure freshwater. Wide variations in their talents for water balance give each species its own peculiar limit of tolerance. In the marine section of an estuary, where salinity is high and stable, the most animal species are usually found. But upstream, diversity falls as the steadily fresher water floods out more and more species (Rudy and Rudy, 1983). Invertebrates who drop out below about 25 ppt salinity include the rock crab *Cancer antennarius* and the ghost shrimp. Those who survive no farther than 20 ppt include the paddleworm *Eteone lighti*, the red rock crab *Cancer productus*, and the periwinkle *Littorina scutulata*. Those who live down to about 15 ppt include the lugworm *Abarenicola pacifica*, the threadworm *Capitella capitata*, the common shrimp *Lissocrangon stylirostris*, the Dungeness crab, the hairy shore crab, and the northwest shipworm *Bankia setacea*. Those who remain down to 10 ppt include the polychaete *Lumbrineris zonata*, the paddleworm *Eteone pacifica*, the spionid worm *Polydora nuchalis*, and the blue mud shrimp. Among those who can survive in near-freshwater are the edible mussel, the mussel worm *Nereis limnicola*, and the amphipod *Corophium spinicorne* (Rudy and Rudy, 1983).

Of course these are all more-or-less marine animals who have only recently adjusted to the estuaries. At the opposite end of the spectrum are the more advanced species already specialized for a freshwater existence, but who for competition or other reasons have done an about-face to recolonize the estuaries from the other direction. Other than some of the bony fishes, however, there are few of these, probably because the water loss in moving from fresh to salt is a much more disastrous and insurmountable problem than the water gain in migrating from salt to fresh.

Among the meager collection of freshwater-derived estuarine invertebrates are the insects, many of whom feed and lay their eggs in salt marshes, and the pulmonate, or lung-breathing, molluscs. Among the latter, the bristle-bearing ear shell *Ovatella myosotis* is often the most common invertebrate near the high-tide line in salt marshes. Although it avoids immersion, this introduced snail tolerates all salinities (Rudy and Rudy, 1983).

A third category of aquatic estuarine animals comprises the few species so highly specialized that they can no longer survive in either river or ocean, but must always remain in the sheltered brackish waters of the estuary. Most are recent arrivals from the sea eliminated from freshwater by their poor osmoregulatory powers, and from salt water usually by competition or the heavy surf. Among the most common are the edible mussel, the oyster, and most of the burrowing mudflat animals. Many estuarine animals can migrate safely into wave-protected areas on the outer coast, but stop short in the heavy surf. Most of the eelgrass-inhabiting animals, for example, also conceal themselves safely in the dense beds of seaweeds and surfgrass on the outer coast. One unusual species, however, must remain in the estuary because it fails to meet the osmotic demands of either fresh- or seawater. The sacoglossan sea slug *Alderia modesta* survives only in *Salicornia* salt marshes on mats of its only food, the alga *Vaucheria*. Although its eggs can develop in seawater, the adults survive only in brackish water, preferably a 50/50 mix of fresh- and seawater (16–17 ppt) (Rudy and Rudy, 1983).

Clearly, the osmotic punishments cruelly inflicted by estuaries present a stony barrier to any potential inhabitants from the sea. Although a few species have adjusted to them and even thrive with them, the great majority avoid them at all costs. Most modern estuaries came into existence only since the last ice age some 10,000 years ago, and their youthfulness has prevented many marine species from colonizing them. It takes time for a sea animal to accumulate enough osmoregulatory adaptations to survive an estuary, and 10,000 years is only an instant of evolutionary time. As the earth enters the next ice age in the coming millenia, the estuaries will fill in and dry up, and most of the newly adapted estuarine animals will probably become extinct. As the glacial epoch once again comes to an end, however, the cycle will begin once more as the melting glaciers create a whole new assortment of estuaries, which in turn receive a new collection of pioneering marine animals. For these reasons, marine species greatly outnumber estuarine species worldwide. A few ancient estuaries, such as the brackish Caspian Sea and some of the river mouths in Southeast Asia, are unusual in that they have existed over 30 million years, long enough for a rich and colorful estuarine fauna to evolve (McLusky, 1981). But in Northwest and most other temperate estuaries, youth and immaturity are the rule.

Although none of us will see the whole evolutionary parade from beginning to end, we can see a flickering instant of it in some detail. If we look closely at the animals we net from the estuary water or sediments, we will discover that many supposed identical specimens actually differ in subtle structural ways that allow them to exploit different regions and resources of their environment. In other words, estuaries are inhabited by clusters of closely related species who only recently evolved from the same common ancestor. We know that these "geminate clusters" arose only recently in estuaries because of the close resemblances among their members. If the estuaries survived the next few ice ages these sibling species would undoubtedly continue to diverge, perhaps evolving striking dissimilarities.

One of the most common geminate clusters is a group of burrowing and swimming crustaceans similar to sand fleas, who constitute the genus *Corophium* and inhabit most estuaries worldwide. Some four species inhabit the Northwest Coast, each with a slightly different habitat preference. While *Corophium spinicorne* tolerates all salinities and sometimes even lives in freshwater, *C. brevis, C. stimsoni,* and *C. salmonis* remain in higher-salinity waters. *Corophium brevis* builds and takes shelter in its own snug sediment tube. In European estuaries, *C. volutator* tolerates low salinities, while *C. arenarium* prefers higher salinities and sandier substrates (Rudy and Rudy, 1983).

Another such group is the sand worms of the genus *Nephthys,* of which some eight species reside in the Northwest. While *N. caeca* prefers the cold water north of California, *N. caecoides* and *N. parva* remain in the warmer Calfornian bays. *Nephthys californiensis* thrives in the coarse, clean sands of the outer coast, while *N. caecoides* and *N. caeca* prefer the mixed mud and sand of the sheltered bays. Other closely related members of this genus are *N. ciliata* (only in Puget Sound), *N. cornuta cornuta, N. assignis,* and *N. punctata,* whose requirements are poorly understood (Rudy and Rudy, 1983).

Yet another close-knit family of species is the clam genus *Macoma,* whose members are found in nearly every mudflat. Many of the 30-odd species in the northeastern Pacific survive only in the coarse, clean sands of the outer coast. *Macoma calcarea, M. eliminata,* and *M. expansa,* for example, live deeper than about 10 fathoms. Some, however, have advanced into the brackish water and dirty mud of the estuaries, including *M. nasuta, M. balthica,* and *M. inquinita,* three of the Northwest Coast's most common *Macoma* species. The bent-nosed clam *M. nasuta* seems particularly well adapted to estuarine life, for it survives in fine anaerobic muds better than any of the others (Rudy and Rudy, 1983).

These are just three of many possible examples of an evolutionary scenario common to nearly all temperate estuaries. In just the last 10,000 to 20,000 years, the melting glaciers spawned a whole new collection of sheltered bays and estuaries. In order to exploit the wave protection and plentiful nutrients of this promising new environment, however, the marine animals worldwide had to evolve some subtle but profound changes in their feeding and respiration processes. Once able to survive the low and fluctuating salinities, wide extremes in temperature, and soft, oxygen-poor sediments of the otherwise very comfortable estuaries, the animals were free to diversify into the variety of habitats. The many groups of closely related, near-identical species are the result, some of whom have crossed the osmotic barrier with enough aplomb to lead the rest on their evolutionary parade toward land.

5

DUNES AND
FRESHWATER
WETLANDS

Mock on, mock on, Voltaire, Rousseau;
Mock on, mock on; 'tis all in vain!
You throw the sand against the wind,
And the wind blows it back again.

William Blake, Mock On

The prevailing westerlies and powerful winter storm winds have bestowed upon Northwest Coast the most expansive sand dune landscape in North America. Though they range from ripples to mountains, from hillocks to ridges many miles long and contribute an endless variety of graceful shapes and textures to the shore terrain, all dunes share a loose-packed consistency that makes them soft and yielding. Hence they shift and drift in dynamic flux under the chaotic hammering of waves, wind, and rain.

A dune is a hill of sand piled up by the wind. It can be bare or covered with vegetation, from sparse grasses to old growth forest. A bare dune is "active" because it is easily windblown and often rolls freely across level ground. A vegetated dune is "stabilized" because the plants hold it in place. Most dunes on the Northwest Coast are stabilized and therefore nearly unrecognizable as dunes; only the sandy soil betrays their origin. Most active dune sand lies between Florence and Coos Bay, where a beautiful sea of sand surges and swells in the ocean winds (Plate 9). Elsewhere the active dunes are small scattered pockets, many of which are shrinking rapidly from human efforts to eliminate them. Away from the central Oregon Coast, active dunes often lie on the upper reaches of sandy beaches, where storm waves break up stabilized dunes whose loose remnants blow and drift in the wind. The ecology of these smaller areas epitomizes that of the expansive Coos Bay active dunes.

Dunes are born wherever there is plenty of sand, wind, and space; space is critical on Northwest beaches. In scattered places the beach merges with flat or gently sloping land that stretches inland up to 2.5 miles before reaching the mountain front. Beach sand blows easily across such open spaces, creating the most spectacular dune landscapes. Though dunes lie scattered along the entire west coast of North America from Alaska to southern California, they are largest and most impressive along the Oregon and southern Washington coasts. Of the 310 miles of Oregon shoreline, 140 miles or 45% consist of dunes (Cooper, 1958). The Washington dunes occupy only a 60-mile stretch from the mouth of the Columbia north, and hence may be considered part of the Oregon dunes system.

Dune (and beach) sand originates from the vast reservoir of sediments heaped on the continental shelf. Over millions of years, rivers have cut their beds and swirled the finer sediments out to sea, while waves have pummeled the shoreline to sand. Sediments thickened on the sea floor, and in calmer weather the gentle breakers scoop some of them up and lay them on the beach. Here they dry and either blow inland to form dunes, or where they are blocked by cliffs, bluffs, or foothills, they simply cycle back and forth from beach to ocean. Dunes also arise, though on a smaller scale, when north- or southward ocean currents push sediments across a bay mouth, forming a sandspit, and where these currents slow down behind jetties and other obstacles, and drop their load of sand. Sand-tolerant vegetation plays a secondary but crucial role because of its ability to immobilize sand and block its movement from the beach inland.

Sand particle size and mineral composition reflect the hills and headlands whence it originated. In general, yellow-gray particles predominate; these are mostly quartz. The occasional dark specks are miscellaneous minerals such as magnetite, ilmenite, chromite, hornblendes, and pyroxene. Most grains are typically $1/8$–$1/2$ mm in diameter. Where the shoreline rocks are harder and more erosion-resistant, such as in southern Oregon, sand particles are larger, $1/2$–1 mm, and dominated by the dark minerals (Cooper, 1958).

DUNE DEVELOPMENT

Transverse and Retention Ridges

Dramatic conflict and unrest among the forces of wind, sea, vegetation, and sand during the last 20,000 years have battered and thrust the Washington, Oregon, and California dunes into their present size and shape (Figures 55, 56, Plate 10). About 20,000 years ago, ice smothered everything below 8000ft in interior British Columbia and northern Washington and in similar latitudes worldwide (McKee, 1972). The ocean lay about 300 feet below its present level, and the shoreline extended out to where the water is now that deep. As the world climate slowly warmed, the ice melted into the ocean, raising the sea level. As the sea rose, it invaded the land,

Figure 55. Sea level rise and dune advance.
(Kellerman.)

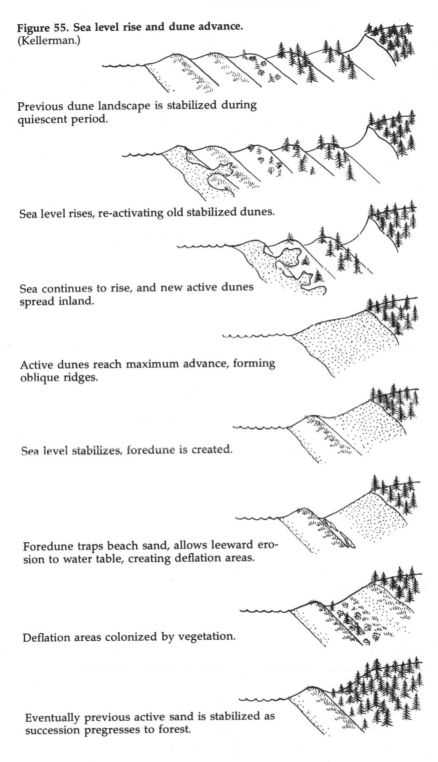

Previous dune landscape is stabilized during
quiescent period.

Sea level rises, re-activating old stabilized dunes.

Sea continues to rise, and new active dunes
spread inland.

Active dunes reach maximum advance, forming
oblique ridges.

Sea level stabilizes, foredune is created.

Foredune traps beach sand, allows leeward erosion to water table, creating deflation areas.

Deflation areas colonized by vegetation.

Eventually previous active sand is stabilized as
succession pregresses to forest.

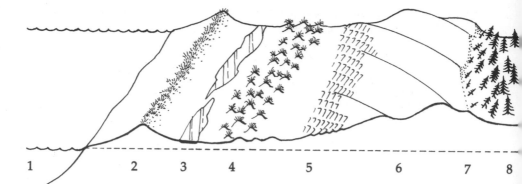

Figure 56. The Dune Landscape. 1 Ocean. **2** Foredune. **3** Deflation plain. **4** Beachgrass hummocks. **5** Transverse ridges. **6** Oblique dunes. **7** Retention ridge. **8** Forest. (Kellerman.)

bringing sediments and creating new ones as the wave front pulverized the shoreline. Waves laid the sediments on the beach, and where a flat, receptive shore lacked any vegetation, the steady, north-west summer winds blew the sand inland in ridges oriented at a right angle to the wind ("transverse ridges"). Where there was forest, the winds blew strongly until the vegetation slowed them down and they dropped their load of sand (Cooper, 1958).

Eventually a continuous ridge of sand rose just inside the forest This "retention ridge" became massive where the trees were tall. Sand grains blew from its windward slope over the top, and landed on the lee slope, and in this way the ridge moved inland about a yard per year, slowly engulfing and burying the forest, leaving masses of decaying logs in its wake (Plate 11). Initially, a sea of sand sloped gently from the beach up to the crest of the retention ridge a few hundred yards inland, which was in turn mantled with smaller trans-verse ridges. Few plants could survive on these dunes, so the sand remained bare and mobile. Winds, however, steadily snatched up the intervening sand and heaped it on the retention ridge, and the ridge grew at the expense of the intervening volume of sand. Continued wind scour eventually exposed the water table in scat-tered places, preventing further sand removal (Cooper, 1958).

Deflation Plains

These wet areas grew and merged, forming "deflation plains" (deflation is the erosion of soil by wind). The wet, stable soil of the deflation plains welcomed the invasion of plants, notably rushes and willows, and these often grew almost overnight into a forest lying between the beach and the retention ridge. The bulk of these forests prevented sand from moving from the beach to the retention ridge, and so the unreplenished ridge slowly shrank and came to a halt. Plants crept up its sides, and it soon was blanketed with forest. Meanwhile, sand blew in incessantly from the beach, encountered the forest, formed a new retention ridge, and the cycle repeated (Cooper, 1958).

In the midst of all this, the sea seems to have stopped rising temporarily, and may have actually fallen slightly. This shut off the supply of beach sand, the dunes dissipated or became forested, and the sand activity of "Episode I" came to an end. The sea then resumed its rise, and active dunes appeared once more; Episode II had begun. This time, however, much of the renewed activity began as waves eroded the old dunes and released them from the grip of the vegetation; this created some special dune forms (Cooper, 1958).

Blowouts and Parabola Dunes

As the waves beat into low bluffs of stable dunes, the wind broke through in the inevitably vulnerable spots, creating long, narrow depressions or troughs lined with loose sand. Wind currents converged on the troughs, directed by the break in the vegetation and by the trough walls in the same way that rainwater converges in a valley. Heightened windspeeds in these troughs tore away their walls, widening and lengthening them in the direction of the wind to form a long, narrow, roughly U-shaped area of active sand. Clouds of sand blew up the central trough and fell where they encountered forest. This created a long, continuous, U-shaped retention ridge along the margin of the trough (Figure 57). As before, wind scour often created deflation plains that became forested, cut off the sand supply, and stabilized the ridges to leeward.

The entire U-shaped arm of sand, trough and ridge, is called a U-dune or parabola dune, and its formation is called a "trough blowout" (Cooper, 1958). During the time of rising sea, blowouts tore through old forested dunes almost instantaneously due to the abundant supply of sand held down only weakly by vegetation. Often nothing more than a burrowing animal or human footpath, aided by sea and wind, have triggered huge blowouts. This second burst of sand activity subsided as the sea's rise briefly halted once again. But this hiatus must have been much shorter than the previous, for only about half the dunes became forested.

Thus, as the sea began its third and latest major rise, it launched an ocean of dunes that merged with those of the previous episode that were yet unforested. The active dunes existing today originated either during this Episode III or as a combination of the second and third. Their size, form, and mode of creation were the same as before: transverse ridges, retention ridges, and trough blowouts. Aerial photographs reveal that they overlie similar dunes, although forested, of the first two episodes; unity of form and process has apparently continued over thousands of years (Cooper, 1958).

About 6000 years ago the sea reached its present level, around which it has fluctuated slightly. Presently it is rising about a millimeter per year worldwide, or 4 inches the last century. This is only a tenth of the average rate during the time when most of the dunes formed: from 20,000 to 6000 years ago (Schneider and Londer, 1984). The coastal lands of the Northwest are also rising, but more slowly, and so the net observed sea level here has risen only a few millimeters the last century. The present relative stability of the ocean may herald an end to the current active dunes, as they become increasingly stabilized during the next few centuries.

Figure 57. Idealized parabola dune. (Kellerman.)

Parallel Ridges and the Foredune

Ironically, the stable sea has allowed a kind of dune formation that was previously impossible. The stabilized parallel sand ridges of the dunes flanking Grays Harbor, Willapa Bay, and the Columbia River mouth did not exist before 6000 years ago. Although parallel ridges cannot be found elsewhere on the Northwest Coast, they are common and similarly created around the mouths of large rivers worldwide (Cooper, 1958).

As the sea began its advance 20,000 years ago, the Columbia estuary, Willapa Bay, and Grays Harbor probably combined to form a single estuary on a broad, flat lowland now undersea. River sediments accumulated into sandbars, but the sea's advance created no dunes because the sand simply blew into the estuary from the sandbars. As the rising sea pushed the bars steadily landward, the three river systems separated. When the sea stabilized 6000 years ago, sediments continued to gush from the rivers, but the sea no longer submerged them. Instead, ocean currents carried them north in winter and south in summer, and they piled up along the beaches from Tillamook Head to Point Grenville. As a result, the shoreline slowly advanced westward and the sea retreated before it, about a foot per year (Cooper, 1958).

Summer waves sorted the sediment particles by weight and heaped the sand-sized ones on the upper beach, forming a ridge or "berm." High winter storm waves in turn scooped up the berm sand and carried it back into the surf where it formed winter bars. So the berm alternately appeared and vanished in summer and winter as sand cycled back and forth from water to beach. But continual sediment accumulation steadily pushed back the sea, until the winter storm waves could no longer reach the berm. This new found stability in turn made the berm habitable to the native sand grasses, which cannot withstand the wave attack (especially American dunegrass, *Elymus mollis*). These grasses not only held the berm in place, but also caught windblown sand, which accumulated and enlarged the berm. A stable, vegetated berm is called a "foredune," and usually runs unbroken along the upper beach (Cooper, 1958) (Plate 12).

Winter waves cleared sand away from near the base of the foredune, making it stand sharply perpendicular to the beach. As sediments accumulated, the summer waves built up a new berm in front of the foredune. Eventually this berm survived the storms, and became a new foredune. Now there were two ridges: a new and old foredune, running parallel to each other along the backshore (Bird, 1969). Sediment pile-up continued, a new berm formed, and the process carried on over the centuries until about 15 successive parallel ridges had formed, one every 400 years or so (Cooper, 1958) (Plate 13). Fluctuations in storm strength and sand supply created scattered irregularities and breaks in the ridges. In some places seawater was trapped between berm and foredune, forming lagoons that later became lakes as the sea receded.

Around 1969, ridge formation stopped in many places, apparently due to diminishing sand supply. On the beach at Fort Stevens, for example, sediment buildup no longer pushes back the ocean, and so storm waves regularly undercut the foredune (U.S. Soil Conservation Service, 1975).

If we travel from Highway 101 west to the beach near Cullaby Lake, Oregon, we traverse over a mile of picturesque, rolling ridges and valleys, some grassy, some forested. Some ridges are so steep and uniform they resemble railroad embankments. Generally 15–40 feet high, they reach 75 feet in places. The well-known Indian trail through mid-Gearhart, the "ridge path," lies on a former foredune about 600 years old (Rankin, 1983).

Geologic time is inconceivably immense, and this history of the dunes encompasses only the last 20,000 years. The latest rise of the dunes is just the most recent in a long series of endless cycles that extends far into the distant past. Over the last 2.5 million years, the mean ocean temperature has fluctuated repeatedly between 72 and 81°F, and the oceans have undergone four major cycles of advance and retreat (Dott and Batten, 1981). Coastal dunes very likely rose and fell in step, in the same way as during the latest advance. Dunes formed during previous interglacial periods are sometimes exposed in roadcuts and other developments, and are weathered to a distinct reddish brown.

Many sea levels of prehistoric times show clearly as wave-cut terraces in shoreline rocks. The highest lie 1500–1600 feet above present sea level on the southern Oregon Coast between Coos Bay and Cape Blanco, and were formed roughly 50,000 years ago. The spectacular dunes between Florence and Coos Bay owe their existence to a broad, near-flat terrace that allows them free and easy movement. This terrace was carved over 200,000 years ago by waves about 150 feet above the present sea level. By chance, it has warped downward in many places and become accessible to beach sand (Cooper, 1958).

THE CURRENT SCENE

Dune forms change abruptly from north to south in response to abrupt changes in sand supply and in the extent of flat lowlands merging with the beach (Cooper, 1958).

A continuous belt of parallel ridges interdigitated with scenic lakes, marshes, and swamps lies between Point Grenville, Washington, and Tillamook Head, Oregon (73 miles). This landscape owes its existence to the voluminous discharge of the Columbia River, a cubic mile or more every 9 days (Proctor, et al., 1980). Since this immense flow pours out much more sand than the offshore currents can possibly carry away, it piles up on the beach in ridges held in place by vegetation.

Of the 125 miles of rocky coast between Tillamook Head and Heceta Head, only 25% is sufficiently flat to receive dunes. A total of 14 scattered localities, eight at river or bay mouths and nearly all with large parabola dunes. By luck, headlands or hills block the northwest summer winds in almost all dune sites, leaving them open only to the southwest storm winds of winter. As a result, the parabolas point northeast (Cooper, 1958).

In only four localities does active sand remain in the parabola dunes: Nehalem Bay, Sand Lake, Nestucca Bay, and Alsea Bay. Here, the beach still merges with receptive shore. The active parabolas have marched over and buried most of the forested dunes from Episodes I and II, but their remnants have endured as unequal fingers fringing the active sand. In most areas, the advancing sea prior to 6000 years ago truncated the seaward ends of the parabolas; the Sand Lake system is most intact, while the Tillamook Bay system has nearly disappeared (Cooper, 1958).

The longest, widest, most spectacular unbroken dune landscape lies between Heceta Head and Coos Bay, the so-called "Coos Bay dune sheet." This sea of sand, unbroken through its entire 45 miles by any rock headlands and crossed by only two rivers, the Siuslaw and Umpqua, is so magnificent that Congress, by 1972 act, protected most of it for public purposes as the Oregon Dunes National Recreation Area (NRA). Its size is due to a fortunate combination of two features: a broad, flat, rock terrace that slopes inland about 3.5 miles and allows easy sand movement, and the size of the Umpqua and Siuslaw rivers, whose discharge apparently lavishes more sand to the nearshore than the ocean can remove.

The dominant active dune form on the Coos Bay dune sheet is the biggest and most awe-inspiring of all: the oblique ridges. These giants loom up to 165 feet high at the crest, stretch to 4000 feet long, and lie in parallel series about 550 feet from crest to crest. They are so named because they trend almost, but not quite, in the direction of the northwest summer winds (Cooper, 1958).

The strong southwest winter winds regularly cut across the ridge system almost at right angles, building up the ridges by scooping sand from the interridge troughs and heaping it on the ridges. The gentle, steady summer winds blow the sand lengthwise down the ridges, lengthening them. When the winds reach the inland forest, they drop their load of sand, forming a retention ridge, and the entire oblique/retention ridge dunescape moves inland as a unit and buries about a yard of forest per year (Cooper, 1958).

Oblique ridges arise in response to full exposure to winds of two widely different directions. Dunes of similar size, shape, trend, and origin are common in the Egyptian/Libyan desert, the Australian deserts, and the Algerian Sahara (Cooper, 1958). The Coos Bay ridges are unique, however, in an unfortunate way: they tend to vanish all too easily. During the summer, there are no south-west winds to heighten the ridges. Instead, the transverse ridges, formed only by the northwest summer winds, march over the oblique ridges and sometimes dissect them into hundreds of scattered pieces. Vegetation can be equally destructive. Forests in the deflation plains between the beach and the oblique ridges starve the ridges by cutting off their sand supply. Starting at their seaward ends, the ridges gradually disappear and are replaced by deflation plains, until only the retention ridge remains, which eventually freezes under cover of forest (Cooper, 1958). The ubiquitous foredune also blocks the sand supply; though it is a recent human addition to the Coos Bay dune sheet, it is devastatingly effective.

The dwindling expanses of transverse dunes and retention/oblique ridges constitute a mixture of Episodes II and III throughout most of the Coos Bay dune sheet. The blending is probably due to a continuous in-pouring of sand by the Siuslaw and Umpqua rivers despite the slight drop of sea level after Episode II.

At the extreme north and south ends of the dune sheet, just north of the Siuslaw River and just north of Coos Bay, Episode II is visibly separate from III and as a stabilized ridge backed by deflation plains. Apparently, these areas experienced a long sand shortage after Episode II, probably because more river sands have consistently moved a short distance further south than north of the mouths during summer, leaving the north and south extremities of the dune sheet in short supply. The greatest masses of sand lie just south of the Siuslaw and Umpqua rivers. Throughout the dune sheet, Episode I can be seen as a meandering, stabilized, retention ridge inland of the active dunes (Cooper, 1958).

South of Coos Bay, the dune landscape shrinks and active dunes nearly disappear. The best examples are the older stabilized dunes between Capes Arago and Blanco, centered at Bandon. Here a broad plain allowed the sand to march great distances inland (over four miles), but a continuing shortage of sand has kept them low and flat. The terminal capes have in part created the shortage, acting as barricades that block any influx of sand from neighboring areas to the north and south. This leaves the Coquille, a river with small discharge, as the primary sand supplier (Cooper, 1958).

South of Cape Blanco, dunes are scarce. The coastline is geologically older, built of harder, more erosion-resistant rocks, and hence steeper, more rugged, and nearly devoid of flat shorefronts receptive to dune sand. Most dunes are in the form of sandspits at river mouths.

In California, parabola dunes dominate. The vegetation here is thinner, though, so directs the wind less effectively, making the parabolas smaller and shorter-lived than in Oregon (Cooper, 1958).

DUNE VEGETATION

Plant Succession in the High Dunes

Though apparently tranquil, over the long run the coastal dunes are vibrant with life-and-death conflict. There is revolution after revolution, pockets of stability within larger pockets of instability themselves held within subtly moving borders. Whole populations are destroyed to make way for new ones, which exist only at the mercy of the constantly moving mountains of sand. The many different levels and intensities of change here create unparalleled opportunities to witness basic successional processes in plants and animals. Within a very small area a spectrum of colorful communities from pioneer to climax are visible.

Anyone struggling through the mountains of shifting sand in the high dunes, or along any upper sandy beach, cannot fail to appreciate the enormous power of the wind in shaping the dunes. During especially strong winds, the hurtling clouds of sand below are sufficiently thick to obscure the ground. These are the active dunes, where bare hills merge, erode, and vanish, and where only the hardiest plants and animals can survive, but plants are especially vulnerable because of their immobility. In addition to tearing winds and sand blasting, these inhabitants must endure occasional sand burial, burning salt spray, intermittent lack of water and nutrients, and shifting, salty soils. Wind and its ravages are usually strongest near the ocean.

Every active dune receives multitudes of wind-borne plant seeds that, unbelievable as it may seem, can eventually blanket it with a thick cover of vegetation, often a forest. The vegetation becomes a hard crust over the dune surface, effectively stabilizing the dune by blocking wind, binding the sand grains in extensive root systems, and building up a layer of dead, decomposing litter and humus that shields the sand from rain. Birds, mammals, insects, and other animals that could not survive on the active dune are drawn seasonally to this "stabilized" dune in search of food, cover, and nesting habitat.

But the conversion of active to stable takes several years and grades through many conspicuous stages that add color and variety to the dune landscape. Dense plant growth cools, moistens, and stills the air near the ground; dead plants fertilize, build up, and moisten the soil. The lack of humus in the young soil of the active dune makes it twice as heavy and half as moist as stable dune soils (Ranwell, 1972). The coating of sea-spray salt around sand grains and the calcium carbonate from shell fragments make young dune soil saltier and less acidic than old soil (Ranwell, 1972). Acidity rises as proliferating decomposers consume the plant litter and release carbon dioxide, and as spreading roots exude increasing amounts of acid. These changes are caused by nothing more than the cover of vegetation, and become more marked with time. The stresses of the active dunes fade and disappear as growth conditions improve for more kinds of plants, boosting diversity and productivity. The pioneers take hold at the base of the dune, nearest the water table, and only creep upwards after building a moist topsoil beneath them. Given time, they eventually reach the top. What was once a hill of loose sand is now a colorful meadow or forest, but only a few inches beneath, the active dune remains. How long the successional process takes depends on the species of plants, their rate of decay after death, and the jumble of seasonal forces that control growth and reproduction.

The lack of humus in the active dune reflects a virtually empty nutrient reservoir. So pioneer plants must rely for their vitamins and minerals on sea spray, dead sea plants and animal material at the high tide line, and rain and fogs that wash mineral salts and ammonia from the atmosphere. Most of the plant's nutrients come from the sea spray, which is rich in potassium and other salts, organic nitrogen, and micro-organisms. In North Carolina, half the spray settles on the seaward slope of a typical foredune, a third on top, and the rest to the back (Valk, 1974). Plants of the upper beach derive most of their nutrients from dead seaweed, birds, and other remains at the high tide line. This organic residue amounts to about 11–15 pounds per hundred yards of beach and after being consumed by sand fleas, birds, and bacteria, is ultimately broken down to nutrient elements, and scattered landward by the winds (Proctor, et al., 1980).

Only a dozen or so plant species are sufficiently robust to tackle the challenges offered by the active dunes. A common strategy is roots that grow deep enough to reach the water table a yard or more underground; the visible portion of the plant is often just the tip of the iceberg. To survive sand burial, a plant must also be able to grow in the darkness through several inches of sand, until it again reaches sunlight, which usually necessitates a thick taproot capable of storing large amounts of starches for emergency use. To withstand wind, sea spray, and sand blasting, an external toughness helps. Woody and coarse stems, dense hairiness, and large, long-lived seeds are typical adaptations. Since sand grains are coarse, the spaces between them are too wide to retain much water. So any plant whose roots have not yet reached the water table must somehow prevent excessive water from evaporating from the leaf-surface pores. Reduced leaf surface area, fleshy, water-storing leaves, and leaf hairiness are common.

Separate pathways of evolution have given each plant of the active dunes its own armory of defenses against the buffetings of earth, wind, and sea. Partial sand burial actually stimulates growth and branching of the unbelievably successful European beachgrass (*Ammophila arenaria*), although complete nonburial, or burial by a yard or more of sand, usually kills it (Ranwell, 1972). During drought, the leaf blades conserve water by curling, thereby closing off the leaf pores and slowing evaporation (Purer, 1942). Its supreme ability to "freeze" sand in place wherever it is planted arises from unrivaled vertical and horizontal growth of underground stems, called "rhizomes" (Ranwell, 1972). Other dune plants have rhizomes but they grow neither as fast nor in both directions. Other plant species create mounds in the active dune, notably yellow abronia and beach silver weed, but these mounds are smaller, looser, and always unstable (Wiedemann, 1966, 1984; Wiedemann, *et al.*, 1969). Hence the Forest Service and other agencies plant European beachgrass along the coast to prevent active dunes from burying roads, buildings, and other developments.

After a beachgrass plant becomes established, sand blows against its leaves and falls to the ground, accumulating at its base, eventually forming a mound. The rhizomes creep throughout the mound, sprouting stems and roots every few inches. The mound eventually becomes compact and hard, and the process continues as the mound broadens and rises, in some places up to 10 yards in height. Mounds grow, multiply, and merge, collectively creating a foredune. Unfortunately, beachgrass and the foredune have created problems. The foredune blocks sand on its way from the beach to the active dunes inland while beachgrass decimates populations of native dune biota, especially colonizing plants and several insect species (Slobodchikoff and Doyen, 1977) (Plate 14).

Chief among the native sand stabilizers are seashore bluegrass (*Poa macrantha*) and large-headed sedge (*Carex macrocephala*) (Wiedemann, 1966, 1984). Both these perennials sprout roots and stems from vigorous underground rhizomes; grow close to the ground where the air is stillest; and have large seeds that disperse easily in the wind. They grow much more thickly than beachgrass, virtually carpeting the sand in some places. The sedge owes its wind-resistance to a dense, sturdy flowering head and a clustering of leaves close to the stem base. Other sand binders are the gray beach pea (*Lathyrus littoralis*) and beach silver-top (*Glehnia leiocarpa*), both of which survive sand burial with stems that grow up through several feet of sand, disperse their offspring with large, easily wind-blown seeds, and easily reach water with deep-growing roots (Wiedemann, 1969, 1984). Beach morning glory (*Convolvulus soldanella*) quickly blankets the ground with vine-like stems that creep over the sand surface and sprout large, pinkish white flowers. This persistent plant survives burial so well that it is nearly impos-sible to weed out of gardens. Other native stabilizers are American dune grass (*Elymus mollis*), which grows most often in the foredune with beachgrass, and is very similar, but has wider, uncurled blue-green leaves; American searocket (*Cakile edentula*), with its thick, water-storing stems and leaves, and small purple flowers; the prostrate beach knotweed (*Polygonum paronychia*), protected from the wind by its woody exterior, and whose tiny flowers bloom all year; and beach pea (*Lathyrus japonicus*), with its large violet flowers and trailing stems much like common garden peas.

These plants are profoundly important in dune ecology, because they initiate the process no other plants can: the often irreversible progression from active dune to forest. They alone can colonize the dunes, and together they make up the "pioneer com-munity" on active dunes. Once established, the pioneers convert the hot, blowing sand to cooler, moister, firm ground, thereby allowing the immigration of less-hardy plants that cannot alone survive sand burial and other stresses.

The presence of these new plants defines a new community, the "dry meadow," which is most striking in June and July, when it is vivid with the deep golden and lemon-yellow hues of seaside tansy (*Tanacetum douglasii*) and hairy cat's ear (*Hypochaeris radicata*), the creamy white of pearly everlasting (*Anaphalis margaritacea*) and yarrow (*Achillea millefolium*), and the purple seashore lupine (*Lupinus littoralis*) (Wiedemann, 1969, 1984). When crushed underfoot, the leaves of seaside tansy release a pungent aroma which, to many natives, is always reminiscent of the seashore. The coast strawberry (*Fragaria chiloensis*) can hardly be seen during the summer because it grows close to the ground, usually beneath the grasses. Seacoast angelica (*Angelica hendersonii*) is a very striking plant in the carrot/parsley family growing up to a few yards tall on the bluffs with white-flowered heads to half a foot across. Of the grasses, red fescue (*Festuca rubra*) is by far the most common and conspicuous. It some-times grows so thickly that it turns the ground into a compact turf. Little-hair grass (*Aira praecox*) is a small inconspicuous annual visible only during the spring months; the aboveground portion of the plant dies before early summer.

By the time this group establishes itself, the pioneers that started the whole sequence are either gone or rare, while their seeds have been dispersed to other open sand areas to begin again the successional process. The beachgrasses, searocket, and others do well in the open sand but cannot compete well enough to survive at such close quarters with so many other species.

The net effect of the dry meadow community is once again a change in growing conditions. Since the plants are taller on average and the growth thicker, they offer more protection from the elements for other plants growing among and beneath them. Some of these newcomers are the larger shrubby species intolerant of high winds and sand deposition.

The emergence of these shrubs gradually converts the dry meadow into the "dry herb/shrub" community (Wiedemann, 1966, 1984). Sparse growths of salal (*Gaultheria shallon*), evergreen huckleberry (*Vaccinium ovatum*), bearberry (*Arctostaphylos uva-ursi*), and seedlings of coast pine (*Pinus contorta*) and Sitka spruce (*Picea sitchensis*) rise above the dry meadow herbs, slowly overshadowing them. Most of the herbs no longer survive in the darkness, but a few remain. These are European beachgrass, coast strawberry, and pearly everlasting. The abundance of western bracken fern (*Pteridium aquilinum*) peaks in this community. By this time, a near-complete soil has developed, and the ratio of bare sand to humus is about 1–20 (Wiedemann, 1966).

The shrubs grow and proliferate into a thick tangle of low, woody growth, sometimes up to 25 feet tall. The dense vegetation darkens the ground and thins the ranks of all herbs except western bracken. This is the dry shrub community, and includes in addition to them hairy manzanita (*Arctostaphylos columbiana*), western rhododendron (*Rhododendron occidentale*), and less commonly California wax-myrtle (*Myrica californica*) and western hemlock (*Tsuga heterophylla*).

Although the shrubs cannot boast as colorful and showy a floral display as some of the earlier communities, they do offer a season of good native berry picking, if a way to can be found through the often thick wall of salal. Coast pine, salal, evergreen huckleberry, western rhododendron, and other shrubs are conspicuous 5 years or so after the pioneer stage. Once they take hold and firmly establish themselves, they almost invariably trigger succession to forest in as little as 20 years (Wiedemann, 1966). The appearance of tree saplings guarantees a future forest because saplings usually grow to adults; if a tree can survive its first 5 fragile years, it is likely to survive the next 15.

The forest vegetation passes through five stages (overstory/understory): coast pine/shrub, pine-spruce/shrub, spruce/shrub, western hemlock-spruce, and hemlock/shrub (Kumler, 1963). Shrubs are mostly salal, western rhododendron, and evergreen huckleberry, all evergreen members of the heath family. Retention of leaves in the winter allows these shrubs to photosynthesize year round in the mild climate, and the thick layer of waxy cutin on the leaves conserves water, making them thoroughly adapted to the dunes. The outstanding wind resistance of coast pine enables it to invade the stable dunes first among the trees. Coast pine grows close to the ground, not usually over 3–5 yards, and exposed individuals often have dramatically contorted branches molded by the salty wind. In areas of especially high-speed southwest winds, all the branches are on the leeward side of the tree, leaving the bare trunk exposed to the wind, as though the branches had been wrenched back and held trembling in position by invisible strings to point the wind's direction.

After the pine and shrubs establish themselves, they block the passage of wind through the forest. This permits the invasion of Sitka spruce, and rarely Douglas fir (*Pseudotsuga menziesii*), whose fragile seedlings are easily wind-damaged. The tops of the faster-growing spruce trees appear above the pines when they are about 10 feet tall, and dominate thereafter (Wiedemann, 1966, 1984). Now the important characteristic of coast pine becomes its shade intolerance. By the pine-spruce/shrub stage, canopy growth is so dense that coast pine seedlings can no longer survive. So the pine fails to reproduce, leaving adults that gradually die out over the lifespan of about 200 years.

But the spruce remains. Individuals along the windswept forest borders often blow down, and those that survive become salt-burned, scrubby, and contorted, much like the coast pine. They and the shrubs nevertheless continue to shelter the interior spruces, which grow straighter and 3–5 times taller.

Sooner or later, seedlings of western hemlock appear. These also break and uproot easily in the wind, and survive only in sheltered places. Eventually, an army of western hemlock trees breaks into the spruce canopy, blocking enough remaining sunlight to kill most of the shrubs, including not only salal, huckleberry, rhododendron, and others, but also the spruce seedlings, because they tolerate much less shade than hemlock seedlings. Thus spruce reproduction wanes and spruces die out as the pines did earlier; an adult spruce lives 500–750 years (Franklin and Dyrness, 1973).

Eventually the remaining hemlocks reach a diseased and decrepit old age; scattered individuals die, making openings to the sun, whose energy again sustains a patchy shrub community.

Hemlocks reproduce easily on the shaded forest floor, and the species composition no longer changes. This is the theoretical climax state.

Strong winds in the dunes, however, prevent all but a few forests from progressing to climax. In most places howling winter southwesterlies uproot enough trees in the spruce/shrub and hemlock-spruce forests to provide space and light for spruce seedlings. Thus the spruce perpetuates itself, and postpones takeover by hemlock indefinitely. Moreover, any force hindering tree establishment can prevent or postpone succession to forest and maintain the meadow. Strong and sustained sand-laden winter winds are probably the commonest agency, and clearly operate in many foredune and other backshore areas, including nondune headlands. Others are periodic flooding, storm tides, and shifting streambeds, all of which maintain sandspits, floodplains, and other dune areas in a perpetual state of disturbance that alternates (usually seasonally) between bare sand and struggling pioneer herbs. Semiactive floodplain areas are common along Siltcoos River, Tahkenitch Creek, and Tenmile Creek in the Coos Bay dune sheet. Of course fire can convert forest to active dunes nearly overnight, and active dunes can bury neighboring forests whose dune soil is thereby reactivated. But human control has increasingly silenced such natural disasters.

Plant Succession in the Deflation Plains

Of course, local growth conditions determine where on the rolling dune landscape plants first appear, and these conditions vary from harsh to hospitable in simple, well-understood ways. As a rule, seedlings cannot stand fast in the high active dunes due to the wind erosion and lack of nutrients. This is true of transverse ridges, oblique dunes, and to a lesser extent, retention ridges. But plants can and do persevere in the wet, rich deflation plains, at the sheltered base of an active retention ridge, and along the detritus-fed strand-line. So the pattern of stabilization across the dunes is not random, but very predictable.

And much to the alarm of many conservationists, the introduction of beachgrass has accelerated the process dramatically. Since the 1900s, the lightning spread of beachgrass up and down the West Coast built up a foredune or "seawall" that now appears so thoroughly natural and fitting that many beach-goers would be shocked and angered if it ever disappeared. The foredune heightens as it intercepts beach sand that would otherwise feed the inland dunes. The result is proliferating deflation plains that have merged to form a long, thin band just east of the foredune. Most of these are now forested and guarantee a premature end to the dunes they wall off. In short, before beachgrass a major long-term climatic change was required to bring stabilization of active dunes, but now, beachgrass can do it nearly overnight. This applies only to dunes south of Tillamook Head, of course; those in the Columbia River area were stabilized by native grasses as they formed, before the wind could blow them inland, and so never boasted any large-scale activity.

Now I turn to a closer look at the stabilization process in an area where it is critically important: the Coos Bay dune sheet. Here, as elsewhere, beachgrass is firmly and perhaps permanently entrenched along the upper beach. The foredune it has built rises to 30 feet in many places and completely walls off the beach sand. The Forest Service first planted beachgrass in the Coos Bay area in 1910 to prevent sand from blowing into navigable river entrances (Cooper, 1958). Soon thereafter the foredune arose and the ground level just east of it steadily dropped as the sands there dispersed in the wind. Beachgrass cannot establish itself in the high active dunes, but it can on ground nearer the water table. Thus it soon spread eastward to the lower areas where it built up an open, hummocky landscape. Islands of green rose above the barren sands as seashore lupine, seashore bluegrass (*Poa macrantha*), beach knotweed, and other plants joined beachgrass on the hummocks. Wind erosion continued mainly in the bare areas between hummocks. The ground level in these areas dipped steadily down to the surface of the water table, which prevented any further deflation. Water-loving plants invaded, mainly rushes (*Juncus* spp.) and sedges (*Carex* spp.). Now the landscape was a mosaic of irregular wet spots interspersed with beachgrass hummocks. Shrubs and tree seedlings sprang up immediately on the wet areas, promising an imminent forest.

Currently, trees or shrubs cover about half the newly deflated areas and are bound to invade the other half soon (Pinto, *et al.*, 1972). As the forest springs up, it will completely cut off the flow of sand to the active retention ridge just inland. As sand movement slows, pioneer plants will creep up its sides, followed by forest, and sand movement will cease.

In recent decades deflation plains have expanded by 100 acres per year, and the Forest Service estimates that the active dunes, the raison d'etre for the National Recreation Area (NRA), will be gone in another century (Pinto, *et al.*, 1972). Thus, conservation groups have urged the bulldozing of paths through the foredune in strategic spots to allow entry of fresh sand, which would convert the deflation plains back into active dunes.

This pattern of stabilization varies from place to place. Where deflation is swift, the water table is bared before beachgrass has a chance to invade. So hummocks are absent and the deflated zone is flat, continuous, and more truly a plain. Flooding frequency increases from either edge of the plain towards the middle (because the middle is lower), and the plant communities respond dramatically.

The community that dominates the drier margins resembles the dry meadow, described earlier, but differs in its slightly wetter soil and hence its greater abundance of red fescue, little-hair grass, false dandelion, and coast strawberry, and its sparser cover of lupine. Water stands on the surface of this "grass" community 2–3 months of the year but drops about a yard below the surface in the summer (Wiedemann, 1966).

In slightly wetter areas the "rush-meadow" community grows, dominated by brown-headed rush (*Juncus nevadensis*), sickle-leaved rush (*Juncus falcatus*), and spring-bank clover (*Trifolium wormskjoldii*) (Wiedemann, 1966, 1984; Wiedemann, *et al.*, 1969). Other regulars are California aster (*Aster chilensis*), golden-eyed grass (*Sisyrinchium californicum*), Pacific willow-herb (*Epilobium watsonii*), centaury (*Centaurium umbellatum*), monkey flower (*Mimulus guttatus*), and several species of bentgrass (*Agrostis* spp.). Water stands on the surface 3–4 months every year and drops about a foot below the surface in summer.

In the wettest areas water stands on the surface at least half the year, and even in the summer is only a few inches beneath it. This is the domain of the slough sedge (*Carex obnupta*), which grows here in dense, spreading mats. Other plants are Pacific silver weed (*Potentilla pacifica*), creeping buttercup (*Ranunculus repens*), Hind's sedge (*Carex lenticularis* var. *limnophila*), and king's gentian (*Gentiana sceptrum*).

These communities often lie in long, thin parallel bands oriented north-south. Each band forms when the wind exposes a new crescent of bare sand each year and scatters over it a new assortment of seeds. Most seeds only germinate after the flood waters recede, usually summer or early autumn when the ground is warm and moist, and the lowest level at which any plant can survive is set by its tolerance of flooding (Ranwell, 1972). Individual preferences eventually sort the plants into the above three communities.

Forest succeeds meadows in the deflation plains in the same way as in the high dunes, and appears in all three communities. In wet areas, seedlings of coast willow (*Salix hookeriana*), wax myrtle (*Myrica californica*), coast pine, and a few spruce constitute the wet shrub community (Wiedemann, 1966, 1984; Wiedemann, *et al.*, 1969). In dry areas, evergreen huckleberry, salal, coast pine, and spruce make up the dry shrub group. Soon the pine and spruce tower above the rest, and eventually the pine disappears. The oldest foredune-initiated deflation plains have progressed only to the pine or pine-spruce stage; slightly older examples such as in the Goose Pasture, near Honeyman State Park, harbor pure stands of spruce. The spruce forest has an uncommonly dense canopy and hence sparse understory, with a lush mossy floor. Many of the earlier deflation plain herbs grow in the occasional openings. In extremely wet areas the spruce cannot survive and gives way to a pine forest, whose open canopy encourages a thick cover of slough sedge.

Of course deflation plains are not just a recent phenomenon, but have formed countless times in the dune cycles of past millenia. Ancient deflation plains that formed during the lull between episodes of dune advance, long before beachgrass, still exist in scattered places along the Oregon Coast (Cooper, 1958). The prime example is a pair of forested plains that spread over about 12 square miles between the Siuslaw River and Sutton Lake. The eastern plain arose after Episode I, and the western after Episode II. They are separated only by the forested retention ridge of Episode II. Though both have been stable for several thousand years, the forest upon them consists of 90% young coast pine about 100–150 years old (Cooper, 1958). This is the result of two fires, at about 1840 and 1870, which together burned 90% of the plains. Coast pine sprang up immediately afterwards because it reproduces after a fire better than any other dune forest tree and is also a resilient dune pioneer. Scattered remnants of the earlier burned forest of Douglas fir, Sitka spruce, and western hemlock are nowhere older than about 300 years, indicating another major fire in the 1600s (Cooper, 1958).

Another ancient deflation plain meanders irregularly for nearly 11 miles among lakes and marshes from Tenmile Creek to Coos Bay, and arose in the lull after Episode II. This also supports a dense coast pine forest, with scattered stands of pure spruce. It is bordered by active dunes, Episode II to the east and III to the west. Since the wind is pushing these slowly eastward, the plain itself is shifting in the same direction by 1–2 yards per year, as the western sands bury it and the eastern are wind-removed (Cooper, 1958).

The deflation plain environment is just the reverse of the high active dunes. While the dunes are harsh and dry, the deflation plains are wet, stable, nutrient-rich, and thoroughly hospitable. More species of plants grow more lushly here than in any other dune habitat. Ironically, the ample water actually eliminates plants of the active dunes because they are adapted to drought. So deflation plain plants are not properly "dune" plants at all, but marsh plants, not specialized for loose sandy soil. They grow in marshy areas everywhere, on or off the dunes.

One reason for the abundance of nutrients in deflation plains is the underground flow of water (Ranwell, 1972). Beneath the dunes, the groundwater seeps upwards in the air spaces among sand grains.

So in the middle of the dunes, where the sand is piled highest, the water table warps upward. Since water flows downwards, ground-water under the high dunes in the middle flows sideways and downward, carrying nutrients with it, toward the outer boundaries of the dune system. Since lakes and deflation plains lie most often at these boundaries, they receive the nutrients from the high dunes. In this subtle way, the rich get richer and the poor get poorer.

ANIMALS IN THE DUNES

Diversity

The dune environment is unique because it offers a dazzling diversity of habitats. A typical acre of dunes embraces a greater variety of plant communities and landforms than an acre of inland forest, and so accommodates a richer variety of animal inhabitants.

This is due simply to the instability of sand, whose vulnerability to the wind has created a perpetual state of disturbance, with biotic communities at all stages of succession from pioneer in the most recently active areas to near-climax in the most protected. This arrangement accommodates an entire series of animals, from the inhabitants of the pioneer meadows, such as the savannah sparrow and northern harrier, to those of the mature forests, such as the pileated woodpecker and osprey. Moreover, moving dunes routinely dam river valleys, creating lakes and ponds (Figure 58). Fringing the eastern margin of nearly every dune system from Washington to northern California is a cluster of lakes, ponds, marshes, and swamps. Among them are Sutton, Mercer, Munsel, Cleawox, Woahink, Tahkenitch, Clear, and Eel lakes of the Coos Bay dune sheet; Smith, Lytle and Town lakes in northern Oregon; Fahys, Bradley, Laurel, Crooks, New, and Floras lakes south of Cape Blanco; and myriad other ponds and marshes. Lakes are also common in the parallel dunes north of Tillamook Head, where they originated somewhat differently as lagoons fronted by sandbars (Cooper, 1958). Among them are Duck, Skating, Island, and Loomis lakes in Washington, and Coffenbury, Smith, Sunset, and Cullaby lakes in Oregon. Scattered among these are seasonal ponds, marshes, and bogs used by local farmers to cultivate cranberries. Wetlands, as already noted, can also arise in dunes as wind erosion creates deflation plains.

It is strange to think of wetlands as an inseparable, integral component of the dune environment, since we normally associate Sahara-like heat and drought with our notion of sand dunes. But it must be remembered that these are coastal dunes, situated in the

Figure 58. Small dune lake near Woahink Lake, Oregon. September, 1987.

heart of the rainy Pacific Northwest, and thus can be thoroughly wet. What is even more intriguing is that they invariably create wetlands where there were none before, thereby bestowing a tempting, swampy oasis on aquatic plants and animals. So our coastal dunes should not be though of as deserts, but as richly varied landscapes, from bare ground through meadows to forests, from dry sand hills to wet hollows, marshes, swamps, bogs, ponds, and lakes.

LAKE SUCCESSION

Probably the single most striking contribution of the dunes to the ecology of the West Coast is their creation of lakes (Plate 15). In the Northwest, mountains rise abuptly from the shoreline, leaving little level ground for lakes. If not for the dunes, perhaps over 90% of the lakes would not exist. A large dune lake contains up to 23 species of fish, and feeds or shelters over 20 ducks, geese, and swans, several shorebirds as well as loons, grebes, herons, gulls, terns, osprey, bald eagles, kingfishers, swallows, and others. Lakes and their margins are also used regularly by over six mammals and numerous amphibians (Pinto, *et al.*, 1972).

Unfortunately for these animals, however, no matter how large or deep, most lakes gradually fill in and dry out from the margins inward. Perhaps the most impressive example of ecological succession is the slow conversion of a lake into a forest. Just as estuaries fill with sediments and detritus, gradually surrendering to the slowly creeping salt marshes, lakes also undergo a slow transformation into a marsh, then swamp, and finally an upland forest, displaying a colorful series of distinct animal and plant habitats (Milne and Milne, 1971; Proctor, *et al.*, 1980).

The process begins imperceptibly with the pioneers, the microscopic, green plants drifting in the nutrient-poor water. As these die, their remains settle on the lake bottom and accumulate into a thin layer of detritus. This layer becomes food and shelter for an abundance of bacteria, which convert some of the detritus into nutrients that can be used again by the plants. Rising nutrient levels fuel the invasion of larger plants such as pondweeds. Detritus builds up even faster as these spread throughout the lake, die, and sink to the bottom. At the same time, sediments swirl constantly into the lake with river currents, and muds wash in along the margins with the rain.

Assorted animal corpses add to the rising layer of lake-bottom muck. The film of algae and diatoms on underwater surfaces feeds snails and grazing insects such as mayflies and caddisflies. The open water diatoms and algae feed zooplankton (copepods, rotifers). The insects and zooplankton feed various predatory invertebrates, which in turn feed fish, amphibians, and waterfowl. Insects begin their lives in the water, and emerge as adults in the air, on the water surface, or underwater depending on their specialty. Dragonflies and damselflies are marvelous aerial predators. Diving beetles, water boatmen, backswimmers, and giant waterbugs dive, paddle, and careen about adeptly in underwater pursuit of their mostly insect prey. Whirligig beetles (family Gyrinidae) and water striders (family Gerridae) scurry and skim over the surface and snatch up insects that emerge from, or land on, the water. Mosquitoes of course are common, but they feed only on detritus and bacteria.

As insects proliferate, they serve as food for various kinds including yellow perch (*Perca flavescens*), rainbow trout (*Salmo gairdneri*), Dolly Varden trout (*Salvelinus malma*), cutthroat trout (*Salmo clarki*), sockeye salmon (*Oncorhynchus nerka*), and whitefish (*Caulolatilus princeps*). The northern rough-skinned newt (*Taricha granulosa granulosa*); various frogs: Cascades (*Rana cascadae*), red-legged (*Rana aurora*), Pacific tree (*Hyla regilla*); and salamanders: brown (*Ambostoma gracile gracile*) and sometimes Pacific giant (*Dicamptodon ensatus*) also thrive on the abundant insects. As waters become warmer and more enriched, larger fish-eating fish settle in, such as largemouth bass (*Micropterus salmoides*), large trout, perch, and crappie (*Pomoxis nigromaculatus*).

As sediments and detritus continue to accumulate, the lake

bottom rises and lake margins become shallow. Flowering plants from wet areas in the surrounding forest or dunes take root in the shallow margins, and the lake steadily shrinks as its borders change into wetlands. Among these "emergent" plants are cattail (*Typha latifolia*), yellow pond lily (*Nuphar polysepalum*), pondweed (*Potamogeton* spp.), bulrush (*Scirpus*), rushes, and sedges. These attract various waterfowl and other birds, who feed on the marsh plants. Most surface-feeding ducks prefer to eat the starchy seeds of marsh and lake-margin plants, but also eat roots, stems, and leafy parts of the plants, and occasionally aquatic insects. The mallard (*Anas platyrhynchos*), gadwall (*Anas strepera*), pintail (*Anas acuta*), teals (*A. crecca, A. discors, A. cyanoptera*), widgeon (*Anas americana*), shoveler (*Anas clypeata*), and wood duck (*Aix sponsa*), feed by dabbling and upending at the surface and rarely diving. The exceptional shoveler usually filters out surface plankton with the lamellae of its spoon-shaped bill, much like clams, mussels, and baleen whales. Diving ducks also eat aquatic plants, but additionally feed on insects, crustaceans, molluscs, and fish in varying amounts. The fish-eaters include the double-crested cormorant (*Phalacrocorax auritus*), Caspian and Forster's tern (*Sterna caspia* and *Sterna forsteri*), osprey, herons, Bonaparte's gull (*Larus philadelphia*), loons (*Gavia* spp.), grebes (*Podiceps* spp.), kingfisher (*Ceryle alcyon*), and bald eagle, although some of these also eat aquatic insects, amphibians, crustaceans, and occasionally seeds of water plants. Bald eagles prefer dead fish, notably spawned salmon. All these birds visit estuaries, rivers, and any lakes whose margins sustain the emergent marsh plants. Among the other vertebrates, fish and amphibians are food for mink (*Mustela vison*) and river otter (*Lutra canadensis*), which take cover among the reeds; muskrat (*Ondatra zibethica*), beaver (*Castor canadensis*), and raccoon (*Procyon lotor*) are primarily vegetarians.

By this time, the lake is warm, turbid, and thick with life of all kinds. But more life means more death, and eventually, inescapably, the lake fills with heaps of mud, sand, clay, rocks, rotting leaves, stems, roots, shells, casings, skeletons, and so on, first around the margins but unremittingly towards the center.

So several decades after its birth, the lake becomes a "marsh," or treeless wetland. Gone are the fish, most waterfowl, river otters, and submerged pondweeds; in their place is the typical marsh community that first appeared around the edges of the old lake. Winter runoff may bring a few feet of standing freshwater, but this may evaporate in the summer drought.

The old emergent plants dominate the vegetation. In addition, duckweed (*Lemna* spp.), skunk cabbage (*Lysichitum americanum*), pitcher plant (*Darlingtonia californica*), sundew (*Drosera rotundifolia*), and Douglas spiraea (*Spiraea douglasii*), extend their roots into the mucky soil. Skunk cabbage attracts pollinating bees and beetles with its vaguely carrion-like odor. If the moss *Sphagnum* becomes abundant, its acid secretions decimate the decomposer community, resulting in extremely slow decomposition, poor nutrient conditions, and buildup of detritus known in this case as peat. The plant community is then called a bog, and dense populations of carnivorous plants may spread across open areas. The pitcher plant compensates for the low nitrogen by consuming marsh insects that become trapped in its tubular leaves (Plate 16). The tiny sundew snares insects in its sticky, knobbed leaf hairs. These hairs also have glands that secrete digestive enzymes, and other glands on the leaf surface absorb the juicy remains of the insect.

Lake-born marshes offer an environment for animals nearly identical to the incipient deflation plains. The habitat is somewhat different from a lake because the water is shallow and often absent in dry months. Fish cannot survive here, and mammals and waterfowl cannot depend on an unbroken body of water for surface swimming and diving. So gulls, terns, phalaropes, and certain ducks are usually absent, as well as some lake- or river-dependent mammals (Canadian river otter, nutria, Yuma bat, and muskrat). Taking their place are various owls, hawks, shorebirds, geese, the red-winged blackbird (*Agelaius phoeniceus*), long-billed marsh wren (*Cistothorus palustris*), common yellowthroat (*Geothlypis trichas*), American bittern (*Botaurus lentiginosus*), and several of the more terrestrial mammals.

Continuing accumulation of detritus displaces more water, and the ground hardens and dries in many places along the marsh margins. Several water-loving tree species appear. Red alder (*Alnus rubra*), and willows sprout, bear fruit, and proliferate into a tangle of low, woody brush. On the coast, California wax-myrtle and Labrador tea (*Ledum glandulosum*), are also common, and black cottonwood (*Populus trichocarpa*), inland. The roots of red alder support actinomycete fungi that pull nitrogen from the air and convert it to a form that plants can eventually use. The soil becomes enriched as the fungi produce more nitrogen than the alder can use, and nutritional conditions improve for other kinds of plants.

Seedlings of western redcedar appear among the shrubs, and grow steadily higher until they eventually tower above the rest. Other conifers follow suit, such as Sitka spruce, coast pine, and western hemlock, but the cedar often dominates. The marsh now has a forested appearance, and so becomes, by definition, a swamp. But since the water table is still high, most of the thick, shrubby marsh vegetation remains. Salal grows into a dense wall 6 feet high or more, and other lush-growing shrubs include rustyleaf (*Menziesia ferruginea*), Alaska huckleberry (*Vaccinium alaskaense*), evergreen huckleberry (*Vaccinium ovatum*), red huckleberry (*V. parvifolium*), willows (*Salix* spp.), and salmonberry (*Rubus spectabilis*). In the wetter areas, water-loving herbs remain, such as skunk cabbage, false-lily-of-the-valley (*Maianthemum dilatatum*), slough sedge, bulrushes, rushes, and ferns.

The unceasing pileup of detritus, however, raises the ground level ever higher above the water table. As the earth dries, plants and animals from the surrounding upland forest steadily invade and displace the swamp inhabitants, and except for some seasonal flooding, the swamp eventually merges into the surrounding forest.

The time required for succession from lake to forest varies depending on lake size, rainfall, slope and topography, runoff, soil, and other conditions, and is measured in decades or centuries. The story can be interrupted by the same disasters that created the lake in the first place. A landslide or moving dune, for example, can bury the lake or create a new one, or the lake water could simply break its barriers and drain out. Some of the best examples of lakes and marshes in all stages of succession are the two previously described ancient deflation plains on the Coos Bay dune sheet.

Clearly, the dune wetlands support a kaleidoscopic abundance of animals. The only nonmarine habitat with a greater diversity of aquatic animals is the estuary/salt marsh, visited by an extra 20 species of birds and over 70 total fishes.

TUNDRA SWAN AND OTHER WATERFOWL

Many visitors frequent the dune wetlands near Florence specifically to watch a breathtakingly beautiful waterfowl, the tundra swan *Cygnus columbianus*. Like many other waterfowl, this elegant and dignified bird breeds in Canada and Alaska and winters in wetlands along both U.S. coasts and occasionally inland (Bellrose, 1976). From November to April 50–200 of these showy, statuesque birds winter in the deflation plain marsh on the south spit of the Siuslaw River, as they have for only the last 10–12 years (Pinto, *et al.*, 1972). Dozens more overwinter along scattered lakes, marshes, and estuaries throughout the Coos Bay dune sheet. The most important wintering areas, however, are large estuaries; more than 30,000 whistling swans overwinter in the delta marshes behind the San Francisco Bay, and a few thousand at the Columbia estuary. Like most ducks and geese in the dune wetlands, whistling swans graze on the leaves, stems, tubers, and seeds of aquatic plants. They usually feed in water so shallow that they need immerse only the head and neck to reach the desired food items but they sometimes tip up like mallards.

In mid-February the swans begin the northward migration to

their nesting grounds. Like other swans, geese, and ducks, they migrate in family units, several families to a flock, and the flocks travel day and night in magnificent V's, some 3000–5000 feet above land. The birds navigate using cues in the landscape below them, usually lakes and rivers, but they may also use the sun, moon, and stars, and possibly even the earth's magnetic field (Bellrose, 1976).

By mid-May, the swans have arrived in their tundra nesting grounds. Most of the individuals that winter along our coast breed in western Alaska, along the Alaskan Peninsula, but tundra swans in general breed along the Arctic Circle from Alaska eastward across northern Canada. The nest is built usually by early June, and consists of a foot-high platform of moss, grass, and sedges along a lake margin or on a lake island. The female incubates 3–5 eggs, one of which usually fails to hatch, and generally less than half the mating pairs succeed in rearing young. Egg predators destroy the rest.

The young swans are able to fly in about a month, and migrate back south with their parents from late September to early October. By late November, the same individuals have reassembled back on the Siuslaw sandspit, but some have brought along a few new swans to continue the tradition.

Most of the lake and marsh birds have the same migratory rhythm, including the loons, grebes, and most of the ducks; about 30 species total. Others follow different regular patterns. Individuals of about 15 species never reside in the region more than about a week at a time, to rest briefly during twice yearly migrations in spring and fall. These include shorebirds for the most part, but also shearwaters, geese, jaegers, terns, and some gulls. About six marsh or lake birds nest in the region in spring and summer but migrate south in the winter; these are the teals, osprey, rail, yellowthroat, and Lincoln's sparrow. Finally, over 20 assorted species reside in the region's freshwater wetlands throughout the year.

Of course, all these species may use wetlands not created by dunes, notably estuaries, but many converge on the dunes due to the absence of freshwater lakes and marshes elsewhere.

DUNE FOREST DIVERSITY

But dunes, needless to say, are not just wetlands. They offer unusually diverse habitats in which nearly every kind of crawling, scuttling, slithering, and flying terrestrial animal can find the right kind of food and shelter.

In addition to the wetlands, the mature dune forests create more diversity than the inland mountain forests. This is because the canopy rarely closes completely due to poor soils and high winds, resulting in greater penetration of sunlight and denser understory. The combination of brush and trees of all ages make these forests the most cosmopolitan of all dune habitats. They are seasonal or year-round haven for nearly 150 terrestrial vertebrates; some 100 birds, 40 mammals, and 10 amphibians and reptiles (Pinto, *et al.*, 1972). The more than 80 songbirds are attracted primarily by the huckleberries, salmonberries, blackberries, salalberries, elderberries, and other summer shrub fruit, and by the prospect of building a nest under the protection and comfort of the thick brush. Especially common are the common crow (*Corvus brachyrhynchos*), winter wren (*Troglodytes troglodytes*), song sparrow (*Melospiza melodia*), golden- and ruby-crowned kinglets (*Regulus satrapa* and *R. calendula*), black-capped and chestnut-backed chickadees (*Parus atricapillus* and *P. rufescens*), dark-eyed junco (*Junco hyemalis*), wrentit (*Chamaea fasciata*), rufous hummingbird (*Selasphorus rufus*), varied thrush (*Ixoreus naevius*), and orange-crowned warbler (*Vermivora celata*).

The allure of the shrubs is augmented by another magnet to wildlife: the abundance of large, dead trees, or "snags." Several vertebrates require large snags for a variety of purposes: nesting, courtship display, roosting, panoramic observation of the landscape, and so on, but nesting is most important. Some 36 bird species nest in cavities in snags; some dig their own holes, others must make do with any hollow or cavity they can find. In the dune forests, the more common cavity-nesting birds are the common flicker (*Colaptes auratus*), tree swallow (*Tachycineta bicolor*), downy woodpecker (*Picoides pubescens*), screech owl (*Otus asio*), and kestrel (*Falco sparverius*). Many of the 13 birds of prey use snags as lookouts when searching for prey (due to lack of obstructing foliage); the majestic but uncommon osprey also nests in snags. Racoons, flying squirrels, (*Glaucomys sabrinus*), and some bats also use snags as dens or roost sites (see Chapter 6 for more details). Clearly, wind makes a dune forest more structurally diverse than an inland forest of the same age, and so gives it more habitats that can be used by more animal species.

However, the human-built foredune may change all this. Its interception of beach sand strangles the principal diversifying force: the large sand hills that invade and smother forests, lay nearby trees open to the wind, and dam the coastal streams. So the foredune may soon convert much of dunes from rich, colorful mosaics to drab unbroken forest suitable for a much smaller complement of wildlife.

Animals of the Active Dunes

Ironically, the active dunes themselves harbor vanishingly few animals; most vertebrates use them only for migrating between vegetated habitats. The only permanent residents are grazing insects, spiders, and ants that remain unstudied and little-known. Many are admirably suited to the dune environment, with gray-

Figure 59. The snowy plover (*Charadrius alexandrinus*). (Kellerman)

speckled camouflaging coloration or pale hairs, special water conservation systems, and adaptations for scurrying over the sand
surface or burrowing beneath it.

One well-publicized shorebird, however, actually nests in
areas of dry, open sand. The plump, sand-gray snowy plover
(*Charadrius alexandrinus*) digs a small hollow in the sand where it lays
its clutch of three buff, speckled eggs (Figure 59). Although the
species ranges from the Gulf of Mexico and Great Plains west to the
Pacific Coast, all snowy plovers share the stubborn and unwavering
instinct of laying eggs only in flat, open spaces. Inland-nesting birds
seek out the clay flats of saline and alkaline deserts (Wilson, 1980;
Wilson-Jacobs and Meslow, 1984).

Coastal snowy plovers nest in remote areas where driftwood
covers less than half the near-horizontal sand surface and vegetation less than 5%. The logs, sticks, and branches around the nest help
conceal the eggs from predators and provide raised lookouts on
which the adults can watch for skunks, coyotes, crows, ravens, gulls,
shrikes, dogs, beachcombers, and other threats. The shady gray color
of both adults and eggs camouflages them against the sand background. The absence of hills and vegetation improves the visibility
for the adult and prevents predators from hiding nearby. Nesting on

or near high dunes would also raise the risk of sand burial or the eggs' rolling off the nest.

These strict requirements have confined the snowy plover nests to just a few locales along the north coast. The spread of European beachgrass has overrun most of the nesting habitat and corralled the birds into the few places where high water periodically sweeps away the grass. This is usually on bay-backed sandspits or near stream outlets. From 10 to 25 pairs nest on the north spit of Coos Bay where the Army Corps of Engineers regularly dumps its dredged-up mud and sand. A few plovers also nest east of the foredune on the bare sandflats exposed as the deflation plains dry.

Snowy plovers have defied the beachgrass with unusually flexible breeding strategies. A male and female stay together until their eggs hatch, and then the female deserts the nest, leaving the male to raise the brood. She then mates with another male at a new location and repeats the cycle as often as time allows. Although a male usually pairs off with a second female only after his brood fledges, he apparently has a few options. He can incubate two nests simultaneously or tend chicks in one and incubate another, and he can leave the female to care for the hatchlings. Sometimes both sexes together raise the brood. In these ways the birds can produce a maximum number of broods depending on the food and space available on the nesting habitat, the number of nesting birds, and the incidence of predators, floods, and other threats.

For the population to maintain itself at a constant size, every four snowy plover breeding pairs must produce at least three young. This is because about 25% of the adults and 33% of the hatchlings die each year. Not enough nest sites in enough seasons have been studied to know if this rate is maintained; in those studied at least one egg hatches successfully in 13% to 100% of the nests, depending on the locale.

At the close of the May-June nesting season, the inland-nesting snowy plovers stream over to the coast, where the plover population swells into the thousands. Most merge into the feeding flocks of sanderlings, with whom they scamper and jab at water's edge (somewhat less adroitly), in search of flies, worms, sand fleas, beach hoppers, and other small crustaceans.

At dusk they flit into the driftwood tangles and beachgrass to the upper beach, where their ghost-gray plumage fades easily into the dry sand.

6

FORESTS

The Pine of fur [fir] species, or spruce Pine grow here
to an emence size & hight maney of them 6 & 7 feet
through and upwards of 200 feet high.

William Clark, Tuesday, Nov. 12, 1805.

DOMINANCE OF CONIFERS

The forests of the Pacific Northwest have no equal on earth. The largest and heaviest trees in the world, and most of the runners-up, grow in the lush, fog- and rain-drenched forests of the Coast Ranges. The total weight of trunk, branches, and foliage in a mature forest ranges from 330 to 790 tons per acre in Oregon Cascades and Coast Range non-redwood forests, and up to 1800 tons/acre in the coastal redwoods. Forests in the eastern U.S. and elsewhere, including the tropics, rarely accumulate more than 300 tons/acre (Waring and Franklin, 1979). Not coincidentally, the dominant trees in these forests are magnificent evergreen conifers rather than deciduous hardwoods. Twenty-five conifer species grow in the Northwest, several times the number in any other region in North America. By comparison, only 12 hardwood tree species are native to the Pacific Northwest. Moreover, both abundance and biomass of conifers in the Oregon Cascades and Coast Range are 1000 times that of the hardwoods (Harris, 1984); hardwoods dominate in nearly all other North Temperate forests.

What is the explanation for this? As early as 30 million years ago, a diverse hardwood forest occupied the lowlands of the Pacific Rim from northern California to Alaska, Siberia, and Japan, consisting of beech, elm, oak, hickory, and many other genera now common in the eastern U.S (Waring and Franklin, 1979). At this time the conifers were small, stunted, and restricted to the more stressful conditions at high elevations. By about 10 million years ago the Cascade and Coast ranges had arisen, and promoted a wetter, cooler climate on their western slopes. During the late Pliocene, some 2.5 million years ago, many of the hardwoods became extinct, and the rest gradually shrank into specialized habitats, as the conifers spread down into the lowlands. By early Pleistocene, about 1.5 million years ago, the Northwest forests had developed an overwhelming preponderance of coniferous species, and appeared more-or-less the same as today.

What happened in the late Pliocene to usher in the conifers? Apparently, this was the period when the two distinctive features of the present Northwest climate coincided for the first time: the low rainfall of summer, and the mild temperatures of winter. Why should these favor conifers?

Mild Winter Temperatures

Botanists believe that deciduous trees evolved about 100 million years ago in areas with wet soils, perhaps river bottoms or flooded meadows (Stebbins, 1974). By this theory, in these places the leaves of plants were saturated with water most of the year, most importantly in the winter when temperatures often plunged below freezing. To prevent ice from forming in the soft, vulnerable tissues of the leaves and young stems, some trees effectively "hardened" themselves by dropping their leaves well before the first frost. These were the first deciduous trees. The deciduous strategy still abounds in wet areas of the Northwest: alder, willow, maple, and ash are common in bogs, fens, and along riverbanks. Before the leaves fall, most of their metabolites, notably chlorophyll, and energy reserves are transferred back into the tree to be recycled next spring. As these substances exit and unveil the minor pigments, the leaves flush crimson and yellow. Since our forests lack the abundant deciduous trees of the eastern U.S., we have nothing to compare with the brilliant "New England autumn."

On the Northwest Coast, however, the proximity of the ocean warms the winter air enough to prevent frequent freezes. Even in the mountains subfreezing day temperatures are rare. In the subalpine zone, although snow often accumulates and persists until July, the soil usually remains unfrozen all winter. As a result, photosynthesis is possible throughout the Northwest winter, but only for those plants that retain their leaves, namely, the conifers and evergreen hardwoods. While the deciduous trees lay dormant, the conifers gain a tremendous advantage by continuing photosynthesis, from October to April accumulating 30% to over 50% of their total budget of carbohydrates (Waring, 1982).

Another aid to winter photosynthesis is the crown shape of conifers. While the bowl-shaped crowns of deciduous trees capitalize on abundant direct summer sunlight, the long, conical crowns of the conifers maximize the absorption of the oblique, reflected light common in the winter.

Finally, the needle-like shape of the leaves helps to maximize nutrient uptake during the winter. The stomates, or pores on the leaf surface, function as evaporation ducts during the process of transpiration, in which water and nutrients enter a plant. Since water molecules adhere tightly together, evaporation of water from the stomates pulls a long string of molecules from the roots, through the trunk and branches, all the way to the leaves, and out the stomates into the atmosphere; the water chain drags in dissolved nutrients as it slides into the root. The large surface area of the needle-shaped leaves allows them to dry off faster than broadleaves, thereby accelerating transpiration and nutrient uptake. Whereas conifers typically bear 15 acres of leaf surface for every acre of forest floor, deciduous hardwoods average about six acres per acre.

Summer Drought

In hot and dry climates, plants are usually faced with a dilemma. Stomates need to remain open in order to take in the carbon dioxide necessary for photosynthesis, and to allow nutrient absorption by roots during transpiration. But on the other hand, open stomates allow water loss. Moreover, the fungi and bacteria whose waste products provide the soil nutrients are active only when moist; thus soil becomes impoverished during dry periods. In the Northwest, 90% of the precipitation falls from late fall to early spring, during the so-called dormant season; in Oregon, the ground is so dry in July and August that decomposition of the litter on the forest floor is too low to be detected. This contrasts with nearly all other temperate forest climates, in which rain falls evenly throughout the year and decomposition rates stay relatively constant (Waring and Franklin, 1979). As a result, the summer drought in the Northwest leads to a loss of photosynthesis in both hardwoods and conifers, but for several reasons conifers fare much better.

First, the large size of the conifers allows them to store more water in the sapwood of the stem (trunk). Roughly half of a Douglas fir's (*Pseudotsuga menziesii*) daily water requirement is met by water absorbed by the roots the night before and stored in the stem and branches. A single 270-foot Douglas fir may contain 4 tons of water, and an entire stand some 100 tons of water per acre (Waring and Franklin, 1979).

Second, the enormous surface area of the needle-shaped conifer leaves tends to increase their water uptake. As upwelling-induced summer fogs move inland, the water vapor condenses on the foliage and drips to the ground. Summer fog drip can increase the annual precipitation along the coast by as much as 20%.

Third, a variety of adaptations allow conifers to conserve and recycle nutrients much more efficiently than deciduous trees. While deciduous trees drop all their leaves, conifers lose only 15–20% of their foliage each winter, and as a result suffer a smaller annual nutrient loss and require a smaller uptake. Moreover, conifers seem to be able to recycle more nutrients from dying leaves still on the tree than hardwoods. The nitrogen salvaged in this way satisfies about half the nitrogen needs of a typical 100-year-old Douglas fir, but only a third the needs of an average hardwood tree. Interestingly, for unknown reasons conifers contain less nutrients per unit weight than hardwoods; foliage of a 450-year-old Douglas fir contains only 0.8% nitrogen (by dry weight), about half that of most hardwoods, and the wood of most conifers contains less calcium than hardwoods (Waring and Franklin, 1979). Perhaps for these reasons, conifers require 30–50 pounds of nitrogen per acre per year, while hardwoods need about 70. The small conifer leaves conserve nutrients in two ways. Since their large cumulative surface area allows them to dissipate heat faster, the internal tissues stay cooler; as a result respiration is slower and nutrient demand less. The abundant surface area also filters out minerals from the air, which leach to the ground during the next rainstorm (Waring, 1982). Significantly, those hardwoods that compete successfully with the conifers are often those capable of extracting their nitrogen from the atmosphere rather than the impoverished summer soil. Red alder (*Alnus rubra*) and snowbrush (*Ceanothus velutinus*), for example, fix about 45–180 lbs/acre of nitrogen annually, often germinating in the ashes left by a fire (Waring, 1982).

OLD GROWTH

For thousands of years before the first pioneer settlements of the Northwest, forest blanketed the landscape from the Cascades to the ocean. Over 70% of this area, some 75% of the biomass, lay unscathed by humans, fires, landslides, windstorms, or other forces for at least 200 years, and is called "old growth." Its great age endows old growth with several unique features, not only huge trees living and dead, but also a highly conservative system of nutrient recycling and energy flow. Since it dominated the landscape probably since the early Pleistocene, it can reasonaby be assumed that it directly influenced the evolution of many animal species, and as a result of this, some have grown so thoroughly adapted to old growth that their survival is seriously threatened in younger forests. Over 40 vertebrate species in the Northwest appear old growth dependent, and an additional 78 are common in both old growth and other habitats. But old growth and its inhabitants are swiftly vanishing. Current harvest rates could annihilate all unprotected old growth in western Oregon by about 2020 (Franklin, *et al.*, 1981); what remains will be that of National and State Parks, Wilderness, Research Natural Areas, and so on, or about 5% of the landscape. The largest expanses of coastal old growth in the Northwest lie within the Olympic and Redwood national parks; in Oregon, a few state parks (e.g., Ecola, Oswald West, and Cape Lookout) and federal Wilderness areas (e.g., Cummins Creek and Drift Creek) protect a modicum of older coastal forest. Perhaps the oldest forest on the Northwest Coast is the western redcedar stand on Long Island in Willapa Bay; this may have remained unburned for over 2000 years. To understand why the evolutionary fate of many plants and animals hinges on the preservation of old growth, it is necessary to first understand how old growth differs from younger forests.

Forest Succession and Old Growth Development

In the past, an old growth forest eventually succumbed to rare disasters such as forest fires, landslides, windstorms, and insect epidemics. In its place a "natural young growth" forest slowly emerged after a preliminary succession of herb and shrub communities. Nowadays human disturbances predominate (highways, development complexes, clearcutting), and their more-or-less permanent nature bodes ill for both old growth and natural young growth. Clearcutting usually involves removal of woody debris, slash burning, spraying of herbicides and insecticides, replanting of the desired species of tree seedlings, and periodic thinning. So the forests that emerge on a clearcut site are not natural, but "managed" and generally poorer in habitats, nutrients, and biotic diversity than natural young growth (Franklin, *et al.*, 1981). Nevertheless both types of young forest are interesting because of the dynamic changes ongoing in function, structure, and composition as they progress (usually theoretically) to old growth (Figure 60).

FUNCTION

As succession advances from grassland to shrub to young forest, several trends in forest function (i.e., in energy and nutrient flow) can be hypothesized. First, as the plants grow, they of course gain weight, and thereby raise the biomass of the site. Nutrient uptake from the soil must be initially high to support the increase in biomass. Since photosynthesis occurs only in the leaves and green stems, the slow rise in foliage biomass mirrors a slow rise in gross primary productivity. These both peak at about 50 years (in the young forest stage), and then level off. Meanwhile, wood biomass continues to rise with the growing branches, trunks, and roots, and levels off only after 400–600 years. So though gross productivity

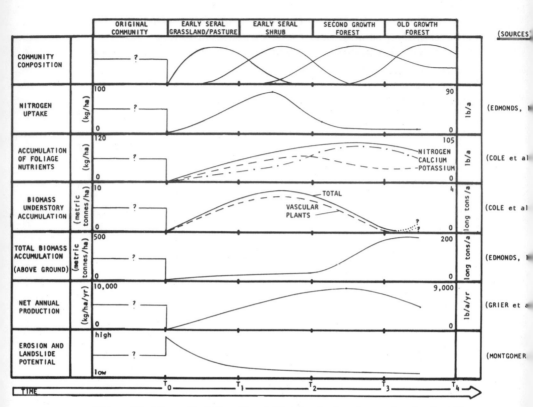

Figure 60. Theoretical Functional Trends during Succession in the Western Hemlock Forest. (From Proctor *et al.,* 1980.)

stays constant, net productivity actually drops because the trees burn more and more sugars simply to keep the enlarging trunks and branches alive (Franklin, *et al.,* 1981). Net productivity reaches a minimum when the wood biomass levels off. At the 43-year-old Thomson site on the west Cascades of Washington biomass is 200 tons/acre, giving an average wood accumulation of 4.5 tons/acre/year (Proctor, *et al.,* 1980). At the 450-year-old H.J. Andrews accumulation averages 1.9 tons/acre/year and biomass 860 tons/acre. At the Sitka spruce forest on Cascade Head, Oregon, growth and yield has been monitored periodically since 1935, when the forest was 83 years old. At 83, the rate of accumulation of canopy wood (from spruce, western hemlock, and Douglas fir) was 3.0 tons/acre/year and biomass 320 tons/acre; at age 116 the rate of accumulation was 2.2 tons/acre/year and bole biomass 400 tons/acre (Smith, *et al.,* 1984). Since total rates of wood accumulation do not include gains in foliage and branch biomass of the canopy let alone understory, they represent an absolute minimum (typically about half) of the total net productivity (Waring and Franklin, 1973).

The highest net productivity yet measured in a coniferous forest was a 26-year-old coastal hemlock stand, which produced some 16 tons/acre/year (Fujimori, 1971). By contrast, net productivity of old growth coast redwood (*Sequoia sempervirens*), on prime alluvial flats is 6.4 tons/acre/year, and on hillsides 5.7 tons/acre/year (Westman and Whittaker, 1975). Coastal productivity is generally assumed to be higher than inland because of the milder temperatures and higher rainfall.

Eventually tree mortality rises to a level where rotting logs return as much nutrients to the soil as the live roots absorb: recycling pathways dominate the nutrient economy. The mass of dead wood probably peaks after 1000 years (Franklin, *et al.*, 1980). The vanishingly rare climax forest embodies a stable balance between reproduction and death, nutrient uptake from the soil and input into the soil, energy trapped and energy used. By this definition most old growth forests are centuries removed from climax.

STRUCTURE

These functional trends underly some simple adjustments in the spatial arrangement of plants, or forest structure (Franklin and Dyrness, 1973; Figure 61). Typically, the initial grass/forb stage lasts about 5 years. By this time the shrubs stand tall enough to overtop and overshadow the herbs, which soon wither and die in the darkness. The shrubs live 20–25 years, until a legion of equal-aged,

Figure 61. Structural Trends during Forest Succession 1 Logs and snags remain from previous stand. **2** Young trees recruit with several shrub species. **3** The next generation of trees dominates after about 20 years. **4** Mortality of canopy trees allows the development of understory trees and shrubs. **5** A multi-layered canopy and many age classes of logs and snags are hallmarks of old growth. (Kellerman)

evenly spaced trees overtops them. From this time on, the dense canopy blocks the sun and nearly eliminates the understory. The canopy dominates until the forest becomes old growth. At this time, an occasional old, decadent tree blows down, opening the canopy and inviting sunlight to stream to the forest floor. A community of herbs and shrubs springs up in this pool of light, and eventually a quiltwork of patchy understory emerges in the mosaic of sunlight wrought by randomly windblown trees.

COMPOSITION

The kinds and numbers of herbs and shrubs that first appear after a disturbance in any forest zone depend on the type of disturbance, environmental conditions (especially moisture), and the kinds of seed available and hence nearby plants. On clearcut areas, the first herbs to appear are typically those present in the original forest, because seeds blow in from nearby sites. By the second year, the site will have welcomed a cloud of windborne seeds from distant weedy plants, which soon dominate. In the hemlock zone, these include woodland groundsel (*Senecio sylvaticus*), fireweed (*Epilobium angustifolium*), bull thistle (*Cirsium vulgare*), and bracken fern (*Pteridium aquilinum*) (Franklin and Dyrness, 1973). Some of the shrubs that dominate after the fifth year are residual, such as vine maple (*Acer circinatum*), trailing blackberry (*Rubus ursinus*), and Oregon grape (*Berberis nervosa*), while others are invaders (willows and snowbrush).

Moisture conditions often control this sequence. In dry areas in the hemlock forest, the commonest seral (=transient successional) shrubs are salal, Douglas fir, and sometimes bigleaf maple (Franklin and Dyrness, 1973). Medium-wet seral communities are shrubbier, with dense tangles of huckleberry (red and evergreen), salmonberry, and salal. Moist to wet areas almost always grow red alder, salmonberry, and sword fern in seral communities, and often vine maple and thick-leaved lotus. Sometimes western hemlock and western redcedar appear from the very beginning and remain through to the climax stage; other times the hemlock does not appear until after 50 to 100 years but eventually takes command because it reproduces better under shade than nearly all other Northwest forest trees. Western redcedar tolerates slightly less shade than western hemlock, and remains through the climax stage only in wet- to very wet sites. Further details of plant composition will be seen later.

Forest Function, Structure, and Habitat

The inhabitants of a forest live sheltered lives. The blanketing canopy shields them from the sun and wind, traps heat, raises humidity, conserves moisture in and above the soil, and hastens the buildup of nurturing carbon dioxide. Old growth is especially comfortable because its age grants it not just one but several layers of deep canopy. As the saying goes, the forest is a poor man's overcoat.

As a general rule, the animal species that live in a particular forest cannot be predicted from knowledge of the plant species growing there, but can usually be predicted on the basis of the relative amounts of trees, shrubs, and herbs, regardless of the species. This is because most animal species depend more narrowly on a certain kind of plant structure for safety and warmth or shade than on a plant species for food. Roosevelt elk, for example, eat several species of palatable herbs, but need thick shrubby growth for cover and bedding. A northern flying squirrel eats underground fungi of several species, as well as nuts, fruits, green vegetation, insects, and meat, but to a large extent needs large trees with previously excavated trunk holes to nest in. Even the dependence on plant structure is unconnected to plant species; an elk accepts most shrub species and a squirrel any species of large tree.

So, using the above terms, forest animal composition does not depend on plant composition so much as on plant structure. And in any ecosystem, structure and function are as interdependent and inseparable as the limbs and roots of the same tree. In old growth western hemlock forests, the most important structural elements are massive trees: alive and dead, standing and fallen, on the ground and in streams. As described below, each of these performs its own special function and provides its own unique habitat.

LARGE LIVE TREES
Function. Western redcedar reaches a maximum diameter of 21 ft. at 1200+ years, Sitka spruce 17.5 ft. at 750+ years, coast redwood 16.7 ft. at 2200 years, and Douglas fir 14.5 ft. at 1200 years; typical diameters are a little less than half these values (Franklin and Dyrness, 1973). Although the average diameter of live trees in old growth is about the same as in young growth (1.5 ft.), the largest young growth trees reach only about 2–3 feet in diameter (Franklin, et al., 1981). Typical old growth heights are 250–330 ft. for coast redwood, 230–260 ft. for Douglas fir, 230–250 ft. for Sitka spruce, and over 200 ft. for western redcedar (Franklin and Dyrness, 1973). Trees of these sizes are truly mountainous (Plate 17).

These massive live conifers are responsible for the huge biomass of Northwest forests. In the 450-year-old H.J. Andrews

Experimental Forest east of Eugene, Oregon, canopy trees amount to about 98% of the plant biomass or 300 tons/acre; 78% of this is tree boles, 12% roots, 8% branches, and 1% foliage (Proctor, *et al.*, 1980). So the trunks of the large live trees make up over three-fourths of the plant weight of a typical western hemlock old growth forest.

The conifers, large and small, also perform most of the photosynthesis and primary production. The long crowns, large leaf surface area, multilayered canopy, and 4–12 tons/acre of leaves capture the sun's energy with supreme efficiency (Franklin, *et al.*, 1981). The result is around 2–3 tons/acre of new plant material raised and unfolded each year. This is about half as much as young growth in the shrub/tree stage and salt marshes, and about the same as the phytoplankton production in the ocean upwelling zone (Proctor, *et al.*, 1980).

Production of course varies in daily and seasonal cycles. A coastal Douglas fir reaches peak photosynthesis in spring and drops to a minimum in winter; much more growth is outside the summer "growing season" than in eastern deciduous forests (Waring and Franklin, 1979). Photosynthesis is moisture-limited in summer and temperature-limited in winter; the optimum temperature is about 66°F (Proctor, *et al.*, 1980). Nitrogen is usually the limiting nutrient and comes ultimately from the air. Thus the few living things that can pull nitrogen out of the air are indispensible.

Besides nitrogen, a tree needs phosphorus, potassium, calcium, magnesium, and sulfur in large amounts, and about seven other nutrients in minute amounts, as well as of course water and carbon dioxide. The minerals it extracts from the soil water, while the carbon dioxide diffuses as a gas through the leaf stomates. We might imagine that a forest eventually exhausts its nutrient supply and deteriorates gradually into a shrubfield or grassland. Although this occasionally occurs in dunes and other stressed habitats, as a rule it is prevented in Northwest forests by a constant recycling of nutrients, from rotting wood to soil to tree and back to rotting wood. Ultimately, however, the nutrients originate from rock. As the temperature rises, for example, the gases in pockets within rocks expand, and the rock repeatedly shatters, baring more and more surface to the constantly flowing groundwater and streamwater, which erode away the minerals and wash them through the soil and into plant roots (Proctor, *et al.*, 1980).

The passage of water and nutrients from soil to roots hinges on an amazing and little-known but crucial interaction between the trees and certain kinds of fungi. Few people are aware that the underground strands of Boletus, truffles, and other fungi wrap tightly around the thin, absorbent ends of plant roots, and other kinds of fungi actually grow inside the root cells. These mycorrhizal (myco = fungus, rhizal = root) associations benefit both plant and fungus in several ways, and in many cases, neither could survive without the other.

For example, water and dissolved nutrients absorbed by the fungi pass directly into the plant roots. The extra absorbing surface offered by the fungi augments the overall water and nutrient uptake of the plant, and facilitates absorption of rare nutrients. The antibiotics manufactured by some of these fungi help to protect the plant from infections, and the tolerance of fungi to high temperatures reinforces the plant's high temperature tolerance. The fungi also produce growth regulators that can stimulate root growth, and prolong the life of the rootlets. And the benefits go both ways. The fungi, which cannot photosynthesize, absorb carbohydrates and other valuable photosynthetic products from the plant (Proctor, et al., 1980).

The benefits bestowed by mycorrhizal fungi are indispensable to many plants that die without them, usually during the first summer drought. Countless other species gain competitive advantage associating with the fungi even though they can survive in hospitable habitats alone. Perhaps because they rarely associate with mycorrhizal fungi, most ferns, rushes, and sedges grow optimally where the substrate remains moist or wet throughout the summer. A fascinating quality of this symbiosis lies in its lock-and-key quality: the fungus that works for one plant species may not work for another. For example, the mycorrhizal fungi of bearberry and Pacific madrone are compatible with Douglas fir and pine, but are incompatible with vine maple and other trees (Proctor, et al., 1980). As a result, seedlings of Douglas fir and pine survive and grow easily in woods of bearberry and madrone, but seedlings of vine maple must compete for nutrients with their bare roots, often unsuccessfully. Clearly, these lock-and-key partnerships can influence forest composition.

In addition to the plants, many small mammals benefit from mycorrhizal fungi. When their underground spores mature, the fungi give off a new odor that attracts squirrels, chipmunks, mice, voles, and shrews. About 80% of these consume fungi as a dietary staple, and many feed extensively on truffles and other mycorrhizae-forming species, whose spores pass through their bodies and scatter intact throughout the forest, thus inoculating the soil and litter to the benefit of future seedlings (Maser and Trappe, 1984). Some rodents, such as the California red-backed vole (outlined in the following), are so dependent on the fruit of the mycorrhizal fungi that they cannot survive in a recent clearcut.

The tremendous size of Northwest conifers demands that a thick flood of nutrients be fed from fungi to roots. Consequently, nearly all the nutrients in any forest are bound up in the massive trees; only minute amounts remain in the soil. So a large tree can be thought of as a storehouse for nutrients that it eventually releases after it dies. At H.J. Andrews, the 30 tons of a typical old growth conifer contain 1.8 tons of nitrogen, 3 tons calcium, 1.2 tons potassium, and 0.24 tons phosphorus. These flow constantly from log to soil to mycorrhizae to roots (Edmonds, 1982).

Plant roots themselves are quite remarkable in the way in which they can chemically enhance nutrient uptake. Since many of the dissolved nutrients are positively charged when dissolved in the soil water (potassium, calcium, magnesium), they are chemically attracted to the negatively charged soil clay particles and organic colloids. To absorb these minerals a plant must somehow pull them off the particles and into solution. The roots accomplish this by secreting acids into the soil. The acids release hydrogen ions, which stick even more tightly to the soil particles than the nutrients. So as the hydrogen ions attach, they displace the nutrients, which are then free to dissolve in the interstitial water, and eventually move into the root hairs.

This relationship between acid and minerals has played a central role in the creation of a special kind of soil in the Northwest. In general, soil acids loosen nutrients that then flush or "leach" with rainwater downward to deeper soil layers. Here they may enter plant roots or diffuse into the groundwater, which washes them out of the forest into streams and eventually to the estuaries. During normal metabolism, soil organisms give off carbon dioxide, which, when dissolved, raises soil acidity and intensifies leaching (Proctor, *et al.,* 1980). Fungi are responsible for most of the soil biomass and carbon dioxide. In the Northwest, a further major source of acid is the conifer foliage, which exudes more acids into the forest floor during decomposition than do deciduous trees. Soil acidity, coupled with the heavy Northwest rains and cool climate, have combined over thousands of years to create "podzolic" soils. Such soils display only a thin layer of organic material near the surface, and an accumulation of mineral nutrients and other materials at deeper levels due to leaching (Spurr and Barnes, 1980). Most leaching, however, occurs after disturbances such as fires, clearcuts, and landslides, when there are no live roots to capture the nutrients at the soil surface before they sink out of reach. In an old growth forest, nutrient flow is extremely conservative, as nutrient loss and input are extremely small, and the majority of minerals taken up by a plant have only recently been liberated from decomposing litter.

Large old growth trees help sustain and enhance the nitrogen economy of low to mid-elevation forests. The microclimate created by the large canopy encourages the growth of several nitrogen-fixing lichens uncommon in young growth. The most important, *Lobaria oregana*, makes up about half the biomass of all lichens and mosses growing on live trees in midelevation hemlock forests; also present are *L. pulmonaria, Pseudocyphellaria rainierensis*, and *Peltigera aphthosa* (Franklin, *et al.*, 1981). These lichens pull enough nitrogen out of the air to manufacture about 2–5 lbs/acre of nitrates per year, which enter the soil from fallen, decomposing lichens (Franklin, *et al.*, 1981). These lichens are an important source of protein (synthesized from the nitrogen) for several mammals. The northern flying squirrel feeds preferentially on lichens during the winter when seeds are scarce; both elk and deer feed heavily on lichen litter during winter starving times, especially in the Cascades (Harris, 1984).

Habitat. Typical heights of old growth conifers greatly exceed those of any other forest on earth. Since animal habitat is three-dimensional, this height translates into an immense habitat volume. As old trees die and an understory of both conifers and hardwoods develops, a tremendous diversity of crown heights results, and with it a diversity of birds and arboreal mammals. Partly because of this, western Oregon contains more bird families than any other region in North America, and unusually large numbers of resident mammal species (Harris, 1984).

Within a single old growth tree, the most important habitat is probably the long, dense, massive crown. The crown is ball-shaped in dense stands and cylindrical otherwise. A typical cylindrical crown of a 400-year-old Douglas fir 7 feet in diameter begins half to a third of the way up the trunk and runs, usually with some irregular gaps and dead branches, about 100 feet to the oft-broken top of the tree, which is usually replaced by vertically growing branches (Franklin, *et al.*, 1981). The thickest branches may exceed a foot in diameter, total branch weight is about 3 tons, and foliage weight a half-ton (Proctor, *et al.*, 1980). The crown weight of a young (3ft. diameter) Douglas fir is only about a half-ton (Snell and Anholt, 1981).

The important triumph of a large dense canopy is the milder air temperatures within it. In the west Cascades, when the canopy is wet, the air temperatures inside range from 32°F in the winter to 60°F in the summer; in dry weather the range is 14°F to 104°F. This regime ensures the survival of "epiphytes" (plants, usually lichens and mosses, growing on the trees), and insects, birds, and mammals either because of the mild microclimate or the nourishment offered by the epiphytes or both (Franklin, *et al.*, 1981).

For example, the dominant, nitrogen-fixing lichen *Lobaria oregana*, which flourishes on upper surfaces of branches and twigs, is active when wet and dormant when dry. So its vulnerable active state switches on only during mild temperatures, and it avoids lethal extremes (Franklin, *et al.*, 1981). Other epiphytes probably enjoy similar lifestyles; in any case, a total of 30–40 lbs of 100 species of mosses and lichens blanket virtually 100% of the surfaces of a typical old growth tree (Franklin, *et al.*, 1981). Many of these have yet to be found in young growth forests in comparable biomass. They do, however, grow on young trees in old growth forests probably due to the microclimate created by dense crowns on surrounding mature trees.

When the epiphytes die, those on horizontal surfaces sometimes remain and decompose on the tree, building a primitive soil called "perched soil" on top of large branches. Perched soils, nourished by decomposing needles, bits of bark, twigs, dust, and other litter trapped in the lichens and mosses, and by the dissolved mineral nutrients that the epiphytes remove from the rainwater that flows over them, feed and shelter numerous insects (Franklin, *et al.*, 1981). Fly larvae, mites, and springtails consume the fungi and bacteria that thrive on the perched soils; the most abundant arthropods, the predaceous spiders, devour the flies. Most of the 1500 canopy insect species in a forest stand are adults that hatch in streams or on the forest floor. Caddis fly adults exploit the mild crown temperatures when they overwinter in the Douglas fir canopies (Franklin, *et al.*, 1981).

Vertebrates that perhaps could not survive without the crown's buffering of the climate include the northern spotted owl (*Strix occidentalis caurina*) and red tree vole (*Arborimus longicaudus*), both of which prefer to nest in large, live old growth conifers rather than dead ones (Figure 62). In addition, the marbled murrelet (*Brachyramphus marmoratus*) strangely enough appears to nest to a large degree on wide branches of mature or old growth trees; the evidence appears to be strongest for the redwood forests and certain remnant old growth stands on the central Oregon Coast, such as near Loon Lake. No nests have yet to be found in Oregon, but researchers are searching intensively in several locations along the Northwest Coast. Northern spotted owls are known to tolerate only a very narrow body temperature range (Barrows, 1978). In warm weather they roost in the deep shade of the old growth understory, and in cold weather fly up to the canopy to escape the dark and cold near the ground (see below). The red tree vole is perhaps the most specialized vole in the world, spending its entire life in the canopy of an old growth conifer, using its needles as a sole source of both food and nesting material (Maser, *et al.*, 1981). Several generations may successively inhabit the same tree, making this vole the most arboreal mammal in all North America (Harris, 1984; Maser, *et al.*, 1981). This and another vole restricted to western Oregon

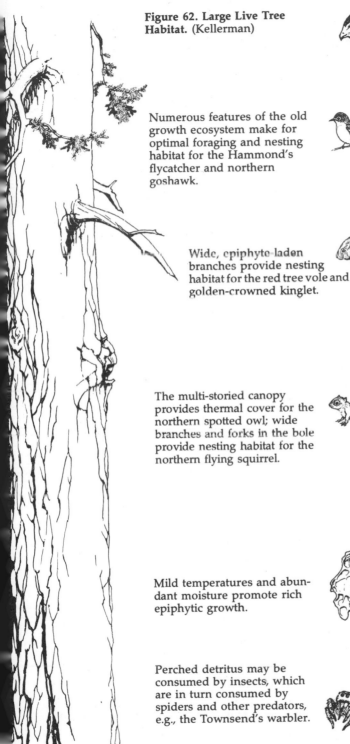

Figure 62. Large Live Tree Habitat. (Kellerman)

Numerous features of the old growth ecosystem make for optimal foraging and nesting habitat for the Hammond's flycatcher and northern goshawk.

Wide, epiphyte-laden branches provide nesting habitat for the red tree vole and golden-crowned kinglet.

The multi-storied canopy provides thermal cover for the northern spotted owl; wide branches and forks in the bole provide nesting habitat for the northern flying squirrel.

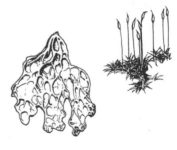

Mild temperatures and abundant moisture promote rich epiphytic growth.

Perched detritus may be consumed by insects, which are in turn consumed by spiders and other predators, e.g., the Townsend's warbler.

coniferous forests, the rare white-footed vole (*Arborimus albipes*), are the only mammals in North America who feed primarily on foliage. At least 10 vertebrates require the canopy of an old growth forest as a part of their optimum habitat.

LARGE DEAD TREES

Function. In all forests, a huge amount of trapped solar energy fuels the production of wood; wood amounts to 98% of the live plant mass (Proctor, *et al.*, 1980). This is unfortunate for most forest animals, because they do not eat wood. But there are some minor exceptions. Deer and elk eat shrubs; woodrats, snowshoe hares, Beechey ground squirrels, Mazama pocket gophers, porcupines, and Townsend voles eat tree bark when greens are scarce; beavers eat the bark of alder and willow as their main diet (Maser, 1981); a single insect outbreak can destroy several years of forest growth. But in general, insect-eating animals prevent epidemics and the indigestibility of wood leaves it unconsumed. Therefore, the total mass of primary consumers (animals that eat live plant material), and of the animals that prey on them, is small. The total biomass of consumers is less than 1/10,000 of the vascular plant biomass, and amounts to less than 50 lbs/acre on the average (Proctor, *et al.*, 1980). (The numbers of species and of individual consumer organisms, however, is much greater than that of plants.) Slugs have the greatest consumer biomass (35 lbs/acre, but slugs are also decomposers), followed by large mammals (5–11 lbs/acre), birds and small mammals (0.2 lbs/acre each), and insects. These grazers eat only about 2% of the plant material produced each year or a few hundred pounds per acre, as there simply is very little in the way of nuts, berries, and soft palatable foliage as compared to wood (Proctor, *et al.*, 1980).

As a result, forest food webs are not built on primary production, but instead, on detritus. In other words, the trees must die and lose their defense systems before they relinquish the immense energy and nutrient reserves bound in their boles and branches. The organisms that "eat" them are the decomposers, or insects, fungi, actinomycetes, and bacteria. The decomposers play a crucial role in the ecosystem as nutrient recyclers, and predictably, have a huge amount of woody debris at their disposal. About a third of the old growth hemlock forest floor is covered with decomposing logs that weigh about 65 tons/acre, or about a fifth of the total biomass (Franklin, *et al.*, 1981).

Clearly, almost all the solar energy trapped by a forest ends up as woody debris; therefore, most of the invisible inner workings beneath the tough, furrowed skin of the forest depend on the processing and rechanneling of this debris. Understanding forest function requires knowledge of tree death, litterfall, decomposition and decomposers.

Litter, or dead plant matter such as leaves, twigs, branches, and logs, falls to the forest floor continuously. In Northwest forests, most leaves fall in early November, cones in January, and twigs, bark, and wood in September (Proctor, *et al.*, 1980). The decadence of the crumbling, time-worn, old growth trees makes litterfall greater than in young growth. Most litter is logs and dead branches; most foliage litter falls from understory shrubs and not from the canopy (Proctor, *et al.*, 1980).

Northwest forest trees generally reach astonishing ages before their death converts them to litter; coast redwood can reach over 2000 years of age, and Douglas fir and western redcedar over 1000 years. Several forces and parasites usually combine to administer the coup de grace. A common pattern is heart or root rots, which weaken a tree, followed by windthrow or insect infestation (Proctor, *et al.*, 1980). Rots, caused by fungi (e.g., *Poria werii* or *Fomes pini*) are often invited by wounds from fires or heavy limb-breaking snows (Proctor, *et al.*, 1980).

Consumption by decomposers converts litter to "humus." Humus, a mass of wholly and partly decayed plant matter, lies like a skin over the top of the soil, just beneath the litter. Nutrients from the humus leach with rain to deeper soil layers where they are taken up by plant roots. Decomposition is thus the pivotal process of soil formation and nutrient recycling. Without decomposers there would be just rock, litter, and scant usable nutrients. Decomposition races along in warm and moist soil and, like photosynthesis, is water-limited in summer and temperature-limited in winter (Proctor, *et al.*, 1980). As already seen, slow summer decomposition in Northwest forests has encouraged the dominance of conifers.

The most important and striking components of old growth litter are the abundant, massive logs and snags strewn riotously over the hills and canyons. In a typical stand of old growth Douglas fir, a tree falls every two years, and about half the annual litterfall is woody debris (Proctor, *et al.*, 1980). Although amounts up to 270 tons/acre have been measured, the mass of logs and snags averages about 80 tons/acre (about a 25% of the total biomass), an amount far greater than in the mature hardwood forests of the eastern U.S (Franklin, *et al.*, 1981). Fallen trees in the Olympics and western Cascades cover 10–20% of the forest floor. Natural young growth has nothing of its own to compare with this; its large logs and snags are all relics from the previous old growth stand.

Old growth logs and snags help conserve and recycle nutrients in three ways. They curb the mischief caused by wildfires; they contain nitrogen-fixing bacteria; and they shield the soil from rain, thereby minimizing topsoil erosion and nutrient loss.

Forest fires impoverish the soil by sweeping a cloud of nutrients into the atmosphere. Nitrogen, carbon, and water vaporize out of burning leaves, branches, and the forest floor. But the large, water-saturated boles of live trees, snags, and logs usually do not burn through, so much of their large energy and nutrient reserves remain intact. Thus large, charred tree boles lie or stand pillarlike as a new young forest slowly emerges from the ashes. Their 200–500 lbs/acre of nitrogen, and about 6 lbs/acre of phosphorus slowly and continuously feed the soil in partial restitution for the losses to fire, ensuring a speedier recovery (Franklin, et al., 1981). In general, logs and snags decay very slowly. Large logs lose 90% of their density only after 500–600 years, while exposed snags disappear in less time, usually about 75 years (Franklin, et al., 1981). So they persist through fires and other disturbances, always slowly trickling nutrients into the litter layer.

The presence of nitrogen-fixing bacteria in logs and snags of old growth forests was an astonishing recent discovery. Previously, biologists assumed that these various bacteria lived either free in the soil or in league with the roots of legumes and other plants. Bigger, wetter, and more decayed logs usually fix nitrogen faster; the estimated rate is about 4 lbs/acre/year for old growth western hemlock (Franklin, et al., 1981). Nitrogen is in high demand in most ecosystems because of the great energetic expense of extracting it from the atmosphere; as a result, productivity in most ecosystems is limited by the concentration of usable nitrogen in soil or water, and thus by the activity of nitrogen fixers.

Habitat

Large logs on land. A steady parade of insects, centipedes, spiders, mites, fungi, microscopic decomposers, plants, amphibians, mammals, and birds exploits a fallen tree as a source of food and nutrients and a site for protection and cover, roosting, nesting, courtship, food storage, and observation. A well rotted log is a complete ecosystem in its own right, with producers, decomposers, and all orders of consumers (Figure 63). Most of the following is described in detail in Maser and Trappe's (1984) excellent book, *The Seen and Unseen World of the Fallen Tree*.

Since the intact skin of outer bark still shuts out fungi and bacteria, the first invaders of a newly fallen tree are the wood-boring insects, primarily beetles, carpenter ants, termites, and mites. With specially adapted mouthparts, these arthropods bore through the dense outer bark and into the thin layer of soft, nutritious tissues sandwiched between the outer bark and the heartwood. Just beneath the outer bark, the secondary phloem (or inner bark), vascular cambium, and secondary xylem (or sapwood) are the only living

Wrens feed and nest in protected areas under the log.

Chickarees store winter food supplies in hollow interior.

Several bird species (e.g., dark-eyed junco) nest in root wads.

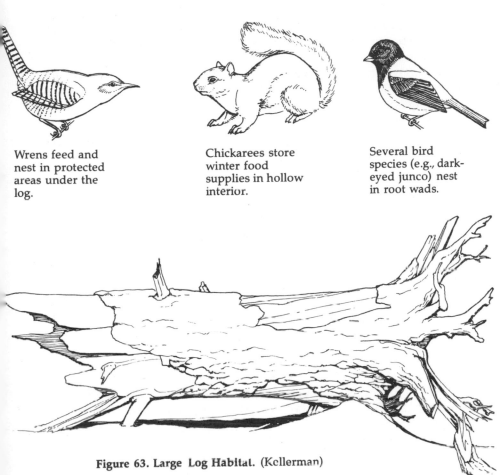

Figure 63. Large Log Habitat. (Kellerman)

The bushy tailed woodrat finds cover and denning habitat in the hollow interior.

The Pacific tree frog finds cover in spaces between loose bark and wood.

Many rodents spread spores of mycorrhizal fungi throughout the rotting wood.

Woodpeckers (e.g., the common flicker) feed on termites, carpenter ants, and other insects.

tissues of an intact tree bole, and are the first to be consumed because of their higher concentration of proteins and digestible carbohydrates.

The Douglas fir bark beetle (*Dendroctonus pseudotsugae*) spends its entire life cycle within these fresh green tissues. In early spring, an egg-bearing female bores through the outer bark and chews a 2-foot-long tunnel along the inner bark and cambium. On both sides of this main tunnel, she then builds a series of short, alternating grooves at right angles. In each of these grooves she lays about 20 eggs. As soon as the eggs hatch, the new larvae feed voraciously on the inner bark, and in the process pack the enlarging tunnel system with wood refuse and excrement. This banquet continues unceasing through the spring, summer, and fall, when the first cold spell brings it to a halt. The larvae then chew out a pupal cell and overwinter in a dormant state. By the following April, they emerge as adults, mate, and resume the cycle.

Among other wood borers, ambrosia beetles (*Monarthrum* spp.) do not eat wood, but instead have evolved an intriguing method of farming their food, the ambrosia fungi. Female and often male ambrosia beetles collect the fungal spores in specialized body cavities called mycangia, and disperse them throughout the egg galleries in the sapwood of newly fallen trees. Each beetle species carries its own species of fungus. As the fungal spores germinate and the hyphae extend throughout the sapwood, both adults and larvae consume the fungus, and pack the tunnels with excrement and uneaten wood powder, which often accumulates conspicuously outside the log.

Although carpenter ants (*Camponotus* spp.) prefer to nest in live trees, any fresh log or stump will serve temporarily until a suitable live tree can be found. In early spring, the young adults grow wings and leave the nest to mate and disperse. As if on cue, the ants often emerge simultaneously from many widely scattered nests and merge into several thick swarms. Beach drift logs often contain carpenter ant nests, and as the mating swarms are swept upward in the wind, they attract great swirling hordes of gulls, who devour them in mid-air. After mating, the males die and the females may replace older females in an existing nest or found a new colony. If the female finds suitable uninhabited wood, she nestles into a small cavity, seals herself in, breaks off her now-useless wings, and lays her eggs. The larvae hatch in about 10 days, and feed entirely by secretions from the queen's salivary glands, after which they grow, spin their cocoons, and crawl out as adults some 30 days later. These new adults assume the role of workers, and immediately begin the task of excavating a complex new network of egg chambers for the queen in any region of soft, semi-decayed wood, showing extraordinary care for the queen, and later her eggs and larvae. The workers routinely move the eggs and larvae to the most comfortable locations within the nest, feed them with their own mouth secretions, and help the new adults out of their cocoons.

Carpenter ants do not eat wood, but rather discard it through specially constructed "windows" to the outside, where it accumulates in sawdust piles beneath the tree. They feed on caterpillars, butterflies, and other insects, and seem to crave the sweet honeydew secreted by aphids. Surprisingly, carpenter ants have been observed to carry aphid eggs into their nests in winter (presumably to shelter them), carry them out in the spring, and plant them on vegetation where they develop and secrete the honeydew. East of the Cascades, predation by carpenter ants keeps the spruce budworm population under control, and in Europe, foresters explicitly manage the ant populations to control several species of defoliating insects.

The tunneling and feeding activities of the wood borers expose the vulnerable, moist, internal wood surfaces to air, which are immediately colonized by an enormous variety of fungi, bacteria, and other decomposers that could not before penetrate the intact outer bark. Some of them hitchhike in on the exoskeletons of the insects themselves, while others drift in on air currents through the tunnel openings and the original breaks. The well tunneled, partially consumed layer of green tissue just beneath the outer bark offers an unusually favorable habitat for decomposers. It contains an abundance of nutritious, nitrogen-rich frass (insect excrement), which the outer bark protects from summer heat and drought and winter cold. This new wave of decomposers rapidly consumes the inner bark and cambium and in the process excretes waste carbon dioxide and water, which maintains the moist incubation environment beneath the outer bark. New fungi with specialized enzyme systems soon arrive, and begin the digestion of the sapwood cellulose and lignin. Many of this wave of immigrants are mutually antagonistic, so the first species to invade a region often dominates. As the food supply dwindles, many fungi sporulate en masse, depending entirely on the emerging insect larvae to disperse their spores to new trees. By the time the fungi become well established, most of the green tissues are gone and most branches under an inch in diameter have decomposed.

At this stage, another wood-boring insect, the Pacific dampwood termite (*Zootermopsis angusticollis*), enters the scene. Termites choose a nest log on the basis of a strong attraction to acids and aldehydes produced by certain species of fungi in the wood, and once in the log, preferentially consume and burrow in the wood that contains those same chemicals. On warm evenings in August, September, and October, the mature adults take wing and embark on their clumsy nuptial flights. Like the carpenter ants, they swarm conspicuously and are preyed on by bats, flickers, gulls, crows, pileated woodpeckers, and other predators. After a short time, they cast their wings, and if opposite sexes meet, the male follows behind the female as she walks about in search of a suitable log, in which they excavate a small chamber and copulate. The resulting colony develops an intricate social organization, with fertile migrants, sterile workers, and nymphs. The fertile members usually do not appear for about 4 years, when the colony has grown to 400 or 500 individuals. A tight symbiotic relationship with two species of gut-inhabiting microorganisms enables the termite to digest the wood cellulose. A zooflagellate protozoan engulfs the wood particles ingested by the termite, and digests the cellulose with its own system of enzymes. Among its waste products is acetic acid, which the termite absorbs as an energy source. Also living in the gut, a nitrogen-fixing bacterium benefits from the digestive products of both termite and protozoan. When the termite's nitrogen intake is low, however, the bacterium immediately raises its rate of nitrogen fixation to make up the deficit, and thereby ensures the survival of its own comfortable habitat.

While all this is going on inside, dead leaves, twigs, and other litter steadily accumulate in the moist, sheltered furrows of the outer bark. Seeds of western hemlock, Sitka spruce, salal, and huckle-berries germinate in these litter clumps, but the roots cannot pene-trate the dense, intact, outer bark. Only if the bark has been broken by insect boring or some other injury can the roots penetrate into that protected, moist incubation zone beneath the bark, where the inner bark, cambium, and sapwood has already been softened and partially cleared away by insects, fungi, and other decomposers. Without an easy entrance, the roots must remain outside, where they dry up and die during the first summer drought. Even those that manage to penetrate, however, cannot yet pierce the heartwood, and this restriction, coupled with the initial lack of mycorrhizae, severely constrains early growth. Once into the incubation zone, the roots of most trees and shrubs secrete compounds that selectively stimulate or inhibit the growth of certain fungi and bacteria. Some of the roots nevertheless fall prey to root pathogens, while others escape but still remain naked, and in either case die during the first summer drought. The lucky ones are clothed early with a soothing coat of mycorrhizal fungus, which provides moisture, nutrients, vitamins, growth regulators and antibiotics in return for photosynthetic sugars. The fungus not only cushions a seedling from the summer drought, but also gives it a competitive edge by accelerating nutrient uptake and growth. Plants that seldom form mycorrhizae (e.g., sedges and rushes) rarely grow among these vigorous mycorrhizal plants on rotting logs.

Of course for any of this to happen, the fungal spores must somehow enter the wood and come into contact with the roots. Since the spores cannot pierce the bark, they must enter through the same openings as the roots. But air currents will not suffice for transport because virtually all species of mycorrhizal fungi produce their spore-bearing structures underground or in rotting wood. Hence the burrowing activities of beetles, carpenter ants, termites, mites, springtails, small mammals, and other animals are indispensable for the dispersal of mycorrhizal fungi.

The healthy plant cover and growing population of fungi in the incubation zone provide shelter and food for an increasing abundance of animals. As nematodes, aphids, collembolans, and others proliferate, they devour the protein-rich bacteria and fungi, both mycorrhizal and non-mycorrhizal. Eventually this dense consumer population exhausts its supply of rich inner bark and cambium, and when this cementing material is gone, the outer bark sloughs off and the incubation zone ceases to be. Any seedlings rooted solely in the inner bark and cambium also fall off, while those whose roots extend well into the sapwood in fungus-softened areas are more likely to survive. But this is only a temporary reprieve, because now that the remaining sapwood is completely naked, it disappears practically overnight, and will take any plants with it whose roots fail to extend into the underlying stable heartwood. The greater its complement of mycorrhizae, the faster a seedling's growth and the greater its chances of survival.

Meanwhile, the chunks of sloughed outer bark and sapwood accumulate on the ground alongside the log, creating a moist mulch immediately exploited by slugs, snails, salamanders, and small mammals. Rodents usually burrow into this material before they enter the decayed heartwood to build nests, and in so doing they enrich it with feces and urine, making it an excellent seed bed.

One such animal, whose life on the forest floor epitomizes the concept of symbiosis, is the California red-backed vole (*Clethrionomys californicus*). This poorly known rodent spends most of its time in subterranean burrows, where it mates, raises young, and, unlike any other North American mammal, feeds preferentially on the underground fruiting bodies of mycorrhizal fungi. Its diet includes the species *Rhizopogon vinicolor*, which fruits mostly in rotten wood and forms mycorrhizal associations with Douglas fir roots. The spores consumed by the vole pass through its digestive system intact, and are scattered in fecal pellets throughout the vole's runways. The fungi thus depend on the vole's feeding and burrowing to disperse spores from decrepit logs and stumps to new, fresh wood, where they once again infect any resident roots. The vole itself cannot survive without mycorrhizal fungi; after a clearcut in which all woody material is removed or burned, mycorrhizae stop fruiting and the voles die. In an old growth forest, the vole population is limited by the abundance of fallen trees. The optimal logs are those with well decayed sapwood or heartwood, in which the fungi have exhausted most nutrients and have begun to fruit. In this three-way symbiosis, both voles and trees die without the fungi, and the fungi might die without the photosynthetic products of the trees and the endless scurrying of the California red-backed voles that share their woody habitat.

In addition to the voles, all other rodents west of the Rockies feed heavily on the underground fruiting bodies of mycorrhizal fungi, including mountain beavers, squirrels, chipmunks, pocket gophers, beavers, mice, rats, woodrats, muskrats, porcupines, and nutrias. Recent studies show that the fecal pellets of deer mice, chickarees, and northern flying squirrels contain not only live, healthy spores of mycorrhizal fungi, but also a yeast and a nitrogen-fixing bacterium that lives within the fungal cells. The bacterium, azosporillin, is the most efficient nitrogen-fixing bacterium known. It apparently absorbs water and nutrients solely from the fungus, and perhaps indirectly from the plant roots, because it is incapable of surviving outside the fungus. It in turn supplies the fungus (and perhaps the plant roots) with nitrogen. Both fungus and bacterium grow more rapidly in the presence of the yeast, suggesting that the yeast secretes some regulatory compound. A single deer mouse produces an average of 66 fecal pellets every hour, and each pellet contains several hundred live mycorrhizal spores with their associated bacteria and yeast. Since it takes 1000 to 10,000 spores to inoculate a seedling, five deer mice produce enough pellets in 3 nights to inoculate 300–3000 seedlings. The pellets of other rodents contain similar amounts, and many of these species, especially voles, chipmunks, and squirrels, depend heavily on the feeding, cover, and nesting habitat offered by fallen trees, in whose crevices and cavities they liberally scatter these minute vitamin tablets. For these reasons, forest tree reproduction tends to be more rapid in stands with a greater abundance of fallen trees.

At about the time the outer bark sloughs off and the seedling roots penetrate the heartwood, the community of plants and animals in and on a fallen tree reaches its maximum diversity. Insect tunnels begin to penetrate the heartwood, permitting easier access for plant roots. The fungal white pocket rot consumes the spring growth in the heartwood faster than the summer, thereby separating the annual growth rings and creating openings for the hemlock roots to follow along the axis of the tree. The highly lignified heartwood nevertheless decays very slowly, presenting a stable environment for roots, with no threat of sudden exposure and loss of substrate. As decay

proceeds, the heartwood fills with water produced by the decomposers, making it wetter during the summer drought than the
rooting zone of the surrounding soil. This appears to be the main
reason tree seedlings, especially western hemlock, are more abundant on rotting logs, "nurse logs," than the forest floor. Brown cubical
rot soon makes life for the young trees even easier as it cuts trans-
versely through the heartwood, breaking it into large chunks and
allowing roots easy penetration straight through to the soil. By this
time a lush plant community blankets the log, and includes conifer
seedlings (mostly western hemlock, but also Sitka spruce and
others), salal, two or three species of huckleberry, licorice fern, and a
great variety of mosses, liverworts, and lichens.

The vegetation provides more shelter for animals, some of
whom (mites, insects, slugs, and snails) graze on the leaves and
stems. By this time the myriad grazers and decomposers have
attracted a large following of predators, including mites, spiders,
pseudoscorpions, centipedes, salamanders, and shrews. The
smallest are a group of mites, whose long, fast legs and strong mouthparts help them capture and consume other small arthropods (e.g.,
springtails), arthropod eggs, and small roundworms that they find in
the soil surface, in mosses, humus, rotten wood, and animal wastes.
A relative of the spider, a pseudoscorpion has pinchers but no tail or
stinger. It weaves a silken nest, waits at the opening with head and
pinchers protruding, and grabs any passing flies, small beetles and
larvae, ants, and small earthworms. The largest spider on fallen trees,
the Pacific folding door spider (*Antrodiaetus pacificus*), does not build
a web, but chases down and subdues its prey. For a nest it seeks out a
horizontal crack in the outer layer of a tree and lines it with silk.
Centipedes have strong, poison jaws that they use to paralyze their
prey; the jaws of the largest Northwest species are big enough to
subdue a small winter wren or chickadee. Centipedes overwinter in
rotten wood and other cover and lay eggs in spring and early
summer.

Among the vertebrate predators, the salamanders enter the
scene about the time the bark sloughs off, and inhabit the cool wet
mulch under and alongside the log. The interface between the soil
and large rotting logs usually remains cool and wet throughout the
summer, and appears to be crucial to the salamander survival during
hot, dry spells. The Oregon salamander (*Ensatina eschscholtzi*) spends
most of its time in rodent burrows, but during cold or dry weather
seeks out the shelter of the woody debris alongside rotting logs. A
female lays her clutch of 11–12 eggs under the bark or in the cracks
and cavities of well rotted sapwood and heartwood. Both sexes dine
preferably on springtails and spiders, but also on isopods,
millipedes, and adult beetles. Clouded salamanders are found most

often in the cool, moist, well tunneled spaces beneath the loose outer bark. The best climber of Northwest salamanders, the clouded salamander (*Aneides ferreus*) has been found up to 20 feet high in live trees, apparently hunting for food. Adults consume mainly sowbugs and beetles year around, but include ants, earwigs, and other invertebrates in the summer. Juveniles find smaller foods, such as mites, springtails, flies, and minute beetles. Like the Oregon salamander, the female lays her eggs in loose bark and cavities. In northwestern California and extreme southwestern Oregon, the California slender salamander (*Batrachoseps wrighti*) inhabits the wood-boring beetle and termite tunnels in sapwood and heartwood. Surprisingly, adults are such discriminating eaters that they favor specific families of springtails and mites (respectively Sminthuridae and Oribatidae) over other types of food, mainly flies, spiders, and small snails.

Among the mammalian predators, probably the most common are shrews (*Sorex*) and shrew-moles (*Neurotrichus gibbsii*). These tiny animals are well known for their gargantuan appetite and extremely nervous, restless, and aggressive temperament. Though not restricted to woody debris, they commonly dig burrows and build nests in the shelter of well rotted logs and stumps and under large pieces of bark, and prey heavily on the neighboring wood fauna. Upon discovering an occupied termite gallery, a marsh shrew was observed to attack it with a frenzied intensity, bracing its claws against the tree as it tore through the soft wood with its teeth, plucking out the living termites with head movements so quick as to be nearly invisible.

Although the most common shrew in the Northwest, the Trowbridge shrew (*Sorex trowbridgii*), is also the most cosmopolitan in both diet and habitat, it shows a clear preference for fallen trees. It feeds heavily on the log fauna, especially on centipedes, spiders, the internal organs of beetles and other invertebrates, and slugs and snails. The American shrew-mole is a consummate burrower, and is much better adapted to active tunneling in rotting wood than the rodents and other shrews. Although its large front feet with thick claws are well adapted for digging, the shrew-mole constructs shallow burrows without molehills. Because it can place its front feet directly under its body, with palms flat on the ground, the shrew-mole is much more agile, graceful, and shrew-like than other western American moles. In a ceaseless search for food, the shrew-mole digs shallow tunnels through the duff on the forest floor, barely an inch below the surface, and patrols these constantly for any earthworms, centipedes, flies, or other animals that have crawled or fallen in. The animal also forages above-ground, often turning over leaves and twigs, pushing aside pieces of bark and duff, and occasionally even climbing into the shrubbery. The shrew-mole makes up for its blindness and poor senses of hearing and smell with a highly developed sense of touch, which it uses to identify its prey. Its most important tactile organ appears to be its long, flexible, whiskered nose, because the mole keeps it in perpetual motion, waving it high in the air, hooking it under its belly, rapping it on the ground, and thrusting it into crevices. Even if a prey item passes within a millimeter of the nostrils, the mole still fails to notice unless it touches the nose.

In the final stages of tree decay, the heartwood is moist and well decomposed, with only the highly lignified tissues remaining. While lignin indigestibility makes it a poor animal habitat, the year-around moisture provides excellent conditions for the plants already present. Newcomers, however, do poorly because of the competition and the thick layer of forest litter that has buried the tree by this time. The now-dominant mycorrhizal fungi remain active throughout the summer in the moist wood, in contrast to the dormant forms in the neighboring soil. New species of mosses, liverworts, and lichens slowly appear with the changing substrate. Eventually the log sags and slumps over the ground, and may remain as a soft, duff-covered hillock for several centuries. In a typical old growth Douglas fir forest, about 50% of the humus is woody debris of all decay stages.

Large snags. Many of the same decomposers also attack standing dead trees, or snags, but since they stand safely out of reach of most predators, large snags furnish indispensible habitat for a different community of birds and mammals (Figure 64). At least 46 birds and 6 mammals in the region depend wholly or heavily on snags for nesting and overwintering, sites for courtship rituals, food sources, and other activities (Proctor, et al., 1980; Franklin, et al., 1980). Among the birds are bald and golden eagles, osprey, peregrine falcons, mergansers, wood ducks, buffleheads, various hawks, owls, woodpeckers, chickadees, nuthatches, and bluebirds. The dependent mammals are martens, fishers, raccoons, chickarees, western gray squirrels, and northern flying squirrels. The largest snags are the most useful to these animals; hole-nesting birds prefer snags over 2 feet in diameter and 50 feet tall (Thomas, 1979). Birds that dig their own holes, such as the pileated woodpecker, (Dryocopus pileatus) require a hard (more recently dead) surface as well. Generally, the larger the snags, the denser and more diverse is the community of birds that inhabit them (Franklin, et al., 1980).

Logs in streams. Falling trees tumble down the canyons and pile up in great tangled heaps in the streams and rivers that flow through an old growth forest. A typical small stream contains 200–700 tons per acre of woody debris, much greater than that of the neighboring higher ground. Some might imagine that this collection would destroy the aquatic animals and their habitats, or at least

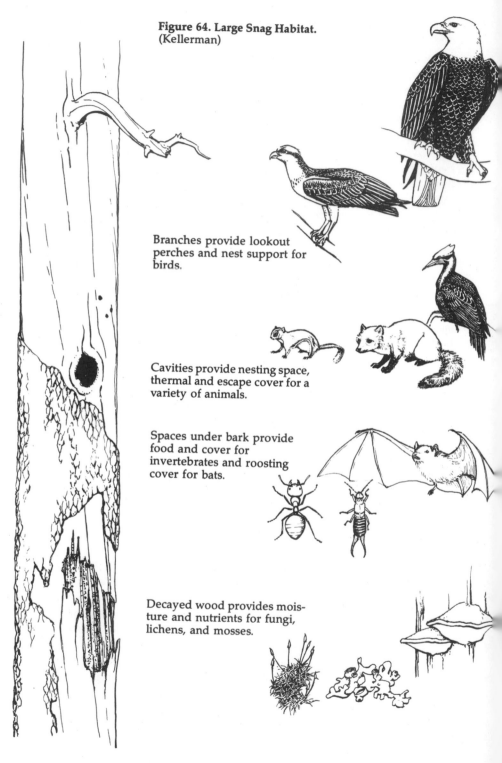

Figure 64. Large Snag Habitat.
(Kellerman)

Branches provide lookout perches and nest support for birds.

Cavities provide nesting space, thermal and escape cover for a variety of animals.

Spaces under bark provide food and cover for invertebrates and roosting cover for bats.

Decayed wood provides moisture and nutrients for fungi, lichens, and mosses.

cause stagnation, but they would be wrong. Stream organisms appear well adapted to the debris, and most populations dwindle or disappear without it.

As on land, trees in streams both create habitat and offer an ample reservoir of food and nutrients. Debris produces habitat by diversifying the flow of the stream and the shape of its channel, thereby generating new gradients in flow rate, water depth, and size of sediment particles, all useful to a wider variety of species. Trees that dam a small stream create ponds and trap fine sediments, while those that partly obstruct it redirect its flow and shape new meanders and smaller pools. In most first and second order streams, the jumbled mass of logs creates a stepped stream profile, in which the stream flows alternately from the still pools behind the logs to the short cascades in front. In such a stream the energy of the current is concentrated not along the banks where it could cause erosion during high flows, but instead in the relatively harmless cascades. Larger streams carry out most debris except where large logs or topography constrict the current. In large rivers logs come to rest on the flood plains or along the outside shore of bends. In the smallest streams, however, the numerous logs trap 70% of the fallen leaves, twigs, branches, and other litter long enough for it to be consumed.

As with logs on land, those in streams are occupied by a steady progression of organisms belonging to all trophic (=feeding) groups. A newly fallen tree immediately attracts fish, aquatic insects, and other invertebrates who seek out the cracks, holes, and spaces under loose bark for shelter from the current and refuge from predators. Before long, decomposition begins as a crop of microbes and algae spreads over the wood surface, and these in turn are consumed by mayflies, snails, and other grazing invertebrates.

Waterlogged wood decays much more slowly than dry because oxygen cannot diffuse into the interior; decomposition is initially restricted to a thin 0.25-inch layer on the surface. Soon, however, fungi attack the surface and soften it enough to permit oxygen penetration, and decomposition progresses inward. A varied group of obligate wood grazers and shredders (beetles, caddisflies, stoneflies, and others) consumes the fungus-infested wood, which contains five times as much nitrogen as clean wood.

Wood-boring insects (primarily fly larvae, but also beetles) tunnel into the fungus-softened wood, carrying in their own fungal symbionts that stain the wood brown around the tunnel openings. Decomposition accelerates as these and other microbes find their way through the tunnels to the newly exposed inner surfaces. By this time the outside has become richly textured, and suitable for caddisfly larvae (order Trichoptera), who build and attach their filter-feeding nets to the roughened surface. Where currents and wood are optimal, 10 caddisfly nets can be found per square inch of wood. Continued softening, fragmentation, and mineralization eventually permit the penetration of earthworms and other detritivores, and finally the wood resembles wet upland soil.

During just the last 10 years biologists have gathered increasing evidence that an important group of Northwest animals, the fish of the salmon family, depends heavily on large woody debris in streams. The slower, safer current around logs allows suspended food particles to settle, and the wood itself provides concealment from predators. Surveys show that 50% of adults in first order streams spawn in wood-related habitat, and 25% in third order streams. Coho salmon, cutthroat trout, and steelhead take cover in the pools and backwaters around large, stable woody debris, and in coastal Oregon streams, the greater the pool volume, the greater the coho biomass. In several surveys of old growth streams in western Washington before and after clearcutting, in which all large logs in streams were removed, the only salmonid remaining in any abundance was an expanded population of steelhead trout, mostly under a year old.

Even in larger streams and rivers, woody debris is an important salmonid habitat. Where they come to rest along the shore, large logs create side channels and small backwaters. In slowing the current, they allow settlement of sediments and organic particles. Red alder, willows, and other plants often take root in these stable areas, and the development of vegetation and soil provides flood control. After winter storms the raging streamflows in the main channel often spare these marginal backwaters, and the salmon congregate in these areas until the floods subside.

Clearly, dead and dying plant material is as crucial in promoting energy flow and habitat diversity in old growth forest as it is in estuaries, whose organic needs are satisfied to a large extent by forest debris washed in by rivers. The theme of big trees spans the entire Northwest Coast, from the mountains to the sea.

Northern spotted owl (*Strix occidentalis caurina*). Enmeshed in a heated political controversy between timber interests and conservationists, the spotted owl (Figure 65) is an instructive example of just how an animal comes to be dependent on old growth, so dependent that its existence is seriously threatened by routine timber harvest. Before 1970, most information about the owl was sketchy and anecdotal, and conventional wisdom held that it was extremely rare, skittish, and partial to large conifers. Since then, biologists have fitted several hundred owls with radio transmitters and followed their movements over several weeks and months. As a result, we now have solid information about home ranges, habitat use, and age-specific

Figure 65. Young spotted owls. (Forest Service.)

mortality. The preponderance of evidence shows convincingly that the owl is heavily dependent on forests with several attributes of old growth, such as a multilayered canopy, patchy understory, and large trees both standing and on the ground.

The foraging and roosting movements of some 27 radio-tagged owls in Washington, Oregon, and northern California, suggest that the average home range of an individual owl is 5180 acres. Similar tracking of nine pairs of mated owls indicates that the average home range of a pair is 5610 acres (Forsman, 1986; Carey, 1985; U.S. Forest Service, 1987). In most of these studies, the owls were followed only in spring and summer; those followed throughout the year expanded their home ranges in the winter. Hence, these averages probably underestimate the total area used by the owls over the entire year. In Oregon, the territories of mated individuals overlap 40–93%, and the territories of adjacent nonmated owls overlap 3–25% (Forsman, *et al.*, 1984). On average, the total extent of old growth forest within a territory amounts to 2480 acres for individual owls, and 2790 acres for mated pairs (Forsman and Meslow, 1985; U.S. Forest Service, 1987). Of all Oregon territories studied between 1969 and 1986, 93–98% were dominated by coniferous forests at least 100 years old, and the rest contained scattered old growth conifers (U.S. Forest Service, 1987; Forsman, 1986). In the Coast Range, old growth is scarcer than in the Cascades, and owl home ranges tend to be larger presumably to accommodate sufficient old growth. Although these figures indicate that old growth comprises only 48–50% of a typical territory, owls forage, roost, and nest almost entirely within the old growth of their territories, and tend to occupy younger forests only in transit (Carey, 1985). In the Oregon Cascade Range, owls forage 64–99% of the time in old growth, 0–16% of the time in mature stands (100–200 years old), and 0–36% of the time in young stands (61–80 years). Spotted owls also nest and roost preferentially in old growth. In Oregon, 42 of the 47 observed nests were in old growth (89%), and the other 5 in forests that contained scattered old growth conifers; of the over 1600 roosts, 91–98% were in old growth forests (Forsman, *et al.*, 1984). Overall, spotted owls in Oregon are 12 times more abundant in old growth than in younger forests (Forsman, *et al.*, 1977).

Since old growth constitutes only 5–10% of forested land in the Northwest, the probability is infinitesimal that the owls would show such a strong old growth bias purely by chance. Rather, they must actively seek it out. But perhaps this preference is nothing but meaningless, ritualized behavior, and in reality, the owls could live perfectly well in younger forests. Is there any direct evidence that the owls are *incapable* of surviving in younger forests? If this were true, we would expect the owl population to decline as old growth is harvested, and indeed this is the case. The only practical means of counting spotted owls is the call transect, in which a researcher drives or hikes along logging roads after dark periodically broadcasting a spotted owl call, and listening for responses. In California, call transects uncovered some 1317 territories in 1975. Censuses in 1985 indicated that 1259 of these were still occupied, a loss of 4.4% over those 10 years (Gould, 1985). Historically in California, spotted owls were clumped at roughly 125 locations; in 1985, they were no longer present in at least 30 of these sites (Gould, 1974, 1985). In the Cascade and Coast ranges of Oregon, call transects indicate an annual population decline of 1.1% in a sample of 98 pairs from 1972 to 1978 (Forsman, 1986). The results of radio-tagging, however, predict a much greater decline (Barrowclough and Coats, 1985).

Based on 20 adult owls tracked for 1–3 years, and another six tracked for 4 months, a typical adult (age 2–10) has an 85% chance of surviving the next year; virtually no adults survive beyond 10 (Barrowclough and Coats, 1985). Only 2 of 13 radio-tagged fledglings survived a full year, a survivorship of only 19% for this age class. Direct observation suggests a constant annual birth rate of 0.28 for all adult females. These figures indicate a net replacement rate of only 0.24; in other words, for each four females who die, only one replacement female is produced, giving an overall rate of population decline much higher than the 1.1% suggested by the call transects. Why the discrepancy? Perhaps the weight of the radio transmitters interferes with foraging, and tagged owls have an unrealistically high mortality rate; in the call transects, perhaps the same owls follow the researchers along, calling over and over again, giving unrealistically high population estimates. In any case, the spotted owl populations are shrinking, and at rates high enough for the U.S. Forest Service to predict extinction in sometime between 20 and 500 years (U.S. Forest Service, 1986).

In what ways is the spotted owl dependent on old growth? Several features of the owl's natural history allow us to speculate (Carey, 1985; Gutierrez, 1985). First, the owl for unknown reasons fails to build its own nest, and so requires a pre-existing cavity in a tree, or a nest previously built by another species. Suitably large, sheltered cavities are likely to exist only in large, decadent old growth conifers. A common spotted owl nest site is the stovepipe-like cavity formed in the top of a large conifer after the top breaks off; often side branches grow vertically to replace the top, and thereby shelter the nest from wind and rain. Of course, the large size of the owl necessitates a large tree; diameters of nest trees average about 5–6 feet (Gutierrez, 1985; Forsman, et al., 1984). The owls also nest on natural platforms created where twigs and other debris accumulate on a broad fork in a conifer limb, and in stick nests built by other birds and mammals. In Oregon and northern California, 64–92% of the spotted owl nests studied were in cavities, for the most part in live trees (Gutierrez, 1985; Forsman, et al., 1984).

Second, the spotted owl plumage is cold-adapted, having presumably evolved in more northern ancestors and retained now by chance (Barrows and Barrows, 1978; Barrows, 1981). As a result, the owl has difficulty keeping cool during the breeding season, and may require the deep, protected, and open shade of an old growth forest. Behavioral observations bear this out. On warm summer days, when the temperature exceeds about 80°F, the owls stay close to the ground where the air is cooler, often roosting on hardwood trees in the understory, such as vine maple and dogwood. In younger stands low roosts are rare because the understory is sparse or absent, and if they roosted on the ground, the owls would expose themselves to predators. In winter, the owls tend to roost high in the canopy, taking advantage of the buffering effect of the old growth crowns. Given the problem of heat stress, one might expect that natural selection should gradually thin out the plumage of owls in future generations, and thereby increase their fitness in both old and young growth. Whether this happens, however, depends on the degree of flexibility in the growth of plumage; at present, we have virtually no information on the degree of natural variability in feather morphology or density, and the prevalence of heat stress behavior suggests that any such changes are unlikely.

Third, spotted owls feed heavily on the dusky-footed woodrat (*Neotoma fuscipes*) in mixed-conifer forests in California and Oregon, and the northern flying squirrel (*Glaucomys sabrinus*) over the rest of Oregon and Washington, as well as on a variety of other small mammals. Although the flying squirrel reaches its greatest abundance in old growth forests, and like the owl, is active only at night, it is unclear whether the owl's preference for it is a cause or effect of the owl's old growth dependence. Nevertheless, small mammals of all kinds are more abundant in old growth than in mature or young forests because the abundance of downed timber provides nesting and feeding habitat and refuge from predators (Maser, et al., 1981; Raphael and Barret, 1984).

Finally, great horned owls (*Bubo virginianus*) prey on both young and adult spotted owls, and goshawks (*Accipiter gentilis*) on young (Forsman, et al., 1984). Undoubtedly, spotted owls flying over or roosting in clearcuts or young forests are more exposed to predation than those concealed in old growth. The fledglings are especially vulnerable to predation as they begin to disperse from their nest areas, flying over acres of clearcuts in search of suitable old growth to settle in. But great horned and spotted owls coexist in many places, with no apparent harm to the spotted owls, and for this reason most researchers suspect that the spotted owl would require old growth regardless of the predation pressure.

Because of the scarcity of old growth, nesting parents have trouble forming territories with a sufficient proportion of decadent stands with abundant small mammals, and are faced with a tradeoff between (1) the costs of traveling great distances between hunting areas, and (2) the benefits of including as many high-quality stands as possible in their home ranges to maximize the fitness of their offspring. As a result, 65% of fledglings die by the end of summer, even before they start to disperse, and only one or two out of every 10 survive the first winter (Forsman, et al., 1984; Barrowclough and Coats, 1985). At present there is no reason to hope that the genetic versatility of the owl will extricate the species from the trap in which it finds itself; rather, its future appears to hang on the sympathy of its human neighbors.

Forest Composition

Although the foregoing discussion of the nature of old growth emphasizes forests dominated by Douglas fir and western hemlock, the most common type of old growth forest in the Northwest, it applies with only minor amendments to old growth stands containing other large, long-lived species, such as Sitka spruce, western redcedar, and coast redwood, all of which are common on the Northwest Coast. But what determines which of these species comes to dominate a particular site? Is it possible to identify the subtle network of forces that control the mix of plant species in some stand, and predict the long-term course of successional change?

As pointed out in Chapter 3, one of the ongoing problems in ecology is the attempt to understand the factors that set the distributional limits of a population or species. Collectively, these boundaries create an overall pattern, or "community structure." We can consider the coast ranges of the Northwest as a broad community of forest species, and ask what structure we see, and what factors control it. At the outset, it is easily predicted that, as with most plants, the most important forces in the life of a forest tree are temperature and moisture. These more than anything else control where and when a certain species of tree can and cannot survive. But for several reasons, a species very seldom occurs at all locations with a tolerable, or even optimal, regime of temperature and moisture. First, barriers such as rivers, topographic discontinuities, or prevailing wind patterns severely restrict seed dispersal and vegetative propagation. Most conifer seeds, for example, are dispersed by wind and rodents, so seldom settle far from the parent.

Second, other species might interfere with or stimulate a plant's growth and reproduction in some places but not in others. For example, in the Olympic rain forest, Roosevelt elk browse preferentially on the soft foliage of hemlock rather than on the stiff spruce needles, and apparently reduce the representation of hemlock in the canopy. Sporadic epidemics of the spruce aphid kill Sitka spruce throughout its range, especially after uncommonly mild winters. Vine maple often grows poorly in pure stands of Douglas fir because of the scarcity of maple-specific mycorrhizal fungi. Conifers often recruit extremely slowly into cutover or burned areas because of a massive invasion of faster-growing shrubs or trees, such as salmonberry and red alder, that compete for sunlight and nutrients.

Third, the "optimal" temperature and moisture regime is not always constant, but instead varies depending on the amount of stress experienced from other physical and chemical factors, such as soil nutrients, pH, salinity, and light; if a plant is already suffering, it will have a harder time bearing up under any additional stress. For example, Douglas fir tolerates shade much better on dry than on wet sites.

Fourth, needs and tolerances change with age. Seedlings, for instance, suffer from snowpack damage, grazing, fire, seasonal dearth of nutrients and moisture, and other insults much more than adults. Hence the reasons for the absence of juveniles might differ considerably from those for adults.

Finally, simply because temperature and moisture appear to be favorable most of the time does not imply that they are favorable in the long run. Northwest conifers are extremely long-lived, and the reason for the present lack of a certain canopy species might involve a fire, drought, or cold snap some hundred years ago. Douglas fir, for example, invades rapidly after a fire, and can dominate the canopy for centuries even though conditions are perfect for western hemlock.

Clearly, a confusion of loosely connected forces in a plant's environment adds a random element to the distribution of its offspring, and its own future survival. A casual observer standing in a forest rarely has a chance to see these forces at work, let alone read their past history in the vegetation. Nevertheless, even though understanding is often hard to come by on the small scale, on the broad regional scale variations in temperature and moisture are restrictive enough to produce noticeable patterns.

The interior of the Northwest Coast is a land of gentle mountain slopes. Land rises abruptly from the beaches to the mountain summits, and forest composition changes in response. Most Coast Range peaks are not particularly high and have only two forest zones; higher slopes boast another one or two zones. In Oregon, the wet, mild, foggy, sea-sprayed Sitka spruce zone extends from sea level to usually less than 490 ft, but up to 1900 ft on mountain masses abutting the ocean; in California this merges with the coast redwood zone, which reaches as high as 3000 ft (Figure 66). Usually just above this, from 450 ft or less to about 1800–3700 ft lies the cooler, wetter, non-sea-sprayed western hemlock zone. Many "peaks" in the coastal mountains are no higher than this and so support no additional zones. But many scattered higher peaks support another. The cool, wet, Pacific silver-fir zone extends from the hemlock zone to about 3900ft. An even higher zone occurs in the Olympic Mountains; this is the very cold, snowy mountain hemlock zone, which extends from the silver firs to timberline, about 4800 to 5500 ft. Some alpine meadows exist even above this, but above these permanent snowpacks are common in the Olympics, as on 7965-foot Mount Olympus.

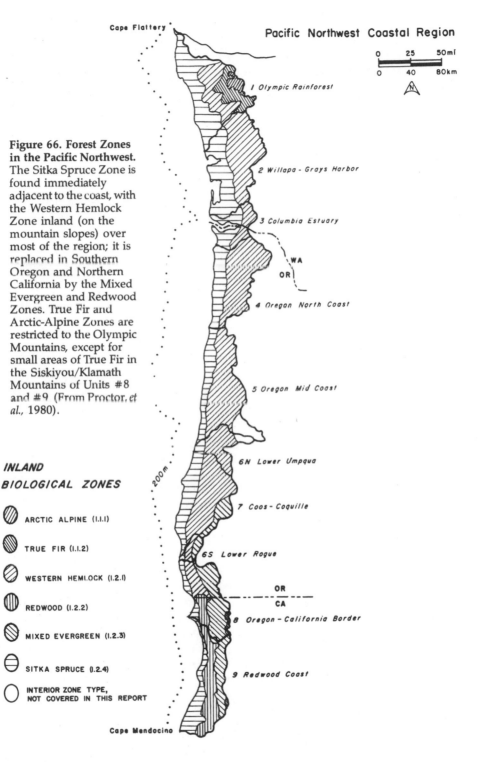

Cape Flattery

Pacific Northwest Coastal Region

0   25   50mi
0   40   80km

1 Olympic Rainforest

2 Willapa - Grays Harbor

3 Columbia Estuary

WA
OR

4 Oregon North Coast

5 Oregon Mid Coast

6N Lower Umpqua

7 Coos - Coquille

6S Lower Rogue

OR
CA

8 Oregon - California Border

9 Redwood Coast

200m

Cape Mendocino

Figure 66. Forest Zones in the Pacific Northwest. The Sitka Spruce Zone is found immediately adjacent to the coast, with the Western Hemlock Zone inland (on the mountain slopes) over most of the region; it is replaced in Southern Oregon and Northern California by the Mixed Evergreen and Redwood Zones. True Fir and Arctic-Alpine Zones are restricted to the Olympic Mountains, except for small areas of True Fir in the Siskiyou/Klamath Mountains of Units #8 and #9 (From Proctor, et al., 1980).

INLAND BIOLOGICAL ZONES

ARCTIC ALPINE (1.1.1)

TRUE FIR (1.1.2)

WESTERN HEMLOCK (1.2.1)

REDWOOD (1.2.2)

MIXED EVERGREEN (1.2.3)

SITKA SPRUCE (1.2.4)

INTERIOR ZONE TYPE, NOT COVERED IN THIS REPORT

Within each of these zones many variations in moisture and temperature create localized differences in the community composition, such as on riverbanks, or on north- vs. south-facing mountain slopes. The most conspicuous mature forest communities in these zones, along with some of the variations, are described below.

SITKA SPRUCE ZONE

Here the heavy winter rains, warm winter temperatures, cool summers, and heavy summer fogs that condense in the tree crowns and drip to the ground, create the most favorable growing conditions and the lushest plant growth in the region. The zone is a thin band that stretches from the Kenai Peninsula, Alaska, to Cape Mendocino, California, and is usually about 7 miles wide but up to 15 miles where it extends up river valleys. Annual precipitation averages 80–120 inches and temperature averages 59–63°F in July and 40–46°F in January. Fog drip takes the edge off the summer drought by adding as much as 25% to the total amount of precipitation reaching the ground. The typical Sitka spruce forest type includes the Olympic rain forest and in part the coastal redwood forest.

Northern Oregon spruce forests. Two major old growth spruce community types can be found on the northern Oregon Coast: the coastal and the inland communities (Hines, 1971) (Figure 67). The dominant trees in both are Sitka spruce and western hemlock, with lesser amounts of western redcedar, Douglas fir, and red alder. Both have lush understories of shrubs, flowering herbs, ferns, mosses, lichens, and liverworts, although the coastal community is shrubbier.

The coastal community grows 90% of the time on soils derived from marine sediments and from 1–6 miles inland (Hines, 1971). The shrub salal is always present and covers 42% of the ground area. Other important shrubs are ovalleaf and red huckleberries (*Vaccinium ovalifolium* and *V. parvifolium*) and rustyleaf (*Menziesia ferruginea*). Major herbs are deer fern (*Blechnum spicant*, 37% cover), sword fern, and Oregon oxalis (*Oxalis oregana*). About half the ground is covered with mosses, liverworts, and lichens.

The inland community occurs on both marine sediments and basalt soils, and lies from 7 to 12 miles inland (Hines, 1971). Salal is absent on 80% of the locales and when present only covers 4% of the ground. Dominant shrubs are ovalleaf and red huckleberries (each about 15% cover), vine maple, and rustyleaf. Less common shrubs are devilsclub, salmonberry, salal, and Oregon grape. Major herbs are sword fern and Oregon oxalis (each 50% cover), with lesser amounts of deer fern, false-lily-of-the-valley, and evergreen violet. More than two-thirds of the ground is covered with mosses, liverworts, and lichens.

Figure 67. Old growth Sitka spruce (*Picea sitchensis*) at Cummins Creek, Oregon. July, 1986.

All trees save western hemlock have greater cover in the inland than the coastal community, and western redcedar, nevertheless, is more frequent near the coast than inland. Perhaps the hemlock grows better in the poorer, sandier soils of the coastal community because of its low nutrient needs.

Interestingly, the only tree that is reproducing in these two communities is western hemlock. The deep shade of the understory kills shade-intolerant saplings, and western hemlock saplings are much more tolerant to shade than Douglas fir, Sitka spruce, and western redcedar. Spruce seedlings are rare, and pole-sized saplings are absent, while all ages of western hemlock are present. This probably means that these communities are not yet at climax, and western hemlock will eventually replace the other tree species. If

Figure 68. The Old Man Cedar (*Thuja plicata*) with western hemlock growing from its bole, Rockaway, Oregon. August, 1986. Old growth western redcedar forests such as this may have been common pre-settlement on the coastal plain of Washington and northern Oregon.

these others are to reproduce in the future, they will need shafts of sunlight brought in when the hemlocks die and blow down. In any case, the spruce, cedar, and Douglas fir are all long-lived species, and though old and decadent, will probably remain for a few more centuries.

Although these communities are typical of the spruce zone, there are conspicuous variations. In general, Pacific silver-fir (*Abies amabilis*) is more common in Washington spruce forests, and grand fir (*Abies grandis*), tanoak (*Lithocarpus densiflorus*), Port-Orford cedar (*Chamaecyparis lawsoniana*), and California laurel (*Umbellularia californica*) in southwest Oregon and northwest California. Throughout the spruce zone, the mixed stands of spruce, hemlock, western red-cedar, Douglas fir, and others are being slowly replaced by western hemlock. On moist to wet sites, however, the cedar and in some cases the spruce remain as climax species along with the hemlock (Franklin and Dyrness, 1973) (Figure 68). Coast pine is a common species on unfavorable sites such as stabilized sand dunes and steep ocean-facing slopes. Dense shrubby understories are typical here with salal, Pacific rhododendron, evergreen huckleberry, and other heath plants dominating (see Chapter 5). The pine is very tolerant of drought, excess moisture, and frost, but is killed by heavy shade (Minore, 1979). It reproduces well close to the beach because high winds and poor sandy soils keep the canopy sparse and the ground sunlit.

Ever-increasing human activity on the coast, including logging and the construction of vacation houses, businesses, and roads, has perpetuated an early successional forest within the spruce forests, especially in Oregon. This red alder/salmonberry community has spread like wildfire in the past few decades wherever the land has been bulldozed or otherwise disturbed. Alder produces multitudes of minute seeds that travel long distances on the wind, and tend to sprout wherever the ground has been laid bare. The disturbed sites are soon smothered with fast-growing red alder seedlings, followed by thick, shrubby salmonberry and red elderberry. Usually hemlock, spruce, and other conifers are present, but their reproduction is brought to a near standstill by the dense vegetation and taller, faster-growing red alders. After 20 years, the alder shades itself out of existence and gradually disappears (Franklin and Dyrness, 1973). If conifers are present, they eventually take over; if not, the salmonberry does.

Red alder forests also flourish along streams and rivers in the spruce zone. Originally, before human settlement, this tree was much more restricted and scarce than it is now, and probably grew in few places other than this "riparian alder" community (Franklin and Dyrness, 1973; Maser, 1981). The alder grows taller and brush is taller and denser along the wet, cool stream banks than in the alder/salmonberry community. Initially, grass and herbs are abundant, such as common velvetgrass, common chickweed, western springbeauty, foxglove, trailing blackberry, and great hedge nettle. As the stand matures, shrubs and ferns such as deer fern, lady fern, and salmonberry take over (Maser, et al., 1981). Large rivers (e.g., on the southern Oregon Coast) often are lined with a dense mixture of hardwoods, typically bigleaf maple, red alder, Oregon ash, willows, sometimes black cottonwood, and in southern Oregon, California laurel. Since these trees subsist on the stable supply of groundwater, they are more-or-less independent of rainfall (Spurr and Barnes, 1980).

Figure 69. The largest known Douglas fir (*Pseudotsuga menziesii*), Queets rain forest, Olympic National Park. July, 1984.

Olympic rain forest. This old growth community is the magnificent culmination of the Northwest coniferous forest. Abundant moisture and rich river bottom soils created the largest western hemlock, Douglas fir, western redcedar, and red alder in the world (Kirk, 1966; Figures 69 and 70). Though a variant of the Sitka spruce forest, this community deserves special mention. For reasons unknown, the Olympic rain forest is found only in the Hoh, Queets, Quinault, and possibly Bogachiel river valleys in the western slopes of the Olympic Mountains (Franklin and Dyrness, 1973). In the thick of the forest, one is struck from all sides by an overall quality of lush, verdant growth. A thick drapery of moss, lichens, liverworts, and ferns blankets everything, giving soft, cushioned contours and blurred outlines (Figure 70). Ancient spruces 10 feet across loom ghost-like

Figure 70. An epiphyte-draped bigleaf maple (*Acer macrophyllum*) in the Hoh rain forest. July, 1984.

in indistinct twilight, and all sounds seem softly muted in the faint, windless air. Flowing luxuriance contrasts with an overwhelmingly spacious immensity, and the result is unforgettably dream-like and surreal (Plate 18).

The abundant mossy growth is created primarily by the heaviest rains in the spruce zone, about 135 inches average per year, only 7% of this from June to August (Franklin and Dyrness, 1973). Proximity to the ocean, the high altitudes, and resultant cool temperatures bring the rain. The spaciousness or open canopy and understory are created by heavy grazing of seasonal Roosevelt elk herds on the shrubs, especially salmonberry. The Sitka spruce dominates the hemlock because the elk prefer the hemlock seedlings and generally prevent enough tree growth to close the canopy. Thus the spruce reproduces well and is considered a climax tree while the hemlock reproduces poorly.

Scattered through the forest are areas of shallow, stony soil where groves of tall, moss-draped bigleaf maples grow. In the shrub layer, vine maple grows in occasional thick clumps, while all other species provide very little cover (Franklin and Dyrness, 1973). Huckleberries (ovalleaf and red), trailing blackberry, and salmon-berry are characteristic. The forest floor is carpeted with Oregon oxalis, sword fern, and assorted other herbs, including western cool-wort (*Tiarella unifoliata*), Dewey sedge (*Carex deweyana*), nodding trisetum (*Trisetum cernuum*), false lily-of-the-valley (*Maianthemum dilatatum*), strawberry-leaf blackberry (*Rubus pedatus*), and others. A thick moss layer is also typical. One of the most abundant epiphytes is *Selaginella oregana*, a club moss.

Succession usually begins with red alder on the river flood plain, followed by black cottonwood and bigleaf maple on the first terrace, spruce and hemlock on the second terrace, which is the site of the classical rain forest, and lastly, near-climax hemlock on the third terrace. Usually western redcedar and Douglas fir grow only on the steep slopes between the terraces and not on the terraces them-selves (Franklin and Dyrness, 1973).

Redwood forests. The coast redwood (*Sequoia sempervirens*) is an example of how nature at times refuses to conform to our preconceived categories. Redwood forests overlap at least three forest zones: the Sitka spruce, western hemlock, and mixed evergreen; although at most sites the species appears climax and therefore deserving independent status, at least in Oregon its place is sufficiently vague to foreclose any special recognition (Franklin and Dyrness, 1973). In California, the coast redwood represents the southernmost limit of the northwest coniferous forests. Although we might expect that, near their distributional limits, conifers should experience espe-cially intense stresses and poor growing conditions, the coast redwoods are the tallest, most massive trees in the world, forming monumental old growth stands with the highest biomass yet measured anywhere in the world. In moist, undisturbed sites, a redwood must reach 200 years of age and 2 feet in diameter before it even enters the forest canopy (Veirs, 1982)

Redwoods grow along the coast from the Chetco River (a few miles north of the Oregon border) south to Monterey, with some scattered trees as far south as Morro Bay. From the Eel River north, virtually the entire redwood forest is unbroken old growth, protected in the Redwood National Park. Intolerant of salt spray, redwoods avoid the exposed ocean bluffs, instead growing well sheltered from the storms behind at least a thin band of Sitka spruce or Douglas fir. Some peculiarities of this distribution suggest a heavy dependence on soil moisture provided by summer fog drip. First, redwoods are restricted to the lowlands adjacent to the ocean, and the center of their distribution corresponds to the region of greatest upwelling on the west U.S. shoreline, along the Mendocino coast (Huyer, 1983). Second, redwoods extend far inland only where the topography is sufficiently low to allow fog penetration. For example, redwood penetrates farthest inland, some 40 miles along the Eel River east of Cape Mendocino, where the coastal mountains dip down to near sea level, allowing free penetration of summer fog from the northwest. Here is the famous "Avenue of the Giants" and Humboldt State Park, where the world record biomass of 1800 tons/acre was measured. In contrast, redwood is absent from the cape itself just a few miles to the west, apparently because steep mountains, primarily the King's Peak Range, 1246 feet in elevation and less than three miles inland, rise abruptly from the ocean and block the fog.

Three attributes of redwood physiology might explain this fog dependence. First, coast redwood lacks root hairs, the primary water-absorbing structures in most plants (Roy, 1966). Hence it is likely that redwood is unable to extract enough water during drought stress of summer. Second, redwood appears to lack anatomical or physiological means for controlling transpiration, and as a result transpires more rapidly than most other conifers (Roy, 1966), thus depleting soil moisture earlier in the summer. Finally, perhaps because of vulnerability to infection by bacteria or fungi in the forest duff, redwood seedlings show a strong preference for clean mineral soil (Roy, 1966). If seedlings in mineral soil are non-mycorrhizal, they are at a serious disadvantage in areas not refreshed by summer fog.

Botanists recognize two categories of coast redwood forests: alluvial and mountain slope. On the deep, lowland alluvial soils, such as the Stout Grove (Del Norte Redwoods) and the Humboldt Redwoods, the species reaches its maximum biomass and canopy density, often dominating in spectacular, pure stands, or with a scant representation of California laurel (*Umbellularia californica*) and red alder. The dense canopy shades out all shrubs save a few scattered California rhododendron (*Rhododendron macrophyllum*) and ever-green huckleberry (*Vaccinium ovatum*). Small shade-loving herbs, however, carpet the ground. Common species include vanilla grass (*Hierochloe occidentalis*), sword fern, Oregon oxalis, wild ginger (*Asarum caudatum*), trillium, fetid adder's tongue (*Scoliopus bigelovii*), and fairy bells (*Disporum smithii*). The dominance of redwood on alluvial flats is due perhaps to an unusual tolerance to periodic flooding (Stone and Vasey, 1968; Zinke, 1977). For example, the alluvial stand at Bull Creek (Rockefeller Grove of the Humboldt Redwoods) has experienced major floods every 30–60 years, some of which dumped 30 feet of new gravel and sand on the ground. Redwood responds to this by growing a new set of roots close to the surface, while most other canopy species die from a lack of root aeration. Some ancient redwoods uprooted at Bull Creek have a fascinating multistoried root system, each corresponding to a different ancient flood, whose date of occurrence can be estimated by ring counts of the trees. Interestingly, some understory herbs, such as Oregon oxalis, survive the floods by sending long shoots upwards to the surface, where they produce new flowers that gradually reseed the new forest floor (Stone and Vasey, 1968).

The slope redwood stands, beautifully exemplified by the Prairie Creek State Park north of Orick, extend inland with the fog, and upwards as high as 3000 feet on a few western slopes. Conditions are drier and somewhat less than optimum for redwood, which shares a sparser canopy with several other species. On low western slopes western hemlock is the most common associate, and on high eastern slopes, Douglas fir (Veirs, 1982). Inland, redwood gradually gives way to more drought tolerant species such as tanoak, Douglas fir, and madrone (*Arbutus menziesii*). The shrub layer is often dense, and includes tanoak, California hazelnut (*Corylus cornuta* var. *californica*), evergreen huckleberry, wild rose (*Rosa gymnocarpa*), thimbleberry, and salal. On the ground layer, Oregon oxalis, sword fern, and other alluvial species are less common, giving way to bracken, clintonia (*Clintonia andrewsiana*), trillium (*Trillium chloropetalum*), false Solomon's seal (*Smilacina racemosa*), vanilla leaf (*Achlys triphylla*), and others.

In the past, botanists have suspected that coast redwood is, like Douglas fir and the giant sequoia, a successional species dependent on fire and floods for the elimination of its competitors (Stone and Vasey, 1968; Franklin and Dyrness, 1973). This theory, however, has been largely rejected, at least for the old growth stands between Orick and Crescent City (Veirs, 1982). In this region, fire frequency varies from one every 250–500 years on the coast, to one every 50 years in the driest inland stands. Certainly redwood seeds-in rapidly after a fire, as does Douglas fir and western hemlock. Redwood, however, also has an unusual ability to reproduce vegetatively, by sprouting from the base of the trunk (Roy, 1966). When only six months old, a redwood seedling begins to develop a burl just beneath the ground surface, which soon produces several dormant buds. If the seedling is injured by fire, grazing, or other means, the buds sprout into several new redwood stems, each of which develops a new burl. Adult trees usually have burls scattered the entire length of the trunk, so if the crown is damaged mechanically or by fire, numerous buds sprout and leaf all along the trunk, creating a "fire column" and the tree eventually grows a new, normal crown. Since these buds are supported by the parent's root system, they grow surprisingly fast, up to 7 feet in a single growing season. Although two other conifers can sprout in this manner, *Taxus brevifolia* and *Torreya californica*, they are much slower than coast redwood, which sprouts during any season within just 2 months after logging or fire. In most old growth stands, three or four generations of sprouts around a massive, ancient, often fire-scarred parent can be identified.

Unlike Douglas fir, however, redwood is not dependent on fires (Veirs, 1982). Redwood seedlings are highly shade tolerant and are usually present in all old growth stands, regardless of fire history. Although seedlings almost never survive in duff, they are common on logs, root wads, and in mineral soil. They can survive suppressed in the shade for 50–150 years, resprouting whenever burnt or wind damaged, and can eventually enter the canopy without disturbance, or grow explosively after a fire. Because redwood mortality rates are extremely low (the maximum measured age is just under 2200 years), only four new trees per acre need recruit into the canopy every century to maintain the typical redwood canopy of 16 trees per acre (Veirs, 1982) present in old growth stands not recently burned. Douglas fir, on the other hand, almost never occurs in the understory of dense, less-disturbed stands, and in moderately moist sites occurs in just one or two age classes. Fire scars on nearby redwoods clearly show that these firs recruited into the stand only after fires destroyed enough redwood foliage to open the ground to sunlight. Redwood, tanoak, and western hemlock, however, are usually present in all ages, suggesting that these persist in the canopy indefinitely.

WESTERN HEMLOCK ZONE

The old growth hemlock forests were the most extensive plant community in the region in prelogging days (Franklin and Dyrness, 1973). This zone is today more important than any other to the region's timber production, and is famous for the stands of massive Douglas fir. On wetter sites fir does not reproduce because its seedlings do not tolerate the deep shade of the forest, and though temporarily dominant because of its size and longevity, it theoretically dies out and is replaced by climax western hemlock and western redcedar. But in the meantime, even old growth stands up to 600 years old frequently contain as much Douglas fir as hemlock, and the fir is much bigger, typically 5–7ft diameter as opposed to 3–4ft. Since western hemlock and western redcedar require more water than Douglas fir, the fir is actually the climax tree on the driest sites in the zone.

Moisture stresses are a major factor in determining the plant species present in any particular community in the zone. This is mainly because of the summer drought; only 6–9% of the total precipitation falls in June through August, and the greater distance from the ocean makes the relief of summer fogs much rarer than in the spruce zone (Franklin and Dyrness, 1973).

With some variations, the typical sequence of old growth communities encountered in the Coast Range when moving from dry to wet is as follows (canopy/understory/ground layer) (Franklin and Dyrness, 1973):

Dry   Douglas fir/creambrush oceanspray/salal
      Western hemlock-Douglas fir/western rhododendron/Oregon grape
      Western hemlock/big huckleberry/common beargrass
Moist Western hemlock/vine maple/salal
      Western hemlock/salal/sword fern
      Western hemlock/sword fern
Wet   Western hemlock/sword fern/Oregon oxalis

Other common conifers are western redcedar in wet areas and, of course, Douglas fir. Less common throughout are grand fir (*Abies grandis*) and western white pine (*Pinus monticola*). In southern Oregon some incense-cedar (*Libocedrus decurrens*), sugar pine (*Pinus lambertiana*), Port-Orford cedar (*Chamaecyparis lawsoniana*), or even ponderosa pine (*Pinus ponderosa*) occur. Hardwoods are rare for reasons given above and occur early in succession or on watercourses. Most widespread are red alder, bigleaf maple, and golden chinkapin. Along major rivers black cottonwood, Oregon ash, bigleaf maple, and red alder thrive. Pacific madrone and Garry oak occasionally grow in drier lowland areas, and California laurel and tanoak occur in the southern coastal mountains (Franklin and Dyrness, 1973).

Notably absent from all these communities, except sporadically near the coast, is Sitka spruce. It is uncertain why the spruce grows and reproduces poorly away from the ocean but several guesses have been made. Although the drought-relieving summer fogs, the milder temperatures, and soils near the ocean influence spruce dominance, the deciding factor may be the salty ocean air. Sitka spruce needs more magnesium and is less tolerant of insufficient magnesium than nearly all other Northwest forest trees, and dissolved magnesium salts are abundant in sea water. When the winds blow the wave froth loose, magnesium and other salts fly in a fine mist inland where they enter the soil directly or after serving as nuclei for raindrops. Widespread metal corrosion on cars and boats of beach residents testifies to the ionic content of the air. Beyond about 10 miles inland, the salt content is insufficient to permit the survival of the spruce, and here the hemlock zone begins. The only places where spruce grows farther inland are on river bottoms, whose soil is unusually rich in calcium and magnesium.

Western hemlock, on the other hand, needs less nutrients of all kinds and actually dies in overly-rich soils. The situation is complicated, though; hemlock is more common than spruce in some wetter areas close to the ocean, such as north-facing headland slopes. In these favorable sites, dense tree growth shades the forest floor so hemlock's shade tolerance permits it to reproduce somewhat better than spruce, which gradually becomes scarcer.

Abundant Douglas fir makes up for the scarcity of spruce in the hemlock zone. The former grows in all the above communities, though is less common than hemlock in all but the driest areas, where it is a climax species.

MIXED EVERGREEN FORESTS

All forest types in the western United States converge, mingle, and interact in complex interdigitating patterns in the Siskiyou/Klamath Mountains of southern Oregon and northern California, and the center of contact is the mixed evergreen forest, perhaps the most all-inclusive transitional forest in western North America. A hike through the mixed evergreen will reveal representatives of the pine-oak foothill woodland and chapparal of California, the coniferous forest of the Pacific Northwest lowlands, the true fir forests of higher elevations, and the northern oak woodland of the interior Oregon valleys. Over geological time, the Klamath Mountains have experienced a minimum of disturbance from glaciation, floods, and fires, and as a result have served as an intact source reservoir of immigrants capable of recolonizing the surrounding landscape after major geologic transitions (Whittaker, 1960, 1961).

The mixed evergreen zone lies along the middle western slopes of the Siskiyous and Klamaths and northern Coast Range of California, just east of the western hemlock zone in Oregon and the Sitka spruce or coast redwood zone in California. The mixed evergreen experiences greater extremes in temperature than coastal locations; January temperatures average 32–36°F, some 10° colder than in the Sitka spruce zone; and June temperatures average 62–66°F, about 5° warmer than the spruce (Franklin and Dyrness, 1973). Drought tolerant species dominate forests of all ages. In old growth stands of average moisture, Douglas fir, Port-Orford cedar (*Chamaecyparis lawsonia*), and sugar pine (*Pinus lambertiana*), characterize the upper canopy; tanoak, madrone (*Arbutus menziesii*), golden chinkapin (*Castanopsis chrysophylla*), and canyon live oak (*Quercus chrysolepis*) the lower canopy; Sadler oak (*Q. sadleriana*), huckleberry oak (*Q. vaccinifolia*), Oregon grape (*Berberis nervosa*), trailing blackberry (*Rubus ursinus*), baldhip rose (*Rosa gymnocarpa*), and poison oak (*Rhus diversiloba*) the shrub layer. The herb layer is sparse (generally less than 10% coverage), and includes whipple vine (*Whipplea modesta*), vanilla leaf (*Achlys triphylla*), starflower (*Trientalis latifolia*), and bracken.

Successional relationships are poorly known in the mixed evergreen zone, but some patterns are obvious. As in other forests, Douglas fir often seeds-in after fires and eventually forms dense, even-aged stands. In addition, knobcone pine (*Pinus attenuata*), is strictly fire dependent because its cones shed their seeds only after fires. Dense brushfields often dominate soon after fires, and some appear to persist on especially dry sites even without fire, and can perhaps be considered climax. Brushfields of hard-leaved species such as hoary and green manzanitas (*Arctostaphylos canescens* and *A. patula*), are assumed to be climax, and often occupy hot and dry southern or eastern slopes. Those of soft-leaved shrubs such as tanoak and madrone probably succeed to coniferous forest (Franklin and Dyrness, 1973).

SILVER FIR FORESTS

These forests are conspicuous on the rocky slopes of the Olympic Mountains and occur in scattered high-elevation patches in the Coast Range; in the Cascades they form a continuous zone. The critical environmental factors that create the silver fir forests are cold and snowfall. Average January temperatures are subfreezing and July temperatures average 57–59°F; precipitation is over 80 inches per year (Franklin and Dyrness, 1973).

The silver fir is rare and nonclimax in the lower elevations partly because of its intolerance, compared to hemlock, of drought and fire, both of which occur more often in the hemlock zone due to its warmer, drier climate (Minore, 1979). Another factor is the slow growth of the silver fir seedlings.

The kinds and amounts of the trees, shrubs, and herbs vary widely, depending on the stand age, history, moisture, and soils. Moisture and soil differences have created at least three different communities in the northern Oregon Coast Range (Franklin and Dyrness, 1973). In the wetter areas around 14 miles inland is the western hemlock-silver fir/ western rhododendron/bunchberry dogwood community; western redcedar also has high cover. In somewhat drier areas closer to the ocean, the vegetation is much more open and reminiscent of a city park. On higher-elevation rugged slopes, the western hemlock-silver fir/ salal/western cool-wort community occurs, and downslope from this, on the cool, gentler east and north slopes is the western hemlock-silver fir/ ovalleaf huckleberry/Oregon oxalis community. Each of these lies from 2000 to 3000 feet above sea level.

Succession occurs as in the lower forest areas; seral tree species include Douglas fir, noble fir, and Sitka spruce.

MOUNTAIN HEMLOCK ZONE

This is the highest-forested zone in the Northwest and, on the coast, occurs only in the Olympic Mountains. At these elevations western hemlock finally disappears completely, surrendering ground to mountain hemlock. Pacific silver-fir and Alaska cedar (*Chamaecyparis nootkatensis*), are other common trees; less common are Douglas fir, subalpine fir (*Abies lasiocarpa*), and western white pine (*Pinus monticola*) (Franklin and Dyrness, 1973).

The force that creates this zone is cold. Subfreezing temperatures prevail 5–6 months of the year; snow accumulates from 10 to 30 feet and persists through late June and July, which leaves a cruel brief growing season, and most Northwest trees, including western hemlock, cannot survive it. Those that can must endure a harsh and oppressive climate. Mountain hemlock (*Tsuga mertensiana*), for instance, needs more water and tolerates frost and the excess moisture during snowmelt much better than western hemlock (Minore, 1979).

The upper edge of the mountain hemlock zone is timberline, where forest meets tundra. In contrast to most mountainous regions, forests in northwest high lands do not break off abruptly at timberline. Rather, they give way gradually from closed canopy to scattered clumps of full-sized trees surrounded by wildflower meadows to the highest level where trees can survive, only in stunted form. Timberline is thus not a line, but a wide band of scenic, park-like forest and meadows that usually extend over 900 feet up the slopes. The cause of this distribution may be the deep, late-lying snowpacks.

The colorful variety of the meadow flora, the dynamic interactions between meadow and forest, and the spectacular alpine scenery make the parklands attractive to scientists and laypersons alike. The tree clumps develop on scattered hummocks and ridges because the snowpack melts sooner there and gives them a longer growing season (Franklin and Dyrness, 1973). Over several decades, the clumps enlarge as new seedlings spring up around the margins under the warm cover of the adult trees. Eventually, the trees spread into the lower areas and surrounding meadow, and remain until fire, slides, or other disturbances remove them and recreate the meadows. During warm years trees invade meadows by the hundreds, and may or may not be wiped out again later.

Tree composition in the parklands is somewhat different from the main mountain hemlock forest. Lodgepole pine (*Pinus contorta*) and whitebark pine (*Pinus albicaulis*) replace the Douglas fir and western white pine. Pacific silver-fir and Alaska cedar are less common, subalpine fir is more common, and mountain hemlock about equally common. Often several whitebark pines will spring up together from a forgotten seed hoard of a Clark's nutcracker.

Surrounding the picturesque tree clumps are sharp variations in soil depth, type, moisture, and duration of winter snowpack. These create about eight distinct and colorful meadow wildflower or shrub communities that, in turn, give food and shelter to the grazing animals of the parklands (Franklin and Dyrness, 1973). Often these communities develop where fire destroys a stand of trees.

In cool places where the snow stays until mid- to late July the shrubby heath community grows. This conspicuous assemblage of red heather (*Phyllodoce empetriformis*), blueleaf huckleberry (*Vaccinium deliciosum*), and western cassiope (*Cassiope mertensiana*), is unique and characterizes the parklands.

Wet places support lush herb growth often 3 feet high or more. Tall herbs stand above understory herbs, and creepers spread over the ground surface. On steep, well-watered northeast-facing slopes lies the valerian community, dominated by Sitka valerian (*Valeriana sitchensis*), American false hellebore (*Veratrum viride*), arctic lupine (*Lupinus latifolius* var. *subalpinus*), showy sedge (*Carex spectabilis*), and smallflower paintbrush (*Castilleja parviflora*). The tall sedge community grows at higher elevations of various aspects and topography; typical plants are showy sedge, American bistort (*Polygonum bistortoides*), arctic lupine, fanleaf cinquefoil (*Potentilla flabellifolia*), black alpine sedge (*Carex nigricans*), and peregrine fleabane (*Erigeron peregrinus*). In shallow gullies kept moist by melting snowbanks or shallow streams is the colorful saussuria community, dominated by saussurea (*Saussurea americana*), cow parsnip (*Heracleum lanatum*), western waterleaf (*Hydrophyllum occidentale*), western groundsel (*Senecio integerrimus*), western meadow rue (*Thalictrum occidentale*), and pale larkspur (*Delphinium glaucum*).

On cold, wet soils of higher elevations where snow remains until late July or early August the dwarf sedge community develops, where black alpine sedge forms a low, dense mat and red heather, western cassiope, blueleaf huckleberry, and others grow in smaller amounts.

The poorly developed, pioneer cushion plant community grows on exposed knolls, ridge tops, and south-facing slopes. The mat-forming spreading phlox (*Phlox diffusa*), dominates, along with gray rockcress (*Arabis cobrensis*), littleflower collinsia (*Collinsia parviflora*), and smooth-leaved Douglasia (*Douglasia laevigata*).

Two grassy communities grow on steep, dry, south- to west-facing slopes and are best developed in the dry rain shadow on the eastern side of the Olympics. In the moist grass community grows green fescue (*Festuca viridula*), arctic lupine, and spreading phlox. The dry grass community grows only on the nutrient-rich basaltic soils, whose dark color traps heat, which evaporates the water and keeps most nights above freezing. Typical plants are green fescue, Cascades aster (*Aster ledophyllus*), Gray's lovage (*Ligusticum grayi*), and American bistort.

Some of these assemblages have their own herbivores. The mountain beaver (*Aplodontia rufa*), eats plants of the saussuria and valeriana communities, and the Olympic marmot (*Marmota olympus*), feeds on and digs burrows under the grass communities. The Columbian black-tailed deer (*Odocoileus hemionus*), grazes mainly on the grass, saussuria, and tall sedge communities, and the Olympic elk (*Cervus elaphus*), on the valeriana and tall sedge.

Above the parklands is the alpine zone, where several stresses eliminate trees and perpetuate meadows similar to those in the parklands. Glaciers, snowfields, bare rock, and rubble dominate the steep, rugged landscape. Cold, whipping winds; deep, late-lying snow; short growing seasons; and thin, youthful soils kill upright trees, shrubs, and all but a few hardy herbs. And these cannot survive in most alpine areas on the western side of the Olympics because of the greater snowfall and deeper snowpack. Even in the northeast Olympics, where conditions are better, the alpine zone is narrow and desolate compared to the expansive alpine of the Rockies and other ranges.

Alpine meadows in the northeast Olympics replace the trees at about 5100 ft., grow best at about 5500 ft., and disappear above about 6800 ft. due to rock and permanent snow and ice (Franklin and Dyrness, 1973; Kuramoto and Bliss, 1970). This is lower than the alpine of the Rockies and other inland ranges because the ocean brings greater snowfall at lower elevations (Franklin and Dyrness, 1973).

Communities are varied and follow the same patterns as those in the parklands. Stronger winds, however, keep the plants closer to the ground where the air is stiller; often the flowers of the abundant mat-formers and cushion plants barely poke out from underneath the blanketing leaves.

Low productivity and slow regeneration make the alpine plant communities helplessly vulnerable to disturbances, and they support only a few grazing and predatory animals. Several species of endemic ground beetles feed on each other and are fed upon by horned larks (*Eremophila alpestris*), water pipits (*Anthus spinoletta pacificus*), brown salamanders (*Ambostoma gracile gracile*), western long-toed salamanders (*Ambostoma macrodactylum*), western toads (*Bufo boreas*), and masked shrews (*Sorex cinereus*). These animals also eat frozen insects that are carried up to the alpine by warm air rising from the valleys below.

Meadow plants are summer food for slugs, the rosy finch (*Leucosticte arctoa*), rufous hummingbird (*Selasphorus rufus*), white-tailed ptarmigan (*Lagopus leucurus*), the introduced mountain goat (*Oreamnos americanus*), black tailed deer, Olympic elk, mountain pocket gopher, (*Thomomys monticola*) and heather vole (*Phenacomys intermedius*). Carnivorous animals include the red-tailed hawk (*Buteo jamaicensis*), common raven (*Corvus corax*), American kestrel (*Falco sparverius*), and rarely, the golden eagle (*Aquila chrysaetos*), peregrine falcon (*Falco peregrinus*), mountain lion (*Felis concolor*), and weasels (*Mustela* spp). The common deer mouse eats plants and insects alike.

Most of these animals migrate downslope when the heavy snows hit and bury the plants, returning when summer warmth again exposes the ground. The water pipits fly to the beaches and open fields and marshes along the coast to feed. The elk move down to the lowland forests, and the ptarmigans winter just downslope below the timberline.

7

HUMAN IMPACTS

*When the Pleiades and the wind in the grass are no
longer a part of the human spirit, man becomes . . . a
cosmic outlaw. . . .*

Henry Beston, foreword to
The Outermost House *(1928).*

MARINE MAMMALS AND SEABIRDS

Whales

Since 1900, the whaling industry has brought death to over 2 million whales worldwide, severely depleting some 20 different populations of great whales (Breiwick and Braham, 1984) (Figure 71-table). This was done primarily to fill the market for a variety of oils, cosmetics thickeners, and assorted other conveniences now available synthetically. Three stocks are now considered extinct or virtually extinct: the North Pacific right whale(s), the western North Pacific gray whale, and the East-Greenland-Spitsbergen bowhead whale. Of the 16 additional populations nearing extinction worldwide, three are native to the Pacific and are seldom seen now in Pacific Northwest waters: the North Pacific blue whale, down to 29–39% of its original abundance; the North Pacific humpback whale(s), down to 8%; and the North Pacific fin whale, down to 32–44%. Japan and the Soviet Union are the most active whaling nations, with Japan taking 13,000–14,000 whales per year in the early 1980s.

One of the reasons these animals are close to extinction is the historically common misconception that they should respond to harvesting in roughly the same manner as commercial fish populations. But unlike fish, whales of course do not lay millions of rapidly developing eggs each year, and are not capable of fast population growth, so are much more vulnerable to overharvest. The large size of virtually all baleen whales makes birth, nursing, and care of offspring extremely costly, and generally prevents females from bearing more than one offspring, and more than once each year.

By the 1970s, popular concern over the situation resulted in protective federal legislation. In 1971 and 1972, the United States and Canada stopped all whaling on their shores. In 1972 Congress passed the Marine Mammal Protection Act, which restricts the

Figure 71. Initial (precommercial whaling) and current population size estimates of large whales currently listed as "endangered" under the ESA; n.e. = no estimates. (From Breiwick and Braham, 1984.)

Species, stocks, or reporting area(s)	Population sizes Initial	Population sizes Current	Approximate percent of initial
Gray whale			
Eastern North Pacific	15,000–20,000	13,450–19,210	Recovered
Western North Pacific	n.e.	n.e.[1]	n.e.
Blue whale			
North Atlantic	1,100–1,500	100	6–9%
North Pacific	4,900	1,400–1,900	29–39%
North Indian Ocean	n.e.	n.e.[4]	n.e.
Antarctic[2]	150,000–210,000	1,000–8,000	<1–5%
Subantarctic Indian Ocean[3]	10,000	5,000	50%
Fin whale			
North Norway	Several thousand	n.e.	n.e
West Norway/Faeroe Isl.	>2,700	n.e.[4]	10%?
Spain, Portugal, British Isles	>5,000	n.e.	n.e.
Denmark Strait	n.e.	1,791–11,584	n.e.
W. North Atlantic	n.e.	3,590–6,300	n.e.
North Pacific	42,000–45,000	14,620–18,630	32–44%
Antarctic[2]	400,000	85,200	21%
Sei whale			
North Atlantic	n.e.	4,957	n.e.
North Pacific	45,000	22,000–37,000	49–82%
Southern Hemisphere[2]	>63,100–64,400	>9,800–11,760	15–19%

Species, stocks, or reporting area(s)	Population sizes Initial	Population sizes Current	Approximate percent of initial
Humpback whale			
E. North Atlantic	n.e.	n.e.	n.e.
W. North Atlantic	>4,400	5,257–6,289	Recovered?
Northern Indian Ocean	n.e.	n.e.	n.e.
North Pacific	15,000	<1,200	8%
Southern Hemisphere	100,000	2,500–3,000	2–3%
Bowhead whale			
E. Greenland-Spitsbergen	25,000	n.e.[1]	<1%?
Davis Strait	11,000	n.e.[4]	<5%?
Hudson Bay	680	n.e.[4]	n.e.
Western Arctic	18,000	3,617–4,125	20–23%
Sea of Okhotsk	n.e.[5]	n.e.[4]	5–10%?
Right whale[6]			
North Atlantic	n.e.	n.e.[4]	n.e.
North Pacific	n.e.	n.e.[4]	n.e.
Southern Hemisphere	n.e.	3,000?	n.e.
Sperm whale[7]			
Eastern North Pacific	166,000	99,500	60%
Western North Pacific	311,000	274,000	88%
North Pacific	309,400	198,100	64%
Southern Hemisphere	590,600	410,700	70%

[1] Thought to be nearing extinction or extremely low.
[2] Six stock units or areas of all oceans in the Southern Hemisphere. For population estimates and status see Masaki and Yamamura (1978), Guliand (1981), and Butterworth (in press).
[3] Pygmy blue whales.
[4] Perhaps in the low hundreds.
[5] Perhaps 6,500–10,000.
[6] Stocks are reported here by general area only. See Braham and Rice (1984) for stock boundaries.
[7] Exploitable population size, and includes males and females (from Tables 4–6 in Gosho et al., 1984); all estimates of initial and current abundance are considered provisional. No estimates are available for the number of immature animals.

killing, harrassment, or possession of any whales or pinnipeds within U.S. territorial waters. This legislation was followed in 1973 by the Endangered Species Act, which names and protects endangered species, among which were the blue, bowhead, fin, gray, humpback, right, sei, and sperm whales, the so-called "great whales." Perhaps the most powerful legislation in controlling foreign harvest has been the U.S. Fishery Conservation and Management Act, with its Pelly Amendment (1971) and Packwood-Magnuson Amendment (1979). These require the U.S. Secretary of Commerce to limit the fishing rights in U.S. waters by at least one-half of customary catches of any country violating a resolution or circumventing the decisions of the International Commission on Whaling (IWC). However, a recent Supreme Court decision (June, 1986), in an unanticipated reversal of two lower courts, allowed the Secretary of Commerce some discretion in deciding whether to impose these sanctions (New York Times, July 1, I, 15:1).

In 1982, the IWC resolved to establish a total moratorium on all commercial whaling worldwide, during which time a detailed assessment could be made of the viability of several depleted whale populations. Despite this moratorium, whaling continues at roughly the same levels, with whaling nations such as Japan claiming that the kill is no longer for commercial purposes, but rather for scientific research.

The most encouraging example of the positive influence of decreased kill rates on large whales is the success story of the California gray whale. During the mid- and late 19th century, American whalers attacked the gray whales each winter as they lay helpless in their calving lagoons. From 1846 to 1874 the total catch was roughly 8,000, with a per-year average of 400–500 from 1855 to 1874 (Breiwick and Braham, 1984). As a result, the population plunged from about 10,000 to less than 2,000 by 1880, and the species was, for all economic purposes, extinct. The hunt was suspended until about 1930, by which time the population had recovered sufficiently for modern factory ships to take an average of 48 whales per year from 1933 to 1946; this harvest was almost entirely by the Soviet Union. In 1946, when the IWC was formed, it immediately named the gray whale a "protected stock," thereby banning any further commercial harvest. But the resolution exempted subsistence whaling, which allowed the Soviet Union to continue harvesting an average of 133 gray whales per year from 1948 to 1982, ostensibly to feed the Chukchi Eskimos of the U.S.S.R. Chukotka coast (Breiwick and Braham, 1984). In addition, researchers Rice and Wolman (1971) collected 316 gray whales under special scientific permits between 1959 and 1969. But these harvests were much less intensive than those of the 1850s, and the population slowly increased from 1900 to

1970, reaching a plateau of roughly 16,000–17,000 individuals by 1980. Several computer models suggest that the maximum historical population size was 24,000, but that aboriginal hunting, which may have eliminated 600 whales per year, kept the population at roughly 12,000 in the vicinity of the year 1800 (Reilly, 1981). Thus the gray whale, even with moderate hunting, has completely recovered to a stable population size, and is even more numerous than before the first American whaling expeditions. Moreover, the population appears to have leveled off, probably due to the Soviet harvest. If there were no harvest at all, it would most likely continue to rise, and level off once more at about 24,000 (Reilly, 1981). How this happy state of affairs relates to the situation of other large whales near extinction, such as the blue whale and North Pacific right whale, is unclear; we simply know too little about reproductive rates and population sizes to predict their futures. Nevertheless, the gray whale at least gives us hope.

Following commercial harvest, perhaps the second most significant source of whale mortality is the American yellowfin tuna fishing industry. Tuna fishermen follow dolphins and porpoises because they have learned that tuna schools follow the boisterous small whales, probably because both search for the same food. The fishermen drop nets that entangle and trap the panicking porpoises as well as the tuna. Unfortunately most of the porpoises have drowned by the time the fishermen make their catch. From 100,000 to 600,000 small whales are killed in this way every year (Maser, *et al.*, 1981). About 20,000 of these are dolphins and porpoises of the northeastern Pacific, such as the common, striped, and white-sided dolphins, and Dall's porpoises. The American incidental kill is regulated by the National Marine Fisheries Service, and that of other countries by the Inter-American Tropical Tuna Commission. About 20,000 dolphins and porpoises of Pacific Northwest waters are also killed accidentally each year by the Japanese open-ocean salmon gillnets in the northeastern North Pacific and Bering Sea.

Sea Otters and Pinnipeds

Direct conflict between nonwhale marine mammals and humans occurs in two ways: first, humans have hunted sea otters and fur seals for their pelts for centuries; and second, sea otters and pinnipeds occasionally eat fish that are sought by commercial, recreational, and Indian fishermen.

Overkilling reduced the sea otter population from 150,000 in the 1800s to about 1500 in 1911 (Maser, *et al.*, 1981), and eliminated the species from the Oregon and Washington coasts (Lyman, 1988).

Sea otter bones have been found in archaeological sites 100 to 3000 years old at Seal Rock, Whale Cove, and the mouth of the Umpqua River (Lyman, 1988). Before 1970, the survivors were scattered in small groups mostly along the Aleutians, but also off British Columbia, central California, and Baja California. Since 1911, when sea otters became legally protected, the population has grown to about 40,000. About 2000 of these are in California, and most of the rest along the Aleutians; the Baja population is virtually extinct. In 1970 and 1971, 50 sea otters from Alaska were reintroduced in Washington and Oregon with limited success. Although the Oregon populations died out by the early 1980s, summer 1985 counts indicate that the Washington transplants have survived well at Destruction Island, Sand Point, Cape Johnson, Jagged Island, and Cape Alava (Jameson, et al., 1982, 1986).

The northern fur seal is another marine mammal much sought after for its pelt. From 1889 to 1911, over 600,000 fur seals were shot from ships at sea and their pelts recovered; about the same number were wounded or unrecovered. As a result the population plunged from about 2 million to 300,000, and the species was extirpated from Oregon and California waters (Maser, et al., 1981; Hildebrandt, 1984; Lyman, 1988). Fur seal bones have been found in archaeological sites occupied prior to 100 years ago in Oregon at Seal Rock, Whale Cove, and the mouth of the Umpqua River, and in California at Stone Lagoon, Point St. George, Patrick's Point, Shelter Cove, and the mouth of the Mattole (Hildebrandt, 1984; Lyman, 1988). These sites indicate that Whale Cove and Seal Rock may have even been fur seal rookeries 2500–3000 years ago. An international treaty stopped the killing in 1911, and although Japan has violated the treaty since the 1930s, the fur seal population appears sufficiently stable that U.S. researchers have allowed limited harvesting. Aleuts make a living harvesting about 30,000 a year, and the United States shares the skins with Canada and Japan who, in return, have agreed not to resume the seal hunt (Maser, et al., 1981).

FISHERY CONFLICTS

Northwest commercial fishermen have complained for years that sea otters, sea lions, whales, and seabirds are destroying the industry by robbing and damaging their nets and by depleting the fish population to economically unprofitable levels. Irate fishermen in the 1950s went so far as to dynamite hauling-out areas, creating "Gunpowder Shoals" in Washington, for example. These complaints have sparked a great deal of research and a few symposia, which in most cases have failed to show that these marine mammals are anything more than an occasional nuisance.

The greatest damage occurs when harbor seals and sea lions

accidentally entangle themselves in salmon gillnets while eating the trapped salmon. In Gray's Harbor, Washington, 25% of the catch value is lost in this way; in Willapa Bay, 9%; and on the Columbia, 9% in winter and 2% in the fall (Beach, 1981). The seals and sea lions rob or damage the nets on about half the gillnetters' trips, and while the sea lions are rarely injured, the entangled harbor seals usually drown. Scientists are experimenting now with shrill sirens attached to the nets which drive away the seals and sea lions, but which are too high-pitched to be heard by the fish.

Fishermen are also of the belief that harbor seals and other mammals deplete fish resources in general, especially since harbor seal populations have been rising by roughly 10% per year since the Marine Mammal Protection Act. Although recent research has shown that the direct effects of pinnipeds on salmon and other commercial fish are small, the indirect effects through the consumption of the salmon prey have not been quantified. The harbor seals' Columbia River diet consists of 17% crustaceans, 11% Pacific tomcod, 11% lamprey (a salmon predator), and each of its remaining prey, including salmon, is less than 10% (Treacy and Beach, 1981; Beach, 1981). Only one prey fish of the seal has a commercial ranking of less than 15, and that is the eulachon, which constitutes only 7% of the seals' diet. We do not know how much crab these seals eat, only that it is less than 17% of the diet. In the Coos Bay area, a study of about 200 samples of seal droppings revealed 52 kinds of fish, 60% of which were the three most common species: English sole (juveniles), shiner and surf perch (Graybill, 1981). Similar studies of stomach contents of 50 dead seals beached or drowned in fishing nets in Washington showed their stomachs to contain 40% smelt; 26% anchovy; 16% tomcod; 14% herring; 8% sole, sanddab and sculpin; and only 2% salmon (Beach, 1981). Even during the spring salmon runs, the diet of seals and sea lions in Oregon contains 60% lamprey, 4% steelhead, and less than 1% salmon (Beach, 1981). This is not surprising, as seals and sea lions move too slowly to catch salmon and steelhead, except in unusual circumstances such as extremely cold water, and when fish become trapped in nets and congregated at the bottom of fish ladders. Harbor seals are opportunistic eaters. Since it is to their advantage to get in and out of the cold water as fast as possible, they tend to eat the first fish that they can find and catch, which are usually the small, abundant species.

SEASHORE

One of the greatest enticements to exploring and studying the outer coast rocky intertidal is the knowledge that, of all the habitats on the Northwest Coast, it is probably the most pristine and least abused by humans. The mussel and kelp beds on our shores remain much the same as they were centuries ago. There are at least three reasons for this stability. First, these organisms have already adapted to heavy waves, exposure, and all the other rigors of intertidal life, and in so doing have developed an extraordinary toughness and resiliency. Second, offshore oil exploration and other industries have not mushroomed on our coast as they have in the eastern U.S., on the Gulf Coast, and in Europe, so the waters of the northeast Pacific are consequently among the cleanest and most pollution-free in the world. And third, the never-ending winter rainstorms on our coast have discouraged urban development (especially as compared to southern California), and so reduced the losses due to trampling and overcollecting.

Nevertheless, though the Northwest Coast's rocky intertidal is in good health overall, some scattered sore spots have developed, especially in Oregon. These are the especially scenic areas that have the misfortune of lying near population centers, condominiums, and popular vacation spots. At practically every summer minus tide, hordes of tourists, students, amateur naturalists, photographers, and sometimes commercial collectors descend on these areas, over-turning stones, trampling and crushing barnacles and snails, and so on. The most badly abused areas in Oregon have been Haystack Rock (Cannon Beach), Shell Cove, Otter Rock, Boiler Bay, Yaquina Head, Cape Perpetua, Neptune State Park, Sunset Bay, Cape Arago, and Harris Beach. In the 1950s and 1960s rampant overcollecting by bucket brigades of schoolchildren and other students became so severe and widespread that snails, limpets, shorecrabs, hermit crabs, and seastars were nearly eliminated from some areas. This, coupled with trampling and the gamut of related disturbances, motivated the three western states to enact laws that prohibit or control the collection of marine invertebrates. Nowadays, collection is kept to a minimum and done primarily for scientific research, so the remaining threats to the rocky intertidal of the Northwest Coast are trampling, careless overturning of rocks, and mishandling of the creatures by tourists and students on field trips. The most disturbed area in Oregon continues to be Yaquina Head, where as many as 400 tidepool watchers may converge during a sunny summer minus tide.

The details of the collecting laws vary among the three states. The California Fish and Game Commission adopted theirs on March 1, 1972, largely in response to severe abuse and wastage near coastal cities from Tomales Bay south to San Diego. The California laws simply expanded a section of the California Administrative Code to include not just the most abused intertidal areas but all intertidal areas in the state. As a result, general collecting anywhere between the high tide mark and 1000 feet beyond the low tide mark along the entire coast is prohibited without a permit from the Department of Fish and Game. Permits are granted almost exclusively to qualified researchers, often in conjunction with collecting programs coordinated by county boards of education. Certain food species are exempt from this rule depending on the location. Visitors may take abalones, clams, cockles, crabs, limpets, lobsters, mussels, sand dollars, octopi, shrimp, scallops, sea urchins, and squid except in state and national parks. But most of these have size and bag limits to prevent overharvesting, and persons 16 years and older must have fishing licenses. In state and national parks, several species are excluded from this list: limpets, mussels, sand dollars, octopi, shrimp, and squid are off-limits. Violators may be fined up to $500 and imprisoned up to 6 months.

The Oregon regulations are somewhat more complicated; different locales are closed to the collection of different classes of animals. The two classes are "shellfish" (abalone, clams, mussels, scallops, edible shrimp, and Dungeness and red rock crab) and "marine invertebrates" (sand crabs, kelp worms, mud and ghost shrimp, starfish, urchins, snails, and other nonfood invertebrates). The Marine Gardens at Otter Rock and Cape Perpetua are closed to the taking of "marine invertebrates," clams (except razors at Perpetua), and mussels (except those taken one at a time for bait), and open to "shellfish." Whale Cove is closed to "shellfish" but open to "marine invertebrates."

At seven additional areas "marine invertebrates" may be taken only with permit, while "shellfish" are open to harvest. These are Haystack Rock (at Cannon Beach), Shell Cove, Boiler Bay, Yaquina Head, Neptune State Park, Sunset Bay-Cape Arago, and Harris Beach. Elsewhere both "shellfish" and "marine invertebrates" may be harvested within size and bag limits; all violators are subject to a $41 fine. Since the rules vary slightly from year to year, take along a copy of the current regulations when visiting the tidepools.

Washington permits collection of most clams, oysters, and crabs (within bag limits) without a permit between November 1 and March 31; the rest of the year beaches are closed to harvest of most edible species, except by permit, due to the risk of paralytic shellfish poisoning. Collection of razor clams for any use, however, requires a special permit and may be done only during designated seasons, which have become shorter in recent years. Collection of nonfood invertebrates for scientific research or public display is allowed only with a special scientific collector permit regardless of the number taken or method used. To obtain a permit, one must assemble a research rationale that details the collection times, places, amounts, and methods. Fines for violation vary by county, but average $30-$50. Much of the outer Washington Coast is under the jurisdiction of Olympic National Park or several Indian tribes; collection in these areas requires a separate permit process.

Regrettably, these regulations do not protect the animals completely, because there are unlimited ways to injure the intertidal without ever breaking the law. Therefore, even those of us who collect specimens either legally or not at all still need to follow a few common-sense rules to preserve the intertidal in an undisturbed, pristine, and ecologically interesting condition.

First and foremost are three essentials: be careful where you step, always replace overturned stones and refill holes, and collect nonfood animals only if you have a legitimate professional need for them. While working along the tidepools, wherever possible step only on bare rock or in the patches of mud and sand between rocks; avoid crushing barnacles, periwinkles, urchins, seaweeds, and crabs; never run. The lower the intertidal level, the more care and alertness is needed. When turning over a rock, never leave it "belly up"; always replace it gently face-down. To avoid crushing any animals, move them aside first or lean the rock carefully against a neighboring rock. If a rock is left upside down, all the attached plants, animals, eggs, and larvae on both sides will eventually die. Those formerly on the bottom will dry up, while those formerly on top will drown, starve, or be crushed. Similarly, always scoop the sand back into any holes; otherwise, the unearthed mound will block neighboring burrows and suffocate or starve their inhabitants, and the next wave will sweep the animals from the hole and mound into the water column. If collecting specimens for classroom use, take only as many as can be sustained by lab facilities: either a large, well-managed saltwater aquarium, or the proper chemical preservatives. Study the animals as diligently as possible in their natural habitats before collecting (if at all), and avoid taking rare species in unique habitats. Instead, make full use of specimens on floating docks, pilings, logs, and boat ramps, for these will always be abundant. Take only one of each species unless dissections or involved experimentation are planned, and by no means allow an army of inexperienced students to collect haphazardly anything that catches their eye.

To see the importance of these rules, one need only visit a place like Haystack Rock or Yaquina Head after a particularly unruly group of schoolchildren has trampled through the area. Footpaths are worn through seaweeds; barnacles and urchins are crushed; seastars are conspicuously absent; and areas of overturned rocks are obvious. At first the rocks appear scarred and dirty, then after a few days entire colonies of tunicates, solitary corals, and tubeworms die and fall off, until the once-fertile rock surfaces are barren. An area like this will require at least several weeks or months to recover, and in the meantime it will be a sorry place for the study of intertidal ecology. For this reason serious researchers avoid heavily visited areas and concentrate their efforts on inaccessible beaches and islands, such as Tatoosh and Waadah islands in Washington.

Ironically, the same virtues that make the rocky intertidal one of the most rewarding ecological field laboratories in the world, namely accessibility and ease of spectacular close-hand observation, have also caused the downfall of many of the most diverse and scenic locations. To stem the tide of destructive curiosity, those who teach and lead field trips to the shore can at least pass along fondness and respect for the intertidal by setting an example of conservation that is well informed, responsible, and inspiring.

ESTUARIES

Humans have always lived near the mouths of rivers. The natural productivity, shelter, and free connection with the sea grant estuaries an abundant and profitable supply of fish and shellfish, and make them safe and convenient shipping harbors and transport routes. Moreover, the large cities that inevitably grow up near estuaries empty their wastes into the river and bay, whose currents conveniently flush them out to sea.

The three major Northwest industries—agriculture, fisheries, and lumber—all depend or impinge on the estuaries in one way or another, and over the years have reduced productivity, eliminated or depleted several animal species, and forced some fundamental shifts in plant and animal community patterns. The U.S. government's National Estuary Study in 1970 found that 37% of the estuarine area in the Pacific Northwest is severely disturbed, 50% moderately disturbed, and 13% slightly disturbed (Proctor, et al., 1980).

Agriculture

Dairy farmers discovered early that salt marshes, with their wet, rich soils and flat, open terrain, could be exploited as profitable pastureland. Across the marshes they built long, meandering dikes with one-way gates that prevent the entry of tidal salt water, but allow any freshwater to flow easily out. In many places sediments dredged from the estuary have been spread evenly over salt marshes and bare shallows to raise them out of reach of the tides and within reach of the cattle. These practices of course invite the invasion of terrestrial grasses and eliminate nearly all the plants and animals of the salt marsh, notably the abundant juvenile fishes who find food and safety in the quiet sloughs.

Nearly all estuaries larger than half a square mile have been diked to some extent, and some have, in this way, lost all but a few trifling vestiges of their salt marshes. About 90% of the marshes of Coos and Humboldt bays have been permanently lost to dikes and landfills (Proctor, et al., 1980). Partly in response to the rapid rate of salt marsh disappearance, the U.S. Department of Fish and Wildlife set aside South Slough of Coos Bay as the first National Estuarine Sanctuary (Proctor, et al., 1980). The slough contains the most pristine undiked salt marsh in the bay (mostly sedge and high marshes), and occupies about 10% of the total estuary.

Since the early 1900s, about half the salt marshes of Grays Harbor have been permanently committed to uplands by diking and filling (U.S. Army Corps of Engineers, 1977). Also, the Army Corps of Engineers regularly deepens the shipping channels by dredging, and has set aside about 12% of the total intertidal lands for disposal of dredged mud and sand (U.S. Army Corps of Engineers, 1977). About 65% of the lower Columbia River flood plain from the mouth to Bonneville Dam is protected by dikes and levees, eliminating a surely large but unknown proportion of the original wetlands (Proctor, et al., 1980). In the estuary itself, some 700 acres (about 1%) have been filled. Some 40% of Willapa Bay salt marshes are now diked farmlands, and smaller undocumented amounts have been filled and developed as commercial, residential, and industrial land (Proctor, et al., 1980).

Among their other miscellaneous impacts, agricultural practices tend to increase soil erosion, leading to greater sedimentation in estuaries, and may also introduce pesticides into the coastal watersheds and eventually to the bays (Gaumer, et al., 1983). By far the greatest threat to estuaries here and worldwide, however, is the diking and filling necessary for any kind of development, because the resulting destruction is immediate and permanent.

Commercial and Recreational Fishing

As we have seen, over half the commercial fish species caught in the ocean and bays of the Northwest depend heavily on the shallow flats along the estuary margins so often targeted for reclamation. In Oregon in 1983, commercial landing of these species alone accounted for 8000 tons (20% of all fish) and 13 million dollars (50% of all fish). If both fish and shellfish are combined, the total comes to 11,000 tons (22% of all) and 25 million dollars (50% of all). Among the most valuable fish, the yearly harvest of salmon amounts to roughly 25 million, tuna 20 million, bottomfish 8 million, shrimp 7 million, Dungeness crab 6 million, and oysters 4 million dollars (Proctor, et al., 1980). Of these, only tuna and some bottomfish remain outside estuaries through their entire life cycle. The rest would face extinction without the estuarine habitat, and some (e.g., oysters) spend their entire lives in sheltered bays.

The success of the Northwest fishing industry has undoubtedly taken a heavy toll on the estuaries, but we may never know its exact effects simply because we have little idea what estuaries were like before the industry. One perennial problem is of course overfishing; with supreme efficiency, fishermen remove over 8000 tons of fish in Oregon alone every year. Only 10% of all salmon who make it downstream to the sea ever survive to spawn; fishermen and natural predators take the rest (Proctor, et al., 1980). Commercial crabbers harvest about 90% of all legal Dungeness each year (Proctor, et al., 1980). Overfishing has, at least in part, caused the demise of the Pacific sardine and the "Cannery Row" era, and continues to threaten some species of salmon. Over half of all adult coho caught each year are now products of state hatcheries (Proctor, et al., 1980).

The mushrooming of harbors and marinas has also caused major shifts in estuarine communities. Construction of boat basins usually requires landfills inside estuaries, and the massive piers, docks, and pilings redirect nearby water currents. The altered currents modify the composition of the bottom sediments, inviting a whole new community of benthic animals (Gaumer, et al., 1983). Currents often slow down around boat basins, and the resulting finer sediments benefit the deposit-feeders (e.g., worms) at the expense of suspension-feeders (e.g., clams).

Lumber Industry and Other Forces of Change

Compared to fishing and agriculture, the lumber industry is a Triton among the minnows, a commanding force that dominates both ecology and economy of the entire Northwest Coast. Its impacts on estuaries arise largely from the introduction of a variety of substances both foreign and natural (Gaumer, et al., 1983).

SEDIMENTATION

The industry's most irreversible contribution to estuarine ecology is the rapid sedimentation caused by logging roads and clearcutting. Each year rainfall washes away millions of tons of mud from Coast Range logging roads into streams and rivers, and from here most of the clay, sand, and gravel eventually finds its way to the estuaries, where it piles up along the quiet shoreline. The Clearwater River watershed in the Olympics, criss-crossed by 4 miles of logging roads per square mile of forest, produces 3–4 times the sediment of the neighboring slopes of the pristine Olympic National Park (Gaumer, *et al.*, 1983). About two-thirds of the road-derived sediment enters the streams during landslides, and about a fourth from road-surface erosion (Gaumer, *et al.*, 1983). Roads used by more than 16 trucks per day contribute a thousand times the sediment of abandoned roads (Gaumer, *et al.*, 1983). Of course the clearcuts themselves also contribute sediment, but the quick recovery of vegetation holds the erosion rate below that of the bare roads.

Excessive sedimentation affects estuaries and their inhabitants in a variety of ways (Gaumer, *et al.*, 1983). Most important in the long run, it fills in the bay several times faster than normal. As described in Chapter 4, sedimentation has shrunk Tillamook, Humboldt, and other low-gradient bays to roughly half their original sizes during just the last century. Sediment pile-up has expanded the low marshes at the expense of the clam and shrimp beds, corralling the invertebrates of the sheltered, saline shallows ever closer to the deep central channels and their swift, fresh currents. Marshes have expanded, however, much more slowly than they have been diked and filled for pasture; for each new acre of low marsh, at least one acre of high marsh is diked. If logging sedimentation and diking continue at the present rates, then in roughly another century they will have converted the quiet, open bays essentially into narrow rivers surrounded by cow pasture, eliminating shorebird feeding grounds and forcing the estuarine species out to sea where many will succumb to wave-shock and competition.

Aside from this, sedimentation has several more direct and immediate effects (Gaumer, *et al.*, 1983). First, the clouds of waterborne logging sediments block the sunlight and stunt the growth of estuarine plants, especially benthic diatoms. The reduced plant productivity depletes the food supply and lowers the biomass and productivity of all estuarine consumers, from herbivores to top carnivores, including the commercial clams, shrimp, and fish. Second, logging sediments bury submerged rocks, and thus eliminate all plants and animals who depend on rocks for stable attachment surfaces, such as seaweeds, mussels, barnacles, anemones, seastars, and many others. Third, excessive waterborne sediments clog and injure the breathing and feeding organs of fish and invertebrates. In some oyster species, for example, a silt concentration of just 0.1 part per million cuts the pumping rate in half, and five parts per million cuts it 90% and kills all the eggs (Gaumer, *et al.*,

1983). High concentrations can kill several fish species, and moderate concentrations can damage their gill tissue. Fifth, toxic chemical pollutants from a variety of sources, especially the heavy metals zinc, iron, and manganese, attach spontaneously to sediment particles, thereby hitch a ride into the estuaries, and enter the food chain after being ingested by deposit-feeders. And finally, excessive sedimentation rapidly builds shoals at the turbidity maximum, intensifying the need for dredging, whose impacts can be severe.

Dredging, performed entirely by the Army Corps of Engineers, essentially rearranges the sediments in an estuary, by removing them from shipping channels and dumping them along the bay margins (U.S. Army Corps of Engineers, 1977; Gaumer, et al., 1983).

The act of digging sends billowing clouds of sediments into the water column, and the abrupt rise in turbidity has the effects listed above. In particular, bacteria and other decomposers pounce on the newly liberated sediments, whose increase in surface area invites a surge in bacterial respiration and reproduction. As a result, the oxygen concentration drops and nearby invertebrates often suffocate (U.S. Army Corps of Engineers, 1977; Gaumer, et al., 1983).

The pure physical force of digging crushes benthic invertebrates such as Dungeness crabs, while allowing most of the more active and alert fishes to escape. Dredges in Grays Harbor consume 1–3 crabs with every 7 cubic yards of sediments, for a total of roughly 100,000 to 300,000 every year, depending on the type of dredge (U.S. Army Corps of Engineers, 1977).

Channels deepened by dredging often become worthless to gulls and bottom-dependent waterfowl, such as American widgeon, pintail, and scaup, who can only feed in the shallows. Dredged channels support less than a tenth the waterfowl and a third the gulls that the untouched channels nearby support. In contrast, fish-eating birds such as mergansers seem unaffected (U.S. Army Corps of Engineers, 1977).

Of course the Corps must dispose of their dredged-up mud and sand somewhere, and usually set aside a few locations for this purpose in the shallows or on salt marshes. Predictably, burial under tons of sediments smothers the plants and animals on the disposal sites, save some of the more mobile burrowers. Only 70 invertebrate species out of 200 survived a dump in Grays Harbor, and the invertebrate biomass at the site dropped 97%. Eelgrass and salt marsh plants also die; at Grays Harbor the Corps buries the low silt and sedge marshes more often than any others (U.S. Army Corps of Engineers, 1977).

Though sediment disposal directly kills countless organisms, it brings longer-lasting change by raising the ground level at the dump site. Tides inundate the higher ground less often, bringing fresher water on the average. Salt-tolerant and aquatic plants and animals gradually disappear, and freshwater or upland species replace them. In this way disposal of dredge sediments eliminates tideflats and eelgrass beds permanently, and replaces them with salt marshes or dry uplands. The loss of tideflats obliterates feeding grounds for shorebirds as well as nursery areas for fish, and the destruction of eelgrass removes valuable habitat for countless consumers, most conspicuously brant, widgeon, and other grass-eating waterfowl (U.S. Army Corps of Engineers, 1977).

But sediments would accumulate in the shallows no matter what, and dredging only controls to a small extent where they end up. Erosive logging practices remain the primary cause of sedimentation, and dredging only strikes at the symptoms, while contributing little to the total sediment buildup or removal in any estuary. Currently the Corps dredges only in Grays, Umpqua, Siuslaw, Coos, Yaquina, Siletz, Coquille, and Humboldt estuaries on the Northwest Coast. In 1977 they stopped dredging Willapa Bay, forcing logging companies to ship their logs through Grays Harbor instead, which in turn raised the pressure for development and dredging in Grays Harbor.

WATER CHEMISTRY

Logging practices also modify the chemistry of estuarine waters, and hence the chemistry of the organisms themselves. First, since rainfall of course is no longer intercepted by trees after a clearcut, it simply drains into the rivers and streams and builds into greater peak flows in winter. Estuarine organisms perceive these as sudden floods of freshwater, and those with poor osmoregulatory powers may die or move downstream to the shelter of the tides (Gaumer, et al., 1983).

Second, logging practices and wood-processing factories introduce pollutants into the estuaries. Environmental contaminants in general fall into two categories: the biodegradable, usually nontoxic substances often derived from living things (roughly "organic"), and the toxic, usually artificially synthesized chemicals ("inorganic").

Organic Pollution. For the most part, sewage, pulp mill effluent, wood chips, and other organic pollution, far from poisoning aquatic animals, serve as a food supply similar to, and often as nutritious as, natural detritus. Bacteria and fungi consume these energy-rich materials, ultimately degrading them into carbon dioxide and water. The decomposers, however, use oxygen in the process, and in great abundance can exhaust the supply of waterborne oxygen. While small amounts of organic pollution can be harmless, large volumes can consume nearly all oxygen in their vicinity (Gaumer, *et al.*, 1983).

Although most estuarine animals suffocate in highly stagnant waters, some have evolved a tolerance of low oxygen, and actually thrive in the absence of their more poorly adapted competitors. Most of these "pollution indicators," often the commonest animals near a sewage or pulp mill outlet, are species of oligochaete or polychaete worms, such as the thread worm *Capitella capitata* (U.S. Army Corps of Engineers, 1977). But few others survive nearby, and as a rule heavy organic pollution noticeably reduces the number of fish and invertebrate species in an estuary. The loss is greatest in summer, when river flow is low and the water warm. Since the oxygen content of water falls as salinity and temperature rises, it drops to a minimum in summer, and any pollution at this time compounds the discomfort (U.S. Army Corps of Engineers, 1977).

Sewage contributes by far the greatest volume of organic pollution in Northwest and most estuaries worldwide, followed in the Northwest by pulp mill effluent, wastes from sawmills, slaughterhouses, fish canneries, and so on (Gaumer, *et al.*, 1983). Of course the lumber industry and its spinoffs bear no responsibility for sewage (other than their tendency to promote urbanization near estuaries), but do contribute to organic pollution with a variety of mill wastes. Sewage may undergo three stages of treatment before disposal. "Primary" treatment is simply chlorination to kill all bacteria; "secondary" treatment is a partial or complete removal of organic and other solid waste by burning, seeding with fresh bacteria to induce natural decomposition, and various other means; and "tertiary" treatment is an expensive and chemically complicated attempt to remove all remaining impurities, especially nutrients, to render the water pure and clean enough to drink. Most coastal towns and cities have little money or incentive to go beyond primary treatment, so they can simply flush the sewage into the ocean (either directly or via estuaries). Over 30 billion gallons of sewage enter U.S. coastal waters every day, or 3 cubic miles every year (Phillips and Thayer, 1977). Much of this passes through estuaries, since a third of the U.S. population lives on estuaries. Combined with mill wastes and other organic pollution, sewage converts the upper reaches of some Northwest estuaries into a stagnant no-man's-land in the summer.

Inorganic Pollution. The harm done by chemical poisons depends on their concentration in the water. In small doses they can kill aquatic plants and animals outright, while in minute doses they often inflict a variety of "sublethal" maladies, such as long-term changes in growth, feeding, respiration, reproduction, behavior, osmoregulation, and disease resistance. Even unaffected species suffer because of their dependence on affected species, and in this way inorganic pollution can change the entire structure of the ecosystem (Gaumer, *et al.*, 1983).

Inorganic pollutants most commonly used by the logging industry are chlorinated hydrocarbon pesticides, organophosphate pesticides, and phenoxy herbicides (Gaumer, *et al.*, 1983). These are most often sprayed from helicopters over a clearcut, and make their way to estuaries via rivers and groundwater. Unlike many others, chlorinated hydrocarbons are nondegradable, and for this reason accumulate in the animals' tissues to levels much greater than those of the surrounding water. The process of biomagnification makes top carnivores, such as raptors and many seabirds, the most vulnerable. Happily, organophosphates are generally safer and easily degradable, and have largely replaced the chlorinated hydrocarbons as the preferred pesticides on clearcuts. Because these generally break down to harmless fragments in less than a year, and some in a few days, they seldom accumulate to deadly levels. Nevertheless, many interact synergistically; the combined toxicity of EPN and malathion, for example, is 50 times the toxicity of either alone (Gaumer, *et al.*, 1983). Phenoxy compounds, used commonly as weed killers on clearcuts, also kill or stunt the growth of estuarine algae and some fish. Though they are generally less toxic than organophosphates, they tend to persist longer and accumulate more easily. The phenoxy herbicide 2,4-D is most commonly used now; forest spraying of 2,4,5-T was recently banned.

Despite their potency, these chemicals are dwarfed by many heavy metals. In approximate order of potency, these are mercury, silver, copper, zinc, nickel, lead, cadmium, arsenic, and several others. Like chlorinated hydrocarbons, heavy metals are nondegradable and therefore can accumulate in living tissues, in some cases to several hundred thousand times the concentration in the surrounding water.

Heavy metals enter estuaries in countless ways: they leach from wrecking yard scrap metal into soil and streams, they enter the air in car exhaust and wash to the ground in rain and snow; they accompany nearly every type of industrial waste. In Grays Harbor in 1975, the mercury content in 21 of 50 random water samples exceeded the hazardous level (0.1 micrograms per liter) set by the Environmental Protection Agency; levels of cadmium and copper were also high (U.S. Army Corps of Engineers, 1977).

Oil Pollution. In estuaries, with their naturally sheltered and convenient channels and harbors and their consequently crowded shipping traffic, commercial vessels collide and run aground more often than in the outer coast. Accidents almost inevitably spawn oil spills, from a few hundred gallons to a few hundred tons. Most recently, a Mobiloil tanker hit a reef in the Columbia and lost 170,000 gallons (500–650 tons) of oil, and the 350-foot Blue Magpie broke up on the jetty rock during a dangerous crossing of the Yaquina Bay bar, and released some 70,000 gallons (200–260 tons).

"Oil" is a general term for a complex and variable mixture of thousands of hydrocarbons, each of which acts independently on the aquatic ecosystem. The most lethal are the volatile, water-soluble constituents (such as the benzenes), which kill or injure animals in the same ways as the pesticides mentioned above. The heavier tarry components do more physical damage than chemical, and in large amounts bury and suffocate sessile animals and plants. Since oil is almost entirely organic, it can be degraded and in part eliminated by bacteria, which may unfortunately deplete oxygen in the process.

Oiled birds and mammals, the most conspicuous victims of oil pollution, suffer and die in several ways. They lose body heat because oil destroys the insulating qualities of feathers and fur; they ingest the toxins while trying to clean themselves; they absorb some of the toxins directly through the skin; and when heavily oiled, lose their buoyancy and drown. Oil poisoning causes intestinal inflammation, diarrhea, and eventually severe weakness and fatigue in most birds, making them easy prey for their enemies.

A natural coating of slippery mucus protects fish and many invertebrates by repelling the oil. If oil repeatedly irritates the gill tissue of fishes, however, they produce excess mucus, and in severe pollution they may suffocate as a result. While fishes can escape oil by simply swimming away, sessile invertebrates lay at the mercy of the winds and currents. Their mucus-shields protect them only in the short run, and tarry residues washed up on beaches or sunken to the estuary bottom can smother entire communities of clams, mussels, oysters, worms, and shrimp. Any survivors may absorb the toxins, and suffer from aberrant growth, impaired feeding, and sterility.

By pure luck, the biggest tanker oil spill of all time had the distinction of fouling the waters near several major French and British marine laboratories, whose intensive monitoring of the disaster provided the first broad picture of the behavior and impacts of a large oil spill (Gundlach, 1983). In March 1978, the supertanker Amoco Cadiz hit rocks off the Brittany coast of France, and during the next 2 weeks of rough seas lost its entire load of 220,000 tons of oil, most of it crude. Research vessels discovered that, during the first month, 30% of the oil evaporated, 28% washed into the intertidal zone, 8% sank to subtidal sediments, 14% remained in the water column, 4% was degraded by microbes, and 20% disappeared entirely. After 6 months, all the oil in the water column had apparently disappeared, having by that time washed ashore, sunk, evaporated, or decomposed.

One major finding was the surprising speed of oil disappearance wherever the sea was rough, and conversely, the stubborn persistence of the oil in quiet waters, notably in the upper reaches of bays and estuaries far removed from the waves. The explanation for this appears to lie with the decomposers. The heavy waves on the Brittany coast provide plentiful nutrients (oxygen, nitrogen, and phosphorus), and redistribute the oil as a fine emulsion, thereby providing optimal conditions for speedy decomposition by bacteria and other microbes. Though tons of oil washed up on the beaches and in the shallows, the rough seas periodically swept it into the surf, where all but the heaviest, tarry residues decomposed. After 3 years, the oil had disappeared from everywhere but the estuaries, where two factors combined to immobilize it. First, the slow currents and weak waves failed to draw it into suspension. Second, fine, anaerobic sediments buried much of the oil, and the lack of oxygen nearly stopped biodegradation. In many of these areas the oil hardened into asphaltlike patches that will probably remain for at least another decade (Gundlach, 1983).

Among numerous other ecological impacts, the Amoco Cadiz spill contaminated 5000 tons of oysters, which had to be destroyed to prevent human poisoning; curtailed the reproduction of crabs, lobsters, and bottomfish; and eliminated entire populations from the estuarine bottoms. Happily, however, the fast decomposition of the oil allowed the sea life to recover almost completely after 3 years. The only species still suffering are the inhabitants of the estuaries, whose still waters will protect the oil for years to come.

Since our outer seas rival those of France in power and roughness, a large spill off the Northwest Coast would probably behave in much the same way as the Amoco Cadiz spill, depending on weather conditions, the spill location, and the time spent at sea. But on our coast, supertanker spills are much more probable in calm inshore waters than in the open sea. The supertanker route from Valdez, Alaska, to refineries at Cherry Point, Washington, cuts through the Strait of Juan de Fuca and Puget Sound, both renowned for tricky tidal currents, strong winds, and poor visibility from fog and rainstorms. A spill of Amoco Cadiz proportions could devastate the productive beaches of Puget Sound because the sheltered waters here lack the wave energy needed to emulsify the oil thoroughly. The slick would likely wash ashore or sink to the bottom, in either case covering the shore communities while decaying only slowly.

Luckily, most spills amount to less than a hundredth this size and do little damage if properly tended. Unlike other forms of pollution, the insoluble components of oil lend themselves (at least theoretically) to physical removal. The Coast Guard usually cleans a waterborne slick by barricading it with long, floating booms, and then mechanically mopping it up while it lies trapped and motionless (Sutherland, 1983). Unfortunately, this strategy fails whenever currents exceed about 1 mile per hour, or waves about 2 feet; in either case the oil sloshes under or over the booms easily, and the booms can do little more than redirect the oil away from sensitive areas. Since the currents through main estuarine channels on the Northwest Coast average about 2–3 miles per hour, cleanup crews must usually wait for a slick to move into the calmer peripheral waters before they can set up a useful boom system, and by this time much of the oil breaks up into a dozen separate slicks, sinks to the bottom, or washes out to sea. Tarry residues invariably find their way to beaches, and must be removed by hand. On the open sea, workers have tried burning the oil with flame-throwers, degrading it with bacterial decomposers, and dispersing it with detergents. None of these methods work well in estuaries, however, where the oil slick may lie only minutes away from salt marshes, mudflats, recreational beaches, and marinas.

THE OUTLOOK

In planning for the future of our estuaries, we should keep a few principles in mind. First, most pollution never exits an estuary by the most direct route. Instead, the complex tidal and river currents carry it on a grand tour of the entire bay before it trickles out, if at all, little by little. In other words, everybody lives "downstream" from everybody else; even if we dispose of sewage near the bay mouth, we can be sure that some will still find its way to the upper sloughs. Until detailed research fills the cavernous gaps in our knowledge of estuarine current dynamics, we should zone, manage, and study any estuary as a whole, with the assumption that each part influences every other part.

Second, the same processes that trap sediments and nutrients in estuaries also trap pollutants. Heavy metals, chlorinated hydrocarbons, and other nonbiodegradable toxins may accumulate over long periods of time, and could eventually reach levels dangerous to humans. We should not assume that estuaries simply flush a pollutant out to sea.

Third, since few species live in estuaries, their food chains are short and easily disrupted. If a central species (such as the thread worm *Corophium*) succumbed to pollution, it could take down several others with it, and perhaps change the productivity and community structure of the entire estuary. Moreover, microscopic organisms, such as bacteria, plankton, and benthic diatoms, occupy the base of the food chain, and these tend to be the most sensitive to pollutants. Invisible shifts in bacterial species and decomposition rates could lead to major shifts in fish and shellfish populations. Ideally, we should build our estuary management plans around the needs of the microbes, who seem to have the most to say about estuarine productivity.

Finally, this phenomenal productivity and quiet waters make estuaries invaluable not only to lumbermen, fishermen, and farmers, but to scientists, students, bird-watchers, and early-morning beach-walkers as well. If we let it, the smooth gray calm reflected in our bays will cast its spell on all of us. Estuaries have given us the oyster, the salmon, and the pyramids. If we treat them well, who knows what they will bring next.

DUNES

For the most part, the coastal dunes of Washington, California, and Oregon outside the Coos Bay dune sheet lie beneath city streets. Most vegetated dune land is owned privately, and has been broken up by light- to moderate residential and commercial development into small, widely separated pockets dominated by introduced plants and animals. Towns built on stabilized dunes include Ocean Shores, Westport, Grayland, Oysterville, Ocean Park, and Long Beach in Washington; and Warrenton, Gearhart, Seaside, Rockaway, Manzanita, Garibaldi, Netarts, Neskowin, Lincoln City, Depoe Bay, Newport, Florence, and Waldport in Oregon (Plate 19). San Francisco lies partly on old dunes whose active areas have the distinction of being stabilized by the first introduction of European beachgrass on the West Coast, in 1869 (Cooper, 1967). As in the Clatsop Plains, Oregon, many dune lands are also grazed and farmed.

Nevertheless, in Oregon lies the largest expanse of coastal sandhills in America that remain for the most part in an intact, natural state. This is of course the Coos Bay dune sheet, untrammeled largely because of the impossibility of developing on or anywhere near the huge, threatening masses of sand.

And this is not likely to change soon. On March 23, 1977, the U.S. Congress placed most of the area under public ownership as the Oregon Dunes National Recreation Area (NRA), in recognition of the need to preserve the myriad recreational opportunities it offers. The act put a halt to most development by allowing the Forest Service to acquire all private lands along the western boundary of the area, and any private lands along the eastern that are improved or developed in any way that diminishes the scenic, scientific, or

historical values of the area (McGuire, 1977). So the only development is that initiated or authorized by the Siuslaw National Forest,
whose boundaries then expanded to include the NRA. Presently, the
NRA embraces a total or 50 square miles; 71% of this is National
Forest, 17% private, 10% owned by the state of Oregon, and 2% by
the counties (McGuire, 1977). About 1.8 million people visit the
NRA each year, mostly from Oregon, to engage in a wide range of
recreational opportunities afforded by the inherent diversity of the
dune environment. By the year 2000, a threefold increase in visitors
is likely (McGuire, 1977).

But this seemingly ideal arrangement nevertheless has failed to
prevent some heated controversy and raised several unanswered
questions. In devising a plan to manage the NRA, the Forest Service
has honored the public's wishes and resisted the temptation to build
luxurious campgrounds, boat ramps, and access roads throughout
the area. Instead, they have minimized development and preserved
the pristine beauty of the dunes. But they needed to provide some
accommodation for an expected upsurge in visitorship, and so they
built 18 new parking lots, mostly along the eastern margin of the
NRA where their impact on the dune environment is minimal. This
is enough space for an extra 2300 visitors. They also built assorted
other attractions: one large campground in the south dunes near
Butterfield Lake; four small, primitive lake- or riverside camps for
boaters and hikers; an extra 30 miles of trails through forest,
meadows, and deflation plains; one formal visitor information
center; two unmanned visitor contact centers; and three panoramic
vista points. They also preserved two areas as "Roadless,
Undeveloped Recreation Use Areas," which are also ideal sites for
serious scientific study of the dunes; these are the north spit of the
Umpqua River and the Umpqua Scenic Dunes, just south of the
Umpqua Lighthouse State Park. Finally, they divided the active sand
areas equally between the dune buggy enthusiasts and the hikers. All
in all, the Forest Service struck a reasonable compromise between
conservation of the intact landscape and accommodation of the
multiplicity of visitor uses (McGuire, 1977).

Nevertheless, conservation groups and individuals feel that
the management of the NRA may shift toward increased development or even timber harvest depending on the goals of future federal
administrations. Hence they propose to designate part of the NRA as
Wilderness, which would give it consummate legal protection. The
Mid-Coast Livability Council, the Wildlife Society, and the Oregon
Environmental Council are among those favoring wilderness
designation. Residents of western Oregon who are concerned about
the NRA are pro-wilderness by a margin of 2 to 1, and the regional
and national opinion splits 3 to 1 (McGuire, 1977).

But the Forest Service disagrees. To deserve the Wilderness appellation, an area must have several definitive features. It must lack any obvious signs of human presence or activity, afford the visitor surpassing opportunities for solitude or free, unconfined wandering, and it must be large enough that neighboring developments will not diminish its pristine, remote ambience. However, scattered from end to end across the NRA are grass and tree plantations, roads and parking lots, campgrounds, dams, water wells, pipelines, jetties, navigational aids, telephone poles and lines, logged-over areas, and even Highway 101 in several places. Though 40 miles long, the area ranges from only ¼ mile to a little over 2 miles wide, and visitor use is heavy in the summer. So it could be designated Wilderness only under a liberal interpretation of the words "solitude," "unconfined," or "primeval."

After two lengthy studies, the Forest Service concluded that only the north spit of the Umpqua River is secluded and unspoiled enough to be Wilderness, and that the rest of the NRA either does not deserve the title or defies federal management due to the presence of state and county lands or the lack of clear boundaries. But conservation groups have not given up, and their efforts may yet result in special legal status for some areas.

Beachgrass

As seen in Chapter 5, European beachgrass has dominated the backshore over the length of the West Coast, but its influence is clearest along the Coos Bay dune sheet. To recapitulate, it created a foredune that intercepts beach sand on its way inland, and thereby starves the active dunes, which creep inland, flatten out, and eventually freeze under cover of forest. During the last 40 years, roughly 100 acres of active sand per year has been replaced by deflation plains. Presently the NRA embraces about 10,700 acres of active dunes (⅓ of the total), which at the present rate could disappear in another century, leaving a few scattered blowouts sifting in the wind. This would not only eliminate the massive oblique dunes, but also wipe out habitat for 50–60 wildlife species (Pinto, et al., 1972). The primary wildlife value of active dunes is their ability to generate new niches as they carve out a mottled, rippling mosaic in the landscape. They create lakes, ponds, and marshes; they lay ridges and furrows on the land surface; they provide nesting habitat for the rare snowy plover; they create new edges and unusual proportions of trees and shrubs with their bizarre, forced juxtapositions of textured terrain. In short, they create diversity; they offer optimal habitat for most coastal plant and animal species.

Since the active sand is not just the reason for the colorful mixture of 425 animals in the dunes, but the primary recreational value of the NRA, beachgrass has become something of a management enigma. On the one hand, government agencies have planted it on every sand hill that threatens Highway 101 or other roads, campgrounds, parking lots, homes, and other developments; navigable river channels; and recreational attractions such as Cleawox and Carter Lakes. But at the same time, preservation of the active dunes requires a plan to eliminate it from many sections of the foredune to restore the healthy inflow of new sand. Currently the Forest Service is collaborating with the Oregon Department of Fish and Wildlife in a multi-year project to examine alternatives in beachgrass control. Options include the restricted use of herbicides such as glyphosate, the bulldozing of sand channels through the foredune, and controlled burning. These, however, may be no more than temporary solutions. As long as beachgrass planting continues and healthy neighboring populations exist, there will be potential for its spreading to the upper beach either by rhizomes or windborne seeds, posing a perpetual annoyance.

On the whole, it appears that the beachgrass question will keep our hands full for several years to come. One is encouraged, however, by the fact that active dunes can spread over large areas in very little time, erasing the effects of decades of stabilization.

Off-road Vehicles (ORV's)

A more immediate and emotion-charged issue in the NRA concerns the rights of dune buggy and 4-wheel-drive enthusiasts. This group is an exasperation to many Forest Service employees and is avoided by most hikers and other visitors, who object to its destruction of wildlife habitat and wilderness values. The conflict is intense and mirrors that between the snowmobiles in the Cascades and the snowshoers and cross-country skiers.

The Forest Service has responded by closing exactly half the active dunes to ORV's and imposing strict regulations on their use. Presently ORV's are allowed in three sections that hikers are advised to avoid even though they include the largest expanses of open sand and the highest dunes in the NRA: from the Siuslaw spit beach access road to the Siltcoos River; from the Umpqua Lighthouse State Park to the Douglas County line; and from Tenmile Creek to the southern boundary of the NRA. The Forest Service asserts that ORV's cause no ecological harm to active dunes, but recognizes the need to bar the vehicles from other habitats. So ORV's are prohibited within 200 feet of any lake, pond, river, or stream and within one-half mile of any campground, picnic ground, or other similar area. They must travel on clearly marked trails through vegetated areas and cannot pass through any visibly obvious barriers.

But the Forest Service understandably has difficulty enforcing these rules over such a large and diverse terrain. So the ORV's more than occasionally ignore them by driving through salt marshes, deflation plains, and down the middle of creeks, flushing wildlife from nests and feeding grounds, and sometimes crushing nests, eggs, and nestlings.

Groups such as the Citizens for Untreaded Beaches hope to solve part of the problem by banning ORV's from beaches that border dune areas off-limits to them. This is because the ORV's sometimes gain illegal access to closed areas by driving along the beach (often across small estuaries) and cutting into them across the foredune and deflation plain. Currently, 27 of the 38.25 miles of beaches along the NRA are open year-round to motor vehicles, 9 are closed in summer, and 2.25 are closed year-round (Pinto, *et al.*, 1972).

Snowy Plover

Off-road vehicles, beachgrass, and dune developments have all combined to reduce the coastal population of this small beach-nesting shorebird in Washington, Oregon, and California.

The most serious damage has been inflicted by beach vaca-tioners attracted by expanding tourist accomodations. Typically, an approaching ORV, dog, or beachcomber will flush an incubating adult from the nest, leaving the eggs exposed, and strong winds then scatter the eggs or bury them with sand. Such mishaps apparently extirpated the snowy plover from the southern California coast and perhaps also from South Beach at Newport, Oregon.

Although the influence of beachgrass on the plover in the last 50 years cannot be measured, it must have been great. Before beachgrass, the upper beach in most places was a tangle of drift-wood half-buried by active sand. The sand supported a much lower cover of plants, primarily the mound-builders yellow abronia and American searocket. These open expanses were prime snowy plover nesting habitat. The sudden spread of the grass along the length of the coast usurped most of these grounds and undoubtedly reduced the population. Not only did the grass eliminate open sand areas, it also steepened the beach and added rolling hills and hummocks. Now the birds nest primarily on flat, bay-backed sandspits scoured clean every winter by storm waves, and these make up only a very small proportion of the strandline. Although the snowy plover has not yet provided any proven short-term response to beachgrass, its close eastern relative, the piping plover, has. When storm waves wash beachgrass from a beach in New York, the plover breeding population rises, and when calm weather allows it to return, the population declines (Wilcox, 1959). The primary natural threats to the snowy plovers are high winds, predators (ravens, crows, gulls, shrikes, skunks, and coyotes), and flooding by high river flows, high tides, and storms. Of the 72 nests observed in 1978 and 1979, only nine were successful; 19 were lost to corvid predation, and 11 were destroyed by storms and moving sand (Wilson-Jacobs and Meslow, 1984).

Snowy plovers are not rare enough throughout their range to deserve federal threatened or endangered status. But since the Northwest Coast lies on the periphery of the range, the birds are rare and considered sensitive here. Although the species comprises a total of at least 3500 pairs from the Great Plains to the Pacific including several hundred in Baja, only about 70 pairs breed in Oregon (Wilson-Jacobs and Meslow, 1984). So Washington, Oregon, and California would be first to lose their coastal snowy plovers during a period of widespread decline.

Scientists agree that snowy plover survival on the West Coast will require either the halting of many recreational, residential, and commercial developments near nesting areas or the elimination of beachgrass from large sections of the beaches. Most of the involved government agencies have affirmed the willingness to include the snowy plover's well-being in their management plans. This includes the Forest Service, Army Corps of Engineers, Oregon Bureau of Land Management, and Oregon Department of Fish and Wildlife.

Clearly, the defense of the status quo in the dune environment will require a great deal of cooperation among government agencies and private interests for years to come.

FOREST

Perfect growing conditions have given the Pacific Northwest the most impressive coniferous forests in the world and a lumber industry responsible for about a third of all employment in the region. The method used by this industry to harvest trees, namely clearcutting, targets more acres of old and young growth forests each year than all other disturbances combined. These include wildfires, landslides, insect epidemics, windstorms, or any other natural catastrophe, and include the gamut of other human-caused disturbances, which are considerable. Historically, however, clearcutting and other disturbances progressed hand-in-hand. From 1945 to 1970, over 58 billion board feet were harvested, almost entirely by clearcutting, from National Forest land in western Oregon and Washington (U.S. Forest Service, Timber Cut and Sold annual reports). During the same period, 1 million acres of commercial forest land were permanently liquidated by other human activities: road construction 35%, urbanization and industry 29%, farm and pasture clearing 16%, power line clearing 5%, and water reservoirs and impoundments 5% (Bolsinger, 1973). If these 1 million acres were mature forest, then they contained roughly 100 billion board feet of wood, nearly twice that harvested on public lands. On private lands, nearly all marketable timber is gone and the replanted trees will not be harvestable for 30–80 years. At the present Forest Service harvest rate (about four billion board feet per year in western Oregon and Washington), old, undisturbed forests will very soon be gone on public lands as well; the amount of wood harvested over three typical years is about equal to that consumed in the Tillamook Burns. In just the past decade scientists have studied in detail the ecological effects of repeated clearcutting (at 50–80 year intervals), controlled burning, logging road construction, and other "intensive harvest" practices. Some of the conclusions suggest that, unless harvesting patterns change, Northwest forests and their inhabitants might soon become a non-renewable resource (Figure 72a–e).

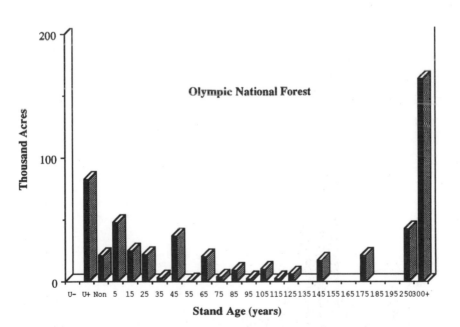

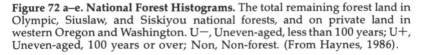

Figure 72 a–e. National Forest Histograms. The total remaining forest land in Olympic, Siuslaw, and Siskiyou national forests, and on private land in western Oregon and Washington. U−, Uneven-aged, less than 100 years; U+, Uneven-aged, 100 years or over; Non, Non-forest. (From Haynes, 1986).

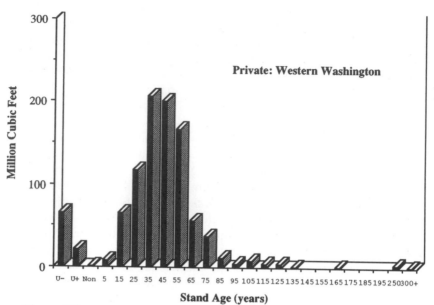

Figure 72b

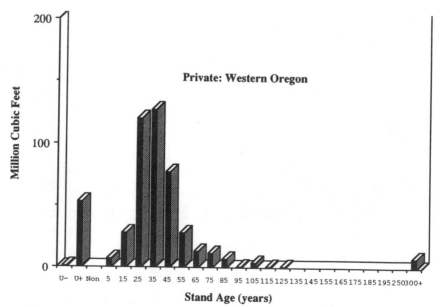

Figure 72c

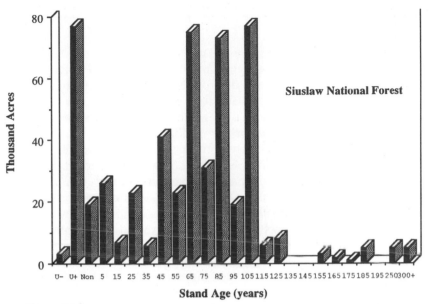

Figure 72d

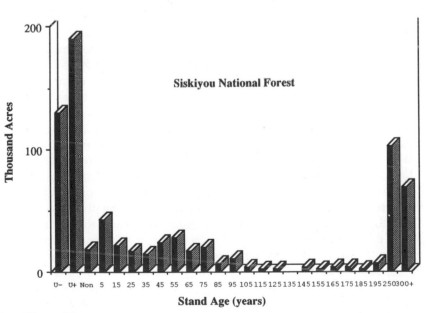

Figure 72e

Clearcutting

ECOLOGICAL EFFECTS

To clearcut is to remove all trees from a stand of timber, typically from 40 acres to a square mile; in addition, all remaining vegetation is usually burned to destroy shrubs that would otherwise outcompete conifer seedlings for light and nutrients. The major ecological impacts of this loss of vegetation are increased erosion, loss of nutrients, and loss of prime wildlife habitat.

Clearcutting increases erosion in two ways (Franklin and DeBell, 1973; Proctor, *et al.*, 1980). First, it kills plant roots. Roots alone hold the soil in place on many steep mountain slopes, and their loss can cause landslides, such as those on the hills above Garibaldi, Oregon, in the winter of 1980–81. Second, clearcutting removes the blanket of vegetation, and so exposes the ground to the physical force of rain, wind, and frost. Plants of course extract water from the soil and send it as vapor into the atmosphere; without them, rainwater accumulates in the soil, making the ground heavier, more fluid, and unstable, prone to slides and other types of erosion. Often the soil becomes so saturated that rainwater no longer soaks into the soil pore spaces, but instead flows in rivulets on the ground surface, carrying the topsoil away to streams and rivers.

On steep slopes where only a thin soil layer rests on bedrock, a major landslide can mean a permanent loss of a forest. Landslides also dam streams and prevent the passage of fish, including breeding salmon, and sediments bury salmon breeding gravels and interfere with feeding and respiration of other stream animals.

A necessary result of erosion is the loss of nutrients, which are washed away with the soil or leached into the groundwater and thence to streams. Loss of limiting nutrients by either route means reduced productivity of the next ecosytem. Measurements of nutrients in streams before and after clearcutting show marked increases in nutrient outflow rates. After clearcutting, yearly losses of potassium, phosphorus, and calcium on typical sites rise two to three times, and nitrogen losses about four to five times (Proctor, *et al.*, 1980). Of course the trees themselves contain nutrients that vanish when the loggers remove them. Tree boles contain about 4% of all the nitrogen in the forest vegetation and soil, 8% of the phosphorus, 8% of the potassium, and 5% of the calcium. Moreover, the destruction of nitrogen-fixing competitors such as red alder and snowbrush reduces the long-term nitrogen input to the soil (Miller and Murray, 1979; Trappe and Bollen, 1979).

Clearcutting of course exposes the ground to elements other than rain, such as wind, heat, and frost, which can cause damage as well. So in general, clearcutting is most destructive where the climate is most severe, magnifying any harshness of climate because it removes the protective cover of the vegetation. One result is wide-spread death of seedlings (both natural and planted), which prevents or slows development of a new forest. On hot, dry sites common in southwestern Oregon and on frost-prone gentle slopes, more protective harvest methods are generally used (see below).

Other miscellaneous effects of clearcutting include major increases in air pollution (suspended particulates, hydrocarbons, and carbon monoxide) as a result of slash burning, increases in stream temperature (due to the elimination of shading foliage), and increases in the volume of stream water (Harr and McCorison, 1979; Proctor, et al., 1980). Of course, clearcutting in the long run slowly liquidates the old growth forest habitat and its dependent wildlife.

Probably the most easily measurable damage, however, is long-term nutrient loss. Recent research in China, whose coniferous forests have been harvested for more than 1000 years by 20–30 year clearcutting rotations, suggests that, in the long run, such intensive harvesting can seriously injure the soil and eventually prevent forest growth altogether (Bergstrom, 1979; Yung, 1986). After just three rotations of clearcutting, burning, and even-aged plantations of Chinese fir (*Cunninghamia lanceolata*), the soil at a typical site can no longer support normal growth of the species. The causes of this appear to be several documented changes in soil chemistry. First, the concentration of several nutrients drops with each rotation. Second, both the abundance and activity of soil microorganisms, including bacteria, decrease; hence decomposition rates and the potential for nutrient regeneration presumably drop. Third, the enzyme activities of the soil change. In particular, the oxidative metabolism deteriorates, and as a result, toxic substances such as vanillin accumulate by the third rotation. These not only inhibit seed germination, but also kill or injure nitrogen-fixing microorganisms, resulting in a new decomposer community whose new waste products interfere with the normal biological functions of the soil.

The end result is stunted, slow-growing trees, and the economic necessity of clearing more old growth, and establishing new plantations on its (temporarily) healthy soil. Similar patterns have been observed in Germany, Britain, and throughout the tropical rain forests. Of course, in the Northwest, most sites have been cutover only once, and in a few areas the second rotation is just beginning. Although we have no hard proof of long-term soil exhaustion, the industry is still young, and the evidence points powerfully enough in that direction for some forest managers to discuss the issue publicly.

ALTERNATIVES

Over the years, the Northwest timber industry has experimented with other harvest methods that eliminate most of these harmful effects. The most common are small patch or strip clearcutting, the shelterwood method, the seed tree method, and the selection method (Isaac, 1956; Williamson, 1973; Curtis, *et al.*, 1973). In addition, some researchers have recently proposed a combination of increased rotation times and the development of a system of strategically-placed old growth reserves (Franklin, *et al.*, 1981; Harris, 1984).

Small patch or strip clearcutting lessens the impact of clearcutting by reducing the area cut at any one time. The total cut is the same, but broken into smaller patches and strips. The shelterwood method removes all canopy trees, but in several cuttings over several years. The first cutting lets in enough light to allow seedlings to survive and grow, but leaves enough canopy trees untouched to shelter the seedlings from extremes in climate. Later cuttings gradually remove the canopy trees so that the vulnerable seedlings are exposed only gradually. The seed tree method also leaves selected trees standing to provide seed for regeneration. Its only difference from small patch harvest is a more complete cut; the scattered remaining trees do not provide enough cover to protect the emerging seedlings. The seed trees are removed as soon as the seedlings appear. The selection method removes only selected mature trees, singly or in small groups. Light and space thus created allow establishment of small scattered groups of equal-aged seedlings. Cuttings are made every few years and continued indefinitely, resulting in a perenially intact, visually appealing forest of all ages of trees. This is the only method that creates an "all-aged" forest; the others leave forests of equal-aged trees and are called "even-age" techniques.

In contrast to clearcutting, each of these methods maintains a continuous cover of vegetation over the ground. The result is a more constant microclimate, firmer soils, unchanged runoff, and stable populations of forest animals. However, only selection cutting of some form can preserve the old growth elements of the stand.

If these methods are so much less harmful, then why are they not used? The answer is not ecology, for the impacts of these methods are no worse than clearcutting, but rather economics (Twight, 1973). Virtually all industry specialists agree that clearcutting generates the most profits, leads to better harvests, and is the only economically feasible harvest technique in areas where maximum timber production is the goal. Clearcutting requires that the logging crew and equipment enter the stand just once, to remove all trees, while the other methods require two to several entries. So clearcutting saves on transportation and related costs. The conservative techniques also are more difficult and demand more skill, planning, and supervision, and thus higher labor costs. Loggers must prevent damage to the residual trees during falling, and during cable hoisting and dragging of logs, or else few trees will survive for future harvests. Other miscellaneous economic advantages of clearcutting include the need for less logging road mileage; an easily-defined cutover area that concentrates problems of thinning, slash disposal, fertilization, and application of pesticides and herbicides; faster growth of trees (because of more light); fewer branches on future trees; and the easier subsequent establishment of Douglas fir, which tends to be outcompeted by western hemlock in more shaded select cut sites. And some mammals benefit from clearcutting. Black bear, black-tailed deer, and Roosevelt elk commonly feed in shrubby regions of recent clearcuts. Coyotes frequent clearcuts and use logging roads in traveling to other habitats. The Oregon vole, deer mouse, Richardson's water vole, and Pacific jumping mouse prefer recently disturbed sites to old growth.

Some conservation groups, on the other hand, suspect that selection cutting has economic values that compensate for its increased costs, and that a carefully controlled field comparison of the two methods should be performed (Twight, 1973). Among the immediate economic advantages of selection cutting are the larger average log sizes, the salvageability of damaged trees, continuous uninterrupted tree growth leading to slightly greater wood production, minimal invasion of shade-intolerant weedy species such as red alder and salmonberry (thus reduced costs of brush control), and the freedom to harvest species only when their market value is high. Of course the major long-range advantage is reduced erosion, but in addition, the preservation through selection cutting of minimal old growth elements may increase nitrogen inputs to the ecosystem. Logs and snags provide sites for nitrogen fixation, and large trees provide habitat for nitrogen-fixing lichens. These benefits would reduce fertilization costs ($42–70 per acre) and boost the long-term productivity.

The preservation of wide-ranging species of wildlife, however, will require integrated management of many habitat elements over a scale of perhaps hundreds of square miles. Mount Rainier National Park has lost 13 species of mammals in the last 60 years, due to its small size and a lack of suitable habitat nearby as a source pool of immigrants (Harris, 1984). If the remaining old growth in the Pacific Northwest were reduced to the present parks and a few small, widely scattered islands, populations of spotted owls and other dependents would similarly fall. For these reasons, several forest managers have proposed a strategy of careful, long-range planning for Northwest coniferous forests to preserve at all times a diversity of forest ages, and sufficient amounts of old growth to maintain viable populations of old growth-dependent wildlife (Harris, 1984).

These plans share several features. First, numerous old growth islands are set aside to remain uncut and undisturbed. These are chosen on the basis of (1) healthy present populations of dependent wildlife; (2) the potential for future occupation, as suggested by the quality of forest structure and other habitat features, such as year-around water sources; and (3) ease of migration between neighboring islands, as a result of older intervening forest and the lack of topographic barriers. Second, a large acreage of forest surrounding each old growth island or between neighboring islands is maintained with a substantial percentage of mature timber, perhaps through lengthened rotation times. Longer rotation times up to 300 years have been formally proposed for portions of the Mt. Hebo region of the Siuslaw National Forest (Franklin, et al., 1981). Third, the remaining areas are used primarily for timber production, and are harvested either with an uneven-aged technique or by clearcutting. But if clearcutting is used, after the second or third rotation the stand is allowed to lie fallow for 200–400 years, so that it develops into a diverse, decadent old growth forest, whose long-term nutrient inputs naturally heal the soil. Then the harvest cycle begins anew.

In only the 200 years since Lewis and Clark first stood in awe of the sylvan magnificence of the Pacific Coast, the era of the giant trees has all but ended, put to rest by a hundred competing interests with little thought of the wider implications. Perhaps in the next 200, a more scientifically informed stewardship will usher a return to some of the former health and stature of these world-class forests, and the Northwest that they symbolize.

BIBLIOGRAPHY

Akins, G., and C. Jefferson. 1973. *Coastal Wetlands of Oregon: A Natural Resource Inventory Report.* Oregon Coastal Conservation and Development Commission: Florence.

Amspoker, M.C., and C.D. McIntyre. 1978. Distribution of intertidal diatoms associated with sediments in Yaquina Estuary, Oregon. Journal of Phycology 14: 387–395.

Anderson, D.W., and F. Gress. 1983. Status of a northern population of California brown pelicans. Condor 85: 79–88.

Anderson, S., and J.N. Jones, eds. 1984. *Orders and Families of Recent Mammals of the World.* John Wiley: New York.

Andrews, H.J., and R.W. Cowlin. 1940. Forest resources of the Douglas fir region. U.S.D.A. Misc. Pub. 389: Washington, D.C.

Anikouchine, W.A., and R.W. Sternberg. 1981. *The World Ocean—An Introduction to Oceanography.* 2nd ed. Prentice-Hall: Englewood Cliffs, New Jersey.

Arnason, U. 1974. Comparative chromosome studies in cetacea. Hereditas 77: 1–36.

Ashmole, N.P. 1971. Sea bird ecology and the marine environment. In *Avian Biology* Vol. 1. D.S. Farner, J.R. King, and K.C. Parkes, eds. Academic Press: New York.

Baldwin, E.M. 1981. *Geology of Oregon.* 3rd ed. Kendall/Hunt: Dubuque, Iowa.

Barbour, M.G., and J. Major, eds. 1977. *Terrestrial Vegetation of California.* John Wiley & Sons: New York.

Barnes, J.R., and J.J. Gonor. 1973. The larval settling response of the lined chiton *Tonicella lineata.* Marine Biology 20: 259–264.

Barnes, L.G., D.P. Domning, and C.E. Ray. 1985. Status of studies on fossil marine mammals. Marine Mammal Science 1: 15–53.

Barnes, L.G., and E. Mitchell. 1978. Cetacea. In *Evolution of African Mammals.* V.J. Maglio and H.B.S. Cooke, eds. Harvard University Press: Cambridge.

Barnes, L.G., and S.A. McLeod. 1984. The fossil record and phyletic relationships of gray whales. In Jones, Swartz, and Leatherwood, 1984.

Barnes, L.G. 1984. Search for the first whale. Tracing the ancestry of cetaceans. Oceans 17(2): 20–23.

Barnes, R.S.K., and J. Green. 1972. *The Estuarine Environment.* Applied Science Publishers: London.

Barrowclough, G.F., and S.L. Coats. 1985. The demography and population genetics of owls with special reference to the conservation of the spotted owl. In Gutierrez and Carey, 1985.

Barrows, C.W., and K. Barrows. 1978. Roost characteristics and behavioral thermoregulation in the spotted owl. Western Birds 9: 1–8.

Barrows, C.W. 1981. Roost selection in spotted owls: an adaptation to heat stress. Condor 83: 302–309.

Barry, R.G., and R.J. Chorley. 1976. *Atmosphere, Weather, and Climate.* 3rd ed. Methuen & Co. Ltd.: London.

Bartholomew, G.A. 1970. A model for the evolution of Pinniped polygyny. Evolution 24: 546–559.

Bascom, W. 1964. *Waves and Beaches.* Doubleday & Co.: Garden City, New York.

Batchelder, H.P., and J.J. Gonor. 1981. Population characteristics of the intertidal green sea anemone, *Anthopleura xanthogrammica,* on the Oregon Coast. Estuarine, Coastal and Shelf Science 13: 235–245.

Battelle. 1975 *Coastal Reconnaissance Study: Oregon and Washington.* For U.S. Army Corps of Engineers: Portland.

Beach, R.J. 1981. Washington Department of Game Marine Mammal-Fisheries Interaction Project: Synthesis and Overview. Abstract and Poster, Fourth Biennial Conference on the Biology of Marine Mammals: San Francisco.

Beadle, L.C. 1972. Physiological problems for animal life in estuaries. In *The Estuarine Environment.* R.S.K. Barnes and J. Green, eds. Applied Science Publishers: London.

Beccasio, A.D., *et al.* 1981. *Pacific Coast Ecological Inventory User's Guide and Information Base.* U.S. Fish and Wildlife Service. FWS/OBS-81/30.

Beeson, M.H., R. Perttu, and J. Perttu. 1979. The origin of the miocene basalts of coastal Oregon and Washington: an alternative hypothesis. Oregon Geology 41: 159–166.

Behrman, D. 1969. *The New World of the Oceans.* Little, Brown: Boston.

Bellrose, F.C. 1976. *Ducks, Geese, & Swans of North America.* Stackpole Books: Harrisburg, Pennsylvania.

Bergstrom, D. 1979. Trees help keep a forest fertile. Forestry Research West. U.S. Forest Service GPO 1979-699-018.

Bernard, F.R. 1974. Annual biodeposition and gross energy budget of mature Pacific oysters, *Crassostrea gigas.* J. Fish. Res. Board Can. 31:185–190.

Berry, R., and K. Brown. 1980. *Pounds and Value of Commercially Caught Fish and Shellfish Landed in Oregon.* Oregon Department of Fish and Wildlife: Portland.

Bertrand, G.A., and J.M. Scott. 1979. *Checklist of the Birds of Oregon.* 3rd ed. by M.S. Eltzroth and F.L. Ramsey. Oregon State University Bookstores, Inc: Corvallis.

Bird, E.C.F. 1969. *Coasts.* MIT Press: Cambridge, Mass.

Blant, C.E. 1980. *Atlas of California Coastal Marine Resources.* California Department of Fish and Game: Sacramento.

Blokhin, S.A. 1984. Investigations of gray whales taken in the Chukchi coastal waters, U.S.S.R. In Jones, Swartz, and Leatherwood, 1984.

Bloom, S.A. 1975. The motile escape response of a sessile prey: a sponge-scallop mutualism. Journal of Experimental Marine Biology and Ecology 17: 311–321.

Boaden, P.J.S., and R. Seed. 1985. *An Introduction to Coastal Ecology.* Chapman and Hall: New York.

Bolsinger, C.L. 1973. *Changes in Commercial Forest Area in Oregon and Washington 1945–1970.* U.S. Forest Service Resource Bulletin PNW-46.

Bottom, D., et al. 1979. *Habitat Classification and Inventory Methods for the Management of Oregon Estuaries.* Oregon Department of Fish and Wildlife: Salem.

Bower, B. 1984. Grammar-schooled dolphins. Science News 126: 346–348.

Braham, H.W. 1984. Distribution and migration of gray whales in Alaska. In Jones, Swartz, and Leatherwood, 1984.

Breiwick, J.M., and H.W. Braham, eds. 1984. The status of endangered whales. Marine Fisheries Review 46(4): 1–64.

Burley, B. 1979. *Critical Species and Habitats of Oregon's Coastal Beaches and Dunes.* Oregon Coastal Zone Management Association: Newport.

Carefoot, T. 1977. *Pacific Seashores: A Guide to Intertidal Ecology.* University of Washington Press: Seattle.

Carefoot, T.H. 1965. Magnetite in the radula of the Polyplacophora. Malacological Society of London. Proceedings 36: 203–212.

Carey, A.B. 1985. A summary of the scientific basis for spotted owl management. In Gutierrez and Carey, 1985.

Chia, F. 1973. Sand dollar: a weight belt for the juvenile. Science 181: 73–74.

Choat, J.H. 1977. The influence of sessile organisms on the population biology of three species of acmaeid limpets. Journal of Experimental Marine Biology and Ecology 26: 1–26.

Clements, F.E. 1916. Plant succession: an analysis of the development of vegetation. Carnegie Institute of Washington Publication 242.

Cline, S.P., A.B. Berg, and H.M. Wight. 1980. Snag characteristics and dynamics in Douglas-fir forests, western Oregon. Journal of Wildlife Management 44: 773–786.

Cole, D.W., W.J. Crane, and C.C. Grier. 1975 The effect of forest management practices on water quality in a second growth Douglas-fir ecosystem. In B. Bernier and C.H. Winget, eds., 1973, *Forest Soils and Forest Land Management,* Proc. 4th N. American Forest Soils Conference, Aug., 1973.

Connell, J.H., and R.O. Slayter. 1977. Mechanisms of succession in natural communities and their role in community stability and organization. American Naturalist 111: 1119–1144.

Connell, J.H. 1961. The influence of interspecific competition and other factors on the distribution of the barnacle *Chthamalus stellatus.* Ecology 42: 710–723.

Connell, J.H. 1970. A predator-prey system in the marine intertidal region. I. *Balanus glandula* and several predatory species of *Thais.* Ecological Monographs 40: 49–78.

Connell, J.H. 1972. Community interactions on marine rocky intertidal shores. Annual Reviews of Ecology and Systematics 3: 169–192.

Connell, J.H. 1975. Some mechanisms producing structure in natural communities: a model and evidence from field experiments. In *Ecology and Evolution of Communities.* M.L. Cody and J.M. Diamond, eds. Harvard University Press: Cambridge, Mass.

Connor, V.M., and J.F. Quinn. 1984. Stimulation of food species growth by limpet mucus. Science 225: 843–844.

Cooper, W.S. 1958. *Coastal Sand Dunes of Oregon and Washington.* Geological Society of America. Memoir 72.

Cooper, W.S. 1967. *Coastal Sand Dunes of California.* Geological Society of America. Memoir 104.

Cubit, J. 1975. Interactions of seasonally changing physical factors and grazing affecting high intertidal communities on a rocky shore. Ph. D. Thesis, University of Oregon: Eugene.

Curtis, R.O., D.L. Reukeme, R.R. Silen, R. Fight, and R.M. Romancier. 1973. Intensive management of coastal Douglas-fir. Pacific Logging Congress Loggers' Handbook 33: 35–37, 134–138.

Dahl, E. 1952. Some aspects of the ecology and zonation of the fauna on sandy beaches. Oikos 4: 1–27.

Daly, G.P. 1981. Competitive interactions among three crab species in the intertidal zone. Ph.D. Thesis, University of Oregon: Eugene.

Darling, J.D. 1984. Gray whales off Vancouver Island, British Columbia. In Jones, Swartz, and Leatherwood, 1984.

Davies, J.L. 1980. *Geographical Variation in Coastal Development.* 2nd ed. Longman: New York.

Dawson, M.R., and L. Krishtalka. 1984. Fossil history of the families of recent mammals. In Anderson and Jones, 1984.

Day, R.H., K.L. Oakley, and D.R. Barnard. 1983. Nest sites and eggs of

Kittlitz's and marbled murrelets. Condor 85: 265–273.

Dayton, P.K. 1971. Competition, disturbance, and community organization: the provision and subsequent utilization of space in a rocky intertidal community. Ecological Monographs 41: 351–389.

Dayton, P.K. 1973a. Dispersion, dispersal, and persistence of the annual intertidal alga, *Postelsia palmaeformis* Ruprecht. Ecology 54: 433–438.

Dayton, P.K. 1973b. Two cases of resource partitioning in a intertidal community: making the right prediction for the wrong reason. American Naturalist 107: 662–670.

Dayton, P.K. 1975a. Experimental evaluation of ecological dominance in a rocky intertidal algal community. Ecological Monographs 45: 137–159.

Dayton, P.K. 1975b. Experimental studies of algal canopy interaction in a sea otter-dominated kelp community at Amchitka Island, Alaska. Fishery Bulletin 73: 230–237.

Defran, R.N., and K. Pryor. 1980. The behavior and training of cetaceans in captivity. In Herman, 1980a.

Denley, E.J., and A.J. Underwood. 1979. Experiments on factors influencing settlement, survival, and growth of two species of barnacles in New South Wales. Journal of Experimental Marine Biology and Ecology 36: 269–293.

Dethier, M.N. 1984. Disturbance and recovery in intertidal pools: maintenance of mosaic patterns. Ecological Monographs 54: 99–118.

Dicken, S.N., C.L. Johannessen, and B. Hanneson. 1961. *Some Recent Physical Changes of the Oregon Coast.* University of Oregon: Eugene.

Domning, D.P. 1977. Sirenian evolution in the North Pacific Ocean. University of California Press: Berkeley.

Dott, R.H., and R.L. Batten. 1981. *Evolution of the Earth.* 3rd ed. McGraw-Hill: New York.

Drake, E. 1982. Tectonic evolution of the Oregon continental margin. Oregon Geology 44: 15–21.

Duxbury, A.C., B.A. Morse, and N. McGary. 1966. The Columbia River effluent and its distribution at sea. Department of Oceanography, Technical Report No. 156. University of Washington: Seattle.

Edmonds, R.L., ed. 1982. *Analysis of Coniferous Forest Ecosystems in the Western United States.* Hutchinson Ross: Stroudsburg, Pennsylvania.

Eilers, H.P. 1975. Plants, plant communities, net production and tide levels: the ecological biogeography of the Nehalem salt marshes, Tillamook County, Oregon. Ph. D. Thesis, Oregon

State University: Corvallis.

Eilers, H.P. 1979. Production ecology in an Oregon coastal salt marsh. Estuarine and Coastal Marine Science 8: 399–410.

Emlen, S.T., and L.W. Oring. 1977. Ecology, sexual selection, and the evolution of mating systems. Science 197: 215–223.

Emlong, D.R. 1966. A new archaic cetacean from the Oligocene of northwest Oregon. Bulletin of the University of Oregon Museum of Natural History 3: 1–51.

Estes, J.A. 1979. Exploitation of marine mammals: R-selection of K-strategists. Journal of the Fisheries Research Board of Canada 36: 1009–1017.

Feder, H.M. 1963. Gastropod defensive responses and their effectiveness in reducing predation by starfishes. Ecology 44: 505–512.

Feder, H.M. 1972. Escape responses in marine invertebrates. Scientific American 227: 92–100.

Forsman, E.D., E.C. Meslow, and H.M. Wight. 1984. Distribution and biology of the spotted owl in Oregon. Wildlife Monographs No. 87.

Forsman, E.D., E.C. Meslow, and M.J. Strub. 1977. Spotted owl abundance in young versus old-growth forests, Oregon. Bulletin of the Oregon Wildlife Society 5: 43–47.

Forsman, E.D. 1986. The spotted owl: a literature review. In U.S. Forest Service, 1986.

Foster, M.S., and D.R. Schiel. 1985. *The Ecology of Giant Kelp Forests in California: a Community Profile.* U.S. Fish and Wildlife Biological Report 85(7.2).

Fox, W.T. 1983. *At the Sea's Edge.* Prentice-Hall, Inc.: Englewood Cliffs, New Jersey.

Francis, L. 1973. Clone specific segregation in the sea anemone *Anthopleura elegantissima.* Biological Bulletin 144: 64–72.

Francis, L. 1973. Intraspecific aggression and its effect on the distribution of *Anthopleura elegantissima* and some related sea anemones. Biological Bulletin 144: 73–92.

Francis, L. 1979. Contrast between solitary and clonal lifestyles in the sea anemone *Anthopleura elegantissima.* American Zoologist 19: 669–681.

Frank, P.W. 1965. The biodemography of an intertidal snail population. Ecology 46: 831–844.

Frank, P.W. 1982. Effects of winter feeding on limpets by black oystercatchers, *Haematopus bachmani.* Ecology 63: 1352–1362.

Franklin, J.F., and C.T. Dyrness. 1973. *Natural Vegetation of Oregon and Washington.* U.S. Forest Service GTR PNW-80.

Franklin, J.F., and D.S. DeBell. 1973. Effects of various harvesting methods on forest regeneration. In Even-Age Management, a symposium held August 1, 1972. R.K. Hermann and D.P. Lavender, eds. School of Forestry, Oregon State University: Corvallis.

Franklin, J.F., and R.H. Waring. 1980. Distinctive features of the northwestern coniferous forest: Development, structure, and function. In R.H. Waring, ed. *Forests: Fresh Perspectives from Ecosystem Analysis.* Proceedings of the 40th Annual Biology Colloquium. Oregon State University Press:Corvallis.

Franklin, J.F., et al. 1981. *Ecological Characteristics of Old-Growth Douglas-Fir Forests.* U.S. Forest Service GTR PNW-118.

Franklin, J.F. 1978. Wilderness ecosystems. In *Wilderness Management.* J.C. Hendee, G.H. Stankey, and R.C. Lucas. U.S. Forest Service MP 1365.

Fujimori, T. 1971. *Primary Productivity of a Young Tsuga heterophylla Stand and Some Speculations about Biomass of Forest Communities on the Oregon Coast.* U.S. Forest Service Research Paper PNW-123.

Furness, R.W. 1978. Energy requirements of seabird communities: a bioenergetics model. Journal of Animal Ecology 47: 39–53.

Gashwiler, J.S. 1970. Plant and mammal changes on a clearcut in west-central Oregon. Ecology 51: 1018–1026.

Gaskin, D.E. 1982. *The Ecology of Whales and Dolphins.* Heinemann: London.

Gaumer, T., S. Benson, L. Brewer, L. Osis, D. Skeesick, R. Starr, and J. Watson. 1983. Estuaries. Manuscript, U.S. Fish and Wildlife Service: Portland.

Gingerich, P.D., D.E. Russell, and S.M.I. Shah. 1983. Origin of whales in epicontinental remnant seas: new evidence from the early Eocene of Pakistan. Science 220: 403–406.

Goldman, B., and F.H. Talbot. 1976. Aspects of the ecology of coral reef fishes. In *Biology and Geology of Coral Reefs.* O.A. Jones and R. Endean, eds. Vol. 3. Academic Press: New York.

Gould, G.I. 1974. The status of the spotted owl in California. California Department of Fish and Game Report No. 74–6: Sacramento.

Gould, G.I. 1985. Management of spotted owls by the California Department of Fish and Game. In Gutierrez and Carey, 1985.

Graybill, M. 1981. Haul Out Patterns and Diet of Harbor Seals, *Phoca vitulina,* in Coos County, Oregon. M.S. University of Oregon: Eugene.

Green, J. 1968. The Biology of Estuarine Animals. University of Washington Press: Seattle.

Grier, C.C., D.W. Cole, C.T. Dyrness, and R.L. Fredriksen. 1974. Nutrient cycling in 37 and 450-year-old Douglas-fir ecosystems. Coniferous Forest International Biome Program Bull. 5:21–34.

Grier, C.C., and R.S. Logan. 1977. Old-growth *Pseudotsuga menziesii* communities of a western Oregon watershed: biomass distribution and production budgets. Ecological Monographs 47: 373–400.

Gundlach, E.R. 1983. The fate of Amoco Cadiz oil. Science 221: 122–129.

Gutierrez, R.J. 1985. An overview of recent research on the spotted owl. In Gutierrez and Carey, 1985.

Gutierrez, R.J. and A.B. Carey. Tech. eds. 1985. *Ecology and Management of the Spotted Owl in the Pacific Northwest.* U.S. Forest Service GTR PNW-185.

Hamilton, P.E. 1973. Oregon estuaries. Division of State Lands: Salem.

Hansell, H. 1983. Aspects of the diving biology of common murres (*Uria aalge*). M.S. Thesis, University of Oregon: Eugene.

Harding, L.W., J.L. Cox, and J.E. Pequegnat. 1978. Spring-summer phytoplankton production in Humboldt Bay, California. California Fish and Game 64: 53–59.

Hare, F.K. 1966. *The Restless Atmosphere.* 4th ed. Hutchinson: London.

Harger, J.R.E. 1968. The role of behavioral traits in influencing the distribution of two species of sea mussel, *Mytilus edulis* and *M. californianus.* Veliger 11: 45–49.

Harger, J.R.E. 1972. Variation and relative "niche" size in the sea mussel *Mytilus edulis* in association with *Mytilus californianus.* Veliger 14: 275–281.

Harr, R.D., and F.M. McCorison. 1979. Initial effects of clearcut logging on size and timing of peak flows in a small watershed in western Oregon. Water Resources Research 15(1): 90–94.

Harris, L.D. 1984. *The Fragmented Forest. Island Biogeography Theory and the Preservation of Biotic Diversity.* University of Chicago Press: Chicago.

Harrison, C. 1978. *A Field Guide to the Nests, Eggs, and Nestlings of North American Birds.* Collins: N.Y. Harrison, C.S. 1979. The association of marine birds and feeding gray whales. Condor 81: 93–95.

Harrison, R.J., and J.E. King. 1980. *Marine Mammals.* Hutchinson: London.

Harrison, R.J., ed. 1972. *Functional Anatomy of Marine Mammals.* 2 vols. Academic Press: London.

Hart, J.L. 1973. *Pacific Fishes of Canada.* Bulletin 180. Fisheries Research Board of Canada: Ottawa.

Hasler, A.D., A.T. Scholz, and R.N. Horral. 1978. Olfactory imprinting and homing in salmon. American Scientist 66: 347–355.

Haven, S.B. 1971. Niche differences in the intertidal limpets *Acmaea scabra* and *Acmaea digitalis* (Gastropoda) in Central California. Veliger 13: 231–248.

Haven, S.B. 1973. Competition for food between the intertidal gastropods *Acmaea scabra* and *Acmaea digitalis*. Ecology 54: 143–151.

Haynes, R.W. 1986. *Inventory and Value of Old-Growth in the Douglas-Fir Region*. U.S. Forest Service Research Note PNW-437.

Hedgpeth, J.W., and S. Obreski. 1981. *Willapa Bay: A Historical Perspective and a Rationale for Research*. U.S. Fish and Wildlife Service FWS/OBS-81/03.

Hedgpeth, J.W. 1966. Aspects of the estuarine ecosystem. In *A Symposium on Estuarine Fisheries*. R.F. Smith, A.H. Swartz, and W.H. Massmann, eds. American Fisheries Society. Special Publication 3. Allen Press: Lawrence, Kansas

Henderson, J.A., and D. Peter. 1982. *Preliminary Plant Associations and Habitat Types of the Soleduck Ranger District, Olympia National Forest*. U.S. Forest Service.

Herman, L.M., and W.N. Tavolga. 1980. The communication systems of cetaceans. In Herman, 1980a.

Herman, L.M., ed. 1980a. *Cetacean Behavior. Mechanisms and Functions*. John Wiley & Sons: New York.

Herman, L.M. 1980b. Cognitive characteristics of dolphins. In Herman, 1980a.

Herman, S.G., and J.B. Bulger. 1981. *The Distribution and Abundance of Shorebirds during the 1981 Spring Migration at Grays Harbor, Washington*. U.S. Army Corps of Engineers. Seattle District: Seattle.

Herzing, D.L., and B.R. Mate. 1984. Gray whale migrations along the Oregon Coast 1978–1981. In Jones, Swartz, and Leatherwood, 1984.

Highsmith, R.C. 1982. Induced settlement and metamorphosis of sand dollar (*Dendraster excentricus*) larvae in predator-free sites: adult sand dollar beds. Ecology 63: 329–337.

Hildebrandt, W.R. 1984. Archaeological presence of the northern fur seal (*Callorhinus ursinus*) along the coast of northern California. Murrelet 65:28–29.

Hines, W.W. 1971. Plant Communities in the Old-Growth Forests of North Coastal Oregon. Oregon State University M.S. Thesis: Corvallis.

Hodder, J., and M.R. Graybill. 1985. Reproduction and survival of seabirds in Oregon during the 1982–1983 El Nino. Condor 87: 535–541.

Hodgson, L.M. 1980. Control of the Intertidal Distribution of *Gastroclonium coulteri* in Monterey Bay, California, USA. Marine Biology 57: 121–126.

Hoffmann, W., D. Heinemann, and J.A. Wiens. 1981. The ecology of seabird feeding flocks in Alaska. Auk 98: 437–456.

Hoffnagle, J., and R. Olson. 1974. *The Salt Marshes of the Coos Bay Estuary.* Oregon Institute of Marine Biology: Charleston.

Hudnall, J. 1981. Population estimate, feeding behavior, and food source of gray whales, *Eschrichtius robustus,* occupying the straits of Juan de Fuca, B.C. Abstract, Fourth Biennial Conference on the Biology of Marine Mammals: San Francisco.

Huyer, A. 1983. Coastal upwelling in the California current system. Progress in Oceanography 12: 259–284.

Ingle, R.M. 1953. The life of an estuary. Scientific American 190(5): 64–68.

Isaac, L.A. 1956. Place of partial cutting in old growth stands of the Douglas-fir region. U.S. Forest Service RP PNW-16.

Jacobs, M.S., P.J. Morgane, and W.L. McFarland. 1971. The Anatomy of the brain of the bottlenosed dolphin (*Tursiops truncatus*): rhinic lobe (Rhinencephalus). 1. Paleocortex. Journal of Comparative Neurology.

Jacobs, M.S., W.L. McFarland, and P.J. Morgane. 1979. The anatomy of the brain of the bottlenosed dolphin (*Tursiops truncatus*): rhinic lobe (Rhinencephalus). Archicortex. Brain Research Bulletin 4: 1–108.

Jameson, R.J., K. Kenyon, S. Jeffries, and G.R. VanBlaricom. 1986. Status of a translocated sea otter population and its habitat in Washington. Murrelet 67:84–87.

Jameson, R.J., K.W. Kenyon, A.M. Johnson, and H.M. Wight. 1982. History and status of translocated sea otter populations in North America. Wildlife Soc. Bull. 10:100–107.

Jefferson, C. 1973. Some aspects of plant succession in Oregon estuarine salt marshes. Ph.D. Thesis, Oregon State University: Corvallis.

Jerison, H.J. 1973. *Evolution of the Brain and Intelligence.* Academic Press: New York.

Johannessen, C.L. 1964. Marshes prograding in Oregon: Aerial photographs. Science 146: 1575–1578.

Johnston, S., and J.R. Carter. 1985. Cavity-nesting marbled murrelets. Wilson Bulletin 97: 1–3.

Jones, M.L., S.L. Swartz, and S. Leatherwood, eds. 1984. *The Gray Whale Eschrichtius robustus.* Academic Press: New York.

Kanwisher, J.W., and S.H. Ridgeway. 1983. The physiological ecology of whales and porpoises. Scientific American 248(6): 110–120.

Keefe, C.W. 1972. Marsh production: a summary of the literature. Contributions in Marine Science 16: 163–180.

Kelly, D. 1986. The decadent forest. Audubon 88(2): 46–73.

Kensler, C.B. 1967. Desiccation resistance of intertidal crevice species as a factor in their zonation. J. Anim. Ecol. 36: 391–406.

Kenyon, K.W. 1969. The sea otter in the eastern Pacific Ocean. North Am. Fauna 68.

Kenyon, K.W. 1981. Sea otter *Enhydra lutris*. In S.H. Ridgeway and R.J. Hanson eds. *Handbook of Marine Mammals*. Vol. 1. Academic Press: New York.

Kenyon, K.W. 1982. Sea otter. In J.A. Chapman and G.A. Feldhamer, eds. *Wild Mammals of North America*. Johns Hopkins: Baltimore.

Kirk, R. 1966. *The Olympic Rain Forest*. University of Washington Press: Seattle.

Kirkland, B.P. 1946. Forest resources of the Douglas fir region. Joint Comm. Forest Conservation, Pacific Northwest Loggers Association: Portland.

Knight-Jones, E.W. 1953. Laboratory experiments on gregariousness during settling in *Balanus balanoides* and other barnacles. Journal of Experimental Biology 30: 584–598.

Kozloff, E.N. 1983. Seashore Life of the Northern Pacific Coast: An Illustrated Guide to Northern California, Oregon, Washington, and British Columbia. University of Washington Press: Seattle.

Kreag, R.A. 1979. *Natural Resources of Sand Lake Estuary*. Oregon Department of Fish and Wildlife: Portland.

Kulu, D.D. 1972. Evolution and cytogenetics. In Ridgeway, 1972.

Kumler, M.L. 1963. Plant succession on the sand dunes of the Oregon coast. Ecology 50: 695–704.

Kuramoto, R.T., and L.C. Bliss. 1970. Ecology of subalpine meadows in the Olympic Mountains, Washington. Ecological Monographs 40: 317–347.

Lack, D. 1968. *Ecological Adaptations for Breeding in Birds*. Methuen: London.

Lauff, G.H., ed. 1967. *Estuaries*. Washington, D.C. American Association for the Advancement of Science. Publication 83.

Leatherwood, S., R. Reeves, W. Perrin, and W. Evans. 1982. *Whales, Dolphins, and Porpoises of the Eastern North Pacific and Adjacent Arctic Waters: A Guide to their Identification*. National Oceanic and Atmospheric Administration Technical Report. National Marine Fisheries Service Circular 444.

Levinton, J.S. 1982. *Marine Ecology*. Prentice-Hall: Englewood Cliffs, New Jersey.

Lewin, J., C.H. Chen, and T. Hruby. 1979a. The chemical composition of the surf diatom *Chaetoceros armatum* and its major herbivore, *Siliqua patula*. Marine Biology 51: 259–265.

Lewin, J., J.E. Eckman, and G.N. Ware. 1979b. Regeneration of ammonium in the surf environment by the Pacific razor clam *Siliqua patula*. Marine Biology 52: 1–9.

Lewin, J. 1978. The world of the razor clam beach. Pacific Search

12(6):12–13.

Lindquist, J.L., and M.N. Palley. 1963. Empirical yield tables for young-growth redwood. California Agricultural Experiment Station: Berkeley. Bulletin 796.

Lyman, R.L. 1988. Zoogeography of Oregon Coast marine mammals: the last 3000 years. Marine Mammal Science 4:247–264.

MacDonald, K.B. 1969. Quantitative studies of salt marsh mollusc faunas from the North American Pacific Coast. Ecological Monographs 39: 33–60.

MacGinitie, G.E., and N. MacGinitie. 1949. *Natural History of Marine Animals*. McGraw-Hill: New York.

MacLachlan, J., and J.S. Craigie. 1964. Algal inhibition by yellow-ultraviolet absorbing substances from *Fucus vesiculosus*. Canadian Journal of Botany 42: 287–292.

Madsen, C.J., and L.M. Herman. 1980. Social and ecological correlates of cetacean vision and visual appearance. In Herman, 1980a.

Mahnken, C., and T. Joyner. 1973. Part III: Developing a coastal fishery for Pacific salmon. Mar. Fish Rev. 35, no. 10.

Mann, K.H. 1982. *Ecology of Coastal Waters*. University of California Press: Berkeley.

Markham, J.W., and J.L. Celestino. 1976. Intertidal marine plants of Clatsop County, Oregon. Syesis 9: 253–266.

Marsh, C. 1983. The role of avian predators in an Oregon rocky intertidal community. Ph.D. Thesis, Oregon State University: Corvallis.

Martin, R.C., and R.E. Frenkel. 1978. *Preserve Analysis: Blacklock Point*. Oregon Natural Area Preserves Advisory Committee to the State Land Board: Salem.

Maser, C., J.M. Trappe, and R.A. Nussbaum. 1978. Fungal-small mammal interrelationships with emphasis on Oregon coniferous forests. Ecology 59: 799–809.

Maser, C.M., B.R. Mate, J.F. Franklin, and C.T. Dyrness. 1981. *Natural History of Oregon Coast Mammals*. U.S. Forest Service. GTR-PNW-133.

Maser, C.M., and J.M. Trappe. Tech. eds. 1984. *The Seen and Unseen World of the Fallen Tree*. U.S. Forest Service GTR PNW-164.

Mate, B.R., and J.T. Harvey. 1984. Ocean movements of radio-tagged gray whales. In Jones, Swartz, and Leatherwood, 1984.

Mathematical Sciences Northwest. 1977. *Washington Coastal Areas of Major Biological Significance. November 1977.* For Washington Department of Ecology: Olympia.

Matthews, L.H. 1978. *The Natural History of the Whale*. Columbia University Press: New York.

McGuire, J.R. 1977. Final Environmental Statement Oregon Dunes

National Recreation Area Management Plan. U.S. Forest Service: Washington, D.C.

McKee, B. 1972. *Cascadia: The Geologic Evolution of the Pacific Northwest.* McGraw-Hill: New York.

McLaren, I.A., and T.G. Smith. 1985. Population ecology of seals: Retrospective and prospective views. Marine Mammal Science 1: 54–83.

McLusky, D.S. 1981. *The Estuarine Ecosystem.* John Wiley: New York.

McRoy, C.P. 1966. The standing stock and ecology of eelgrass, *Zostera marina,* Izembek Lagoon, Alaska. M.S. Thesis. University of Washington: Seattle.

Mead, J.G., and E.D. Mitchell. 1984. Atlantic gray whales. In Jones, Swartz, and Leatherwood, 1984.

Means, J.E., ed. 1982. *Forest Succession and Stand Development Research in the Northwest.* Proceedings of the Symposium of the Northwest Scientific Association, March 1981. Forest Research Laboratory: Corvallis.

Meinke, R.J. 1981. *Threatened and Endangered Vascular Plants of Oregon: An Illustrated Guide.* U.S. Fish and Wildlife Service: Portland.

Miller, R.E., and M.D. Murray. 1979. Fertilizer versus red alder for adding nitrogen to Douglas-fir forests of the Pacific Northwest. In Symbiotic nitrogen fixation in the management of temperate forests: proceedings of a workshop held April 2–5, 1979, Oregon State University: Corvallis. J.C. Gordon, C.T. Wheeler, D.A. Perry, eds.

Milne, L., and M. Milne. 1971. *The Arena of Life. The Dynamics of Ecology.* Doubleday/Natural History Press: Garden City, N.Y.

Minore, D. 1979. *Comparative Autecological Characteristics of Northwestern Tree Species—A Literature Review.* U.S. Forest Service GTR PNW-87.

Mitchell, E., and R.H. Tedford, 1973. The Enaliarctinae: a new group of extinct aquatic carnivora and a consideration of the origin of the Otariidae. Bulletin of the American Museum of Natural History 151: 201–284.

Montgomery, J.M. 1976. Forest harvest, residue treatment, reforestation and protection of water quality. U.S. Environmental Protection Agency: Seattle.

Morgane, P.J., M.S. Jacobs, and W.L. McFarland. 1980. The anatomy of the brain of the bottlenosed dolphin (*Tursiops truncatus*): Surface configurations of the telencephalon of the bottlenosed dolphin with comparative anatomical observations in four other cetacean species. Brain Research Bulletin 5: 1–107.

Morgane, P.J. 1974. The whale brain: The anatomical basis of intelligence. In *Mind in the Waters.* J. McIntyre, ed. Charles Scribner's Sons: New York.

Morris, R.H., D.P. Abbot, and E.C. Haderlie. 1980. *Intertidal Invertebrates of California.* Stanford University Press: Stanford.

Murison, L.D. *et al.* 1984. Foraging of the gray whale along the west coast of Vancouver Island. In Jones, Swartz, and Leatherwood, 1984.

Myers, J.P., P.G. Connors, and F.A. Pitelka. 1979. Territory size in wintering sanderlings: the effects of prey abundance and intruder density. Auk 96: 551–561.

Myers, J.P., S.L. Williams, and F.A. Pitelka. 1980. An experimental analysis of prey availability for sanderlings (Aves: Scolopacidae) feeding on sandy beach crustaceans. Canadian Journal of Zoology 58: 1564–1574.

Nelson, B. 1979. *Seabirds. Their Biology and Ecology.* A & W Publishers Inc.: New York.

Nerini, M. 1984. A review of gray whale feeding ecology. In Jones, Swartz, and Leatherwood, 1984.

Nixon, S.W. 1982. Between coastal marshes and coastal waters—a review of 20 years of speculation and research on the role of salt marshes in estuarine productivity and water chemistry. In *Estuarine and Wetlands Processes.* P. Hamilton and K. McDonald, eds. Plenum Press: New York.

Norris, K.N., and T.P. Dohl. 1980. The structure and functions of cetacean schools. In Herman, 1980a.

Oceanographic Institute of Washington. 1977. *A Summary of Knowledge of the Oregon and Washington Coastal Zone and Offshore Areas.* Vol. 1. Oceanographic Institute of Washington, for the Bureau of Land Management, U.S. Department of the Interior.

Odum, E.P. 1961. The role of tidal marshes in estuarine production. Conservationist 15: 12–13.

Odum, E.P. 1969. The strategy of ecosystem development. Science 164: 262–270.

Odum, E.P. 1971. *Fundamentals of Ecology.* 3rd ed. W.B. Saunders: Philadelphia.

Odum, E.P. 1974. Halophytes, energetics, and ecosystems. In *Ecology of Halophytes.* R.J. Reimold and W.H. Queen, eds. Academic Press: New York.

Osis, L., and B. Kuhn. 1975. *A Guide to Oregon's Rocky Intertidal Areas.* Fish Commission of Oregon Educational Bulletin No. 5.

Page, G.W., and L.E. Stenzel, eds. 1981. The breeding status of the snowy plover in California. Western Birds 12.

Paine, R.T., and S.A. Levin. 1981. Intertidal landscapes: disturbance and the dynamics of pattern. Ecological Monographs 51: 145–178.

Paine, R.T., and R.L. Vadas. 1969. The effects of grazing by sea urchins, *Strongylocentrotus* spp., on benthic algal populations.

Limnology and Oceanography 14: 710–719.

Paine, R.T. 1969. The *Pisaster-Tegula* interaction: prey patches, predator food preference, and intertidal community structure. Ecology 50: 950–961.

Paine, R.T. 1974. Intertidal community structure. Experimental studies on the relationship between a dominant competitor and its principle predator. Oecologia 15: 93–120.

Paine, R.T. 1979. Disaster, catastrophe, and local persistence of the sea palm *Postelsia palmaeformis*. Science 205: 685–687.

Paine, R.T. 1984. Ecological determinism in the competition for space. Ecology 65: 1339–1348.

Parmenter, T., and R. Bailey. 1985. *The Oregon Ocean Book. An Introduction to the Pacific Ocean off Oregon Including its Physical Setting and Living Marine Resources.* Oregon State Department of Land Conservation and Development: Salem.

Percy, K.L., D.A. Bella, C. Sutterlin, and P.C. Klingeman. 1974. *Descriptions and Information Sources for Oregon Estuaries.* Sea Grant College Program. Oregon State University: Corvallis.

Peterson, C.H., and N.M. Peterson. 1979. *The Ecology of Intertidal Flats of North Carolina: A Community Profile.* U.S. Fish and Wildlife Service Biological Services Program. FWS/OBS-79/39.

Phillips, R.C., and G.W. Thayer. 1977. Importance of eelgrass beds in Puget Sound. Marine Fisheries Review 39: 18–22.

Phillips, R.C. 1974. Temperate grass flats. In H.T. Odum, B.J. Copeland, and E.A. McMahan, *A Source Book for Estuarine Planning,* Conservation Foundation: Washington, D.C.

Phillips, R.C. 1984. *The Ecology of Eelgrass Meadows in the Pacific Northwest: A Community Profile.* U.S. Fish and Wildlife Service FWS/OBS-84/24.

Pierotti, R., and D. Pierotti. 1980. Effects of cold climate on the evolution of Pinniped breeding systems. Evolution 34: 494–507.

Pinto, C., et al. 1972. *Resource Inventory Report for the Oregon Dunes National Recreation Area, Siuslaw National Forest.* U.S. Department of Agriculture, Forest Service: Portland.

Pomeroy, L.R., E.E. Smith, and C.M. Grant. 1965. The exchange of phosphate between estuarine water and sediments. Limnology and Oceanography 10: 167–172.

Pomeroy, L.R. 1980. Nutrient cycling in coastal ecosystems. In *Rehabilitation and Creation of Selected Coastal Habitats: Proceedings of a Workshop.* U.S. Fish and Wildlife Service Biological Services Program. FWS/OBS-80/27.

Popper, A.N. 1980. Sound emission and detection by delphinids. In Herman, 1980a.

Proctor, C.M., et al. 1980. *An Ecological Characterization of the Pacific Northwest Coastal Region.* 5 Vols. U.S. Fish and Wildlife Service.

FWS/OBS-79/15.

Purer, E.A. 1942. Anatomy and ecology of *Ammophila arenaria* Link. Madroo 6: 167–171.

Quayle, R.C., and D.C. Fulbright. 1975. Extreme wind and wave return periods for the U.S. Coast. Mariner's Weather Log 19: 67–60.

Queen, W.H. 1975. Halophytes: adaptive mechanisms. In *Physiological Ecology of Estuarine Organisms*. F.J. Vernberg, ed. University of South Carolina Press: Columbia.

Rankin, D.C. 1983. Holocene geologic history of the Clatsop Plains foredune ridge complex. Ph.D. Thesis, Portland State University: Portland.

Ranwell, D.S. 1972. *Ecology of Salt Marshes and Sand Dunes*. Chapman and Hall Ltd.: London.

Raphael, M.G., and R.H. Barrett. 1984. Diversity and abundance of wildlife in late successional Douglas-fir forests. In New Forests for a Changing World. Proceedings of the 1983 Society of American Foresters National Convention. Portland.

Ratti, F.D. 1979. *Natural Resources of the Umpqua Estuary.* Oregon Department of Fish and Wildlife: Portland.

Ray, C.E. 1976a. Fossil marine mammals of Oregon. Systematic Zoology 25: 420–436.

Ray, C.E. 1976b. Geography of phocid evolution. Systematic Zoology 25: 391–406.

Recher, H.F. 1966. Some aspects of the ecology of migrant shore birds. Ecology 47: 393–407.

Reeves, R.R. 1984. Modern commercial pelagic whaling for gray whales. In Jones, Swartz, and Leatherwood, 1984.

Reilly, S.B. 1981. Population assessment and dynamics of the California gray whale (*Eschrichtius robustus*). Ph.D. Thesis, University of Washington: Seattle.

Reilly, S.B. 1984. Assessing gray whale abundance: a review. In Jones, Swartz, and Leatherwood, 1984.

Repenning, C.A. 1976. Adaptive evolution of sea lions and walruses. Systematic Zoology 25: 375–390.

Repenning, C.A. 1980. Warm-blooded life in cold ocean currents. Following the evolution of the seal. Oceans 13(3): 18–24.

Rice, D.W., A.A. Wolman, D.E. Withrow, and L.A. Fleischer. 1981. Gray whales on the winter grounds in Baja California. Report of the International Commission on Whaling 31: 477–493.

Rice, D.W., and A.A. Wolman. 1971. The life history and ecology of the gray whale (*Eschrichtius robustus*). American Society of Mammalogists Special Publication 3.

Ricketts, E.F., J. Calvin, and J.W. Hedgpeth. 1985. *Between Pacific Tides*. Revised by D.W. Phillips. Stanford: Stanford University Press.

Ridgeway, S.H., ed. 1972. *Mammals of the Sea: Biology and Medicine.* Charles C. Thomas: Springfield, Ill.

Riznyk, R.Z., and H.K. Phinney. 1972. Manometric assessment of interstitial microalgae production in two estuarine sediments. Oecologia (Berlin) 10: 193–203.

Robbins, C.S., B. Bruun, and H.S. Zim. 1983. *Birds of North America: A Guide to Field Identification.* Golden Press: N.Y.

Rosenthal, R.J., and J.R. Chess. 1972. A predator-prey relationship between the leather star, *Dermasterias imbricata,* and the purple urchin, *Strongylocentrotus purpuratus.* U.S. National Oceanic and Atmospheric Administration Fishery Bulletin 70: 205–216.

Roy, D.F. 1966. Silvical characteristics of redwood (*Sequoia sempervirens* [D. Don] Endl.). University of California, Pacific Southwest Forest and Range Experiment Station: Berkeley. U.S. Forest Service Research Paper PSW-28.

Rudy, P., and L.I I. Rudy. 1983. *Oregon Estuarine Invertebrates. An Illustrated Guide to the Common and Important Invertebrate Animals.* U.S. Fish and Wildlife Service. FWS/OBS-83/16

Rugh, D.J. 1984. Census of gray whales at Unimak Pass, Alaska: November-December 1977–1979. In Jones, Swartz, and Leatherwood, 1984.

Sanger, G.A. 1972. Preliminary standing stock and biomass estimates of seabirds in the subarctic Pacific region. In A.Y. Takenouti, ed., *Biological Oceanography of the Northern Pacific Ocean,* Idemitsu Shoten: Tokyo.

Scagel, R.F., R.J. Bandoni, J.R. Maze, G.E. Rouse, W.B. Schofield, and J.R. Stein. 1982. *Nonvascular Plants. An Evolutionary Survey.* Wadsworth: Belmont, California.

Schneider, S.H., and R. Londer. 1984. *The Coevolution of Climate and Life.* Sierra Club: San Francisco.

Schoen, J.W., *et al.* 1981. *Wildlife-Forest Relationships: Is a Re-Evaluation of Old Growth Necessary?* Transactions of the 46th North American Wildlife and Natural Resources Conference, Wildlife Management Institute: Washington, D.C.

Schustermann, R.J. 1981. Behavioral capabilities of seals and sea lions: A review of their hearing, visual, learning, and diving skills. Psychological Record 31: 125–143.

Scott, J.M. 1973. Resource allocation in four syntopic species of marine diving birds. Ph.D. Thesis, Oregon State University: Corvallis.

Sealy, S.G. 1973. Interspecific feeding assemblages of marine birds of British Columbia. Auk 90: 796–802.

Sebens, K.P. 1981. Recruitment in a sea anemone population: juvenile substrate becomes adult prey. Science 213: 785–787.

Sebens, K.P. 1983. Population dynamics and habitat suitability of the intertidal sea anemones *Anthopleura elegantissima* and *A. xanthogrammica*. Ecological Monographs 53: 405–433.

Silverberg, R. 1972. *The World Within the Ocean Wave.* Weybright and Tally: New York.

Simenstad, C.A., et al. 1979. *Food Web Relationships of Northern Puget Sound and the Strait of Juan de Fuca: A Synthesis of the Available Knowledge.* U.S. Environmental Protection Agency: Washington, D.C.

Slijper, E.J. 1979. *Whales.* 2nd ed. Cornell University Press: Ithaca, N.Y.

Slobodchikoff, C.N., and J.T. Doyen. 1977. Effects of *Ammophila arenaria* on sand dune arthropod communities. Ecology 58: 1171–1175.

Smith, S.H., J.F. Bell, F.R. Herman, and T. See. 1984. *Growth and Yield of Sitka Spruce and Western Hemlock at Cascade Head Experimental Forest, Oregon.* U.S. Forest Service Research Paper PNW-325.

Snell, J.A.K., and B.F. Anholt. 1981. *Predicting Crown Weight of Coast Douglas-fir and Western Hemlock.* U.S. Forest Service Research Paper PNW-281.

Sollins, P., et al. 1980. The internal element cycles of an old-growth Douglas-fir ecosystem in western Oregon. Ecological Monographs 50: 261–285.

Sousa, W.P. 1979. Disturbance in marine intertidal boulder fields: the nonequilibrium maintenance of species diversity. Ecology 60: 1225–1239.

Sousa, W.P. 1980a. Experimental investigations of disturbance and ecological succession in a rocky intertidal algal community. Ecological Monographs 49: 227–254.

Sousa, W.P. 1980b. The responses of a community to disturbance: the importance of successional age and species' life histories. Oecologia (Berlin) 45: 72–81.

Sowls, A.L., A.R. DeGange, J.W. Nelson, and G.S. Lester. 1980. *Catalog of California Seabird Colonies.* U.S. Fish and Wildlife Service FWS/OBS-37/80.

Spurr, S.H., and B.V. Barnes. 1980. *Forest Ecology.* Wiley: New York.

Starr, R.M. 1979. *Natural Resources of the Nestucca Estuary.* Oregon Department of Fish and Wildlife: Portland.

Stebbins, G.C. 1974. *Flowering Plants. Evolution above the Species Level.* Belknap Press: Cambridge, Mass.

Stehli, F.G., A.L. McAlester, and C.E. Helsley. 1967. Taxonomic diversity of recent bivalves and some implications for geology. Geological Society of America Bulletin 78: 455–466.

Steinberg, P.D. 1985. Feeding preferences of *Tegula funebralis* and chemical defenses of marine brown algae. Ecological Monographs 55: 333–349.

Stephensen, T.A., and A. Stephensen. 1949. The universal features of zonation between tide-marks on rocky coasts. J. Ecol. 37:289–305.

Stephensen, T.A., and A. Stephensen. 1972. *Life between Tidemarks on Rocky Shores.* W.H. Freeman: San Francisco.

Sternberg, R.W., and J.L. Johnson. 1978. The birth and death of estuaries. Pacific Search 12(4): 14–15.

Stimson, J. 1970. Territorial behavior of the owl limpet, *Lottia gigantea.* Ecology 51: 113–118.

Stimson, J. 1973. The role of territory in the ecology of the intertidal limpet *Lottia gigantea* (Gray). Ecology 54: 1020–1030.

Stone, E.C., and R.B. Vasey. 1968. Preservation of coast redwood on alluvial flats. Science 159: 157–161.

Suchanek, T.H. 1978. The ecology of *Mytilus edulis* L. in exposed rocky intertidal communities. Journal of Experimental Marine Biology 31: 105–120.

Sumich, J.L. 1982. Gray whales along the Oregon Coast in summer, 1977–1980. Murrelet 65: 33–40.

Sutherland, G.B. 1983. *A Plan for Protecting the Natural Resources of Coos Bay, Oregon from Oil Spills.* Oregon Department of Environmental Quality.

Sutherland, J.P. 1970. Dynamics of high and low populations of the limpet, *Acmaea scabra* (Gould). Ecological Monographs 40: 184–190.

Szalay, F.S. 1969. Origin and evolution of function of the mesonychid condylarth feeding mechanism. Evolution 23: 703–720.

Szalay, F.S. 1969. The Hapalodectinae and a phylogeny of the Mesonychidae. (Mammalia, Condylarthra). American Museum Novitiates 2361: 1–26.

Tedford, R.H. 1976. Relationship of Pinnipeds to other carnivores (Mammalia). Systematic zoology 25: 363–374.

Thom, R.M. 1981. *Primary Productivity and Carbon Input to Grays Harbor Estuary, Washington.* U.S. Army Corps of Engineers. Seattle District: Seattle.

Thomas, J.W., tech. ed. 1979. *Wildlife Habitats in Managed Forests: The Blue Mountains of Oregon and Washington.* U.S.D.A. Agricultural Handbook 553.

Thompson, K., and D. Snow. 1974. *Fish and Wildlife Resources Oregon Coastal Zone.* Oregon Coastal Conservation and Development Commission: Portland.

Thorson, G. 1964. Light as an ecological factor in the dispersal and settlement of larvae of marine bottom invertebrates. Ophelia 1: 167–208.

Trappe, J.M, and W.B. Bollen. 1979. Forest soils biology of the Douglas-fir region. In *Forest Soils of the Douglas-Fir Region.* P.E.

Heilman, *et al.*, eds. Washington State University Cooperative Extension: Pullman.

Treacy, S.D., and R.J. Beach. 1981. A comparison between prey species of marine mammals and species important to fishermen along the Pacific Northwest Coast. Abstract and poster, Fourth Biennial Conference on the Biology of Marine Mammals: San Francisco.

Trewartha, G. 1961. *The Earth's Problem Climates.* University of Wisconsin Press: Madison.

Trillmich, F., and K.G. Trillmich. 1984. The mating systems of pinnipeds and marine iguanas: Convergent evolution of polygyny. Biological Journal of the Linnaean Society 21: 209–216.

Turner, T. 1983a. Complexity of early and middle successional stages in a rocky intertidal surfgrass community. Oecologia (Berlin) 60: 56–65.

Turner, T. 1983b. Facilitation as a successional mechanism in a rocky intertidal community. American Naturalist 121: 729–738.

Twight, P.A. 1973. *Ecological Forestry for the Douglas Fir Region.* National Parks and Conservation Association: Washington, D.C.

U.S. Army Corps of Engineers. 1976. Willapa River and Harbor Navigation Project, Washington. Final Environmental Impact Statement. U.S. Army Corps of Engineers: Seattle.

U.S. Army Corps of Engineers. 1977. *Maintenance Dredging and the Environment of Grays Harbor, Washington.* Seattle District: Seattle.

U.S. Bureau of Land Management. 1974. The Western Gulf of Alaska. A Summary of Available Knowledge. U.S. Bureau of Land Management: Washington, B.C.

U.S. Department of Commerce. 1968. Climatic Atlas of the United States. Environmental Science Services Administration, Environmental Data Service, National Climatic Center, Federal Building: Asheville, North Carolina.

U.S. Department of Commerce. 1977. Local Climatological Data, Annual Summary with Comparative Data, Eureka, California. U.S. National Oceanic and Atmospheric Administration, Environmental Data Service, National Climatic Center: Asheville, North Carolina.

U.S. Department of the Navy. 1958. Marine Climatic Atlas of the World. Vol. 2. North Pacific Ocean. Navaer 50-1C-529, 1 V. U.S. Department of the Navy: Washington, D.C.

U.S. Fish and Wildlife Service. 1979. Concept Plan for Waterfowl Wintering Habitat Preservation: Washington and Oregon Coasts. Portland.

U.S. Fish and Wildlife Service. 1980. Selected Vertebrate Endangered Species of the Seacoast of the United States. American

Peregrine Falcon, Arctic Peregrine Falcon. Slidell, Louisiana.

U.S. Forest Service. 1973. *Silvicultural Systems for the Major Forest Types of the United States.* Agriculture Handbook No. 445.

U.S. Forest Service. 1986. *Draft Supplement to the Environmental Impact Statement for an Amendment to the Pacific Northwest Regional Guide.* 2 vols. Pacific Northwest Region: Portland.

U.S. Forest Service. 1987. *Habitat Management for the Spotted Owl. Planning Report.* Pacific Northwest Region: Portland.

U.S. National Marine Fisheries Service. 1977. Final Environmental Impact Statement/Preliminary Fishery Management Plan, Trawl Fishery of the Washington, Oregon and California Region. National Oceanic and Atmosperic Administration: Washington, D.C.

U.S. Soil Conservation Service. 1975. *Beaches and Dunes of the Oregon Coast.* Portland.

Valk, A.G. van der. 1974. Mineral cycling in coastal foredune plant communities in Cape Hatteras National Seashore. Ecology 55: 1349–1358.

Van Valen, L. 1968. Monophyly or diphyly in the origin of whales. Evolution 22: 37–41.

VanBlaricom, G.R., and J.A. Estes, eds. 1988. *The Community Ecology of Sea Otters.* Ecological Studies Vol. 65. Springer-Verlag: New York.

Varoujean, D.H., and R.L. Pitman. 1980. *Oregon Seabird Colony Survey 1979.* U.S. Fish and Wildlife Service: Portland.

Varoujean, D.H. 1979. *Seabird Colony Catalog: Washington, Oregon, and California.* U.S. Fish and Wildlife Service.

Veirs, S.D. 1982. Coast redwood forest: stand dynamics, successional status, and the role of fire. In Means, 1982.

Waaland, R.J. 1977. *Common Seaweeds of the Pacific Coast.* Pacific Search Press: Seattle.

Wahl, T.R., and D. Heinemann. 1979. Seabirds and fishing vessels: co-occurrence and attraction. Condor 81: 390–396.

Wahl, T.R. 1975 Seabirds in Washington's offshore zone. Western Birds 6: 117–134.

Waring, R.H., and J.F. Franklin. 1979. Evergreen coniferous forests of the Pacific Northwest. Science 204: 1380–1386.

Waring, R.H. 1982. Land of the giant conifers. Natural History 91 (10): 54–63.

Washington Natural Heritage Program. 1982. *Endangered, Threatened, and Sensitive Vascular Plants of Washington.* Washington State Department of Natural Resources: Olympia.

Washington State Department of Ecology. 1977. *Washington Coastal Areas of Major Biological Significance.*

Washington State Department of Game. 1982. *Wildlife Studies at*

Proposed Disposal Sites in Grays Harbor, Washington. U.S. Army Corps of Engineers. Seattle District: Seattle.

Wells, R.S., A.B. Irvine, and M.D. Scott. 1980. The social ecology of inshore odontocetes. In Herman, 1980a.

Welty, J.C., and L. Baptista. 1988. *The Life of Birds.* 4th ed. Saunders: New York.

Westman, W.E., and R.H. Whittaker. 1975. The coast redwood region of northern California. Studies on biomass and primary productivity. Journal of Ecology 63: 493–520.

Whittaker, R.H. 1960. Vegetation of the Siskiyou Mountains, Oregon and California. Ecological Monographs 30: 279–288.

Whittaker, R.H. 1961. Vegetation history of the Pacific coast States and the "central" significance of the Klamath region. Madrono 16(1):5–23.

Wickham, D.E. 1979. Predation by the nemertean *Carcinonemertes errans* on eggs of the Dungeness crab *Cancer magister.* Marine Biology 55: 45–53.

Wiedemann, A.M., L.J. Dennis, and F.H. Smith. 1969. *Plants of the Oregon Coastal Dunes.* Oregon State University Bookstores: Corvallis.

Wiedemann, A.M. 1966. Contributions to the plant ecology of the Oregon coastal sand dunes. Ph.D. Thesis, Oregon State University: Corvallis.

Wiedemann, A.M. 1984. *The Ecology of Pacific Northwest Coastal Sand Dunes: A Community Profile.* U.S. Fish and Wildlife Service. FWS/OBS-84/04.

Wiens, J.A., and J.M. Scott. 1975. Model estimation of energy flow in Oregon coastal seabird populations. Condor 77: 439–452.

Wilcox, L.R. 1959. A 20-year banding study of the piping plover. Auk 76: 129–152.

Williamson, R.L. 1973. Results of shelterwood harvesting of Douglas-fir in the Cascades of western Oregon. U.S. Forest Service RP PNW-161.

Wilson, R.A. 1980. *Snowy Plover Nesting Ecology on the Oregon Coast.* M.S. Thesis, Oregon State University: Corvallis.

Wilson-Jacobs, R., and E.C. Meslow. 1984. Distribution, abundance, and nesting characteristics of showy plovers on the Oregon Coast. Northwest Science 58: 40–48.

Wolcott, T.G. 1973. Physiological ecology and intertidal zonation in limpets (*Acmaea*): a critical look at "limiting factors." Biological Bulletin 145: 389–422.

Wright, W.G. 1982. Ritualized behavior in a territorial limpet. *Journal of Experimental Marine Biology and Ecology* 60: 245–251.

Yablokov, A.V. 1965. Convergence or parallelism in the evolution of cetaceans. International Geology Review 7: 1461–1468.

Yablokov, A.V. and L.S. Bogoslovskaya. 1984. A review of Russian research on the biology and commercial whaling of the gray whale. In Jones, Swartz, and Leatherwood, 1984.

Yocum, C.F., and M. Keller. 1961. Correlation of food habits and abundance of waterfowl, Humboldt Bay, California. California Fish & Game 47: 41–53.

Yung, W. 1986. Chinese fir. Wild Oregon 13(1): 27.

Zinke, P.J. 1977. The redwood forest and associated north coast forests. In Barbour and Major, 1977.

INDEX

Boldface indicates figure or table. Invertebrates and algae are listed fully only under their latin names, while all other extant species are listed fully only under their common names, and under latin names only where cited in the text. Common names of species are alphabetized by noun if animal, by first word in full name if plant.

365